Notable
New Yorkers
of Manhattan's
Upper West Side

Notable New Yorkers of Manhattan's Upper West Side

BLOOMINGDALE–MORNINGSIDE HEIGHTS

JIM MACKIN

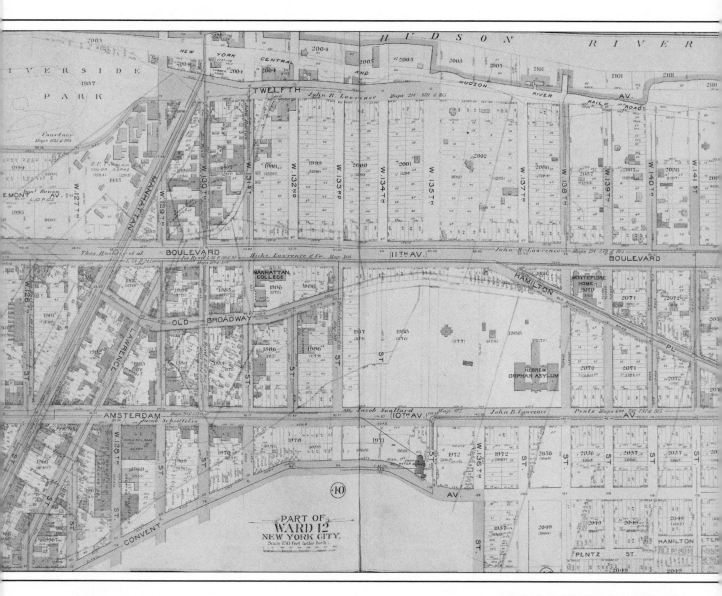

HUDSON RIVER

RIVERSIDE PARK

PART OF
WARD 12
NEW YORK CITY.
Scale 150 feet to the inch

EMPIRE
STATE
EDITIONS

EMPIRE STATE EDITIONS

An imprint of Fordham University Press

New York

2021

for Janet

Contents

Preface

Q. Who is the only person to fly under all four of New York's East bridges?
A. Elinor Smith.

Q. Who joined the army at age 12 years and 9 months to fight in the Civil War?
A. Augustus Meyers.

Q. Which American physicist was friends with Sir Ernest Rutherford, Marie Curie, and Maxim Gorky but was forced to leave Barnard's faculty on becoming engaged?
A. Harriet Brooks.

Have you ever heard of Elinor Smith, Augustus Meyers, or Harriet Brooks?

Two years ago, I hadn't.

I discovered these amazing individuals while researching the history of my neighborhood, the Upper West Side of Manhattan. Intrigued by these and similarly remarkable people, I began searching for more of these neighborhood gems . . . and I became very good at it. Using newspaper articles, obituaries, genealogy databases, historical biographies, local history books, Internet searches, college alumni registers and directories, census data, city directories, telephone directories, oral histories, personal papers, and community collections, I quickly collected a few hundred more accomplished, interesting residents of the Bloomingdale–Morningside Heights area in my files and realized I had a book in the making.

Focusing my attention specifically on the Bloomingdale and Morningside neighborhoods, the northern sections of the Upper West Side that stretch from the 90s to the 120s, my only criterion for inclusion was that the person had to have lived within that area. I found inspiration and a model for shaping my book in Guy Sterling's *The Famous, the Familiar, and the Forgotten: 350 Notable Newarkers,* a book that opens a window into the history of Newark, NJ, through its people. Eventually, my research turned up more than thirteen hundred individuals of note. Out of these, I selected six hundred for this book. My judgment, alone, determined who was notable, and the book contains a broad cross section of people over hundreds of years, including the famous, the infamous, and many who should be better known.

How did I, a kid from Queens, become a historian? It started when I was 12 years old, organizing long walks—fifteen and then twenty-five miles—along the newly built Long Island Expressway and beyond. As a teenager, I took part in a fifty-mile hike as part of President Kennedy's national physical fitness campaign. As an adult, I switched to running and completed several New York City Marathons, including the bicentennial run through the five boroughs.

These events set me on a path to new and interesting places and opened my eyes to the world around me. A walk was not just a walk but an exploration. In my teens, I discovered the Vanderbilt Motor Parkway, one of the first roadways in the country built exclusively for use by cars. I walked it, and then I went home and read everything I could find about its history. In later years, I participated in the "Great Saunter," a thirty-two-mile walk around Manhattan organized by the Shorewalkers. That walk gave me a street-by-street view of the city and a sense of how the early settlers saw the coastline and the rivers. Even my running workouts became more than just preparation for races; I always had a destination. I would read about a place of historic interest and take a run to see it for myself. The marathons gave me a CinemaScopic view of the city's boroughs. To learn more about these areas, I joined the Bronx, Queens, and

Brooklyn historical societies. In my fifties, I took part in a run up the stairs of the World Trade Center, with three hundred others, in a charitable event. From the 104th floor, the view of Manhattan, my hometown, was spectacular—and two of the greatest resources for understanding its history, the New York Historical Society and the Museum of the City of New York, were in my backyard.

My education was in business. I majored in economics at Fordham University and did my graduate work at New York University. I earned an MBA and a CPA license and became a financial executive. My years in finance were successful but also demanding. In spite of that, I never gave up my interest in history. My clients were *Fortune* 500 companies, many of which had books on their institution's history. I devoured them. I also developed an interest in industrial history and became the president of the Roebling Chapter of the Society for Industrial Archeology. And no matter what I was doing, I always had a history book close at hand.

In my retirement, I have made walking my business and my pleasure by creating WeekdayWalks, tours of New York neighborhoods. Every week I take a group of people—new visitors and loyal followers—on offbeat walks throughout the five boroughs (and occasionally into the "beyond" of New Jersey and Long Island), sharing the history of the neighborhood and its people. I also became a member of the Bloomingdale Neighborhood History Group, a small, dedicated group of individuals who are committed to sharing the history of the area through lectures and presentations—which brings me back to the reason for this book.

Having discovered that the history of Bloomingdale and Morningside Heights was comprised of wildly diverse people who shaped the character of the area, I knew I had to write a biographical compilation of the area's fascinating residents. Even more, I wanted to connect personage to place—to see the notables in the context of their community. It became clear to me that each biographical entry had merit on its own but that its value was multiplied when viewed alongside the others. The book became a journey of time "in place."

The location of the neighborhood stays the same, but its residents change over the years, creating a kaleidoscopic view of community and culture.

My research revealed many surprises, including dozens of accomplished women whose histories are little known. Although their opportunities were severely limited, the achievements of these scientists, educators, researchers, social scientists, psychologists, and jurists were outstanding. The bluestockings were among them, but the Upper West Side was also home to women artists, writers, actors, musicians, and singers, some of whom were well known in their day but are now unfamiliar to us. I am glad to give these women the spotlight they truly deserve.

Although the focus of *Notable New Yorkers of Manhattan's Upper West Side: Bloomingdale–Morningside Heights* is on people, I have also included an eclectic collection of interesting facts and colorful stories about the neighborhood itself. The area, well known for its educational institutions, including Columbia University, was also home to the Ninth Avenue El, Little Coney Island, an insane asylum, and an orphanage. It was also notoriously one of the most dangerous streets in the city. I couldn't resist telling these stories. Nor could I resist including the songs that were written about the neighborhood and the movies that were shot there.

There is no better example of what this book is trying to convey than that of The Old Community, a tight-knit African American enclave that once thrived on West 98th and 99th Streets. This microcosm included talented and accomplished residents such as Marcus Garvey, Billie Holiday, Butterfly McQueen, and Arturo Schomburg. That history would have been lost forever had it not been for the efforts of the late Jim Torain. This book honors him, and I thank him for the opportunity to tell the stories that he shared. He helped me to see that this book had to be more than individual bios; that time, place, and community were necessary for a richer understanding.

Writing this book was a daunting task. Because of the short bio format, I was unable to tell the whole story of a person's life—that will be left to others. Instead, I tried to present the most interesting or important accomplishments of each notable to give the reader a quick sense of who they were. Discerning the merit of the sources of data was a challenge. Obituaries can be overgenerous in praise, telephone books can be wrong, census data may be missing, names change or are spelled differently, and sources can present conflicting facts. I have done my best to find the most credible information.

My hunt for notables continues, and I welcome the help of others. I am hopeful that my research will revive an interest in the forgotten notables of the Bloomingdale and Morningside Heights area. So many are, I believe, "plaque-worthy." While there are thousands of buildings in New York City that are landmarked, there are fewer than two hundred plaques honoring individuals. This book provides both an overview of the people who shaped the Upper West Side through their presence and a guide to those individuals who deserve to be recognized and remembered.

How to Use this Book

You might choose to read this book from cover to cover, or just pick a spot at random, or hunt for a certain name, or look up a particular address. I recommend that you tuck the book under your arm and walk the streets of Bloomingdale and Morningside Heights to observe where the interesting people from the past lived. To do this, you should know a few things:

- The book is divided into five geographical sections: the West 90s, the West 100s, the West 110s, the West 120s, and Riverside Drive.
- Addresses are arranged in ascending order within each section, first by street number and then by street address number.
- The cross street for each address is provided in parentheses with each bio.
- If you want to find a particular notable, use the index at the back of this book.
- The names of all notables are highlighted in bold in their individual bios and wherever else they appear in the book.

As you wander the neighborhood, keep your eyes open for new notables. The old chap or cute kid you see along the way may be (or may become) a notable of the future.

SUPERSTAR—There are a few notables who stand out above all the rest because of their accomplishments. They deserve special acknowledgment and the attention of every reader.

PLAQUE-WORTHY—There are buildings that should have a plaque to let all passersby know that it was the residence of a notable of great merit. Unfortunately, there are few buildings with such plaques. This category places a "virtual plaque" on these residences.

NEED TO BE MUCH BETTER KNOWN—There are notables who readers might skip over because their names are not familiar. These individuals deserve greater attention for their accomplishments, and this designation is designed to encourage readers to take the time to find out more about them.

ESPECIALLY INTERESTING—This category is designed to acknowledge notables whose stories are somewhat unique and unusual. Their accomplishments may be few, but their lives are fascinating, and readers are encouraged to find out more about them.

To find out more about the people and places of the Upper West Side, refer to the following highly recommended resources:

- Peter Salwen's book *Upper West Side Story: A History and Guide.*
- Daytonian Tom Miller's website http://daytoninmanhattan.blogspot.com/.
- Bloomingdale Neighborhood History Group's website https://bloomingdalehistory.com/ and https://www.upperwestsidehistory.org/.

- Notable New Yorkers website https://www.notablenewyorkers.com/. This website provides short biographies of hundreds of additional notables who lived in the Bloomingdale–Morningside Heights neighborhood. Because of space limitations, they were not included in this book, but they are deserving of recognition and will be of great interest to readers.

What Is Bloomingdale? What Is Morningside Heights?

BLOOMINGDALE is the area of Manhattan's Upper West Side from the West 90s to 110th Street and between Central and Riverside Parks.

When the Dutch settled on the island of Mannahatta, they kept to the southernmost part of the island. They prospered and protected their community by erecting a wall that came to be known as Wall Street. In the middle of the 1600s, the Dutch moved north of the wall, and by the late 1600s, some settled in the large area from approximately the West 40s up to the West 120s. It was called Bloemendaal, which meant "blooming valley or dale," perhaps because of its natural characteristics, or possibly because the area was populated by people from the Holland community of Bloemendaal, the tulip-growing region near the Dutch city of Haarlem.

After the English took over New Amsterdam in 1664, Bloemendaal became anglicized to Bloomingdale. By 1708, the Bloomingdale Road was constructed and extended to present-day 115th Street and Riverside Drive. When the Bloomingdale Insane Asylum opened on the site where Columbia is today, it was the first institutional use of the name. In time, it would be followed by Bloomingdale Square, the Bloomingdale Public School, the Bloomingdale Branch of the New York Public Library, the Bloomingdale School of Music, and others. A Bloomingdale community came into being near St. Michael's Church, which was built on the east side of the Bloomingdale Road at 99th Street in 1806. A cluster of homes peppered the area along the Bloomingdale Road nearby. As the area developed with the coming of the Croton Aqueduct, along with the construction of the Ninth Avenue Elevated Railroad and the Interborough Rapid Transit (IRT) Subway, the "Bloomingdale" name faded from common usage. In very recent times, however, with new attention to the area's history, the "Bloomingdale" name has been affectionately revived.

Today, Bloemendaal is one of the wealthiest communities in the Netherlands. The Bloomingdale neighborhood of Manhattan's Upper West Side is also rich in many ways.

MORNINGSIDE HEIGHTS is the area from 110th Street to 125th Street between Morningside and Riverside Parks.

In its earliest days, Morningside Heights was considered part of the larger Bloomingdale area, but in the late 1600s it came to be known as Vanderwater's Heights, named after the local landowning family. It later took on the name "Harlem Heights" and was the location of a famous Revolutionary War battle. In the late 1800s, the park's name changed again. "Morningside" was an invented word, possibly coined by parks planner Andrew Haswell Green or by architect Frederick Law Olmsted. It was chosen for the east-facing Morningside Park. The name took hold and the neighborhood became known as Morningside Heights. Today, it is the home of Columbia University, Barnard College, Teachers College, Manhattan School of Music, Union Theological Seminary, Jewish Theological Seminary, the Cathedral of St. John the Divine, Riverside Church, St. Luke's Hospital, and Grant's Tomb.

The rich institutional heritage of Morningside Heights has attracted talented and accomplished individuals, many of whom are described in this book. There is little doubt that similarly interesting people will make Morningside Heights their home in the future.

See also the Timeline of Bloomingdale–Morningside Heights in the next section.

Timeline of Bloomingdale–Morningside Heights

1609—Henry Hudson sails up the North River, later renamed in his honor.

Late 1600s—Dutch farmers settle in the area and call it Bloemendaal, meaning "blooming valley or dale." After the British capture of New Amsterdam in 1664, the name is anglicized to "Bloomingdale."

1708—The Bloomingdale Road is laid out from Eastern Post Road at 23rd Street and Fifth Avenue to 115th Street and Riverside Drive.

1776—The Battle of Harlem Heights takes place.

1811—Colonel John Randel surveys Manhattan and establishes the grid of streets and avenues.

1821—The Bloomingdale Insane Asylum moves from its downtown location to the site now occupied by Columbia University.

1842—The Croton Aqueduct, running south on 10th Avenue, which will be renamed "Amsterdam Avenue" north of 59th Street, is completed to supply fresh water to the city.

1843—The Leake and Watts Orphan Asylum is established on the site of what is now the Cathedral of St. John the Divine.

1857—Central Park is established to 106th Street.

1863—Central Park is expanded from 106th Street to 110th Street.

1866—The Western Boulevard is begun. It is renamed "Broadway" in 1899.

1870—Land is obtained to create Morningside Park.

1875—Riverside Park is begun, is substantially completed by 1910, and is expanded in 1937 with the covering of the railroad tracks and the construction of the West Side Highway.

1870s—Riverside Avenue is constructed, renamed "Riverside Drive" in 1909.

1879—The Ninth Avenue Elevated Railroad is completed and runs through the neighborhood.

1884—The Association for Respectable Aged Indigent Females moves from downtown into its new building on Amsterdam Avenue at 104th Street.

1892—Columbia University arrives in Morningside Heights to occupy the site of the Bloomingdale Insane Asylum.

1897—Grant's Tomb is completed.

1904—The Interborough Rapid Transit Subway, called the IRT, runs through the area under Broadway.

1933—The Independent Subway, called the IND, runs through the area under Central Park West.

Late 1950s—Urban renewal tears down tenements and older structures, and it destroys The Old Community of African Americans living on West 98th and 99th Streets. Soon after, Park West Village and the Douglass Houses are built.

1950s through 1980s—Commensurate with New York City's problems, the Bloomingdale and Morningside Heights neighborhoods suffer economically and experience elevated crime rates.

1990s to present—As crime drops dramatically in New York City, Bloomingdale and Morningside Heights experience prosperity and gentrification while retaining their characteristic diversity.

Notable
New Yorkers
of Manhattan's
Upper West Side

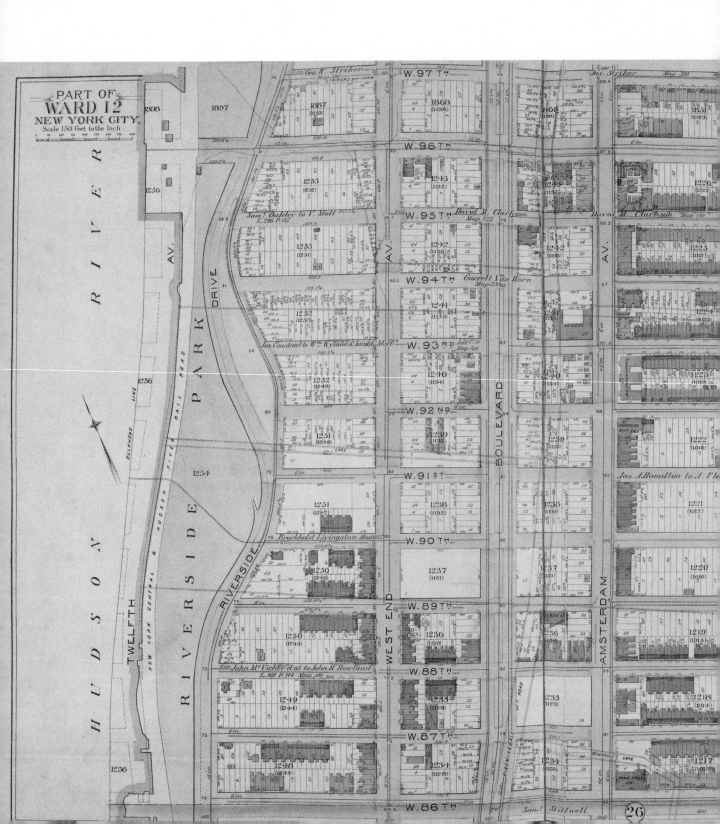

PART OF
WARD 12
NEW YORK CITY.
Scale 150 feet to the Inch.

Geo. W. Striker
Map 580
STRIKER'S BAY FARM

Jas. Striker   Map 580

W. 97TH

1897   1887   1863   1863   1851
            (1253)   (1138)   (1138)   (1023)

1893

W. 96TH

1256   1253   1243   1243   1226
            (1252)   (1137)   (1137)   (1022)

Saml. Oakley to V. Moll.
L. 296 P. 155

David M. Clarkson
Map 722

David M. Clarkson   Map 150

W. 95TH

1253   1242   1242   1225
(1251)   (1136)   (1136)   (1020)

Garrett Van Horn
Map 839

W. 94TH

1252   1241   1241   1224
(1250)   (1135)   SCHOOL   (1135)   (1020)

Jos. Constant to Wm. Wyman & Jacob C. Moll

Map 70
Map 704

W. 93RD

1252   1240   1240   1223
(1249)   (1134)   (1134)   (1019)

W. 92ND

1251   1239   1239   1222
            (1133)   (1133)   (1018)

1254

Jas. A. Hamilton to A. The

W. 91ST

1251   1238   1238   1221
(1247)   (1132)   (1132)   (1017)

Brockholst Livingston Map 635

W. 90TH

1250   1237   1237   1220
(1246)   (1131)   (1131)   (1016)

W. 89TH

1250   1236   1236   1219
(1245)   (1130)   (1130)   (1015)

John McVicker et al to John H. Howland
L. 169 P. 144   Map 565

W. 88TH

1249   1235   1235   1218
(1244)   (1129)   (1129)   (1014)

W. 87TH

1248   1234   1234   1217
(1243)   (1128)   (1128)   (1013)

1256

W. 86TH

Saml. Stillwell

(26)

The West 90s

Beautiful brownstones, elegant apartment buildings,

and the unique Pomander Walk grace the West 90s. The

eastern boundary is a section of Central Park that boasts

a pond and scenic landscaping. The western boundary,

Riverside Drive, bears the curvature of the long-gone

Stryker's Bay. The intersection of 96th Street with

Broadway was a preeminent stop on the "subway circuit,"

featuring a host of motion picture theaters. Park West

Village is a story unto itself and The Old Community was

a city treasure.

Plate 36 [Map bounded by W. 97th St., Central
Park W., W. 86th St., Hudson St.]. (George
Washington Bromley, Cartographer.)

5 West 91st Street (near Central Park West)

de Forest, Lee (1873–1961) ◼ ▢

INVENTOR

The 1950s television show *What's My Line* introduced their mystery guest de Forest as the "Father of Radio and the Grandfather of Television." He was born in Iowa and earned his BS degree at Yale's Sheffield Scientific School. He was expelled from the graduate program there for conducting experiments that blew too many fuses, which resulted in building-wide blackouts. Not to be defeated, he developed 180 patents. His 1906 Audion triode vacuum tube advanced electronics fundamentally by enabling broadcast radio, long-distance telephone transmission, talking motion pictures, radar, and even computers before transistors. Unfortunately, his efforts were usually undermined by partners who exploited and defrauded him. His first financial venture of the De Forest Wireless Telegraph Company in 1902 failed, as did his De Forest Radio Telephone Company in 1907, which successfully broadcast speech and music on an experimental basis in New York City. In 1910, he broadcast a live performance of Enrico Caruso at the Metropolitan Opera. By 1912, he was employing Audions to significantly amplify signals by a "cascading" grid arrangement. But much litigation forced him to sell his important patents, most of which found their way to the American Telephone and Telegraph Company. In the early 1920s, he invented a sound-on-film process that he branded as "Phonofilm." His Phonofilm company went bankrupt in 1926, but history recognized that movies became talking pictures with a process not unlike the one pioneered by de Forest.

Near West 91st Street and Columbus Avenue, Site of the Apthorp Mansion

Apthorp, Charles Ward (ca. 1726–1797)
LOYALIST, LANDOWNER, AND MERCHANT

Apthorp was a Loyalist, but his son-in-law, Hugh Williamson, was a patriot and signer of the Constitution. Apthorp had inherited his father's importing business and properties, and he had

The Apthorp Mansion.

accumulated additional properties in Massachusetts and Maine. In 1755, he married Mary McEvers, settled in the city, and served on the Governor's Council from 1763 until the end of the Revolutionary War in 1783. He also acquired nearly three hundred acres on the Upper West Side of Manhattan, built a mansion known as Elmwood, sold off some land to Gerrit Striker, and created two crossroads through his property that connected the Bloomingdale Road to the Harlem Commons. As a loyalist to the crown, he had to forfeit his properties. Further, he was arrested and tried for treason but was allowed to keep Elmwood. His son-in-law and patriot Hugh Williamson purchased Elmwood sometime after Apthorp's death and consolidated much of the Apthorp properties under his name. At a later date, a wealthy Englishman, William Jauncey, purchased Elmwood and its remaining land. The building was demolished in 1891.

THE WEST 90S   7

White Oaks Farm Site (near 91st Street and Riverside Drive)

Livingston, Henry Brockholst (1757–1823) ▪ 👈

JURIST

Appointed by Thomas Jefferson, Henry Brockholst Livingston was
an associate justice of the Supreme Court. He served through the
administrations of Madison and Monroe and under Chief Justice John
Marshall. Livingston was born in New York City and graduated in 1774
from the College of New Jersey (now Princeton University). During the
Revolutionary War, he served on the staff of General Philip Schuyler
and was an aide-de-camp to Major General Benedict Arnold at the
Battle of Saratoga. From 1779 to 1782, he was a private secretary to John
Jay, who was serving as minister to Spain. For twenty years, he had a
private law practice and then served as a justice on the Supreme Court
of the State of New York. In 1806, he was appointed to the highest court
in the land. Livingston's uncle Philip was a signer of the Declaration of
Independence, and his uncle Robert administered the oath of office to
George Washington, made the Louisiana Purchase, and enabled Robert
Fulton's steamboat. The Brockholst apartment building, on West 85th
Street at Columbus Avenue, undoubtedly was named in homage to
Livingston.

316 West 91st Street (near Riverside Drive)

Fox, William (1879–1952) ★ ▪

MOTION PICTURE EXECUTIVE

Today, Fox News and 20th Century Fox bear his name. In his day, he
was thought to have had a fortune as high as $35 million and controlled
more movie theaters—hundreds—than anyone else. Born Wilhelm
Fuchs in Hungary, his parents brought him to the United States in

his birth year. He worked as a newsboy and in the fur and garment industries until he bought his first nickelodeon in 1904. After acquiring some theaters and building others, he formed Fox Film Corporation in 1915. Fox Film was developing into a sizeable competitor and prospecting a merger with Loew's interests, but in 1929 Fox was badly hurt in an automobile accident and suffered financially from the stock market crash. The following year, a hostile takeover pushed him to the edge of bankruptcy and into retirement from the movie business. In 1935, Fox Film Corporation merged with Twentieth Century Pictures to become 20th Century Fox. In 1985, it merged into Rupert Murdoch's News Corporation, and in 2019 it became part of the Walt Disney Company.

7 West 92nd Street (near Central Park West)

Salk, E. Jonas (1914–1995) ★ ▪

VIROLOGIST

One of the architectural treasures in the United States is the Salk Institute for Biological Studies in La Jolla, California, designed by the great architect Louis Kahn. The institute honors Jonas Salk, who developed a successful vaccine for polio, eliminating the spread of the crippling disease. A native New Yorker, Salk was raised in East Harlem, the Bronx, and Queens. In 1934, he graduated from City College and, in 1939, received his medical degree from New York University. After a brief internship at Mount Sinai Hospital, he received a research fellowship and went to the University of Michigan to study the influenza virus. That research led to his development of a polio vaccine. In a few years his vaccine, introduced in 1955, was supplanted by one developed by Albert Sabin that had the added advantage of being an oral vaccine.

303 West 92nd Street (near West End Avenue)

Adler, Pearl "Polly" (1900–1962) ☞

MADAM

Adler operated Polly's Apparel Shop at 2719 Broadway (near 104th Street) before she turned to managing houses of prostitution. Adler was born in Russia, came to the United States at age 12, and began working when she was 17 years old. In the years right after World War I, prostitution thrived so well in the neighborhood that, during fleet week, the US Navy placed the blocks between 110th and 113th Streets and between Broadway and Amsterdam Avenue off-limits. Her life as a madam of houses of prostitution is recounted in her best-selling book *A House Is Not a Home*. In it, she writes about her connections with mobsters such as Arthur "Dutch Schultz" Flegenheimer and Charles "Lucky" Luciano. In 1920, she moved into an apartment on Riverside Drive that belonged to a friend that she identified as "Joan Smith." In this apartment, she made the acquaintance of a bootlegger and mobster, who enticed her into the procurement trade. In 1923, one of her business locations was 303 West 92nd Street. Some of her clients were thought to be playwright George S. Kaufman, humorist Robert Benchley, and author **Dorothy Parker** (all members of the Algonquin Round Table), *New Yorker* co-founder Harold Ross, actors John Garfield and Desi Arnaz, comedian Milton Berle, gangsters Al Capone and "Legs" Diamond, and Mayor Jimmy Walker. Adler also had a residence somewhere on Riverside Drive near Riverside Church.

37–43 West 93rd Street (near Central Park West), the Norman and 46 West 93rd Street (near Central Park West)

Freschi, John J. (1876–1944)
JUDGE

Freschi was known for presiding over more than sixty trials of kidnappers, communists, and gangsters, such as Louis "Lepke" Buchalter, who was executed for murder. Born in Greenwich Village, Freschi attended New York University and then graduated from New York Law School in 1895. His career on the bench began when Mayor Gaynor appointed him as a magistrate in 1910. During World War I, he was chairman of Manhattan's draft boards. Five years later, he was promoted to the Court of Special Sessions. Although Mayor Hyland didn't reappoint him in 1925, Mayor Jimmy Walker did so in 1930. In 1932, Governor Franklin Roosevelt appointed him to a fourteen-year term on the General Sessions bench. Freschi raised most of the funds to create Columbia University's Casa Italiana on Amsterdam Avenue at 117th Street.

59 West 93rd Street (near Columbus Avenue) and 66 West 93rd Street (near Columbus Avenue)

Mumford, Lewis (1895–1990) ★ ■
URBANIST AND INTELLECTUAL

Mumford was one of a small group of scholars responsible for the re-discovery of Herman Melville. Mumford's writings covered architecture—he was the architecture critic for the *New Yorker* magazine for over thirty years—technology, and history, with a concentration on sociology and cities. He was born in Flushing, Queens, but grew up in the Bloomingdale neighborhood, attended PS 165 on West 109th Street

and Stuyvesant High School, then on East 15th Street. He studied at
City College and the New School for Social Research, but because of a
bout with tuberculosis, he never finished. Among his thirty-some-odd
books, *Technics and Civilization* in 1934, and *The City in History* in 1961
are standouts. His interest in city planning led him to co-founding
the Regional Planning Association of America and becoming involved
with Sunnyside Gardens in Queens where he chose to make his home.
President Reagan awarded him the National Medal of Arts in 1986.
Mumford also lived at **100 West 94th Street** (near Columbus Avenue) and
at **200 West 105th Street** (near Amsterdam Avenue).

67 West 93rd Street (near Columbus Avenue)

Rothstein, Arnold (1882–1928) ☞
RACKETEER

Rothstein is usually remembered as the man who fixed the 1919
baseball World Series. He arranged payments to the Chicago White Sox
team to lose to the Cincinnati Reds. It tarnished baseball and became
infamously known as the "Black Sox Scandal." He was a gangster of all
trades: gambling, loan-sharking, and bootlegging. A native New Yorker,
Rothstein dropped out of high school at age 16. His mental skills were
impressive, and so after becoming bored as a traveling salesman, he
decided to concentrate on gambling. By the time he was 30, he was
a millionaire and based his operations in the Tenderloin district of
the West 20s in Manhattan. He was one of the first racketeers to see
the opportunity to profit from prohibition. Meyer Lansky and Lucky
Luciano were part of his crew. Dutch Schultz is thought to be the one
most likely responsible for assassinating Rothstein at a high-stakes
poker game in a midtown hotel. It remains one of crime history's most
remarkable events and an unsolved one at that. Rothstein also lived at
319 West 94th Street (near Riverside Drive).

123 West 93rd Street (near Columbus Avenue)

Stein, Andrew (1945–)
LAWYER AND POLITICIAN

Stein was borough president of Manhattan and the last president of the New York City Council. He was born Andrew J. Finkelstein, grew up in New York, and later attended Southampton College. His father, Jerry Finkelstein, was the founder of the *New York Law Journal* and a Democratic Party power broker. In 1969, Andrew Stein was elected to the New York State Assembly. In 1977 he was elected borough president, and in 1986 he was elected president of the City Council. He failed in attempts to win the Democratic primary for mayor and the office of public advocate. In 2010, he was arrested and convicted for lying about his involvement with money manager Ken Starr, who conducted a Ponzi scheme that impacted many Hollywood celebrities. Stein also lived at **784 Columbus Avenue** (near 97th Street).

175 West 93rd Street (near Amsterdam Avenue)

The Ronnette's and Murray the K.

Kaufman, Murray "Murray the K" (1922–1982) ■ ☞
RADIO DISC JOCKEY

Known as "the Fifth Beatle," Kaufman played emcee and introduced the Beatles at their first concert in New York at Shea Stadium in 1964. As a popular radio host, he was a tireless and effective advocate for moving rock and roll from the AM to the FM radio band. He also helped popularize the revolutionary music brought on by the "British invasion" of the 1960s. Born Murray A. Kaufman into a showbiz family, Kaufman served in the US Army in World War II by organizing entertainment for the troops. He did the same after the war in the Catskill Mountains' "Borscht Belt" and did promotional work for sports figures such as Willie Mays and Mickey Mantle. He also plugged songs such as "How Much Is That Doggie in the Window." In 1958, he joined WINS radio, home of Alan Freed, and Kaufman's *Swingin' Soiree* radio show soon catapulted to the top. "Murray the K" was known for such antics as his "Ah-bey" call and references to "submarine race-watching," a teenagers' euphemism for "making out." The live music shows that he hosted at movie theaters like the Paramount and the Brooklyn Fox presaged the mega rock concerts to come.

301 West 93rd Street (near West End Avenue)

Matthews, Brander (1852–1929) ◼ ▯ ☞

WRITER, EDUCATOR, AND THEATER BUFF

A Brander Matthews Theater was located on 117th Street between Morningside Drive and Amsterdam Avenue. It existed from 1940 to 1958, when urban renewal eliminated the entire street to make way for Columbia's Jerome Greene Hall. Matthews was a theater-phile who collected stage memorabilia that he housed and displayed in Columbia's Philosophy Hall. Born to a wealthy family in New Orleans, Louisiana, but raised in New York City, Matthews graduated from Columbia College in 1871 and from Columbia Law School in 1873. He later earned AM and LLD degrees from Columbia. Never interested in pursuing a career in law, he began writing professionally. From 1892 he was a professor of literature at Columbia, and in 1900 he was appointed Chair of Dramatic Literature, which he held until his retirement in 1924. He served as president of the National Institute of Arts and Letters; was the first chairman of the Simplified Spelling Board; and helped start the Authors' Club, the Players' Club, the Grolier Club, and the Century Club. Four universities conferred honorary degrees upon him. His friends included Mark Twain, Rudyard Kipling, William Dean Howells, and Teddy Roosevelt. He wrote more than thirty books, and one of his plays, *A Gold Mine*, is mentioned in Theodore Dreiser's novel *Sister Carrie*. Matthews also lived at **681 West End Avenue** (near 93rd Street).

Site near West 93rd Street on the Bloomingdale Road

Mott, Valentine (1785–1865) ★ ◼ ▮ ☜

SURGEON

Historian Peter Salwen described Mott as "a surgical rock star." He has been called "the father of vascular surgery" in America. Supposedly, he performed one thousand amputations. Born on Long Island, Mott graduated from Columbia College in 1806, studied with a noted surgeon in London, England, and was appointed professor of surgery at Columbia in 1809. Along with Alexander Hamilton's physician, David Hosack, and others, he established Rutgers Medical College in 1826. His surgical practice and reputation grew, and in 1834 he went to Europe for seven years where he met many notables and reveled in the exchange of professional information. Returning to the United States in 1841, he was employed on the founding faculty of NYU School of Medicine. He was an early president of the New York Academy of Medicine. He lived at 1 Gramercy Park West, but in 1833 he built a country house off the Bloomingdale Road near 93rd Street. Story has it that he died just days after hearing the shocking news of President Lincoln's death.

61 West 94th Street (near Columbus Avenue)

Dixon, Thomas, Jr. (1864–1946) ☜

LAWYER, MINISTER, LECTURER, AND AUTHOR

Dixon wrote the 1905 book *The Clansman*, which **D. W. Griffith** made into the 1915 movie *Birth of a Nation*. Blatantly racist, he was a tired but formidable advocate for racial segregation and the old values of the Southern Confederacy. Born in North Carolina, Dixon received an MA degree from Wake Forest College in 1883, studied at Johns Hopkins University for two years, and earned an LLB from Goldsboro Law School in 1886. At age 21, he became a Baptist minister and one of the most popular lecturers in the country. In 1889, he came to New York to be the minister at the 23rd Street Baptist Church. His twenty-some-odd novels, as well as a few screenplays, are replete with his racist views.

66 West 94th Street (near Columbus Avenue)

Rosenblum, Doris Sandra (1925–1996) ■
COMMUNITY ACTIVIST AND MANHATTAN BOROUGH HISTORIAN

Doris Rosenblum Way on West 94th Street honors her role in the community. She was affectionately known as "the Mayor of the West Side." Born on the Lower East Side and raised in the South Bronx, Rosenblum arrived on the Upper West Side in 1959. In addition to serving as district manager of Community Board 7 on Manhattan's Upper West Side for twelve years, she was an original member of the Mitchell-Lama Residents' Council and president of the Stryker's Bay Neighborhood Council. She was a constant central force from the 1960s, when the public school system was decentralized, into the 1970s and 1980s, as the Upper West Side was managing gentrification and development. In 1990, Borough President Ruth Messinger named Rosenblum to the voluntary position of Borough Historian.

100 West 94th Street (near Columbus Avenue)

Mumford, Lewis (1895–1990), Urbanist and Intellectual

(See bio for Mumford at **59** and **66 West 93rd Street**.)

147 West 94th Street (near Columbus Avenue)

Moskowitz, Belle (1877–1933) ◼
SOCIAL AND POLITICAL ACTIVIST

Moskowitz was a close aide and advisor to Governor Al Smith and was his campaign manager when Smith became the Democratic candidate for president in 1928. Born in Harlem, Moskowitz left Teachers College to be the director of entertainments and exhibits at the Educational Alliance on the Lower East Side. There she met her first husband, who died in 1911, and **Henry Moskowitz**, who would become her second husband. After the Triangle Shirt Waist fire, she was at the forefront of numerous reforms and, as a result, became acquainted with Al Smith. She died tragically from complications after falling down the steps in front of her home on West 94th Street.

Moskowitz, Henry (ca.1879–1936) ◼ ▮
SOCIAL AND POLITICAL ACTIVIST

Moskowitz was the founding executive director of the American Theater Wing, the theater group that bestows the Tony Awards. Born in Romania, Moskowitz graduated from City College in 1899 and from the University of Erlangen-Nuremberg in Germany in 1906, where he received his PhD in philosophy. His earliest civic activities were on the Lower East Side and with the Henry Street Settlement and the Society for Ethical Culture. In 1914, Mayor John Purroy Mitchel appointed him head of the Civil Service Commission and, in 1917, commissioner of Public Markets. Belle Lindner Israels became **Belle Moskowitz** when she married Henry in 1914, and they both worked closely with Governor Al Smith. Henry co-authored the Smith biography, *Up from the City Streets.*

250 West 94th Street site (near Broadway)

Stanton, Elizabeth Cady (1815–1902) ★ ■
SUFFRAGIST

Stanton was an alumna of the Troy Female Seminary, renamed the Emma Willard School, whose other activist graduates included Kirsten Gillibrand, Mrs. Russell Sage, and Jane Fonda. Elizabeth Cady Stanton was born in upstate New York to a one-term Federalist congressman. Her mother's ancestors included Livingstons and Schuylers. Stanton learned the law and developed an activist bent from her father, from a brother-in-law—the son of a Delaware Senator—and from her cousin and prominent abolitionist Gerrit Smith. She met her husband, Henry Brewster Stanton, through her involvement in the temperance and abolition movements. Stanton, Lucretia Mott, and other women organized the Seneca Falls Convention in 1848 and declared that women were equal to men and should have the right to vote. In 1851, Susan B. Anthony joined the cause. It would take nearly seventy years until the Nineteenth Amendment would be passed to give women the right to vote.

Elizabeth Cady Stanton.

250 West 94th Street (near Broadway), the Stanton

Allen, Joan (1956–)
ACTOR

Joan Allen has been lauded for her work on stage, on-screen, and on television. She was born in Illinois, and while attending Eastern Illinois University, she performed on stage with John Malkovich. In 1977, he had her join the Steppenwolf Theatre Company. Meanwhile, she had graduated from Northern Illinois University with a BFA degree in theater. After receiving acclaim for her roles on film, such as *Compromising Positions* and *Peggy Sue Got Married*, Allen won the

1989 Tony Award for Best Actress in Lanford Wilson's play *Burn This*, with Malkovich as her co-star. That same year, she starred in Wendy Wasserstein's Pulitzer Prize–winning play, *The Heidi Chronicles*. She has been nominated three times for an Academy Award: first, in 1995 for her portrayal of Pat Nixon in *Nixon*, again for her role in the 1996 movie of Arthur Miller's play *The Crucible*, and then for her role in the 2000 film *The Contender*. Her TV work is extensive, notably in series such as *The Mists of Avalon*, *Luck*, *The Killing*, *The Family*, and the Lifetime movie *Georgia O'Keeffe*, for which she received two Emmy nominations.

Land, Edwin Herbert (1909–1991) ★ ■
INVENTOR

Only Thomas Edison and six others had more patents than the 533 held by Land in his day. Born in Connecticut, Land went to Harvard University to study chemistry. After freshman year, he left for New York City to use the New York Public Library and to sneak into Columbia University's laboratories to begin inventing polarized film. He returned to Harvard but did not finish his studies; he would have to be satisfied with the honorary doctor of science degree they conferred upon him in 1957. In 1932, he formed a company to commercialize the polarization technology. Renamed Polaroid Corporation, it produced the first "instant camera" in 1947. By the 1950s, the Polaroid camera could claim, in advertising, that it took and developed pictures in sixty seconds. Land's company also aided the US effort in World War II with technology using aerial equipment that uncovered the enemy's camouflaged positions. Similarly, Polaroid aided Cold War intelligence efforts, such as the U2 program.

Mailer, Norman (1923–2007) ★ ■
NOVELIST

In 1969, Mailer ran in the Democratic Party primary for mayor, proposing that New York City become the fifty-first state. Born in New

Jersey and raised in Brooklyn, Mailer graduated from Harvard in 1943. In 1948, he wrote his novel *The Naked and the Dead,* which was based, in part, on his limited experiences in the US Army. Another of his dozen novels, *The Executioner's Song*, which was published in 1980, won a Pulitzer Prize. Some of his political activities included protesting the Vietnam War, having sympathy for Cuba, and urging the release of arrested Black Panthers. He was also one of the founders of the *Village Voice.* Frequently quarrelsome and combative, he was an entertaining presence on talk shows and gained additional notoriety by stabbing his second of six wives.

Oppenheimer, Julius Robert (1904–1967) ★ ◼
THEORETICAL PHYSICIST

Oppenheimer's childhood home on Riverside Drive contained works by Pablo Picasso, Édouard Vuillard, and Vincent van Gogh. A native New Yorker, Oppenheimer graduated summa cum laude in three years from Harvard University with an induction to Phi Beta Kappa. After a frustrating experience at Cambridge University in England, he adjusted his interest to theoretical physics at the University of Gottingen in Germany. Studying under Max Born, he established friendships with fellow students Wolfgang Pauli, Enrico Fermi, Edward Teller, and Werner Heisenberg. Back to the United States in 1927, he was awarded a fellowship at the California Institute of Technology. Soon he had additional shared responsibilities at the University of California, Berkeley, and Harvard. So much in demand, he would be tapped for the Manhattan Project and become "a father of the atomic bomb." He served as head of the Los Alamos Laboratory during World War II and as chairman of the General Advisory Committee of the brand-new Atomic Energy Commission. He advocated for control of nuclear power but had his loyalty to the United States tested in a very public 1954 hearing. History, however, has weighed in his favor. Oppenheimer also lived at **155 Riverside Drive** (near 88th Street).

J. Robert Oppenheimer.

308 West 94th Street (near West End Avenue)

Royle, Edwin Milton (1862–1942)
ACTOR AND PLAYWRIGHT

Royle wrote the one-act play *The Squaw Man*, which **Cecil B. DeMille** made into the silent movie classic in 1914. It is thought to be the first motion picture made in Hollywood. Born in Missouri, Royle graduated from Princeton University in 1883. He also attended Edinburgh University, Scotland, and Columbia Law School for a brief time. His first play, *Friends*, reached the New York stage in 1892. Approximately fifteen plays followed, including *The Squaw Man* in 1905; its four revivals; and additional productions in Australia, Canada, and New Zealand. William S. Hart, who would become a silent film star, appeared in the original cast. Royle also authored books such as *Edwin Booth as I Knew Him*, *English as She Is Spoke*, and *The Why of It All*. He was a life member of the Lambs Club and became its "shepherd," or president, in 1930. Further, he was vice president of the Episcopal Actors Guild and a trustee of the Percy Williams Home for Indigent Actors. The character actress Selena Royle is his daughter. He also lived at **780 West End Avenue** (near 98th Street).

310 West 94th Street (near Riverside Drive)

Gilbreth, Frank Bunker, Sr. (1868–1924) ■
INDUSTRIAL ENGINEER

Gilbreth's son, Frank Gilbreth, Jr., wrote the best seller *Cheaper by the Dozen*, which is about growing up as one of twelve children of his exceptional parents. Gilbreth, Sr., and his wife, **Lillian Gilbreth**, were pioneers in industrial management. They created one of the earliest management-consulting firms that made work processes more efficient and profitable. Their work complemented that of Frederick Winslow Taylor, whose focus, with the stopwatch always in hand, was on reducing processing times. Born in Maine but raised in Massachusetts, Gilbreth chose to forgo higher education to support his family. With a start in bricklaying, he developed a method of finding "the one best way" of executing tasks that constituted a given job. He made innovations in concrete construction, started his own building firm, patented his inventions, and became what we now call a management engineer. His service in World War I enabled small arms to be assembled and disassembled more efficiently. He also lived at **380 Riverside Drive** (near 111th Street).

Gilbreth, Lillian Moller (1878–1972) ∎
PSYCHOLOGIST AND INDUSTRIAL ENGINEER

Gilbreth is most likely the first industrial and organizational psychologist. She was a pioneer in industrial management, being one of the first female engineers with a PhD, and she was a partner with her husband, **Frank Gilbreth**, in one of the earliest management-consulting firms. Born in California, Gilbreth graduated from the University of California with a degree in English literature. She attended Columbia to earn a master's degree, but because of health reasons, she returned to study at the University of California. Frustrated in her attempt to earn a doctorate in California because of residency requirements, she achieved her PhD in psychology in 1915 at Brown University. She also lived at **380 Riverside Drive** (near 111th Street).

315 West 94th Street (near West End Avenue)

Lebron, Dolores "Lolita" (1919–2010)
PUERTO RICAN NATIONALIST

On March 1, 1954, Lebron and fellow assailants entered the House of Representatives and fired some thirty shots. They were proud of their

POMANDER WALK

Pomander Walk is an enclave of quaint houses on both sides of a path that runs from 94th Street to 95th Street, about halfway between Broadway and West End Avenue. There are 16 two-story houses, numbered 3 to 22, facing the path. In addition, there are 9 three-story and 2 two-story houses facing the streets with addresses of **261 to 267 West 94th Street** and **260 to 274 West 95th Street**. As a private haven, Pomander Walk is gated against public access.

An English dramatist, Louis Napoleon Parker (1852–1944) wrote the George III period novel *Pomander Walk* and a stage play of the same title. After its run in London, it came to New York in late 1910 and ran for 143 performances. Parker's daughter, Dorothy (no relation to the notorious Upper West Side wit), was in the cast. The stage set—a street in Georgian London—caught the attention of restaurant owner and businessman Thomas Healy.

After 15-year-old Healy arrived from Ireland in 1886, he worked at a restaurant on 103rd Street and Broadway. In time he catered two racetracks and owned five restaurants, the most notable being the Golden Glades on Columbus Avenue at 66th Street, with customers like the King of the Belgians, Teddy Roosevelt, and Admiral Dewey. It sat one thousand patrons

actions wounding five congressmen in the melee. Born Dolores Lebron Sotomayor in Puerto Rico, she acquired her nationalistic ideology after the "Ponce Massacre" killings of peaceful demonstrators in 1937. She came to the United States in the 1940s and became a member of the Puerto Rican Nationalist Party. Convicted of attempted murder and other crimes, she served time in prison but was pardoned in 1979 by President Carter. In the 1980s, she was arrested twice for protesting the US military base in Puerto Rico.

319 West 94th Street (near Riverside Drive)
Rothstein, Arnold (1882–1928), Racketeer

(See bio for Rothstein at **67 West 93rd Street**.)

Pomander Walk: 94th to 95th Street between Broadway and West End Avenue
Carroll, Madeleine (1906–1987) ■
BRITISH ACTRESS

Carroll was thought to be the highest-paid actress in the world in 1938, —with earnings of $250,000. Appearing in nearly fifty movies, she is perhaps best remembered for her role in Alfred Hitchcock's 1935 film *The 39 Steps*. Born Marie-Madeleine Bernadette O'Carroll near Birmingham, England, she graduated from Birmingham University majoring in French. The film industry recognized her talent and beauty from her first movie in 1928. She stopped acting for a while after her sister died in the London Blitz. In 1943, she became an American citizen. All four of her marriages, including one to the actor Sterling Hayden, ended in divorce. Madeleine Carroll lived at 265 West 94th Street.

Pomander Walk in the early 1920s, when it was first built.

Gish, Dorothy (1898–1968) ★ ◼

ACTRESS

Born in Ohio, the Gish sisters were brought to New York City by their mother. They were employed by silent film director **D. W. Griffith**, who, in order to tell them apart, had them wear ribbons: a red one for Dorothy and a blue one for Lillian. At the age of 8, Dorothy made her stage debut and, like her older sister, experienced the earliest days of motion pictures. After a busy career as a child actress, she developed into a featured star as a young adult. She especially excelled as a comedienne in such films as *Battling Jane*, *Peppy Polly*, *I'll Get Him Yet*, and *Remodeling Her Husband*. Unfortunately, a significant amount of film stock that evidenced Dorothy's talents has been forever lost. Although she didn't live as long as her sister, Dorothy appeared in some one hundred films, the last one being *The Cardinal*, produced and directed by Otto Preminger in 1963. Dorothy's remains, along with those of her sister Lillian, reside in the columbarium of St. Bartholomew's Episcopal Church near Park Avenue and 51st Street.

who could watch a sixty-person cabaret show.

In 1917, Healy acquired the Astor Market on Broadway between 94th and 95th Streets. His plan to develop a sixteen-story hotel did not materialize, but part of the property was developed as Pomander Walk. In 1921, Healy hired the architects King & Campbell to design the enclave based on the Old English feel of the *Pomander Walk* stage set designed by George Tylor. In 1966, Pomander Walk was rejected for landmark status. In 1982, it was landmarked.

Gish, Lillian (1893–1993) ★ ■
ACTRESS

Lillian Gish was the last of the great silent film stars with a professional career on the stage, in movies, and on television that spanned eighty-five years. Born in Ohio, she began acting at an early age. Her mother brought Lillian and her sister Dorothy to New York City. There, they became friends with Gladys Smith, who changed her name to **Mary Pickford** and introduced the sisters to **D. W. Griffith**. Lillian made her film debut with her sister Dorothy in 1912 in a D. W. Griffith short. Her cute face and expressive manners were perfect for silent films, and she starred in many Griffith films, including his classics, *Birth of a Nation* and *Intolerance*. Decades later, in 1946, she was nominated for an academy award for best-supporting actress in the **David O. Selznick** western, *A Duel in the Sun*. In 1971, she was given an Academy Honorary Award for her significant contribution to the motion picture industry. Lillian never married, despite numerous proposals from drama critic George Jean Nathan.

Goddard, Paulette (1910–1990) ★ ■
ACTRESS

Paulette Goddard and Charlie Chaplin introduced his composition "Smile" in the classic 1936 feature *Modern Times*. Born Marion Levy in Queens, Goddard gained fame at age 13 as "the girl on the crescent moon" in Ziegfeld shows. In 1926, she made her acting debut in the Ziegfeld production *No Foolin'*. She found her way to Hollywood in 1929 and a few years later became one of the twenty original Goldwyn Girls, along with Betty Grable, Ann Dvorak, Ann Southern, Jane Wyman, and Lucille Ball. Her career pivoted to stardom when Charlie Chaplin cast her in *Modern Times* and, later, in *The Great Dictator*. Goddard first married at age 16; Chaplin was her second marriage; her third was to actor Burgess Meredith; and her fourth was to Erich Maria Remarque, the author of *All Quiet on the Western Front*. In all, she made some sixty movies and was nominated for an Academy Award for best supporting actress in the 1943 picture *So Proudly We Hail*. Her $20 million contribution to New York University created the freshman residence, Goddard Hall.

McLaglen, Victor (1886–1959) ▇
ACTOR

Early in his career, McLaglen boxed Jack Johnson and Jess Willard, two heavyweight champions. McLaglen was born in England, grew up there and in South Africa, and wound up in Canada as a professional wrestler and boxer. After military service in England, he acted in silent films. After moving to Hollywood, he became a sought-after character actor with a talent for playing drunks. He starred in the silent World War I classic *What Price Glory*. His transition to talking films was seamless, and he won an Academy Award in 1935 for Best Actor in *The Informer*. During his career as an actor, he was in such films as *The Lost Patrol*, *Gunga Din*, *Fort Apache*, *She Wore a Yellow Ribbon*, *Rio Grande*, and *Around the World in Eighty Days*.

Morehouse, Ward (1895–1966) ▇
THEATER CRITIC

Morehouse wrote the screenplays for the 1932 movie *Central Park* and the 1935 film *It Happened in New York*. He also wrote two Broadway plays: *Miss Quis* in 1937 and *Gentlemen of the Press* in 1928, which was made into a motion picture. Born in Georgia, Morehouse started as a reporter on newspapers in Savannah and Atlanta. He arrived in New York in 1919 and first wrote for the *Tribune*, but in 1926 he launched his column *Broadway After Dark* in the *New York Sun*. It outlasted the paper's folding in 1950, continuing in other publications. Morehouse lived at 8 Pomander Walk and **420 West 119th Street** (near Amsterdam Avenue).

Russell, Rosalind (1907–1976) ■
ACTRESS

Russell had a distinguished career on both stage and screen. She won Tony Awards for her performances in *Wonderful Town* and *Auntie Mame*. She was also nominated for an Academy Award for Best Actress four times for her roles in *My Sister Eileen* in 1942, *Sister Kenny* in 1946, *Mourning Becomes Electra* in 1947, and *Auntie Mame* in 1958. Born Catherine Rosalind Russell in Connecticut, she attended Rosemont College in Pennsylvania; attended Marymount College in Tarrytown, New York; and graduated from the American Academy of Dramatic Arts in New York City. She started as a fashion model and acted in regional theater before debuting in a Broadway revival of *The Garrick Gaieties* in 1930. She moved to Los Angeles and became a contract actress for Universal Studios, but she shifted to Metro-Goldwyn-Mayer and appeared on the screen for the first time in the 1934 motion picture *Evelyn Prentice*. Never a sex goddess, she excelled in portraying sophisticated females, sometimes as "the other woman." Her notable appearances were in such films as *The Women* in 1939, *His Girl Friday* and *No Time for Comedy* in 1940, *Design for Scandal* in 1941, and *Picnic* in 1955.

Sternhagen, Frances (1930–) ■
ACTRESS

Sternhagen was nominated for seven Tony Awards and won twice: in 1974 for her role in *The Good Doctor* and in 1995 for her role in a revival of *The Heiress*. She was prominent in such Broadway staples as *Steel Magnolias*, *On Golden Pond*, and *Equus*. Her television work was extensive, and she was a regular on *The Closer*, *ER*, *Sex and the City*, and *Cheers*. In addition to motion picture work, including *Misery*; *Bright Lights, Big City*; *Independence Day*; *Outland*; and *The Hospital*, she did more off-Broadway and summer theater than would seem possible. Born in Washington, D.C., in 1951, Sternhagen graduated from Vassar College where she was head of the drama club. In the 1960s, she studied with Sanford Meisner at the Neighborhood Playhouse.

Stothart, Herbert (1885–1949) ★ ■ ▯
COMPOSER

Stothart won his 1939 Academy Award for the score to the classic movie *The Wizard of Oz*. He received twelve Academy Award nominations over his lifetime. His other movie scores included *Mutiny on the Bounty*, *A Tale of Two Cities*, *A Night at the Opera*, *Northwest Passage*, *Pride and Prejudice*, *Madame Curie*, and *National Velvet*. He collaborated on many of the standard American operettas including *New Moon*, *Rose-Marie*, *Maytime*, *Sweethearts*, *The Chocolate Soldier*, and *I Married an Angel*. They yielded such song classics as "Lover Come Back to Me" and "Indian Love Call." He also composed the music for the song "I Want to Be Loved by You," sung by Helen Kane as Betty Boop. Born in Wisconsin, Stothart graduated from the University of Wisconsin-Madison and joined its faculty. He was hired by the impresario Arthur Hammerstein to be a musical director of touring Broadway shows. That put him in touch with Arthur's nephew, **Oscar Hammerstein II**, and they collaborated on the operetta *Rose-Marie*.

Swanson, Gloria May Josephine (1899–1983) ★ ■
ACTRESS

Gloria Swanson is best remembered for her role as Norma Desmond in the 1950 film classic *Sunset Boulevard*. She was the first person to win back-to-back Oscar nominations for *Sadie Thompson* in 1928 and *The Trespasser* in 1929. Swanson was born in Illinois but was raised mostly in Puerto Rico where her father was stationed with the US Army. Her acting career began at age 14 with a crowd scene and led to Mack Sennett's short films. **Cecil B. DeMille** employed her as a romantic lead in silent features that emphasized her brazen and sexy persona. The 1919 *Lion's Bride* is memorable for her scene with a real lion. She was one of the highest-paid actresses of her day and made a successful transition from silent films to "talkies." Before her final appearance on the screen in the 1975 comedy *Airport*, she had made some seventy motion pictures. Swanson married five times. She also famously had affairs with Joseph Kennedy and actor Herbert Marshall. Her last husband, the writer William Duffy, was a friend of John Lennon and Yoko Ono, and he co-wrote *Lady Sings the Blues* about Billie Holiday. Swanson's remains are in the columbarium of the Church of the Heavenly Rest on Fifth Avenue at 90th Street.

15 West 95th Street (near Central Park West)

Knopf, Alfred Abraham (1892–1984) ◼

BOOK PUBLISHER

Knopf rejected the following authors: Vladimir Nabokov, Anais Nin, Jorge Luis Borges, Isaac Bashevis Singer, and Jack Kerouac. His personal tastes were somewhat refined and mildly conservative. A New York native, Knopf received his BA degree at Columbia in 1912. Supposedly, he was writing a paper for his Columbia professor Joel Spingarn, which led to correspondence with the English author John Galsworthy. That summer, after he traveled to Europe and met Galsworthy, he decided to forgo the study of law and became a publisher. He started his publishing firm at age 23, and within a year he had a best seller with W. H. Hudson's *Green Mansions*. Knopf's very simple but very effective strategy was to offer high-quality European literature that was largely ignored in the United States. But in addition to such Europeans as Thomas Mann, W. Somerset Maugham, E. M. Foster, D. H. Lawrence, and Freud, and Sartre, and Kafka, he published Americans such as Theodore Dreiser, Dashiell Hammett, Langston Hughes, and Willa Cather, among others. Great historians such as Arthur Schlesinger, Jr., Samuel Elliot Morrison, and Richard Hofstadter were also in the Knopf catalog.

46 West 95th Street (near Columbus Avenue)

Kazin, Alfred (1915–1998) ■
AUTHOR AND LITERARY CRITIC

Kazin's 1951 book about his childhood, *A Walker in the City*, is essential New York City reading. Born in Brooklyn, Kazin graduated from City College with a BA in 1935 and an MA in English in 1938. Starting in his college days, he wrote book reviews and numerous essays for the *New Republic*, *Harper's Magazine*, *Partisan Review*, the *New Yorker*, and other magazines. Working alongside his Columbia friend Richard Hoftstadter at the New York Public Library, he authored a massive review of American literature in his 1942 book *On Native Grounds*. It set a standard for literary criticism and solidified his intellectual reputation. He wrote, taught at many universities, and endured the changing political views of many of his liberal friends. One good friend was **Hannah Arendt.** Kazin also lived at **545 West 111th Street** (near Broadway).

56 West 95th Street (near Columbus Avenue)

Knopf, Alfred Abraham (1892–1984), Book Publisher ■

(See bio for Knopf at **15 West 95th Street**.)

115 West 95th Street (near Columbus Avenue)

Douglas, Virginia O'Hanlon (1889–1971) ■ 🖝

SANTA CLAUS BELIEVER

"Yes Virginia, there is a Santa Claus" was the title of an 1897 editorial in the *New York Sun*, thought to be the most reprinted editorial of all time. Eight-year-old Virginia O'Hanlon asked the question in a letter to the newspaper, and editor Francis Pharcellus Church responded by writing the paper's editorial. The story has been made into movies, a television show, a musical, and a cantata. Born Virginia O'Hanlon in New York City to a family of doctors, she married, divorced, and used her married name. A Hunter College graduate, she received a master's in education at Columbia in 1912 and a doctorate at Fordham in 1930. In 1959, and after a life of teaching, she retired to Valatie, New York. Her father was the physician and medical examiner Philip F. O'Hanlon.

137 West 95th Street (near Columbus Avenue)

Kohn, Robert D. (1870–1953)

ARCHITECT

Kohn designed the magnificent River Mansion at 337 Riverside Drive, as well as the adjacent and elegant 322 West 106th Street. A native of Manhattan, Kohn attended City College, earned a PhB in Architecture at Columbia, and studied four more years at the École des Beaux-Arts in Paris. The New York Evening Post building, with sculptured work by Gutzon Borglum and his wife, Estelle Rumbold, was his first notable design. After an earlier collaboration with Carrere & Hastings on the Ethical Culture school building, he soloed on the adjacent Society for Ethical Culture hall. From 1917, he partnered with Charles Butler, and they designed the largest part of Macy's Herald Square, and buildings for Mount Sinai and Montefiore hospitals. Along with Clarence Stein, they designed the Temple Emanu-El on Fifth Avenue. Kohn was president of the American Institute of Architects for a few years and president of the New York Society for Ethical Culture for more than twenty years. As an acknowledged expert on low-cost housing, he was director of the housing division of the Public Works Administration, and he chaired the architectural committee for the 1939 World's Fair and designed some of its buildings.

141 West 95th Street (near Columbus Avenue)

Walsh, Raoul (1887–1980) ★ ■

FILM DIRECTOR

Walsh grew up on the same block as **Virginia O'Hanlon Douglas** of "Yes Virginia, there is a Santa Claus" fame. He is best known as the director of such stars and movies as **Humphrey Bogart** in *High Sierra* and *They Drive By Night*, Errol Flynn in *Objective Burma* and *Gentleman Jim*, and James Cagney in *The Roaring Twenties* and *Strawberry Blonde*. Born Albert Edward Walsh in Manhattan, he interrupted his studies at Seton Hall College in New Jersey to sail on his uncle's cargo schooner to Cuba. A hurricane placed him in Mexico, where he learned enough about cowboy life to find his way into motion pictures in 1912 as a western movie actor. He advanced to directing movie shorts and learned his craft from **D. W. Griffith**, whom he assisted in directing *The Birth of a Nation* in which he also played the part of John Wilkes Booth. His 1915 silent film *Regeneration* is sometimes considered the first gangster film. Through the years he directed nearly one hundred films and such stars as Theda Bara, **Gloria Swanson**, John Wayne, Lawrence Olivier, Olivia de Havilland, Marlene Dietrich, Jane Wyman, Ronald Reagan, Gregory Peck, Clark Gable, Sidney Poitier, and Rock Hudson.

148 West 95th Street (near Amsterdam Avenue) (birthplace)

Cadmus, Paul (1904–1999) ■
SUPER-REALIST PAINTER

Cadmus's 1934 Works Progress Administration, or WPA, painting *The Fleet's In* caused uproar and launched his career. Because of its depiction of sailors, prostitutes, and a homosexual encounter, the Navy had it pulled from an exhibition in the Corcoran Gallery. The following year, his frolicking *Coney Island* had certain Brooklyn realtors in a tizzy. His sketches for the Port Washington, Long Island, post office resulted in a cancellation of his commission. Controversies aside, Cadmus's work was in great demand for gallery and museum shows—in part because he was a master of depicting distinctively suggestive male bodies. He was born on the Upper West Side, and his parents were artists. His sister married Lincoln Kirstein, who founded the New York City Ballet with George Balanchine. Cadmus studied at the National Academy of Design and the Art Students League. Considered one of the great artists of the twentieth century, Cadmus's circle included accomplished figures, such as George Balanchine, E. M. Foster, Christopher Isherwood, and W. H. Auden. He also resided at **150 West 103rd Street** (near Amsterdam Avenue).

153 West 95th Street (near Amsterdam Avenue)

Hawks, Everett Merle (1877–1970) ☜
OBSTETRICIAN

Hawks was the physician at the birth of Charles Augustus Lindbergh, Jr., in 1930. The child was kidnapped and found dead two years later. Hawks also delivered the second and fourth children of the author Anne Morrow Lindbergh and her husband, Charles A. Lindbergh, the aviator. A New York native, Hawks graduated from Columbia's College of Physicians and Surgeons with an MD. He practiced obstetrics and gynecology at the Women's Hospital, which was built in 1906 and located at 141 West 109th Street. In the course of his long career, he was connected with New York Hospital, Bellevue Hospital, and the New York French and Polyclinic Hospital.

157 West 95th Street (near Amsterdam Avenue)

Lincoff, Gary (1942–2018) ★ ■
MYCOLOGIST

Lincoff was the undisputed mushroom expert of New York City. In spite of no formal training in the science of mycology, he taught about mushrooms for more than forty years at the New York Botanical Garden, he led thousands of tours and expeditions to more than thirty countries, and he authored the *National Audubon Society Field Guide to North American Mushrooms*. For nine years, he was president of the North American Mycological Association. He was a constant presence in Central Park, introducing thousands of people to the world of fungi, and popularizing year-round exploration. Born in Pittsburgh, Lincoff graduated from the University of Pittsburgh in 1963 with a bachelor's degree in philosophy. He decided to leave law school at George Washington University and moved to New York in 1968.

159 West 95th Street (near Amsterdam Avenue)

Clarke, Joseph Ignatius Constantine (1846–1925) 🖙
JOURNALIST, POET, PLAYWRIGHT, AUTHOR, AND IRISH NATIONALIST

Clarke perpetrated the Central Park Zoo hoax of 1874. He reported in the *New York Herald* that a rhinoceros escaped and gored his keeper to death, followed by a polar bear, a panther, several hyenas, a lion, and a Bengal tiger. At the end of the lengthy article was a brief indication that the story was a hoax. Born in Ireland, Clarke came to the United States in 1868. In 1883, after thirteen years on the *New York Herald* editorial staff, he shifted to the *New York Journal* where he was managing editor for twelve years. In 1900, he became Sunday editor for the *Herald*. He created a publicity bureau for the Standard Oil Company and received a salary of $20,000 (over half a million dollars today). For years, he was on the executive council of the Irish Historical Society. He was also president of the National Art Theater Society and a director of the American Dramatists. In addition to an autobiography and numerous Ireland-inspired poems, he wrote books about two of his friendships: with the Japanese chemist **Jokichi Takamine**, and with the Irish Nationalist Robert Emmet.

200 West 95th Street (near Amsterdam Avenue)

Jacobs, Michael "Mike" Strauss (1880–1953) 🖎
TICKET BROKER AND FIGHT PROMOTER

Jacobs was the most powerful figure in boxing in the late 1930s and early 1940s, controlling all boxing in Madison Square Garden and exclusively promoting Joe Louis during his rise to heavyweight champion of the world. The first boxing shows at the Hippodrome and the Bronx Coliseum were Jacobs's productions. A New York native, Jacobs was raised on the Lower West Side where he dropped out of school after the sixth grade to hawk newspapers and to sell snacks to tourists in Battery Park. He learned how to buy tickets to concerts, shows, and sporting events and sell them for a profit. By 1907, he had his own ticket agency. Expanding into promotion, he once earned $80,000 by booking Enrico Caruso for 10 one-night stands. He specialized in boxing promotion under the legendary Tex Rickard. Author Budd Schulberg wrote a book on the life of Jacobs entitled *The Machiavelli of 8th Avenue*.

251 West 95th Street (near Broadway)

Runyon, Damon (1880–1946) ★ ▪
JOURNALIST AND SHORT STORY WRITER

The year Runyon died, his close friend, newspaper columnist Walter Winchell, established the Damon Runyon Cancer Research Foundation. Bob Hope, Joe DiMaggio, Marlene Dietrich, and Marilyn Monroe were some of the foundation's supporters. In 1949, Milton Berle raised $1.6 million for it on the first-ever telethon. Runyon is most readily connected with the stories he wrote about the characters on Broadway, which **Frank Loesser** adapted into the 1950 musical *Guys and Dolls*. Runyon was born in Manhattan, Kansas; was raised in Pueblo, Colorado; served in the US Army in the Spanish-American War; and worked for various newspapers in Colorado. In 1910, he came to New York, started writing stories, and reported on boxing matches and the New York Giants baseball team for the Hearst *New York American* newspaper. Runyon wrote nearly one hundred stories and authored approximately thirty books. Some twenty of his stories were made into movies such as the 1934 *Little Miss Marker*, which introduced Shirley Temple; the 1934 and 1951 remake of *The Lemon Drop Kid*; the 1938 and 1953 remake of *A Slight Case of Murder*; and in 1942, *The Big Street*. He also lived at three other addresses in the neighborhood: **320 West 102nd Street** (near Riverside Drive), **330 West 113th Street** (near Manhattan Avenue) and **440 Riverside Drive** (near 116th Street).

311 West 95th Street (near West End Avenue)

Harland, Marian (1830–1922) ▪ ▯
AUTHOR OF FICTION AND HOME ECONOMICS

Before Martha Stewart, there was Marion Harland. In 1872, her book, *Common Sense in the Household: A Manual of Practical Housewifery*, made her rich and made her pseudonym a household name. In her lifetime, she would write some twenty-five homemaking books in addition to an equal number of popular novels. Born Mary Virginia Hawes in Virginia, she began writing for magazines and adopted her pen name, Marian Harland. By the publication of her second novel and her marriage to the young Presbyterian minister Edward Payson Terhune in 1856, she had become successful as a writer. In 1859, she moved to Newark, New Jersey, where her husband had pastoral duties. With separation from her family during the Civil War years and the loss of three of her six children from illness, she engaged ever more in writing. She was president of the Woman's Christian Association in Newark, and she was the first woman inducted into the Virginia Historical Society. Her son, Albert Payson Terhune, was a renowned dog breeder and the most prolific author of dog stories in his day.

317 West 95th Street (near Riverside Drive)

Arendt, Hannah (1906–1975), Political Theorist ★ ▪

(See bio for Arendt at **370 Riverside Drive**.)

330 West 95th Street (near Riverside Drive)

Herriman, George Joseph (1880–1944) ▪
CARTOONIST OF "KRAZY KAT"

Herriman was the creator of "Krazy Cat," a popular cartoon strip in its day. It became one of the first comic strips to be taken seriously as an art form by intellectuals. The poet e. e. cummings wrote the introduction to the first book to compile a collection of comic strips. Herriman was born in New Orleans and grew up there and in Los Angeles from age 10. At age 20, he hopped a freight train to New York, where he rapidly found a liking for comic art. In addition to having fans like President Wilson, "Krazy Kat" influenced many later comics strip artists from Art Spiegelman to Robert Crumb to Charles Schultz. Herriman launched his creation in the William Randolph Hearst newspaper the *New York Evening Journal* in 1910 and then gave "Krazy Kat" his own comic strip in 1913. Although New York gave him his first opportunity, he lived most of his life in California, where he died.

George Herriman.

336 West 95th Street (near Riverside Drive)

Pendleton, Nathaniel "Nat" Greene (1895–1967) ◼

ACTOR AND WRESTLER

Pendleton played one of the two college football players who kidnapped Chico and Harpo in the 1932 Marx Brothers film *Horse Feathers*. Born in Iowa, Pendleton graduated in 1916 from Columbia where he was on the wrestling team. He won a silver medal in wrestling in the 1920 Olympics in Antwerp. His acting career in motion pictures followed. Although he usually played bit parts, he appeared in more than one hundred movies, including such classics as *The Thin Man*, *The Great Ziegfeld*, *Young Dr. Kildare*, and *Buck Privates Come Home*. His ancestor Nathaniel Pendleton was Alexander Hamilton's "second" in the duel with Aaron Burr. The Revolutionary War general Nathaniel Greene was another ancestor, as was the presidential contender George H. Pendleton, who authored the "Pendleton Civil Service Reform Act" in 1883 that established merit as the basis for government employment. Pendleton is also one of the twenty names commemorated in the architectural drum of Columbia's St. Paul's Chapel.

7 West 96th Street (near Central Park West)

Caro, Robert (1935–) ★ ■ ☞
BIOGRAPHER

Caro's 1974 biography of Robert Moses, *The Power Broker*, was edited down from 2,000 pages to 1,336. In his works, the author seeks not to write biographies per se, but rather to find the sources of power, first with Moses, and then with President Lyndon B. Johnson. His research on Johnson resulted in a first volume in 1982, and a fifth and likely last volume is awaiting publication. A native New Yorker, Caro graduated in 1957 from Princeton majoring in English. After working as a reporter for a New Jersey newspaper, he distinguished himself as an investigative reporter with the Long Island newspaper *Newsday*. The proposed bridge across the Long Island Sound from Oyster Bay to Rye caught his attention and served as the seed to his work on Moses. Caro's 2019 book *Working* recounts the incredible effort and relentless methodology he employs in crafting his masterpieces, especially citing his invaluable "research department of one," his wife, Ina. He has earned numerous awards including two Pulitzer Prizes for Biography. Caro plans to turn his attention next to Moses's mentor, New York State governor Alfred E. Smith.

12 West 96th Street (near Central Park West)

Ahlert, Fred E. (1892–1953) ■
COMPOSER AND SONGWRITER

Ahlert gave us memorable songs such as "I'm Gonna Sit Right Down and Write Myself a Letter" (with Joe Young), first popularized by Fats Waller in 1935 and, again, by Billy Williams in 1957. He is also responsible for putting "Walkin' My Baby Back Home," with lyrics by Roy Turk and sung by the crying Johnny Ray, on the charts in 1951. Amongst his many other compositions is the popular standard "Mean to Me" (lyrics by Roy Turk). His education at City College and Fordham Law School served him well in running his own music publishing company and as president of the American Society of Composers, Authors, and Publishers.

20 West 96th Street (near Columbus Avenue)

Salsbury, Nathan "Nate" (1846 –1902) ■ 👉

SHOWMAN AND ENTERTAINER

Salsbury was the producer, manager, and co-owner of Buffalo Bill's Wild West Show. Born in Illinois, Salsbury enlisted as a teenager in the Union Army during the Civil War. First a drummer boy, then a soldier, he fought in Georgia, Texas, and in Tennessee. After the war, he acted in various stock companies and formed his own troupe, the Salsbury Troubadors. In 1883, he helped create the show built around the personality of William F. Cody, who was known as Buffalo Bill. Over the years, the show included Chief Sitting Bull and Annie Oakley. It performed all over the country and in Madison Square Garden. In 1895, Salsbury produced a show entitled *Black America* that featured singing, acting, dancing, and gymnastics, and employed six hundred African Americans.

27 West 96th Street (near Central Park West)

Sackler, Arthur M. (1913–1987) ★ ■

ENTREPRENEUR AND PHILANTHROPIST

There are Sackler galleries of art at the Metropolitan Museum of Art, Harvard University, the Smithsonian, Princeton, and the Royal Academy in London. There are Sackler medical and science units at New York University, Long Island University, Tufts and Clark

University in Massachusetts, and Tel Aviv University. The funding came from Arthur Sackler's biweekly newspaper the *Medical Tribune,* with a circulation of six hundred thousand, and from the development of new drugs including the infamous Oxycontin, which is at the source of the opioid epidemic. Sackler was born in Brooklyn, studied at New York University and Cooper Union, and graduated from NYU School of Medicine with an MD. In the 1940s he began collecting art that ranged from the pre-Renaissance to post-Impressionism to modern American. His collection of ancient Chinese art is in the Smithsonian and is among the best in the world. Harvard received his other Asian and Near-Eastern art.

41 West 96th Street (near Columbus Avenue)

Holbrooke, Richard (1941–2010) ▪

PUBLIC OFFICIAL, DIPLOMAT, MAGAZINE EDITOR, AND INVESTMENT BANKER

Because of his work on the 1995 Dayton Peace Accords, Richard Holbrooke is likely most responsible for ending the war in Bosnia. He also had a long and remarkable career in public service under Presidents Johnson, Carter, Clinton, and Obama. In addition to serving as US Ambassador to the United Nations from 1999 to 2001, he was the Special Representative to Afghanistan and Pakistan from 2009 to 2010, and Ambassador to Germany from 1993 to 1994. Additional experience included work with the Peace Corps, editor of *Foreign Policy* magazine from 1972 to 1976, and a senior role at the investment banking firm Lehman Brothers from 1981 to 1993. A Manhattan native, Holbrooke graduated in 1962 from Brown University where he majored in history. After graduation, he joined the United States Foreign Service for six years of experience related to the Vietnam War. His further role as part of a select team that advised President Johnson led to increased and new responsibility in the State Department, including participation in the 1968 Paris Peace Talks and work on drafting some of the notorious

Pentagon Papers. Holbrooke also lived at **378 Central Park West** (near 97th Street).

44 West 96th Street (near Central Park West)

Kantor, John Leonard (1890–1947) ▪

GASTROENTEROLOGIST

Kantor's stature in the field of gastroenterology is due in part to his work on Kantor's string sign, indicating the narrowing of a cavity in the colon, and the Golden-Kantor syndrome, revealing an intestinal anomaly. Born in Russia, Kantor came to the United States as a youngster and graduated from Columbia University, receiving MD and PhD degrees in 1912. He interned at Mount Sinai Hospital and then joined the US Army during World War I. From 1919 to 1935, he was the chief of the Vanderbilt gastroenterologist clinic at Columbia-Presbyterian Hospital. Concurrently, he served Montefiore Hospital; Beth David Hospital; Sharon Hospital in Connecticut; Will Rogers Hospital in Saranac Lake, New York; and National Jewish Hospital in various capacities.

50 West 96th Street (near Columbus Avenue)

Pomeroy, Marcus Mills "Brick" (1833–1896) ☞

JOURNALIST AND AUTHOR

Pomeroy raised $6 million to build a five-mile-long railroad tunnel west of Denver. It was often referred to as "Pomeroy's folly" and "the West's Greatest Failure" because the tunnels dug from the east and west didn't meet. Born in Elmira, New York, he became an apprentice on a local newspaper. He then started small, local newspapers in Pennsylvania and Wisconsin before becoming city editor for the Milwaukee *Daily News*. As a member of the Copperhead faction of the Democratic Party, he supported Steven Douglas against Lincoln. Believing that Pomeroy's writings inspired John Wilkes Booth's assassination of

Abraham Lincoln, a lynch mob formed in its aftermath and Pomeroy barely escaped. A few years later, he started a newspaper in New York, the *Daily Democratic*, with the backing of the infamous Boss Tweed. His few books were all best sellers, but he retired to New York and died almost bankrupt. In 1894, he hosted an event at his home on West 96th Street to support women suffragists, and local public official Thomas A. Fulton was one of the speakers.

60 West 96th Street (near Columbus Avenue)

Packard, Eleanor Gould (1917–2005) ★ ■
GRAMMARIAN

It was said that she once found four grammatical errors in a three-word sentence. Known affectionately at the *New Yorker* as "Miss Gould" and occasionally called a "grammar goddess," her grammatical scrutiny was applied to some of the best writers of our age, such as John McPhee, Roger Angell, Joseph Mitchell, and J. D. Salinger. E. B. White gave her special mention in the 1952 edition of *Elements of Style*. Born Eleanor Gould in upstate New York, her family moved to Ohio. She won a scholarship to Oberlin College and graduated summa cum laude in 1938 with a major in English. She arrived at the *New Yorker* in 1945 where she met Frederick A. Packard. They married in 1946, and the couple dedicated ninety-nine years in total to the magazine. She also lived at **415 Central Park West** (near 101st Street).

125 West 96th Street (near Columbus Avenue)

Zacherle, John (1918–2016) ☞
RADIO AND TELEVISION PERSONALITY

Zacherle came into some national prominence as host to the television show *Shock Theater* where movies were shown and interrupted by

---

GRANTS', NOT GRANT'S

New Yorker grammarian and neighborhood resident **Eleanor Packard** might roll over in her grave. "Grant's Tomb" should be "Grants' Tomb"; it should be plural possessive, not singular possessive, since Julia Dent Grant is in the tomb with her husband, Ulysses. Furthermore, every New York City tour guide likes to ask, "Who's buried in Grant's Tomb?" An astute response is "no one," since the Grants are entombed, not buried.

his ghoulish persona. Zacherle's professional colleague, Dick Clark, gave him the moniker "The Cool Ghoul." With Clark's help, he had a 1958 minor hit "Dinner with Drac." Zacherle was born and raised in Philadelphia, and he graduated from the University of Pennsylvania with a bachelor's degree in English literature. When he moved his TV character to New York, he changed the spelling of his name to "Zacherley." He hosted cartoon shows, dance shows, rock and roll radio shows, and *Chiller Theater* on TV. His shtick continued for many years in many different venues and even included his appearance with the Grateful Dead rock and roll band at the Fillmore East.

153 West 96th Street (near Amsterdam Avenue)

O'Brien, Pat (1899–1983) ▪

ACTOR

O'Brien's last acting role was in the television show *Happy Days*, which took place in his hometown of Milwaukee, Wisconsin. Early in his career, he worked in numerous plays, but his breakthrough came when he was cast a lead role in the movie *The Front Page*. Over his long career, he appeared nine times with his friend, James Cagney, in films including *Angels with Dirty Faces* and *Ragtime*. O'Brien's best-remembered movie moment was his "win one for the Gipper" speech given in his role as legendary Notre Dame University football coach Knute Rockne. The role of the Notre Dame player, George Gipp, was played by Ronald Reagan. The O'Brien legacy includes nearly one hundred motion pictures, including *Some Like It Hot.* Interesting fact: O'Brien attended Marquette Academy high school with fellow actor and friend **Spencer Tracy**. In New York City, where they were budding actors, they roomed together on West 96th Street.

Tracy, Spencer (1900–1967) ★ ▪
ACTOR

Tracy joined the US Navy in World War I and soon after studied at Ripon College in Wisconsin. His activities in debating and acting led to a scholarship at the American Academy of Dramatic Arts in New York. He had acted in stock company productions, but when he got to Broadway, he was "discovered" by the legendary George M. Cohan. His opening night performance in a 1930 production, *The Last Mile*, earned him a standing ovation of fourteen curtain calls and led him to Hollywood. Some of his nearly one hundred films include *Dr. Jekyll and Mr. Hyde*, *Adam's Rib*, *Father of the Bride*, *The Old Man and the Sea*, *Inherit the Wind*, *Judgment at Nuremberg*, and *Guess Who's Coming to Dinner*. He won Academy Awards for *Captains Courageous* and *Boys Town*. He received a total of nine Oscar nominations, a record he shares with Sir Laurence Olivier. His nine films with Katherine Hepburn, with whom he had a long-term relationship, are cinema treasures.

160 West 96th Street (near Amsterdam Avenue)

Tanguay, Eva (1878–1947) ▪
VAUDEVILLE SINGER AND ENTERTAINER

In 1909, Eva Tanguay appeared on Broadway in one of her typically extravagant costumes—a coat made entirely of newly minted Lincoln pennies. Known as the "Queen of Vaudeville," she made a phenomenal $3,500 a week at the peak of her career. Born in Canada, she began in the entertainment business by winning amateur contests. When she was 10 years old, her big break came in a stage adaptation of Frances Hodgson Burnett's novel *Little Lord Fauntleroy*. In 1909, she appeared in the Ziegfeld Follies with Nora Bayes and Sophie Tucker. Tanguay is best known for her alluring rendition of the song "I Don't Care," which she introduced in the 1904 Broadway musical revue *The Chaperone* but

Eva Tanguay.

recorded years later in 1922. In 1953, Mitzi Gaynor portrayed her in the biographical movie *The I Don't Care Girl*.

204 West 96th Street (near Amsterdam Avenue)

Juettner, Emerich (1876–1955) 🖾
COUNTERFEITER

Juettner, originally known as Edward Mueller, came to the United States at age 13 from Austria, where he had learned photoengraving. He was a building superintendent, but he also worked as a junkman in the Bloomingdale neighborhood. In 1938, he started making counterfeit $1 bills. The first one appeared at a cigar store on Broadway near 102nd Street. That caused the Feds to open a file, which grew with hundreds of other counterfeit $1 bills. But Juettner eluded the Feds from 1938 until 1948, longer than any other counterfeiter. In late 1947, his apartment on West 96th Street caught fire. In early 1948, some boys playing in the snow found copper plates in his rubbish and they took them to the police station on West 100th Street. Secret Service agents found more counterfeiting paraphernalia in his basement. Juettner was profiled in the *New Yorker* magazine, and the movie *Mr. 880* was made about him.

Park West Village (97th Street to 100th Street between Columbus Avenue and Amsterdam Avenue)

Angelou, Maya (1928–2014) ■
MEMOIRIST, POET, AND ACTIVIST

Angelou received over fifty honorary degrees for her body of work and for her activities with Martin Luther King and Malcolm X. Her seven autobiographies, starting with *I Know Why the Caged Bird Sings*, have become required reading for appreciating the African

Maya Angelou.

American experience. She was also a journalist, playwright, television and movie screenwriter, poet, and presidential inaugural speaker. In the early part of her career, she danced professionally in clubs, toured in a production of Gershwin's *Porgy and Bess*, and appeared in the acclaimed television show *Roots*. Her address was **372 Central Park West** (near 97th Street).

Chamberlain, Wilton "Wilt" Norman (1936–1999) ★ ■ 👉
BASKETBALL PLAYER

Which is true about basketball great Wilt Chamberlain: (A) He scored 100 points in a game, or (B) He had sex with 20,000 women? The correct answer is "A." Although he made the claim of a prolific sex life in his 1991 book *A View from Above*, answer "B" is impossible. A true basketball legend, Chamberlain holds many records that are likely to stand for a long time. The 100-point game is one, but so are the records for a 50-point season scoring average and for being the only player to average 30 points and 20 rebounds in a season—and for seven consecutive seasons! He was born and lived in Philadelphia where he would play for the 76ers. In high school, he was a track star whose records would be competitive at the college level, but he chose basketball as a career. After dazzling the sports world at the University of Kansas, he went professional. He never fouled out of a game. And let's not forget that he challenged Muhammad Ali to a fight, albeit for the publicity. Chamberlain lived at **784–792 Columbus Avenue** (between 97th and 100th Streets).

Charles, Ray (1930–2004) ★ ■
SINGER AND COMPOSER

Charles was called "the Genius" for good reason. His singing could turn "The Star-Spangled Banner" into an art piece. From his earliest classics on Atlantic Records, including "I Got a Woman" and "Lonely Avenue," Charles's novel style was unmistakable. His 1959 classic "What'd I Say" impacted rock and roll music thereafter. And how can we even begin to evaluate his rhythm-and-blues interpretations of such country standards as "You Don't Know Me" and "I Can't Stop Loving You"? He was born Ray Charles Robinson in Albany, Georgia. By age 7, he had lost his sight and was sent to the Florida School for the Deaf and Blind in St. Augustine, where he learned to read braille music and play classical piano. Through many ups and downs, the world came to realize his genius. He composed, performed, and recorded music across many genres. In 1979, his version of "Georgia on My Mind" was proclaimed the state song of Georgia. In 1986, he was one of the first inductees into the Rock and Roll Hall of Fame. In 2004, the actor Jamie Foxx received an Academy Award for Best Actor for his portrayal of Charles in the film *Ray*.

Ellington, Edward Kennedy "Duke" (1899–1974) ★ ■
COMPOSER, PIANIST, AND BANDLEADER

Ellington was a beloved musician. More than twelve thousand people turned out for Ellington's funeral at the Cathedral of St. John the Divine. The Cathedral houses his signature white piano. Ellington, along with Louis "Satchmo" Armstrong and Charlie "Bird" Parker, occupies the pinnacle of the Pantheon of Jazz. Born in Washington, D.C., Ellington took up the piano at an early age and composed "Soda Fountain Rag" when he was only 15 years old. By age 18, he began assembling musical groups to play at social occasions including society balls and embassy parties. By 1923, they had a four-year engagement. The following year, they recorded for the first time, and in 1926 Ellington signed with the agent and publisher Irving Mills. That led to more recordings and the start of a long and profound association with the Cotton Club. "Take the A Train," "Sophisticated Lady," "It Don't Mean a Thing (If It Ain't Got That Swing)," "Caravan," "Don't Get Around

Much Anymore," "Mood Indigo," and "Satin Doll" are only some of his compositions. A successful Broadway musical revue, *Sophisticated Ladies,* was a tribute to him and his music. He was a Pulitzer nominee, and statues of him stand in New York, Los Angeles, and Washington, D.C., where a bridge is also named after him. Ellington's image is on a US postage stamp and coin. Ruth Ellington Boatwright is his sister, and Mercer Ellington is his son.

Feliciano, Jose (1945–) ▪

SINGER AND GUITARIST

No Christmas holiday sing-along would be complete without a few choruses of "Feliz Navidad" sung as Jose Feliciano sang it. His version of the Doors' "Light My Fire" hit the charts and was remarkable for transforming the driving psychedelic-infused composition into a heartfelt love song. Feliciano was born in Puerto Rico and was blind since birth. His family migrated to Spanish Harlem in New York City when he was five years old. He is self-taught on the guitar in jazz and classical idioms. His folk singing experience is extensive, including Greenwich Village nightclubs during the period of Dylan; Baez; and Peter, Paul, and Mary. His style has continued to evolve but his voice is distinctly his own, with respect for the Ray Charles influence. His address was **382 Central Park West** (near 97th Street).

Greer, William Alexander "Sonny" (1895–1982) ★ ▪

JAZZ DRUMMER

Greer was one of the first drummers to use cymbals, gongs, and other percussive instruments to create the "jungle" beat that attracted so much attention in the 1920s. Greer was born in Long Branch, New Jersey. He knew Ellington from 1919 in Washington, D.C., and became the Duke's first drummer in 1924. Over time Greer accumulated so many drumming accessories that when he sat in front of his drum set, it looked like he was on a throne. He was the driving force behind the Duke Ellington Orchestra at the Cotton Club and in many other places all over the world. Ellington was somewhat kind when he suggested that Greer's drumming was reactive. The *New Yorker* magazine jazz critic Whitney Balliett was less kind in suggesting that Greer gave the impression "that he was testing his drums." He was a smooth talker and classy dresser, but by 1951, because of alcohol addiction, he was encouraged to find employment elsewhere.

Hawkins, Coleman (1904–1969)
SAXOPHONIST

The 1939 recording of "Body and Soul" by Hawkins is one of the most revolutionary in the history of jazz and a perfect harbinger for bebop music. Born and raised in Missouri and in Chicago, he studied music theory for two years at Washburn College in Topeka, Kansas. After playing with local bands from age 14, he came to New York and did the same. In 1934, he joined the Fletcher Henderson Orchestra, and that led to studio work with the likes of Benny Goodman. In much demand, he traveled overseas and played in numerous bands and ensembles with the new breed of musicians, including Thelonious Monk, Sonny Rollins, Miles Davis, John Coltrane, and Max Roach.

Holbrooke, Richard (1941–2010), Public Official, Diplomat, Magazine Editor and Investment Banker ■

Holbrooke's address in Park West Village was **378 Central Park West (near 97th Street).** (See bio for Holbrooke at **41 West 96th Street**.)

PARK WEST VILLAGE

Park West Village is a complex of apartment houses and commercial establishments located from 97th to 100th Streets and between Central Park West and Amsterdam Avenue. The dozen or so buildings in the complex contain approximately three thousand apartments and occupy some twenty acres on six blocks.

Park West Village was a product of urban renewal brought about under the Title 1 section of the United States Housing Act of 1949. Robert Moses put it into effect as slum clearance, more politely called "urban renewal." The lurid details of how the $15 million worth of tenements were sold for $1 million, and how it took multiple developers and owners to create Manhattantown, later renamed Park West Village, is outlined in Robert Caro's 1974 biography of Robert Moses, *The Power Broker*. Jim Epstein's video, *The Tragedy of Urban Renewal* (viewable on YouTube) details how the African American community that lived on West 98th and 99th Streets suffered immeasurably from the creation of Park West Village. (See The Old Community.) In all, eleven thousand people were displaced as hundreds of brownstones and tenements were bulldozed.

Despite the tragic past of the area, Park West Village developed into a dynamically diverse community with a new proud heritage, and it became home to many notable residents.

Lang, Pearl (1921–2009)
DANCER AND CHOREOGRAPHER

Pearl Lang taught both the rock star Madonna and the German dancer and choreographer Pina Bausch. Born Pearl Lack in Chicago, Lang studied acting at the renowned Goodman Theater and attended classes at the University of Chicago. When she came to New York City in 1941, she found a place in the Martha Graham Dance Company. In time, she would dance roles that Graham premiered, such as in *Appalachian Spring*. She also originated many roles in Graham productions and celebrated her technique and creativity in her own choreography and in teaching at Yale, the Neighborhood Playhouse, and Julliard. Lang also danced on Broadway in such notable musicals as *One Touch of Venus*, *Finian's Rainbow*, and *Carousel*. She was married to the actor **Joseph Wiseman**. Lang's street address was **382 Central Park West** (near 97th Street).

Lincoln, Abbey (1930–2010)
JAZZ SINGER AND ACTRESS

In the 1956 rock and roll movie *The Girl Can't Help It*, Lincoln made her film debut wearing the dress that Marilyn Monroe wore in *Gentlemen Prefer Blondes*. She acted extensively in movies, including *For Love of Ivy* with Sidney Poitier, and on television shows, from *Marcus Welby, M.D.*, to *Mission Impossible*. Born Anna Marie Woolridge in Chicago but raised in Michigan, she began as a singer in Chicago nightclubs and adopted the stage name Abbey Lincoln. The name was suggested by her manager and songwriter, Bob Russell, who wrote "He Ain't Heavy, He's My Brother." Her singing talents were admired by **Max Roach**, who became her husband for eight years in the 1960s. In her later days, her singing grew in sophistication and critical appreciation. She frequently cited the influence of **Billie Holiday** on her singing. In turn, she influenced the next generation. Lincoln lived also at **415 Central Park West** (near 101st Street).

Luciano, Felipe (1947–) 🖘
POET AND COMMUNITY ACTIVIST

In the 1960s, Luciano was arrested for a killing. He said that he was
beaten so badly by the police who arrested him that his mother didn't
recognize him. He served two years for manslaughter, began writing
poetry, and co-founded the Young Lords Party, a militant group
advocating for social change and independence for Puerto Rico. Born in
Spanish Harlem, Luciano attended Queens College after he was released
from prison. There he joined the original group of poets and musicians
known as The Last Poets. The Young Lords separated from the national
organization to become the Young Lords Party. In 1969, they, along with
members of the Black Panther Party, received much media attention
when they battled the police while being holed up in a church in East
Harlem. In 1998, Mayor Giuliani appointed Luciano, then a 49-year-old
father of three and a radio personality, to a task force on police behavior
because Luciano had studied police behavior and knew it firsthand.
Luciano's street address was **382 Central Park West** (near 97th Street).

MacDowell, Edward Alexander (1860–1908) ★ ■
COMPOSER

In 1904, MacDowell's accident with a hansom cab on Broadway
contributed to his developing mental illness. Financial help for the
care he required was provided by Andrew Carnegie, Seth Low, Victor
Herbert, Grover Cleveland, J. P. Morgan, and other well-wishers. Prior
to his accident, MacDowell studied piano and music composition
under private tutors before attending the Paris Conservatory under a
competitive scholarship. He continued his studies at a conservatory
in Germany, where he performed, composed, and gave piano lessons.
One of his American students in Germany became his wife, and they
chose to settle in the Boston area where he would perform with the
Boston Symphony Orchestra. In 1896, appointed the first professor

of music at Columbia, he created their music department. He also directed the Mendelssohn Glee Club and composed numerous pieces for piano, orchestra, and voice. His second piano concerto and his New England sketch pieces are staples of American classical music. Many people will recognize his popular song "To a Wild Rose." He resigned from Columbia in 1904 under administrative and personal pressure for issues most likely related to his accident. In 1907, he and his wife established the MacDowell Colony in New Hampshire for use by future generations of artists of all types. MacDowell's address was **381 Central Park West** (near 97th Street).

MacNeil, Claudia (1917–1993) ■
ACTRESS

MacNeil appeared in the motion pictures *The Last Angry Man* and *A Raisin in the Sun*, which she reprised on Broadway to earn a Tony Award nomination. Born in Maryland but raised in New York City, McNeil started singing in nightclubs in Harlem, in Greenwich Village, and on 52nd Street. She received critical acclaim after having been selected by Langston Hughes for his 1957 musical *Simply Heavenly*. Her television work included *New York Confidential*, *The Doctors and the Nurses*, *CBS Playhouse*, *The Mod Squad*, and *Roots*. Her second Tony Award nomination came in 1962 for her role in *Tiger, Tiger Burning Bright*, whose cast included Roscoe Lee Browne, Cicely Tyson, **Alvin Ailey**, and Diana Sands.

Makeba, Zenzile Miriam (1932–2008) ■
SOUTH AFRICAN SINGER

After seeing her in the 1959 film *Come Back, Africa*, Harry Belafonte arranged for Miriam Makeba to come to the United States, perform in concert, and get a contract with RCA records. Makeba was born in South

Africa and began singing in groups as a teenager. A 1953 song, "Laku Tshoni 'Ilanga," recorded with a jazz group, the Manhattan Brothers, became a national hit and made her a prominent figure in her country. She was exiled to the United States in 1959, appeared on television and in concert, and made more recordings but was frustrated with financial difficulties when her passport was revoked by the South African government. She was briefly married to Hugh Masekela, another South African who was exiled. She later married the civil rights activist Stokely Carmichael, who lived with her in Guinea where her diplomatic work for the United Nations earned her the Dag Hammarskjöld Peace Prize. Makeba lived at **382 Central Park West** (near 97th Street).

Mankiewicz, Herman (1897–1953) ■
JOURNALIST AND SCREENWRITER

Mankiewicz and Orson Welles wrote the screenplay for the movie classic *Citizen Kane*. It won them Academy Awards in 1941. Mankiewicz won another Academy Award the following year for his screenplay for *The Pride of the Yankees*, about baseball great and one-time Columbia student Lou Gehrig. Born in New York to the son of a City College professor, Mankiewicz received a BA degree from Columbia in 1916. He began his career in journalism as a managing editor of the *American Jewish Chronicle* but left to serve in World War I. Staying in Europe, he served as Isadora Duncan's publicist, became director of the Red Cross News Service in Paris, and then operated as a foreign correspondent for the *New York World*. When he returned to New York, he joined the *New York Times* to write book and play reviews. He contributed to *Vanity Fair*, the *Saturday Evening Journal*, and many other magazines, and he was briefly the drama critic for the *New Yorker* magazine. Renowned for his wit, he wrote plays with Marc Connelly and George S. Kaufman until he was lured to Hollywood. His brother was the producer, director, and screenwriter Joseph Mankiewicz.

Masekela, Hugh (1939–2018)
TRUMPETER

Masekela had a number one hit in 1967 with the catchy jazz-pop tune "Grazing in the Grass." Born in South Africa, Masekela mastered the trumpet at an early age. He joined the first youth orchestra in his country, took leadership with other ensembles, and then played in prominent groups. Like his future wife, **Miriam Makeba**, he was befriended and encouraged by Harry Belafonte when he visited New York. From 1960 to 1964, he studied classical trumpet at the Manhattan School of Music. He did studio work on albums for Paul Simon and the Byrds.

Noguchi, Hideyo (1876–1928) ◼
BACTERIOLOGIST

Dr. Noguchi, like Louis Pasteur, saved innumerable lives. Noguchi was born in Japan, and at age one and a half, he burnt his hand very badly when he fell into a fireplace. The attention he received made him vow to help people in need. He trained at the Nippon Medical School, passed the examinations to practice medicine, and came to the United States in 1900. Starting as a research assistant for Dr. Simon Flexner at the University of Pennsylvania, and then at the Rockefeller Institute of Medical Research, he concentrated on venomous snakes. Noguchi discovered the serums that treated rattlesnake bites, rabies, and infantile paralysis. In 1912, he survived some controversy with charges made by anti-vivisectionists. He was a professor of pathology at the Tokyo Dental College, the University of Pennsylvania, and the Carnegie Institute. Japan awarded him their highest medical degree, and the Kings of Sweden, Spain, and Denmark knighted him. He died in the Gold Coast colony in Africa while performing research related to yellow fever. The following year his widow, Mary Dardis Noguchi, moved to **203 West 107th Street**. Interesting facts: Hideyo Noguchi knew poet Yone Noguchi (apparently no relation), whose son was the sculptor **Isamu Noguchi**. The Pasteur Institute at **372 Central Park West** was right down the street from the Noguchi apartment. His Park West Village address was **381 Central Park West** (near 97th Street).

Noguchi, Isamu (1904–1988) ★ ■
SCULPTOR

Isamu Noguchi was born in California. His parents were Yone Noguchi and Leonie Gilmour. Yone Noguchi was a poet of note who read some of his work at a benefit for Barnard College in 1904. Since his father married a Japanese woman in Japan, Isamu Noguchi grew up in Japan traveling around with his mother. In 1918, he came back to the United States and had a less-than-rewarding apprenticeship with the sculptor **Gutzon Borglum** (of Mount Rushmore fame). In 1922, he enrolled at Columbia as a pre-med student. Shortly thereafter, he met the bacteriologist **Hideyo Noguchi**, who knew his father. He dropped out of Columbia in 1924 to study at the Leonardo da Vinci Art School on East 10th Street. His first works were busts of such luminaries as Martha Graham and Buckminster Fuller. He later designed gardens, including ones in Jerusalem, Houston, and Los Angeles. He also designed for choreographers such as Merce Cunningham, Martha Graham, and George Balanchine. His "Sunken Garden" in Chase Manhattan Plaza downtown, his "Red Cube" off lower Broadway, his "Landscape in the Cloud" in the lobby of 666 Fifth Avenue, and his "Unidentified Object" on Fifth Avenue, just south of the Metropolitan Museum of Art, are only part of his lasting legacy. His studio in Queens became the Noguchi Garden Museum. He lived at **381 Central Park West** (near 97th Street).

Odetta (1930–2008) ★ ■
FOLK SINGER

A 2007 tribute to Odetta included performances by Peter, Paul, and Mary; Oscar Brand; Harry Belafonte; Pete Seeger; and many others. Born Odetta Holmes in Alabama, she studied music and opera

singing at Los Angeles City College. She was an ensemble member
of Hollywood's Turnabout Puppet Theater for four years and toured
with a group performing *Finian's Rainbow*. Concentrating on folk
singing, she developed a large following at the legendary folk clubs, the
hungry i in San Francisco, and the Blue Angel in New York. Her rise in
stature included record albums, national television appearances, and
performances at such venues as Carnegie Hall and the White House.
Because of her extensive activism with Dr. Martin Luther King and
numerous performances at protests and marches, she was called "the
voice of the civil rights movement." In 1999, President Clinton presented
her with the National Endowment for the Arts' National Medal of Arts.

Oliver, Melvin James "Sy" (1910–1988) ◼
TRUMPETER

In 1954, Oliver was the first music director of Bell Records, which
recorded the Dorsey Brothers, Roy Rogers, Dale Evans, and the duo Tom
and Jerry, who later used their real names, Simon and Garfunkel. Oliver
was born in Michigan to a musically talented family. He left home at age
17 to play and sing in jazz bands. In 1933, he joined Jimmie Lunceford's
band and demonstrated that he could arrange songs, discipline the
band, and conduct the music. In 1939, he became one of the first African
Americans to become part of a white band, that of Tommy Dorsey. He
arranged material for Dorsey that brought acclaim and popularity,
especially "On the Sunny Side of the Street" and "Opus One." He also
arranged music for Frank Sinatra and Louis Armstrong, and he arranged
and conducted for Ella Fitzgerald for five years at Decca Records. Oliver
also lived at **865 West End Avenue** (near 102nd Street).

Puente, Tito (1923–2000) ★ ◼
LATIN PERCUSSIONIST AND BAND LEADER

Puente wrote Carlos Santana's biggest hit "Oye Como Va." He single-
handedly popularized the mambo and other Afro-Cuban sounds to

mainstream audiences. Playing himself in the 1992 movie "The Mambo Kings," based on the Oscar Hijuelos novel, Puente conveys all the infectious energy that characterized his work. Born in Harlem and raised in Spanish Harlem, Puente served in the US Navy during World War II. He studied at the Julliard School of Music before forming his own Tito Puente Orchestra. Hit after hit earned him five Grammy Awards. The post office in Spanish Harlem is named in his honor.

Roach, Max (1924–2007) ★ ■
PERCUSSIONIST

Roach was probably the first notable jazz drummer to teach at the level of higher education as a faculty member at the University of Massachusetts at Amherst in 1972. The legendary jazz drummer, who had studied composition at Manhattan School of Music, once demonstrated his virtuosity at Columbia's Miller Theater by performing on drums while recounting a history of his percussive instruments and espousing the aesthetic principles of rhythm. Born in North Carolina, he grew up in Bedford-Stuyvesant where he studied the piano and transitioned to drums. As a teenager, he had a brief stint at the Brooklyn Paramount with Duke Ellington's orchestra. While still a teenager, he entered jazz history by jamming with Charlie Parker at Monroe's in Harlem on 134th Street. In the next few years, he and Parker, along with Dizzy Gillespie, Thelonious Monk, Miles Davis, and others would develop bebop jazz. In addition to becoming a seminal figure in the development of bebop, he revolutionized modern jazz and was arguably the greatest drummer in the jazz idiom. Thereafter, he would play with almost all the jazz greats and creatively develop his craft further, especially with the likes of Charles Mingus and Art Blakey. In addition to receiving a MacArthur Foundation "genius" grant, Columbia University and seven other schools awarded him honorary doctorates. He was married to **Abbey Lincoln** for a while in the 1960s. In addition to living in Park West Village, he also lived at **69 West 105th Street** (near Columbus Avenue) and **415 Central Park West** (near 101st Street).

Stein, Andrew (1945–), Lawyer and Politician

Stein's address in Park West Village was **784 Columbus Avenue** (near 97th Street). (See bio for Stein at **123 West 93rd Street**.)

Stritch, Elaine (1925–2014) ◼

ACTRESS

Late in her career, Stritch played Alec Baldwin's mother on the TV series *30 Rock*. She was the niece of Chicago's long-serving Roman Catholic Cardinal Samuel Stritch. She almost landed the role of Trixie Norton in the TV show *The Honeymooners*, which instead went to Joyce Randolph. She also almost landed Gig Young as a husband, but he went instead to Elizabeth Montgomery. Born in Michigan, Stritch came to New York and studied acting at the Dramatic Workshop of the New School. Her classmates included Bea Arthur and Marlon Brando. Her first stage appearance was in a forgettable children's play in 1947. But her talent was noticed along with her delightfully gravelly voice and her spectacular legs, such that in 1950 she became Ethel Merman's understudy in Irving Berlin's *Call Me Madam*. That was followed by the 1952 revival of Rogers and Hart's *Pal Joey* where she took ownership of the strip-song "Zip." Her distinguished career includes four Tony Awards; her first was for her role in William Inge's *Bus Stop* in 1956. In 1971 she graced Stephen Sondheim's *Company*.

Tyson, Cicely (1924–) ◼

ACTRESS

As an unknown actress, Cicely Tyson was in the New York Off-Broadway 1961 production of Jean Genet's absurdist play *The Blacks* that ran for 1,408 performances. The other unknowns in the show included **Maya Angelou**, Louis Gossett, Jr., Godfrey Cambridge, Roscoe

Lee Browne, and James Earl Jones. Tyson is the oldest person to win a Tony Award for Best Performance by an Actress in a Leading Role for her role in *The Trip to Bountiful*. Born in Harlem, Tyson was discovered by *Ebony* magazine and became a leading fashion model. She continued modeling and acted extensively for the stage and television. She won two Emmy Awards for her roles in *The Autobiography of Miss Jane Pittman* in 1974 and *Roots* in 1977. In 2016 she was awarded the Presidential Medal of Freedom.

Wiseman, Joseph (1918–2009)
ACTOR

Wiseman debuted on Broadway in 1938 with a small role in *Abe Lincoln in Illinois*. He is most well known, however, for his title role as the villain in *Dr. No*, the first feature-length James Bond movie. Wiseman was born in Canada, raised in Queens, and educated on the legitimate stage. His stage work was extensive, and his title role in the 1968 Broadway production *In the Matter of J. Robert Oppenheimer* earned him a New York Drama Desk Award. He was a constant presence on television in shows ranging from *The Untouchables* to *Law and Order*. Movies to his credit included *Detective Story*, *Bye Bye Braverman*, *The Night They Raided Minsky's*, and *Viva Zapata*. Wiseman's second wife was **Pearl Lang**, dancer, teacher, and creative force in the Martha Graham Dance Company.

26 West 97th Street (near Central Park West)

Armstrong, Edwin Howard (1890–1954) ★ ▣ ☜
ELECTRICAL ENGINEER AND INVENTOR

Armstrong invented frequency modulation, which is the foundation for FM radio and the audio part of broadcast television. Before that

Edwin Armstrong.

accomplishment in 1939, his theories resulted in the heterodyne circuit that enables radios to have reception. His super-regenerative circuit is essential to two-way radio transmission used in walkie-talkies. Born in the Chelsea neighborhood of Manhattan, Armstrong graduated from Columbia in 1913 with a degree in electrical engineering. He served in both World War I and II, attaining the rank of major. During and after his Columbia days, his work with regeneration circuits led to a lifetime of lawsuits, notably with **Lee de Forest**, the inventor of the three-element vacuum tube. In 1922, Armstrong sold his super-regeneration patent to Radio Corporation of America, more commonly known as RCA, and thereby became its largest stockholder. For complex technical reasons, his relationship with RCA became adversarial, and while developing FM, he was embroiled in extensive lawsuits that undoubtedly led to his suicide, committed by jumping out of his thirteenth floor apartment overlooking the East River.

179 West 97th Street (near Amsterdam)

Israels, Charles Henry (1865–1911) ▆ ☞
ARCHITECT

In 1903 Charles Israels, of the firm Israels & Harder, designed the Hudson Theater, which in 1954 became the home of the *Tonight Show* with Steve Allen. The work of Israels & Harder consisted mostly of hotels and private residences, many of which were on the Upper West Side. The firm is also credited with some of the beautiful exterior of the Hall of Records, sometimes referred to as the Surrogates Court, designed by John Thomas. Israels was born in New York and was trained at the Arts Students League and in Paris. He was on the 1907 Building Code Revision Commission, was secretary of the Municipal Art Society, and was on the executive committee of the Architectural League. Socially responsible architecture was his primary interest. Israels was the first husband of Belle Lindner, who, after her second marriage in 1914, would be known as **Belle Moskowitz**. His uncle was the Dutch painter Jozef Israels.

230 West 97th Street (near Broadway)

Snyder, Charles B. J. (1860–1945) ■ ▯
ARCHITECT

Snyder designed more than four hundred buildings, mostly New York City public schools, including PS 165 on West 109th Street. He designed school buildings to look extraordinarily important so that the attending students would realize that their education was important. Born in upstate New York, Snyder came to New York City and worked for a few years with builders. He earned two certificates from Cooper Union in 1881 and 1884. In 1891, he was appointed Superintendent of Buildings at the Board of Education. His responsibilities expanded tremendously with the Consolidation of the City of New York in 1898, and with the rapidly growing population. Many of the buildings he designed, including PS 165, have a strikingly collegiate appearance. This is most apparent with the high schools, namely, Morris High School in the Bronx; Wadleigh High School at 215 West 114th Street; Flushing High School and Newtown High School in Queens; the original DeWitt Clinton High School, now John Jay College of Criminal Justice on 10th Avenue at 58th Street; and the original Stuyvesant High School on East 15th Street. Snyder retired in 1923.

241 West 97th Street (near Broadway)

Adler, Cyrus "Cy" A. (1927–2018) ☜
SHORE-WALKER AND AUTHOR

If the famous *New Yorker* writers, Joseph Mitchell and St. Clair McKelway, had known about Adler, they would most likely have written about him and his "wild schemes." One of them, a delightful but

170 Foot Croton Water Tower built in 1879—West 97th and 98th Streets between Columbus and Amsterdam Avenues.

challenging annual ritual celebrated each May, is "The Great Saunter," the thirty-two-mile walk around Manhattan's shoreline. Adler's friend, Pete Seeger, with whom he wrote a few ditties, joined him one year on the walk. Adler also proposed a trail along the entire length of the Hudson River. His plan is detailed in his book, *From the Batt to the Bear*, referring to Battery Park and Bear Mountain. Born in Brooklyn, Adler was college-educated, married in 1961, and taught physics at City College of New York and oceanography at SUNY Maritime and Long Island University. In the 1970s, he turned his attention to environmental advocacy with the publication of his first book, *Ecological Fantasies—Death from Falling Watermelons: A Defense of Innovation, Science, and Rational Approaches to Environmental Problems.*

255 West 97th Street (near West End Avenue)

Chambers, Julius L. (1850–1920) 🖒
JOURNALIST

Chambers is credited with ascertaining the source of the Mississippi River. As a journalist for Horace Greeley's *New York Tribune*, he infiltrated the Bloomingdale Insane Asylum, using the fictitious name Felix Somers, to test the Lunacy Laws. A few days after his exposé was published, the governor of New York appointed a commission to investigate the allegations of abuse that Chambers had brought to light. Based on the commission's findings, a new act was drafted to improve conditions in the asylums and to appoint a Commissioner of Lunacy. An Ohioan, Chambers attended Cornell and Columbia College Law School. He worked at the *New York Herald* and managed the *New York World* for Joseph Pulitzer. In 1876, his book entitled *A Mad World and Its People*, based on his experiences at the Bloomingdale Asylum, was published. In his later years, he lectured at Cornell and New York University. Chambers also lived at **202 West 103rd Street** (Amsterdam Avenue), the Hotel Clendening.

Striker Farmhouse Site, West 97th Street and West End Avenue

Morris, George Pope (1802–1864) ■
NEWSPAPER EDITOR, POET, AND SONGWRITER

Morris wrote one of the most popular songs of the nineteenth century. It was called "The Oak" when he wrote it in 1837, and the English singer and composer Henry Russell set it to music. In 1853, it was renamed "Woodman, Spare That Tree." The song originated when Morris was visiting Striker's Bay with a friend and came upon "a grand old elm" that was about to be cut down for firewood. Morris promised ten dollars to the woodman not to cut it down. Morris was born in Philadelphia but was writing verses for the *New York Gazette* at age 15. In 1823, he co-founded the *New-York Mirror*. In 1845, the newspaper published Edgar Allen Poe's poem "The Raven" for the first time. Morris wrote and published his own songs, poems, prose pieces, and a libretto to an opera, *The Maid of Saxony*. In addition, he was a Brigadier-General in the New York State Militia.

The Old Community: West 98th–99th Street, Central Park West to Columbus Avenue

Alston, Charles (1907–1977) ■ ▇
ARTIST AND MURALIST

Alston's bust of Dr. Martin Luther King was the first image of an African American to be displayed in the White House. President **Obama** placed it in the Oval Office along with one of Abraham Lincoln. As one of the great artists of the Harlem Renaissance, Alston's works have been widely exhibited and held in museum collections. He was born in North Carolina to a father who was born into slavery. Young Alston came to New York in 1915 and started drawing posters at PS 179 at 174 West 102nd Street. He graduated from Columbia University in 1929 and

Columbus Avenue, west side, from northeast corner of 100th Street looking southward, showing "El" before demolition, August, 1934.

from Teachers College in 1931 with a master's degree. He and three others, working as WPA artists, produced murals for Harlem Hospital in 1936. They can be seen in the hospital lobby and, more amazingly, projected in a montage on the large façade of the hospital building. His illustrations were published in many magazines, including the *New Yorker*, and he designed album covers for such jazz greats as Duke Ellington and **Coleman Hawkins**. He is related to the great African American painter Romare Bearden by marriage.

Clayton, Buck (1911–1991) ■

Jazz Trumpeter

Clayton might be best known as a distinctive soloist in the Count Basie band. He also played on the early recordings of **Billie Holiday.** A native Kansan like Basie, he mastered the trumpet as a teenager. He also mastered arranging, composing, and promoting by forming and leading an ensemble called 14 Gentlemen from Harlem. They did a two-year gig in, of all places, Shanghai, China. Back in the States, and passing through Kansas City in 1936, Count Basie nabbed him to replace "Hot Lips" Page. Basie utilized his composing and arranging skills, in addition to his solo work. Clayton left in 1943 and joined the army for three years. After the war, he worked extensively in such varied gigs as the Brussels World's Fair, backing up Frank Sinatra, and making a cameo in *The Benny Goodman Story*. He also taught at Hunter College.

Cook, Will Marion (1869–1944) ★ ◼ ▪

VIOLINIST AND COMPOSER

Cook was one of the most important figures in African American music before jazz. His 1898 musical sketch comedy *Clorindy, or The Origin of the Cake Walk*, written in collaboration with Paul Laurence Dunbar, was the first all-Black show to be performed on Broadway. In 1903, *In Dahomey*—with music by Cook, lyrics by Dunbar, and performances by the great vaudeville team of **Bert Williams** and George Walker—made Broadway history as the first musical to star African Americans. Cook was born in Washington, D.C., and was raised there and in Chattanooga, Tennessee. At age 13, he went to Oberlin Conservatory of Music in Ohio. From there, he won a scholarship to study violin in Berlin, Germany, under Joseph Joachim, who was one of the great violinists of the nineteenth century and a collaborator of Johannes Brahms. Cook made his professional debut in 1889 in Washington, D.C., but found musical theater more accepting and less segregated than the classical music world. In 1894 and 1895, however, he studied with Antonin Dvorak, who headed up the National Conservatory of Music in New York. In addition to the dozen or so Broadway shows that he composed music for, he also wrote songs for solo performers and choral groups. In 1898, Cook married 14-year-old singer **Abbie Mitchell**, and she performed in many of his early shows. Their son, Will Mercer Cook, became the US Ambassador to Niger and Senegal and, like his grandfather, a professor at Howard University. Cook lived at **10 1/2 West 99th Street** (near Central Park West).

Garvey, Marcus Mosiah, Jr. (1887–1940) ◼

BLACK NATIONALIST POLITICAL LEADER

Garvey claimed to have four million followers to establish a new nation of Black citizens and, indeed, twenty-five thousand of them attended his rally in Madison Square Garden in 1920. His ideas synthesized into the return of the African diaspora to their ancestral lands. To

THE OLD COMMUNITY

"The Old Community" refers to the African American enclave that flourished from the early 1900s to the late 1950s on West 98th and 99th Streets between Central Park West and Columbus Avenue.

Before African Americans migrated in large numbers from the South to manufacturing jobs in the North, their numbers in New York were not very large. Most lived on the Lower West Side, in the Tenderloin district of the West 20s and 30s, or in a small neighborhood in the far West 60s called San Juan Hill.

Philip Payton is widely known for opening Harlem to African Americans. In 1901, a Mary O'Sullivan, who owned two buildings—10 and 10 1/2 West 99th Street—had a dispute with a neighbor and might have hired Payton to fill the buildings with Blacks to "retaliate." In 1905, Payton purchased 57 and 59 West 99th Street and, later that year, controlled more properties on the street.

Those African Americans on West 98th and 99th Streets coalesced around St. Jude's Chapel, which opened in 1921 at 19 West 99th Street, and St. Luke's Baptist Church, which began in 1937 and grew to a three-story chapel at 55 West 99th Street by 1939. Most of the children went to PS 179 at 174 West 102nd Street. They had an extensively vibrant social life of dances, sports teams, outings, and the like, all of which were brought to a needless end by urban renewal. See Jim Epstein's video *The Tragedy of Urban Renewal* (viewable on YouTube).

that end, funds were raised, and a ship was acquired and renamed the *S.S. Frederick Douglass*. But financial difficulties and charges of mail fraud sank the effort. Further, Garvey's influence declined as some Black leaders, such as W. E. B. Du Bois, thought that leaving America was capitulation. Garvey was born on the Caribbean island of Jamaica. After attending Birkbeck College in London, he returned to Jamaica to start the Universal Negro Improvement Association, which advocated for social, political, and economic freedom for Black people. Inspired by Booker T. Washington, Garvey came to the United States, where he lectured extensively and published his widely distributed newspaper, *Negro World*. Founder of the African Communities League, he was a political leader, publisher, journalist, entrepreneur, and orator who promoted and, in so doing, championed Black Nationalism. Garvey lived at **52 West 99th Street**.

Greene, Belle da Costa (1883–1950) 📖
LIBRARIAN AND ADVISOR TO J. P. MORGAN

Belle de Costa Greene.

Belle Greene was the personal librarian to J. P. Morgan. In that capacity, she acquired many of the treasures that are now in the Morgan Library. After serving Morgan's son in the same capacity, the Board of Directors named her the director of the Morgan Library. Born Belle Marion Greener in Washington, D.C., she grew up in New York City. In a time when it would have been extraordinary for an African American woman to attend college, she developed her intellect and Bohemian sophistication through her accomplished parents and through her work as a librarian at Princeton University. A valued advisor, she managed Morgan's growing library and made significant purchases on his behalf. Her knowledge of rare books gave her a first-rate reputation with bibliophiles and other librarians. Never married, she had an ongoing romantic relationship with the art expert and dealer, Bernard Berenson. When asked if she was Morgan's mistress, she is supposed to have said, "We tried!" Her father was the renowned **Richard Theodore Greener**. Greene's address was **29 West 99th Street**. She also had two other addresses in the neighborhood: **507 West 112th Street** (near Amsterdam Avenue) and **403 West 115th Street** (near Morningside Drive).

Greener, Richard Theodore (1844–1922) ■ ▉ ☞
LAWYER, DEAN, AND DIPLOMAT

Greener was the first African American graduate of Harvard University. He was born in Philadelphia but grew up in Boston. After teaching a bit post-graduation, he went on to graduate from South Carolina University School of Law. He taught at Howard University School of Law and was dean there for a time. His activities in the Republican Party led to his selection as the secretary of the Grant Monument Association. He also did some foreign service work in Russia and was honored by China for his efforts there. Along the way, he wrote for a publication edited by Frederick Douglass and was awarded two honorary doctorates. His daughter was **Belle da Costa Greene**.

Holiday, Billie (1915–1959) ★ ■
SINGER

She was dubbed "Lady Day" by her saxophonist friend and musical partner, Lester Young. Born in Philadelphia, she was named Eleanora Fagan from her mother, but she later took her professional name from her father. Her difficult and sketchy childhood left her truant and in reform school. Joining her mother in Harlem, she began singing in nightclubs as a teenager. Her breaks came in working with Benny Goodman and being discovered by the legendary record producer and talent scout, John Hammond, who also discovered Aretha Franklin, Bruce Springsteen, and Bob Dylan. Her performances and recordings were extensive and

Billie Holiday, July 28, 1945.

essential to jazz history. Diana Ross played her in the movie version of her autobiography *Lady Sings the Blues*. Her uniquely moody voice and distinctive style of phrasing place her alongside Ella Fitzgerald, Sarah Vaughan, and **Nina Simone** in the pantheon of great female jazz singers. Holiday's address was **9 West 99th Street**; her mother Sadie's restaurant was located at **71 West 99th Street** (near Columbus Avenue).

Johnson, James Weldon (1871–1938) ★ ■
COMPOSER AND CIVIL RIGHTS ACTIVIST

Johnson's 1899 poem "Lift Every Voice and Sing" was set to music by his brother **J. Rosamond Johnson** and became affectionately known as the "Negro National Anthem." Born in Florida, Johnson graduated in 1894 from Clark Atlanta University in Georgia. He and his brother moved to New York to write and compose for the Broadway stage. In 1906, President Theodore Roosevelt appointed James Weldon Johnson consul, first for Venezuela and later for Nicaragua. In 1916, he began working for the National Association for the Advancement of Colored People, and by 1920 was executive secretary in charge of the NAACP's daily operations. He organized the 1917 silent march of ten thousand African Americans down Fifth Avenue. Meanwhile, Johnson became a central figure in the Harlem Renaissance with the publication of his novel, poems, and anthologies of poems and Negro spirituals. Johnson lived at **52 West 99th Street**.

Johnson, J(ohn) Rosamond (1873–1954) ★ ■
COMPOSER

Johnson set music to his brother **James Weldon Johnson**'s poem "Lift Every Voice and Sing," also known as the "Negro National Anthem."

Born in Florida, he found his way into vaudeville and musical theater at an early age. Trained at the New England Conservatory of Music, he joined his brother and another versatile talent, Bob Cole, to produce several musicals in the early 1900s. Some of the musicals, such as *Sleeping Beauty and the Beast* in 1901 and *Humpty Dumpty* in 1904 played for "white" audiences on Broadway. More significant, however, were their operettas: *Shoo-Fly* in 1906 and *The Red Moon* in 1908. They featured the first Black actors in respectable roles. Johnson performed, wrote, and composed for vaudeville for years; conducted numerous orchestras; and acted and sang in the original production of Gershwin's *Porgy and Bess*. Johnson lived at **52 West 99th Street**.

Jones, Robert Earl (1910–2006)
ACTOR

Jones was the one-time sparring partner to Joe Louis. Born in Mississippi, he made his way to New York City via Chicago as a prizefighter. His acting career, which began in the 1930s, included stage work, movies, and television. A character actor, rather than a leading man, he might best be remembered as Robert Redford's mentor in *The Sting*. In one of his last performances in 1991 at Lincoln Center, he distinguished his role in Langston Hughes's *Mule Bone*. Adored by the opposite sex, he was married three times. His first marriage yielded another actor, James Earl Jones. Jones lived at **69 West 99th Street**.

McQueen, Thelma "Butterfly" (1911–1995) ◼
ACTRESS

Thelma McQueen was called "Butterfly" in tribute to her constantly moving hands during her performance of the Butterfly Ballet in a production of *A Midsummer Night's Dream*. McQueen is undoubtedly most remembered for her role as Scarlet O'Hara's maid in the 1939 movie classic *Gone with the Wind*. Born in Florida, she began acting in her high school on Long Island, then moved to Harlem where she could work on the legitimate stage. She studied dance with Geoffrey Holder and others and debuted on Broadway in 1937, under the direction of George Abbott. She was cast in *Gone with the Wind* after being seen on the Broadway stage in the 1938 comedy *What a Life*. She had more film work in the 1940s, although she was often cast in stereotypical roles and uncredited. She left filmdom and did some television in the 1950s, including a regular stint in *Beulah* with Ethel Waters and Louise Beavers. In 1975, she received a bachelor's degree in political science at City College.

Mitchell (Cook), Abriea "Abbie" (1884–1960) ▣ ▢
ACTRESS AND SOPRANO

Mitchell was in the premiere performance of George Gershwin's *Porgy and Bess* and was the first to record the song "Summertime." She also appeared in an 1898 musical production *Clorindy, or The Origin of the Cake Walk*. It had lyrics by the poet Paul Laurence Dunbar and music by **Will Marion Cook**, whom Mitchell married the following year. Her lead roles include the historic London performance in the show *In Dahomey*, produced by George Walker and **Bert Williams** with music by her husband. Born in Baltimore, she studied voice in New York in 1897. She appeared as an actress on Broadway in *The Little Foxes*, and in concert with her husband. She was the former executive secretary of the Negro Actors Guild of America.

Payton, Philip A., Jr. (1876–1917) ★ ▣ ▢
PIONEER REALTOR

Philip Payton and his Afro-American Realty Company opened Harlem to Blacks. Born in Westfield, Massachusetts, he attended Livingstone

College in North Carolina. In 1901, an angry white landlord in Harlem had a dispute with a neighboring building owner. Philip Payton was hired as a rental agent to enact revenge by filling the building with African American tenants. That was the start of his involvement in breaking the color lines that had kept African Americans out of Harlem. In that same year, 1901, a woman named Mary A. O'Sullivan acquired two buildings with addresses of **10 and 10 1/2 West 99th Street**. Like the situation in Harlem, she had a dispute with a neighbor that prompted her to retaliate. She ordered the white tenants out of her buildings and hung a sign across the second floor of her buildings that announced that apartments were available for "respectable colored families." It is not known whether Philip Payton was, in fact, hired by Mary O'Sullivan, but in 1905 he purchased numbers **57 and 59 West 98th Street** and **19, 25, 27, 31, 44, and 46 West 99th Street**. During that time, and for the next twenty years, Philip Payton continued to open Harlem to African Americans.

Schomburg, Arturo Alfonso (1874–1938) ■ 🖘

HISTORIAN, COLLECTOR, AND CURATOR

In 1926, the Carnegie Foundation purchased Schomburg's extensive personal collection and appointed him curator of the Schomburg Collection of Negro Literature and Art. It was considered the best in the world. The Carnegie Foundation gave the collection to the New York Public Library and it became the Arthur Schomburg Center for Research in Black Culture. The incredible collection included more than five thousand books, three thousand manuscripts, two thousand etchings and paintings, thousands of pamphlets, and such rarities as slave narratives and materials from colonial times. The New York Public Library was shrewd enough to put Schomburg in charge of his collection, and he used the money from its sale to travel and to expand the collection. Schomburg was born in Puerto Rico and studied what was then called Negro literature at St. Thomas College in the Virgin Islands. He came to New York in 1891 and became active in advocating for the independence of Cuba and Puerto Rico from Spain. He taught Spanish, worked as a clerk and a messenger in a law firm, and worked as a supervisor in the Bankers Trust Company. In 1911, he founded the Negro Society for Historical Research with historian and journalist John Edward Bruce. Fully immersed in the Harlem Renaissance, Schomburg spearheaded wider efforts to collect and value African American history. Schomburg also lived at **205 West 115th Street** (near Adam Clayton Powell Jr. Boulevard).

Torain, James "Jim" E. (1942–2017) ◾

COMMUNITY HISTORIAN, FATHER OF THE OLD COMMUNITY

Jim Torrain.

Torain established The Old Community to celebrate the rich and unique story of the African American residents who had lived on West 98th and 99th Streets and were displaced in 1955 by urban renewal. Along with that effort, he accumulated information about the notables that lived there and mobilized an annual reunion to honor their heritage. Miraculously, residents were still coming to the reunion fifty and sixty years after they left the neighborhood. Born in the Bloomingdale neighborhood, Torain worked as a public relations assistant at Madison Square Garden. Torain lived at two addresses in The Old Community: **14 West 99th Street** and **63 West 99th Street**.

Williams, Egbert Austin "Bert" (1874–1922) ★ ◼ ◾

VAUDEVILLE ENTERTAINER

Bert Williams might have been the greatest vaudevillian of all time. Knowing Williams's work is essential for understanding all African

American entertainment. Williams was born in the Bahamas, but his family moved to Florida and then to California. Performing in different minstrel shows, he met George Walker. As Walker & Williams, they were the rock stars of their day. Although initially they played plantation stereotypes in blackface, they developed into more nuanced characterizations. With dignified demeanor and immaculate dress, they conveyed a mockery to their blackface and cakewalking. As early as 1901, they were recorded on cylinders. The 1903 production of *In Dahomey*, with Laurence Dunbar lyrics and **Will Marion Cook** music, featured Williams as the first Black man to star in a leading role on Broadway. The 1906 show *Abyssinia,* with Williams as co-writer, included the classic song "Nobody." Williams went on to star in numerous *Ziegfeld Follies*, one of which debuted Fanny Brice. W. C. Fields called him "the funniest man I ever saw; and the saddest man I ever knew."

Bert Williams.

Woods, Granville (1856–1910) ★ ▪ ▮
INVENTOR

Woods was known as "the Black Edison." Some sixty patents were attributed to him, and some were sold to General Electric, the Bell Telephone Company, and Westinghouse. One of them, the "troller," enabled streetcars, hence "trolleys," to receive electricity from overhead wires. Another Woods invention was the device that grabbed power from the "third rail." His most important invention was the multiplex telegraph, which enabled voice communication over telegraph wires. Woods was born in Ohio and seemed to be entirely self-taught in his mechanical and electrical engineering abilities. He apprenticed in a machine shop, worked as a fireman on a railroad where he became a train engineer, and worked in a rolling mill and electric shop for a while. Eventually, he settled in New York, and probably through a connection to St. Michael's Episcopal Church was buried in St.

Michael's Cemetery in Queens. He lived at **12 West 99th Street** (near Central Park West).

220 West 98th Street (near Broadway), the Borchardt Apartments

Berrigan, Daniel Joseph (1921–2016)

ACTIVIST PRIEST

Berrigan received national attention in 1968 when he and others burned draft files in Catonsville, Maryland. Thus, they were called the Catonsville Nine, and they contributed to the growing sentiment against the Vietnam War. It is no surprise that he spent years in prison. Born in Minnesota but raised in Syracuse, he was educated by Jesuits into the priesthood. While teaching at Jesuit prep schools, he began writing poetry. He also wrote or co-wrote some fifty books and taught at several colleges and universities, the longest tenure being at Fordham. His activism against war and work on behalf of HIV/AIDS victims never abated.

240 West 98th Street (near Broadway)

Marble (Pollock), Anna (1880–1946) ■ ▢

THEATRICAL PRESS AGENT

Marble might have been the first woman theatrical press agent in the country. She left her job as a feature writer at the *Brooklyn Eagle* newspaper to become the press agent for the 1900 rave musical *Florodora*. In addition to handling publicity for several Elsie de Wolfe plays, she was press agent for **Oscar Hammerstein**'s Victoria Theater and his Manhattan Opera House. She had also handled the press work for the Hippodrome for a period and is credited with making the Rialto Theater one of the nation's most important vaudeville

---

"THE GOAT"—A PLAYGROUND BASKETBALL LEGEND

The playground on the east side of Amsterdam Avenue between 98th and 99th Streets was once named in honor of a basketball legend, Earl "the Goat" Manigault (1944–1998). He was said to be the first basketball player to perform the "double-dunk"—dunking a basketball twice on one leap—although Manigault himself claimed that he never did it. Another myth associated with him was an ability to leap so high that he could take a dollar bill off the top of the backboard and leave change. It should be noted that a basketball rim is ten feet off the ground, but the top of the backboard is thirteen feet.

Born in South Carolina and raised in Harlem, Manigault held court on the court, dazzling one and all with his legendary basketball skills. Manigault played in many other city

venues. Marble was born in Chicago in one of the oldest theatrical families in the country. Her father, Edward Marble, was a renowned actor, as was his father, Danford "Dan" Marble, especially for his role as daredevil jumper Sam Patch. The Library of Congress has the diary Anna Marble donated of another relative, the actor William Warren, who first appeared on the New York stage in 1841. The Yale Collection of American Literature has the Anna Marble Pollock Memorial Collection of Books about Cats. Her husband was the playwright Channing Pollock.

201 West 99th Street (near Amsterdam Avenue)

Peters, John Punnett, Jr. (1887–1955) ■

PHYSICIAN

Peters made national news when, appearing before the Supreme Court, he successfully appealed his dismissal from the surgeon general's office on loyalty grounds. As a prime mover behind the so-called Committee of Four Hundred, he advocated for the expansion of public health, often in conflict with the American Medical Association. As the author of more than 150 books and papers on internal medicine and public health policy, he was an internationally renowned physician and research scientist. Born in Philadelphia, he was raised in Bloomingdale. His father, John Punnett Peters, Sr., was the rector of St. Michael's Church, as was his grandfather **Thomas McClure Peters**. Junior received his BA degree from Yale in 1908 and his medical degree five years later from Columbia's College of Physicians and Surgeons. He served as a captain in the Army Medical Corps in World War I, after which he performed research at Bellevue Hospital and the Rockefeller Institute until he was appointed assistant professor of internal medicine at Yale in 1921 and the John Slade Ely Professor in 1927. Peters also lived at **227 West 99th Street** (near Broadway).

playgrounds, hustling the game with such future greats as Wilt Chamberlain, Connie Hawkins, and Kareem Abdul-Jabbar.

How "the Goat" got his name is up for grabs. Was Manigault economized into "goat," or suggested by his walk and quiet demeanor? Some say "goat" is an acronym for "greatest of all time."

Unfortunately, drug use ruined his opportunity for college and professional stardom. In time, he overcame his addiction and became a respected community leader. In 1996, HBO featured Don Cheadle in the television film *Rebound: The Legend of Earl "The Goat" Manigault*.

Sometime in the 2000s, a decision was made to change the name of the playground to "The Happy Warrior" playground. President Franklin Delano Roosevelt called New York State governor Al Smith "The Happy Warrior" because of his diligence and perseverance. FDR owes credit to William Wordsworth, who, in 1807, penned the poem "Character of the Happy Warrior."

220 West 99th Street (Broadway)

Coakley, Andrew "Andy" (1882–1963) ☞
BASEBALL PLAYER AND COLUMBIA COACH

Coakley played professional baseball for the team that became the New York Yankees. Born in Providence, Rhode Island, Coakley graduated from Holy Cross College, where he was a star on the mound. He pitched in professional baseball for ten years and for four different teams. In his last year, he was with the New York Highlanders, which would be renamed the New York Yankees. In his only post-season game, his pitching opponent was Hall of Famer Christy Mathewson. After professional ball, Coakley coached the Williams College baseball team for three seasons and then served as Columbia's beloved baseball coach from 1914 to 1951 (minus 1919). One of his star players at Columbia was New York Yankee Hall of Famer Lou Gehrig. Another was Sid Luckman, who switched to football and became a Hall of Fame quarterback. Columbia honored him by naming the Andy Coakley Field, a place where today's baseball players can reflect upon the Columbia Lions vs. Princeton Tigers game of May 17, 1939, the first sporting event ever broadcast live on television.

227 West 99th Street (near Amsterdam Avenue)

Peters, John Punnett, Jr. (1887–1955), Physician ■

(See bio for Peters, Jr., at **201 West 99th Street**.)

309 West 99th Street (near Riverside Drive)

Goldberg, Ruben "Rube" Garrett Lucius (1883–1970), Cartoonist ■

(See bio for Goldberg at **420 Riverside Drive**.)

310 West 99th Street (near Riverside Drive)

Loveman, Amy (1881–1955) ▪

EDITOR

In 1924, Loveman, along with Christopher Morley, William Rose Benet, and Henry Seidel Canby, founded the *Saturday Review of Literature* magazine, renamed the *Saturday Review* in 1940. A New York native, Loveman graduated from Barnard College in 1901 and was elected to Phi Beta Kappa. In the earliest days of her career, she wrote book reviews for the *New York Post*. In addition to serving as a longtime associate editor of *Saturday Review*, she also served as its poetry editor from 1950. In 1939, she became head of the editorial department of the Book of the Month Club, where she also contributed numerous book reviews. She edited a few anthologies, including *Varied Harvest: A Miscellany of Writing by Barnard College Women, 1888–1953*, and she wrote a book of literary recommendations entitled *I'm Looking for a Book*.

315 Central Park West (91st Street) and 320 Central Park West (92nd Street)

Hammerstein, William "Willie" (1875–1914) ☞

THEATER MANAGER

Hammerstein masterminded the first theatrical roof garden on Broadway. He was the son of the theater impresario, **Oscar Hammerstein I**, and the father of the lyricist, **Oscar Hammerstein II**. He built a small vaudeville resort in what was called "Little Coney Island" on 110th Street between Amsterdam Avenue and Broadway. He also managed two of his father's theaters in the Times Square area: the Olympia Theater and the Victoria Theater. At one time, he booked the infamous Cherry Sisters vaudeville act on the Olympia roof garden. By all estimates, they were one of the worst acts ever, and that was the basis of their popularity. They sang sentimental patriotic songs to a flurry of tomatoes, cabbages, and eggs tossed their way, and it was said that "they were so bad, they were good." Hammerstein booked Will Rogers before he became famous, and Irving Berlin in 1911, the year he had his first big hit with "Alexander's Ragtime Band." Some of his other bookings included Evelyn Nesbit, who was Stanford White's love interest; heavyweight champion boxer James J. Corbett; and Don the Talking Dog. The honorary pallbearers at his funeral included such theatrical luminaries as Martin Beck, E. F. Albee, William Morris, Marcus Loew, and William Fox.

348 Central Park West (near 94th Street)

Bolton, Guy (1884–1979) ● ▣
PLAYWRIGHT OF MUSICAL COMEDIES

Bolton wrote the books to the Gershwin musicals *Girl Crazy* and *Lady Be Good*, and to Cole Porter's *Anything Goes*. More importantly, he wrote the shows with music by Jerome Kern that became known as the "Princess Theater musicals." By collaborating with the likes of **P. G. Wodehouse**, these highly sophisticated shows ushered in the modern musicals of Rogers, Hart, the **Gershwins**, Porter, Berlin, **Hammerstein**, and Kern. Bolton also wrote numerous screenplays and stage adaptations of novels by Henry James and W. Somerset Maugham. His father was Reginald Pelham Bolton, who wrote a standard history of Washington Heights and Inwood, and whose excavations in those areas documented Native American and Revolutionary War history.

350 Central Park West (near 94th Street)

O'Dwyer, Paul (1907–1998) ▪

POLITICIAN

Judge Benjamin Cardozo, in the New York Court of Appeals, had to give O'Dwyer, not yet a citizen in 1929, special permission to take the bar exam. O'Dwyer emigrated from Ireland to the United States in 1925, but he would not become a citizen until the mandatory period of five years passed in 1930. While working on the docks and in the garment center, he attended night school at Fordham University and St. John's Law School. As a lawyer, and while president of the progressive National Lawyers Guild, he was always the champion of the underdog. He argued loudly with his older brother, Mayor William O'Dwyer, who was ushered out of office with a tarnished reputation. In 1948, he barely lost a congressional election to Jacob Javits. In 1951, he successfully won a suit against Metropolitan Life Insurance Company to ensure that Blacks could live in Stuyvesant Town. In the mid-1970s, after serving two terms in the city council, he was elected president of the City Council. O'Dwyer also lived at **103rd Street and Columbus Avenue** (Mrs. Maguire's Irish Boarding House).

370 Central Park West (near 97th Street)

Burns, Arthur Frank (1904–1987) ▪

ECONOMIST AND FEDERAL RESERVE CHAIRMAN

In addition to his two-term stint as Chairman of the Federal Reserve in the 1970s, Burns served as chairman of the Council of Economic Advisers and as ambassador to Germany. Born in Austria, Burns came with his family to the United States just before World War I. Highly accomplished, in 1925 he graduated from Columbia, was elected to Phi Beta Kappa, and earned a master's degree. From 1927 to 1944, he taught economics at Rutgers University. In 1930, while pursuing his PhD, he came under the wing of the renowned economist, Wesley Clair

Mitchell. In 1933, Mitchell recruited Burns for the organization that he founded, the National Bureau of Economic Research. Burns earned his PhD, concentrated on the study of business cycles and the causes of expansion and contraction, and followed Mitchell as head of the National Bureau. In 1945, he became a Columbia professor and received the John Bates Clark endowed chair in 1959.

375 Central Park West (near 97th Street), the Versailles Apartments

Smythe, J. Henry, Jr. (1883–1956) ☞

PUBLICIST

J. Henry Smythe.

Smythe looked like President Franklin Delano Roosevelt and coined one thousand political slogans. In World War II they included "Swat the Swastika" and "Ax the Axis." For the World War I Liberty Bond campaign, he crafted "Lend to Defend" and "A Bond Is a Prayer That You Send Over There." He gave the British "Lend That Shilling for Shelling." Born in Philadelphia, Smythe graduated from the University of Pennsylvania in 1909. Although rejected for service in World War I because of defective vision, he served in the American Red Cross in Europe. He published children's books for a time but then established a commercial advertising business. A lifelong Republican, whose heroes were Benjamin Franklin and Alexander Hamilton, he produced campaign slogans for every presidential election from 1924. For 1924, it was "Keep Coolidge. He Keeps the Faith." For 1936, he championed Alf Landon, FDR's running mate, with "Let's Make It a Landonslide."

Wodehouse, Sir Pelham Grenville "P. G." (1881–1975) ★ ■

AUTHOR

Wodehouse wrote special lyrics for Cole Porter's "You're the Top" in the musical *Anything Goes* to be used only for English audiences. He wrote many other lyrics for American composers such as **Oscar Hammerstein II**, Rudolf Friml, **George Gershwin**, Sigmund Romberg, and, of course, Jerome Kern. Born and educated in England, Wodehouse wrote numerous humorous pieces for publications and a few novels before he first visited the United States in 1904. Soon he was writing for the stage, and lyrics for musical theater. In 1915, he wrote the first of many "Bertie" and "Jeeves" books that playfully invert English society. In 1916, the wonderful collaboration of Wodehouse with writer **Guy Bolton** and composer Jerome Kern began to advance Broadway toward its golden age with their Princess Theater musicals. Hollywood lured Wodehouse with some hefty bucks, but it didn't work. No matter, he continued writing with a solid reputation. He survived an incident during World War II where his patriotism was challenged, resulting in three missed opportunities for knighthood. He became a citizen of the United States in 1955 but kept his British citizenship as well. In 1975 he was knighted.

385 Central Park West (near 97th Street), no longer extant

Weiss, Louis Stix (1894–1950) ■
LAWYER

He was the Weiss in the well-known law firm of Paul, Weiss, Rifkind, Wharton & Garrison. Weiss recruited Treasury Department General Counsel Randolph E. Paul and War Labor Board chairman Lloyd K. Garrison to join the firm. In addition, he was chairman of the Legal Defense Committee of the National Association for the Advancement of Colored People, and chairman of the Board of Trustees of the New School for Social Research. A native New Yorker, he graduated from Yale in 1915 and from Columbia's Law School, where he was editor-in-chief of the *Columbia Law Review*, in 1920. After his World War I service in in the legal division of the War Industries Board and the United States Housing Corporation, he joined the Simpson, Thatcher

& Bartlett law firm. He left after three years to form Paul, Weiss. Along with Eleanor Roosevelt, he was a founder of the US Committee for the Care of European Children, a trustee of the National Opinion Research Center, and a director of the American Council on Race Relations. He was married to Barnard graduate Aline Pollitzer, class of 1917.

386 Central Park West (near 98th Street), the Elberon Hall Apartments

Waghalter, Ignatz (1881–1949) ■
COMPOSER AND ORCHESTRA CONDUCTOR

By age 13, Waghalter was playing the big drum in a circus band. Less than ten years later, his first professional work in an orchestra was playing the timpani. He would go on to become one of the best conductors in the world. Waghalter was born into a musical family in Poland. In his late teens, he ran away to Berlin, studied the violin, and was accepted into the Prussian Academy of Arts, where he studied composition and conducting. Soon he was conducting opera and his reputation was established. He conducted the premiere performances in Germany of well-known operas such as Verdi's *Tosca* and Puccini's *La Boheme*. He composed operas and operettas, as well as concert pieces for orchestra and string ensembles. Facing danger as a Pole and a Jew, he fled Germany in 1934 and came to the United States. With musical styles changing, he wasn't employed or appreciated as much in the United States as in Germany, where some of his compositions have been revived in recent years.

2450 Broadway (at 91st Street), now the location of Carmine's restaurant

Roosevelt, Franklin, Jr. (1914–1988) ☞
CONGRESSMAN

Six-foot, four-inch Roosevelt was a dead ringer for his president father. Unfortunately, he burned too many bridges with the family's Democratic Party by declaring for Eisenhower in 1948 and not catering to the Tammany political machine. In other circumstances, he might have been governor of New York, but his bad blood with the party resulted in the selection of **Averell Harriman** as the candidate for governor. Harriman won, and Roosevelt, the attorney general candidate, lost. Roosevelt was born on the family compound on Campobello Island in Canada. After graduating from Harvard in 1937 and from the University of Virginia Law School in 1940, he served in the US Navy during World War II, commanding a destroyer and earning the Legion of Merit, the Navy Cross, the Silver Star, and the Purple Heart. He worked in a corporate law firm for a few years but was more interested in politics. In 1949, the Bloomingdale and Morningside Heights neighborhoods mourned the death of Congressman **Sol Bloom**. Without Tammany support, Roosevelt found an opportunity to represent the Twentieth Congressional District by moving into the district and running in the special election as a Liberal Party candidate. He served in Congress from 1949 to 1955.

2469 Broadway (near 92nd Street)

Lewis, Sinclair (1885–1951) ★ ■
AUTHOR

In 1930, Sinclair Lewis became the first American to win the Nobel Prize for Literature. In 1926, he had refused to accept the Pulitzer Prize for his book *Arrowsmith*. He thought all prizes were "dangerous" in that they encourage artists to seek rewards instead of excellence. In addition to being critically acclaimed, his novels introduced names and images into popular vocabulary, and many were reprised into notable movies. Although his first novel was authored in 1914, *Main Street*, which was published in 1920, was his first large success, followed by *Babbitt* in 1922, *Arrowsmith* in 1925, *Elmer Gantry* in 1927, *Dodsworth* in 1929, *It Can't Happen Here* in 1935, and *Cass Tamberlane* in 1945. He wrote some twenty other novels and fifty short stories. He also wrote poems, essays, and a few plays. Born in Minnesota, he graduated from Yale with an AB degree in 1908. He interrupted his education to work in **Upton Sinclair**'s short-lived utopian community, Helicon Hall, near the New Jersey Palisades.

2520–2524 Broadway (near 94th Street), Hotel Monterey, now the Hotel Apthorp

Peck, Anne Smith (1850–1935) ★ ● ▮ ☜

MOUNTAINEER AND SUFFRAGIST

In 1912, Anne Peck climbed the twenty-first tallest mountain in South America, Coropuna in the Peruvian Andes, and planted a flag with the inscription "Votes for Women." After she climbed the fourth highest mountain in South America, Huascaran, its north peak was named

Annie Smith Peck.

Cumbre Ana Peck in her honor. In addition to climbing the Matterhorn in the European Alps, she scaled Pico de Orizaba, the highest mountain in Mexico. Her last climb, at age 82, was Mount Madison in the White Mountains of New Hampshire. Born in Rhode Island, Peck completed her studies at the University of Michigan in 1881 with AB and AM degrees. She studied German and music in Germany for two years before becoming the first woman to study in the American School of Classical Studies in Athens, Greece, where she undertook Greek and archeology. Back in the United States, she taught at various high schools before becoming a professor of Latin at Smith College in Massachusetts and at Purdue University in Indiana. The books she authored included *The South American Tour*, *Flying Over South America*, and *High Mountain Climbing in Peru and Bolivia*. She was a fellow of the Society of Women Geographers and of the Royal Geographical Society.

2561–69 Broadway and 96th Street, NW corner, Riverside Theater-Skuras Circuit building.

Broadway and West 99th Street

Peters, Thomas McClure (1821–1893)

EPISCOPAL PRIEST AND RECTOR

Peters was the fourth rector of St. Michael's Church on Amsterdam Avenue at 99th Street from 1858 to his death. He was thought to be the oldest rector in the city at the time of his death, having served in that capacity for fifty years. Born the son of a prominent merchant in Boston, Peters graduated from Yale in 1841 and received his doctorate in Divinity. During his tenure, the second St. Michael's Church was completed in 1854, and the third and present one in 1891. Peters also acquired the property in East Elmhurst, Queens, that became St. Michael's Cemetery in 1852. His father-in-law was St. Michael's second rector William Richmond. His son, John Punnett Peters, Sr., succeeded him as fifth rector of St. Michael's. **John Punnett Peters, Jr.**, was his grandson. Thomas Peters also lived on **Broadway and West 101st Street**, and **Broadway between 103rd and 104th Streets**.

624 West End Avenue (near 90th Street)

Norworth, John "Jack" (1879–1959) ▪

VAUDEVILLE PERFORMER AND SONGWRITER

Norworth wrote the lyrics to "Take Me Out to the Ball Game." It is thought that only "Happy Birthday" and "The Star-Spangled Banner" are sung more often. Born John Godfrey Knauf in Philadelphia, he came to

New York, changed his name to Norworth, and became a show business performer. Norworth and his second wife, Nora Bayes, starred in the first Ziegfeld Follies in 1908 and co-wrote "Shine on Harvest Moon." The 1944 movie of the same name recounts their story. Norworth and Bayes were married from 1907 to 1913, and they lived together at 624 West End Avenue, yet city directories for 1910, 1911, and 1913 list him also at 606 West 116th Street. Did he keep a separate apartment there? Also, was he related to Margie Norworth? His third wife was the Academy Award–nominated actress Louise Dresser. Norworth staged several early shows on Broadway and built a theater on West 48th Street that he named after himself. It just so happens that **Patty Hill**, who wrote "Happy Birthday" with her sister Mildred, lived at **21 Claremont Avenue**, across the street from Norworth's home at **606 West 116th Street**. The composer of "Take Me Out to the Ballgame," **Albert Von Tilzer**, also composed "I'll Be with You in Apple Blossom Time."

681 West End Avenue (near 93rd Street)

Matthews, Brander (1852–1929), Writer and Educator

(See bio for Matthews at **301 West 93rd Street**.)

685 West End Avenue (near 93rd Street)

Newman, Barnett (1905–1970)

ARTIST

In 2013, Newman's painting *Onement VI* (1953) was sold at auction to Microsoft co-founder Paul Allen for a record $43.8 million. His work can be found in most modern art museums, including the Whitney, the Museum of Modern Art, the Metropolitan Museum of Art, and the National Gallery. His best-known sculpture, *Broken Obelisk* (1969), is outside the Rothko Chapel in Houston. A native New Yorker, Newman graduated in 1927 from the City College of New York where he studied philosophy. He taught, wrote, painted, and married his art teacher, and he made a life decision in 1948 to only paint. His surrealist work transitioned into abstract expressionism. Although his reputation was somewhat overshadowed by the likes of Pollock and Rothko, in time Clement Greenberg and other sophisticates raised Newman's stature significantly.

700 West End Avenue (near 94th Street) and 702 West End Avenue (near 94th Street)

Hall, Edward Hagaman (1858–1936) ■ ▣
HISTORIAN AND PRESERVATIONIST

Hall was the workhorse of the American Scenic and Historic Preservation Society (ASHPS). As secretary of that institution for twenty-seven years, he authored a classic historical guide to the city of New York, as well as works on City Hall Park, McGowan's Pass in Central Park, the Philipse Manor Hall in Yonkers, and the first settlement of Jamestown in Virginia. Born in Auburn, New York, where his father was mayor, Hall worked at various newspapers. He and his associates at the ASHPS saw to the preservation of the Poe Cottage in the Bronx, Philipse Manor Hall, the Palisades, and New York State Parks, including Letchworth and Watkins Glen. As a member of the mayor's committee to plan for a celebration for the Consolidation of the City of New York in 1898, he designed its commemorative medal. In 1900, he devoted himself to researching and writing history. In his role as trustee for the Hudson-Fulton celebration of 1901, he researched Henry Hudson's ship, the "Half Moon." He was also secretary of the Association for the Protection of the Adirondacks, and secretary of the Municipal Art Commission. New York University and Hobart College awarded him honorary degrees. He was president of the Laymen's Club of the Cathedral of St. John the Divine and authored the Cathedral's wonderfully detailed guidebook. Hall lived at two additional addresses in the neighborhood: **12 West 103rd Street** (near Manhattan Avenue) and **60 Manhattan Avenue** (near 103rd Street).

710 West End Avenue (near 95th Street)

Spector, Ronnie (1943–) ■
ROCK AND ROLL SINGER

Spector sang lead with her group the Ronettes on the number one hit song of 1963 "Be My Baby." The list of studio musicians on the recording is a Who's Who of rock and roll talent, and even includes Leon Russell and Sonny and Cher. Born Veronica Yvette Bennett in East Harlem, Spector grew up in the Washington Heights section of Manhattan. Along with a sister and three cousins, she formed a singing group known originally as Ronnie and the Relatives. After a brief stint at Colpix Records, they gained exposure as dancers at the Peppermint Lounge during the height of the Twist dance craze. Reduced to Ronnie, sister Estelle Bennett, and cousin Nedra Talley, the group renamed themselves the Ronettes and found the brilliant up-and-coming record producer Phil Spector. They courted a "bad girl" image and he recorded them in his "wall of sound," producing a string of chart hits including "Baby I Love You" and "Walking in the Rain." Their album of Christmas songs became a perennial classic. Ronnie Bennett was married to Phil Spector from 1968 to 1974. She continued to have a long and successful singing career.

Williamson, Marianne (1952–)
AUTHOR AND PRESIDENTIAL CANDIDATE

Many people know Williamson from having seen her in the Democratic Party presidential debates in the fall of 2019. She eventually dropped

out and endorsed Bernie Sanders. A Texas native, Williamson attended
Pomona College, the University of New Mexico, and the University
of Texas. Arriving in New York City in the mid-1970s, she underwent
a spiritual transformation. Next came a return to Texas, where she
opened a coffee shop and singing cabaret. That was followed by
resettlement to California, where 17-year-old Laura Dern was her
roommate for a while. Her maturing spirituality had her lecturing
about "Divine love" and gaining a following. She joined the ministry of
the Church of Today and grew a following in Michigan that included
congregants, television viewers, and occasional celebrity guests. Her
career transcended her ministerial responsibilities as she returned to
Los Angeles and continued writing some of the dozen or so books, some
of which reached the number one position on the best-seller lists.

711 West End Avenue (near 95th Street)

Weiss, Theodore S. "Ted" (1927–1992) ◼

CONGRESSMAN

During his years as a New York City councilman, Weiss could be seen
riding the M104 bus, often in his rumpled suit carrying a worn-out
briefcase. Writing the city's gun law and fending off the Westway
project are among the many accomplishments of his public service.
Weiss was born in Hungary, but his family fled the Nazis to come to
the United States in 1938. After serving in the US Army for two years,
he graduated from Syracuse University in 1951 and from Syracuse
University College of Law in 1952. He was an assistant district
attorney under **Frank Hogan** in New York County from 1955 to 1959.
In 1961, fighting the DeSapio machine, he was elected a Democratic
councilmember. In 1978, he was elected to Congress, following Bella
Abzug, and preceding Jerry Nadler. After his passing, the Ted Weiss
Federal Building in lower Manhattan was named in his honor.

720 West End Avenue (near 95th Street)

Simpson, Mona (1957–) 🖙
NOVELIST

Apple co-founder Steve Jobs is Mona Simpson's older brother. Because Jobs was put up for adoption at birth, they did not meet until they were adults. She is also the namesake for the television series *The Simpsons*, thanks to her former husband, Richard Appel, who wrote for the show. Born Mona Jandali in Wisconsin, she took the Simpson name from her stepfather. She earned a BA degree from the University of California at Berkeley and an MFA degree from Columbia. While doing graduate work, some of her short stories were published in well-known magazines. Later, while she was an editor at the *Paris Review* for five years, she worked on her first novel. Literary success came in 1986 with the publication of that book, *Anywhere but Here.* It was also made into a film starring Susan Sarandon and Natalie Portman. Five more novels followed, as did numerous awards, including a Guggenheim Fellowship, as well as the Literature Award from the American Academy of Arts and Letters.

740 West End Avenue (near 96th Street), the Della Robbia

Carreño, Teresa (1853–1917) ★ ■ ▯ 🖙
PIANIST, SINGER, COMPOSER, AND CONDUCTOR

Teresa Carreño was the most famous woman concert pianist in her day. She performed for Abraham Lincoln in the White House. Her virtuosity tagged her as the "Valkyrie of the piano." Born in Venezuela to a musical family, Maria Teresa Carrenñ Garcia de Sena came to the United States in 1862 and performed many concerts. She studied with the extraordinary Anton Rubenstein and under America's first great composer, Louis Gottschalk. She was also a teacher of 14-year-old Edward MacDowell. Carreño was especially noted for performing the great piano concertos, especially the Grieg Piano Concerto in A minor. In 1865, she traveled to Europe for more concerts and met Charles Gounod, Franz Liszt, and Gioachino Rossini, who gave her voice lessons. She took on operatic roles, notably in Mozart's *Don Giovanni* and Meyerbeer's *Les Huguenots*. She composed some seventy-five works for piano, voice, choir, and orchestra. The Teresa Carreño Cultural Complex is the home of the Venezuela Symphony Orchestra in Caracas.

Teresa Carreño.

Benny Leonard.

Leonard, Benny (1896–1947) ★ ■
BOXER

Among boxers in all weight categories, Leonard is usually ranked sixth, seventh, or eighth, and he is often considered the greatest lightweight boxer of all time. Leonard won the lightweight title (boxers weighing 130–135 pounds) at age 21. Born Benjamin Leiner on the Lower East Side, he was educated in the school of hard knocks. Legend has it that in 1911, at age 15, Leiner couldn't afford the entrance fee to watch a fight, so he climbed to the skylight above the ring to watch. When he fell through the skylight into the ring, since he couldn't pay for the broken skylight, he offered to replace a fighter who failed to show up—and, he won. His success rebuts the jokes about the lack of Jewish sports stars. From 1912 to 1932, he lost only one fight for a disqualification; seventy of his eighty-nine wins were by knockouts. He died of a heart attack while refereeing a boxing match at the St. Nicholas Arena on West 66th Street. Leonard also lived at 2350 Broadway (near 85th Street) and **884 West End Avenue** (near 101st Street).

Lipton, Margaret Ann "Peggy" (1946–2019)
ACTRESS

Lipton acted with distinction in the TV cult series *Twin Peaks* and is fondly remembered as one of the three undercover, hippie cops in the early 1970s TV series *Mod Squad*. A native New Yorker, Lipton was trained at the Professional Children's School. By age 15, she began a successful modeling career at the prestigious Ford Agency. Two years later she was contracted with Universal Pictures. Her first television role followed shortly on the *John Forsythe Show*. That was followed by roles in episodes of such shows as *Mr. Novak*, *The Alfred Hitchcock Show*, *Bewitched*, *The FBI*, and others. Lipton also sang and had three minor hits. Briefly linked romantically to Paul McCartney, she was married for fifteen years to music producer Quincy Jones. Their daughter is the actress Rashida Jones.

755 West End Avenue (near 97th Street), Amsterdam Nursing Home

Redfield, Liza (1924–2018)
PIANIST, COMPOSER, AND CONDUCTOR

Redfield made history in 1960 when she became the first female musical director and conductor of a major Broadway Show, *Music Man*, during its initial run. After achieving her fame, she managed to defeat the television panel on *What's My Line*. Panelist Dorothy Kilgallen guessed that she was a stripper in *Gypsy*. Born Betty Weisman in Philadelphia, she earned a degree in music at the University of

Pennsylvania. Forsaking the career of a concert pianist, she made her way to New York and put her red hair to use to inspire her new name. Redfield conducted a few other Broadway shows, orchestrated and conducted road productions of Broadway shows, and composed music for the reopening of Ford's Theater in Washington, D.C., in 1968.

777 West End Avenue (near 98th Street)

Levy, Edward (1878–1947) ▮
MEDICAL DOCTOR AND RESEARCHER

Levy studied the effects of compressed-air chambers on the body and gained experience with the maladies affecting the sandhogs who built the New York City subway tunnels. His studies established the limited time periods that workers could tolerate compressed-air conditions. Later, for the Holland Tunnel, he determined the need to limit the period of exposure to carbon monoxide for workers and policemen patrolling the tunnel. In 1931, he was instrumental in designing the first compressed-air chamber in Metropolitan Hospital to treat "the bends." He continued his invaluable work as the Lincoln Tunnel was being built and served as the medical director of the Port Authority of New York. Born on Long Island, Levy received his MD from Columbia's College of Physicians and Surgeons in 1900. After a few years of private practice, he was appointed medical advisor to the Transit Commission. He also lived at **305 Riverside Drive** (near 103rd Street) and **324 West 103rd Street** (near Riverside Drive).

Salvadori, Mario G. (1907–1997)
PROFESSOR OF STRUCTURAL ENGINEERING AND ARCHITECTURE

Although he didn't realize it at the time, Salvadori was a consultant to the Manhattan Project, headed up by his friend and fellow Italian,

Enrico Fermi. His books, *Why Buildings Stand Up* and *Why Buildings Fall Down*, only begin to suggest the life of this professional talent, who designed, among other things, the concrete structural system for Eero Saarinen's renowned CBS Building. Born in Italy, Salvadori earned a doctorate in civil engineering in 1930 and in mathematics in 1933, both at the University of Rome. He taught there for a short while and did some research at University College London. In 1938, he arrived in the United States to be involved with the early development of television. After a short stint with the Lionel Train Company, he taught at Columbia from 1940 until his death, when he was the James Renwick Professor of Civil Engineering and Applied Science and Professor of Architecture Emeritus. In 1975, he volunteered to teach at a junior high school in Harlem, from which came the Salvadori method of instruction and the Salvadori Center on the City College campus.

Von Mises, Ludwig (1881–1973) ★ ● ▪

ECONOMIST

Forbes magazine called Von Mises "the greatest thinker you've never read." Mises was born in what was then Austria-Hungary. By age 12, he spoke German, Polish, and French, could understand Ukrainian, and read Latin. Having graduated from the University of Vienna in 1906 with a doctorate in law, he taught there and found economic theory more to his liking. His students included Karl Popper, Rudolf Carnap, Oskar Morgenstern, and Frederick Hayek. His *Theory of Money and Credit*, published in 1912, was the first explanation of economic expansions based on demand for cash. He also formulated a complete theory of the business cycle based on the expansion and contraction of the money supply. In 1934, he became a professor at the Graduate Institute of International Studies in Geneva, Switzerland. Fleeing the Nazis, he came to the United States and taught at New York University from 1945 until his retirement in 1969. His magnum opus, *Human Action: A Treatise on Economics*, is based on praxeology, otherwise known as the study of how people engage in purposeful behavior. Mises's belief in the marketplace made him a foe of socialism, and so he, along with Friedrich Hayek and **Milton Friedman**, is often associated with libertarian economics.

780 West End Avenue (near 98th Street)

Royle, Edwin Milton (1862–1942), Actor and Playwright

(See bio for Royle at **308 West 94th Street**.)

Wolfe, Linda (1932–2020)
JOURNALIST, CRITIC, TRUE CRIME AND NONFICTION AUTHOR

Her 1989 book *Wasted: The Preppie Murder* only brought more attention to an illustrious career of writing. From restaurant reviews to travel to book reviews to sexuality and social behavior, Wolfe's range was remarkable. First employed at *Partisan Review*, then in the Time organization, followed by *New York* magazine, she wrote numerous articles. Her book reviews appeared in most major newspapers from the *New York Times* to the *Washington Post*. But her sweet spot was true crime, such as her article "The Strange Death of the Twin Gynecologists" for *New York* magazine, and books such as *The Murder of Dr. Chapman: The Legendary Trials of Lucretia Chapman and Her Lover*, *The Professor and the Prostitute and Other True Tales of Murder and Madness*, and, of course, the *Wasted* best seller about "rough sex" gone wrong. Born in Brooklyn, she attended Antioch College, graduated from Brooklyn College, and earned an MA degree at New York University.

West 98th Street and West End Avenue

Lee, Stan (1922–2018) ★ ■
COMIC BOOK ARTIST, AUTHOR, AND EXECUTIVE

Lee collaborated with other comic book artists to create such well-known characters as Iron Man, Doctor Strange, the Hulk, the Fantastic Four, the X-Men, the Black Panther, the Avengers, Captain America, and Spider-Man. He became the head of the Marvel Comics empire that housed all these icons. Lee was born Stanley Martin Lieber in his parents' apartment at the corner of West End Avenue and West 98th Street. He began in the comic book business right out of high school in 1939 and left only for service in World War II in the Signal Corps. In the 1950s, his firm developed into Marvel Comics and, along with other artists, including Jack Kirby and Steve Ditko, he revolutionized the industry with a seemingly endless supply of heroic figures and stories. Most of their creations have rematerialized on television or film to large audiences and enormous profits.

789 West End Avenue (near 99th Street)

Nicholas, Harold (1921–2000) ★ ■ ▣
TAP DANCER

Take Fred Astaire's advice and watch the Nicholas Brothers in the greatest musical sequence ever filmed in the 1943 movie *Stormy Weather*. With numerous leaps and splits, they dance on a piano and soar over performing musicians. No wonder Michael Jackson and many others sought Harold Nicholas's instruction. Harold was born in North Carolina seven years after his brother Fayard. The Nicholas brothers began tap-dancing as youngsters. When Fayard was 16 and Harold only 9, they were good enough to dance at the Cotton Club in Harlem. Twentieth Century Fox motion picture studios kept them busy in such classic flicks as *The Big Broadcast of 1936*, *Down Argentine Way*, and *Sun Valley Serenade*, in which they performed the dazzling "Chattanooga Choo Choo" with Dorothy Dandridge, who would become Harold's wife for ten years. In Cole Porter's 1948 movie musical *The Pirate*, Gene Kelly broke a racial barrier by dancing with them. Harold appeared in more than fifty movies during his remarkable life, including *Uptown Saturday Night* and *The Five Heartbeats*.

800 West End Avenue (near 99th Street)

Kempton, James "Murray" (1917–1997) ■
NEWSPAPER COLUMNIST

Kempton bicycled to work every day, never having learned how to drive. He was awarded a Pulitzer Prize for distinguished commentary in 1985. Born in Baltimore, Ohio, he started out as a copyboy for H. L. Mencken at the *Baltimore Evening Sun*, and he graduated from Johns Hopkins University in 1935. After flirting with communism in a mariners' union and the Socialist Party of Norman Thomas, he joined the *New York Post* and left to serve in the US Army Air Forces during World War II. He returned to the *Post*, wrote for other newspapers, and was an editor at the *New Republic* in the 1960s before finally winding up at *Newsday* in 1981. Kempton's likable style was characterized by the *New York Times* as "of honor and elegant vinegar."

801 West End Avenue (near 99th Street)

Harriman, William Averell (1891–1986) ■
GOVERNOR OF NEW YORK

On 96th Street at Columbus Avenue, just five months before she would marry the future New York State governor, Kitty Lawrence was crushed under the horse she was riding when it reared up. She fortunately survived the accident. Kitty and W. Averell Harriman married in 1916, and they made their home on West End Avenue. The marriage lasted until 1928. He was the son of railroad baron Edward Henry Harriman and graduated from Yale University as a member of the infamous Skull and Bones. Harriman built an investment banking firm that merged into Brown Brothers Harriman & Co. before he entered public service in the Roosevelt administration, serving as ambassador to the Soviet Union and to Great Britain, and serving as Secretary of Commerce. In 1954, he was elected Governor and served one term. His second wife was a Whitney, who left her husband to marry him. After she died, he married Pamela Churchill Harriman, who became ambassador to France, having previously been the widow of Winston Churchill's son, Randolph. Harriman might also be remembered as the founder of the Sun Valley ski resort in 1936.

Spear, Maurice R. (1889–1983) ■

REAL ESTATE EXECUTIVE

Spear was the other half of the real estate empire of Helmsley-Spear Inc. Born Maurice Rabinowitz in Russia, he came to the United States as a toddler. He joined his brother's real estate operation in 1906, just two years after it began. By 1928, he was president of Spear & Co. and saw to its merger with Dwight-Helmsley Inc. in 1955. He lectured extensively on real estate, and after retiring in 1975, he continued to do so. He also taught at City College and Columbia. His philanthropic interests were varied, and he was a president and director of the Young Men's and Young Women's Hebrew Association of Washington Heights and Inwood. In addition, he was trustee of Jewish Philanthropies and a director of the Henry Street Settlement.

808 West End Avenue (near 99th Street), the Allendale Apartments

Goldwyn, Samuel (1879–1974) ★ ■
MOTION PICTURE MOGUL

When Goldwyn was told that he couldn't make a movie because it was based on a book about lesbians, he reportedly said, "That's alright, we'll make them Hungarians." This and other humorous malapropisms attributed to him are known as Goldwynisms. On another linguistic note, Goldwyn is the "G" in "MGM," a.k.a. Metro-Goldwyn-Mayer. Born Samuel Goldfish in what is now Poland, he came to the United States as a young teenager. By age 30, he was a success in the glove business in Gloversville, New York. His entrance into the motion picture business came through his marriage to the sister of Jesse Lasky, who created what became Paramount Pictures. Goldwyn produced such notable motion pictures as *Wuthering Heights*, *The Secret Life of Walter Mitty*, *Guys and Dolls*, and *The Best Years of Our Lives*.

Lasky, Jesse L. (1880–1958) ★ ■
MOTION PICTURE PIONEER

Lasky made the first feature-length motion picture, *The Squaw Man*, directed by **Cecil B. DeMille**. He was also one of the thirty-six people who formed the Academy of Motion Picture Arts and Sciences, which administers the Academy Awards, a.k.a. the Oscars. Lasky was born in California, prospected for gold in Alaska, played professional cornet, performed in vaudeville, and, by 1911, was producing two shows on Broadway. In 1913, he shifted into motion pictures and, along with his brother-in-law **Sam Goldwyn** and **Cecil B. DeMille**, formed a motion picture company, which merged with another one headed up by **Adolph Zukor**. The company, with one studio in Astoria, Queens, and others in Hollywood,

California, was called the Famous Players–Lasky Corporation, and with some more merging and reorganization, it became Paramount Pictures.

Shelnitz, Louis E. (ca.1899–1957) 🖙
PRINTER AND LYRICIST

By day Shelnitz set type at the *New York Times*. By night he used the name Louis E. Shelly to write the lyrics to such songs as "There's No Yellow in the Red, White, and Blue," "Ding-Dong Polka," "Barnyard Boogie," and "I Thought She Was a Local (But She Was a Fast Express)." Various performers recorded "Ding Dong Polka," but the one released by Yodelin' Slim Clark in 1946 appears to be the first. The Muppets do a mean rendition of his "Barnyard Boogie." He is credited with fifty-two songs in the repertoire listing of the American Society of Composers, Artists, and Publishers. Some of them are "Cannonball Yodel"; "Choo Choo Bop"; "Don't Wait to Baby Your Baby"; "Find 'Em, Fool 'Em, and Forget 'Em"; "I'm Gonna Sue Sioux City Sue"; "The Mighty Mickey Mantle"; and "The Okey Dokey Polka." Shelnitz was born in Connecticut. Before he came to New York and worked for the *New York Times*, he was a copywriter most of his working life at the *New Haven Register*.

Zukor, Adolph (1873–1976) ★ ■
MOTION PICTURE PIONEER

Present at Zukor's 100th birthday party were Dorothy Lamour, Gregory Peck, Groucho Marx, George Raft, Liv Ullman, Diana Ross, Gene Kelly, Barbara Stanwyck, Fred MacMurray, Gene Hackman, Bette Davis, Charlton Heston, Jimmy Stewart, Jack Benny, Bob Hope, and many other Hollywood stars. Zukor was born in Hungary, came to the United States, and became moderately wealthy from the fur business. In 1903, Zukor and **Marcus Loew** invested in an early motion picture operation on 14th Street. In 1912, he established the Famous Players Film Company that brought well-known stage players into motion pictures. He later partnered with **Jesse L. Lasky** to form Famous Players–Lasky which went on to become Paramount Pictures Corporation which distributed their films. The rest, as they say, is history. An urban legend has it that the idea for the name came from the Paramount apartment building at 315 West 99th Street. Initially, Paramount had a studio in Hollywood, California, and another in Astoria, Queens, which is known today as the Kaufman Astoria Studios. Zukor was chairman of Paramount until 1959 and, thereafter, chairman emeritus. Zukor also lived at **611 West 114th Street** (near Broadway).

HONORARY STREET NAMES— WEST 90S

Ariel Russo Place (97th Street between Amsterdam Avenue and Broadway) Four-year-old Ariel Russo was killed in 2013 by an unlicensed driver fleeing the police.

Cooper Stock Way (at the corner of 97th Street and West End Avenue) Nine-year-old Cooper Stock was killed in 2014 by a taxicab driver who failed to yield to a pedestrian.

Doris Rosenblum Way (94th Street between Central Park West and Columbus Avenue) **Doris Rosenblum** was a community activist who lived on the street.

James and Rina Garst Way (94th Street between Columbus Avenue and Amsterdam Avenue) James D. Garst and Rina Garst were community activists who lived on the block.

Robert Woolis Way (95th Street between Columbus Avenue and Central Park West) Robert Woolis was a community activist who lived in the nearby Columbus House.

Special Note—See also http://www.oldstreets.com/, the website of historian Gil Tauber, a valued member of the Bloomingdale Neighborhood History Group.

Plate 37 [Map bounded by W. 108th St., Central
Park W., W. 97th St., Hudson River]. (George
Washington Bromley, Cartographer.)

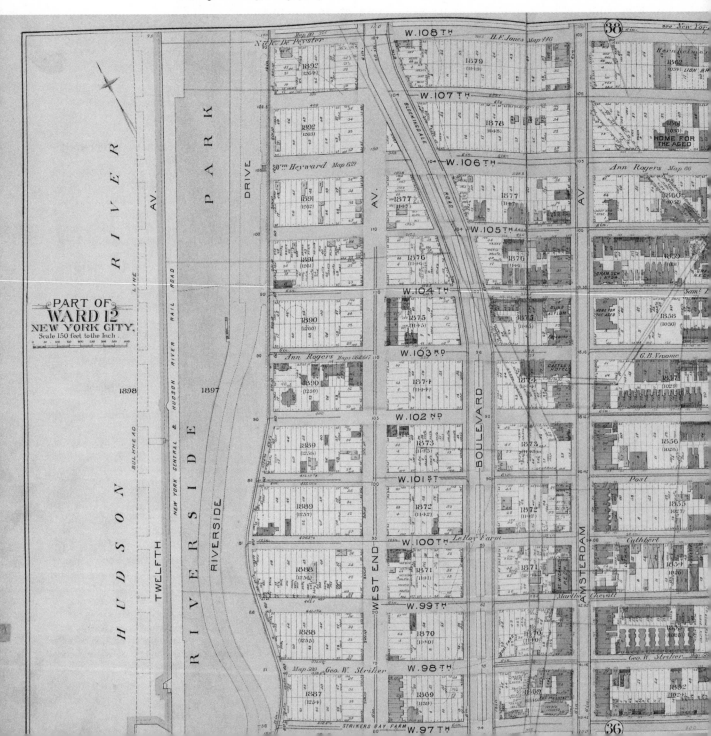

The West 100s

The West 100s came into its own in the latter part of the nineteenth century as a working-class neighborhood. The building of the Croton Aqueduct, the establishment of the Lion Brewery, and the coming of the Ninth Avenue Elevated Railroad populated the area with Irish and German immigrants. The last speculative row-house developments in Manhattan were built in the 1800s in the neighborhood that would come to be known as Manhattan Valley in the 1980s. In the early twentieth century, Italians, French, Jews, and other Europeans arrived. After World War II came Puerto Ricans, followed by other Latinos who filled apartments vacated by earlier residents, many of whom moved to the suburbs. The variety of commercial emporiums, especially on Broadway, and the nearly dozen movie theaters operating in the West 100s testified to the neighborhood's vitality.

West End Avenue and 100th Street ca. 1910 (above). Bloomingdale Square at Broadway and 107th Street ca. 1903 (below).

233 West 100th Street (near Broadway), the Nameoki

Canavan, David Patrick (1872–1914), Excavator

(See bio for Canavan at 333 Riverside Drive.)

250 West 100th Street, Hotel Whitehall (near Broadway)

Gershwin, George (1898–1937), Composer ★ ■

(See bio for Gershwin at 316 West 103rd Street.)

256 West 100th Street (near West End Avenue)

Townsend, Ralph S. (1854–1921) ■ ▣
ARCHITECT

Townsend designed the only building on Columbia's campus that remains from the time when the Bloomingdale Insane Asylum occupied the property. The 1884 building, originally the asylum's Macy Villa, was moved, reused, and renamed Buell Hall. Townsend designed it the same year he designed his own home. He later chose to move his house to 302 West 102nd Street. Townsend was a native New Yorker, and perhaps he learned his trade from his father, Ralph S. Townsend, Sr. The details of his education are not known, but his talents were consequential enough to have allowed him to design houses and stables and large apartment buildings such as the Kenilworth at 151 Central Park West, the buildings at 425 and 640 West End Avenue, and the ones at 190 and 194 Riverside Drive. Townsend also lived at 302 West 102nd Street (near West End Avenue), 172 West 105th Street (near Amsterdam Avenue), and somewhere on 108th Street and Riverside Drive.

306 West 100th Street (near West End Avenue)

Reuhl, Mercedes (1948–)
ACTRESS

One of Reuhl's earliest film appearances was in 1979 in *The Warriors*, which was filmed in the Riverside Park playground at 97th Street. In 1991, she won an Academy Award for Best Supporting Actress for her role in *The Fisher King* and a Tony Award for Best Actress for her role in *Lost in Yonkers*. Born in Jackson Heights, Queens, Reuhl graduated from the College of New Rochelle. After extensive television and movie work, her first starring role on the stage was in the Broadway production of *I'm Not Rappaport* in 1985. Her movie credits include *Radio Days*, *Big*, *Last Action Hero*, and *Married to the Mob*. On television, she was seen in such shows as *Kate and Allie*, *The Cosby Show*, *Law & Order*, *NCIS*, *Frasier*, and *Power*. She is a trustee of the Bay Street Theater in Sag Harbor, Long Island.

315 West 100th Street (near Riverside Drive) ★ ■

Bodanzky, Artur (1877–1939) 👉
VIOLINIST AND OPERA CONDUCTOR

Bodanzky conducted the night that Enrico Caruso sang for his last time at the Metropolitan Opera. Bodanzky conducted many of the great voices at the Met, including Kirsten Flagstad, Lauritz Melchior, Lawrence Tibbett, Lily Pons, and Geraldine Farrar. His specialty was conducting chorus and orchestra in such gems as the Mozart *Requiem*, Hayden's *The Seasons*, Bach's *St. John Passion*, and Beethoven's *Choral Fantasy*. His forte and his reputation, however, rested on his interpretation of the Wagnerian operas. Born in Vienna, Bodanzky studied the violin as a child at the Vienna Conservatory of Music. He played violin in the renowned Society of the Friends of Music, which was conducted by such greats as Brahms, Dvorak, Rubenstein, and Saint-Saëns. After hearing Mahler conduct Wagner's *Lohengrin*, he shifted from his instrument to conducting. Considered Mahler's protégé, he was an assistant conductor to him in 1902 at the Imperial Opera House. His breakthrough came in conducting the first performance in Paris of Strauss's *Die Fledermaus*. He also conducted in Berlin, Prague, and London before coming to the United States in 1915.

Gluck, Alma (1884–1938) ★ ■
SOPRANO

Gluck's 1916 recording of "Carry Me Back to Old Virginny" was the first popular recording by a classical musician to sell a million copies. It was only the seventh gold disc ever awarded. Alma Gluck earned $600,000 in royalties from her recordings. At the height of her career, only Enrico Caruso and John McCormack were thought to be as popular. Gluck defined the modern classical star with her exceptional looks, style, personality, and voice. Born Reba Fiensohn in Romania, she came to the United States at an early age and attended New York City's Normal College (now Hunter College) and Union College in Schenectady. She married Bernard Gluck, an insurance man, but they separated before she began to sing professionally and employ the stage name Alma Gluck. An audition with the great maestro Arturo Toscanini created her opportunity to sing at the Metropolitan Opera in 1909. In her first season, she took on eleven roles. In 1914, she married **Efrem Zimbalist, Sr.,** the violinist and conductor. Both their professional and married lives were successes by every standard. Gluck retired in 1925. When she died thirteen years later, she left $10,000 to Barnard College to establish a scholarship in her name to be awarded annually to a student electing to major in political economics. Her daughter was the novelist Marcia Davenport, and her son was the actor Efrem Zimbalist, Jr.

Zimbalist, Efrem, Sr. (1889–1985) ■
VIOLINIST AND MUSIC CONSERVATORY DIRECTOR

Zimbalist became first violin in an orchestra when he was 9 years old. His father was conductor of the orchestra in Russia where Efrem was born. At 12 years of age, he entered the St. Petersburg Conservatory, which, under the tutelage of Leopold Auer, produced Mischa Elman and Jascha Heifitz. When Zimbalist graduated, he won the Rubenstein Award. He debuted professionally in Berlin in 1908, and in the United States with the Boston Symphony Orchestra in 1911. By that time, he was one of the world's greatest violinists and can be given credit for popularizing some of the well-known violin concertos. In 1928, he joined the faculty of the new Curtis Institute in Philadelphia. He would become its director from 1941 to 1968. He composed as well, including a musical comedy that was produced on Broadway in 1920. He met his Metropolitan Opera soprano wife, **Alma Gluck**, on a ferry to New Jersey. After she died in 1938, he married the widow of the founder of the Curtis Institute. His son, the actor Efrem Zimbalist, Jr., is best known for his role on the 1960s television show *77 Sunset Strip*. The novelist Marcia Davenport was his stepdaughter.

316 West 100th Street (near Riverside Drive)

Harris, Isaac A. (1871–unknown)
CO-OWNER OF THE TRIANGLE WAIST COMPANY

Harris was co-owner of the Triangle Waist Company during the horrific fire on March 25, 1911. The fire killed 146 employees, mostly young Italian and Jewish women who died either in the carnage or while trying to escape the fire by jumping nine stories. Owner Harris and his partner **Max Blanck** had the monikers "Shirtwaist Kings" in the 1890s. Despite their responsibility for locked doors that made a stairway exit impossible, they were acquitted of manslaughter charges. They were awarded insurance proceeds that enabled the business to be reestablished in two different locations, but the costs of legal defense ended operations. Harris also lived at **324 West 101st Street** (near Riverside Drive).

Somewhere on West 100th Street

Griffith, David Wark "D. W." (1875–1948) ★ ■
MOTION PICTURE FILM PIONEER

Primarily known for his 1915 landmark film *Birth of a Nation*, which demeaned African Americans and glorified the Ku Klux Klan, Griffith might be better appreciated for popularizing such film techniques as fadeouts, flashbacks, and close-ups. Griffith was born in Kentucky, the son of a Confederate Army colonel. Arriving in New York City in his twenties, he acted bit parts in many silent movies. He filled in for a director who became ill, and the rest, as they say, is history. Also attributed to him is the early use of such film techniques as the eye-opener effect, the long shot, backlighting, the moving camera, high and low camera angles, and the fade in/fade out. He broke the convention of filming with only one thousand feet of film. His 1916 film *Intolerance* employed sixteen thousand extras in one scene. In 1919, he joined Mary Pickford, Douglas Fairbanks, and Charlie Chaplin in forming the motion picture company United Artists.

Frederick Douglass Houses from 100th to 104th Streets between Columbus and Amsterdam Avenues

Hilton-Jacobs, Lawrence (1953–)
ACTOR

Hilton-Jacobs is uncredited in the original *Death Wish* movie as mugger number two. Born in New York, he graduated from the

High School of Art and Design and attended Wilkes University in Pennsylvania for two years until his acting career took off. His training in acting at Al Fann's Theatrical School and the Negro Ensemble Company led to a role in the 1974 movie *Cooley High*. That, in turn, led to his prominent role in the television show *Welcome Back, Kotter*, and was followed by many movie parts and television roles on such shows as *Hill Street Blues*, *Roseanne*, and *Gilmore Girls*. He also played Michael Jackson's father in the television story of the Jackson Five.

5 West 101st Street (near Central Park West)

Guthrie, Woodrow "Woody" Wilson (1912–1967) ★ ■
FOLK SINGER AND SONGWRITER

Guthrie wrote "This Land Is Your Land" as a reprisal to Irving Berlin's "God Bless America." Many of his earliest songs, so well known and influential to so many subsequent performers, are accumulated in the compilation *Dust Bowl Ballads*. By 1940, he was a resident in New York City inspiring other folk singers, such as the Almanac Singers and the Weavers. His politics were very progressive, and he could be found singing at social-political events alongside other singer-activists, such

Woody Guthrie.

as Lead Belly, Pete Seeger, and Paul Robeson. Born in Oklahoma and named after President Woodrow Wilson, Guthrie left his difficult childhood environment by migrating to California. There he began a musical career that involved much travel, many wives, and constant singing and songwriting. After years of treatment in psychiatric facilities, where he received a visit from Bob Dylan, he died of complications of Huntington's disease. Singer Arlo Guthrie is his son.

210 West 101st Street (near Broadway), designed by Emery Roth in 1926

Roth, Emery (1871–1948) ★ ■ ▤
ARCHITECT

Remnants of the Croton Aqueduct below the Ninth Ave Elevated Railroad, from 100th to 104th Streets.

Roth reshaped the Central Park West skyline by designing the San Remo, the Eldorado, and the Beresford, among other buildings. His other designs included the Hotel Belleclaire on Broadway at 77th Street, the Hotel Ritz Tower on East 57th Street, the Hotel St. George in Brooklyn Heights, and the Normandy on Riverside Drive at 86th Street. Born in Hungary, Roth came to the United States as a young teenager. After some working in Kansas City, he apprenticed as a draftsman in the office of Burnham & Root during their responsibility for the 1893 World's Columbian Exposition in Chicago. There he was invited to work for architect Richard Morris Hunt, but Hunt died soon after. So Roth found work in the office of Ogden Codman, Jr., who designed for the upper-class clientele of New York and Newport, Rhode Island, and who collaborated with Edith Wharton. On his own from the turn of the last century, Emery achieved a first-rate reputation for hotels, apartment buildings, and synagogues. His two sons continued his work as Emery Roth & Sons, and they executed the Pan Am Building, now known as Metropolitan Life, and the World Trade Center in collaboration with the Japanese architect Minoru Yamasaki.

324 West 101st Street (near Broadway)

Harris, Isaac A. (1871–unknown), Co-owner of the Triangle Waist Company

(See bio for Harris at **316 West 100th Street**.)

6 West 102nd Street (near Central Park West)

Dreiser, Theodore Herman Albert (1871–1945) ■
NOVELIST AND JOURNALIST

Dreiser is one of the great American novelists, known mostly for *Sister Carrie* and *An American Tragedy*. Initially, his novels were not given their proper due, as his realism was not appreciated by the critics. He did not sacrifice his voice, but the price he paid was critical isolation. H. L. Mencken was one of his few supporters who had acknowledged Dreiser as a great American novelist years before *An American Tragedy* was published in 1926. A native of Indiana, he started as a journalist with St. Louis and Chicago newspapers, writing about luminaries like John Burroughs, William Dean Howells, and Nathaniel Hawthorne. For his writings, he interviewed an interesting array of people such as Thomas Edison and Andrew Carnegie. By the time he came to New York, his novels were finding trouble. One of his novels, *The Genius*, was targeted by The New York Society for the Suppression of Vice, and *An American Tragedy* was banned in Boston. Dreiser was the brother of songwriter **Paul Dresser**. Theodore Dreiser had lived at two other addresses in the neighborhood: **605 West 111th Street** (near Broadway) and **429 West 123rd Street** (near Morningside Avenue).

74 West 102nd Street (near Amsterdam Avenue)

Brace, Donald Clifford (1881–1955)
PUBLISHER

In 1919, Brace co-founded the publishing firm Harcourt, Brace, and Howe, which became the well-known Harcourt Brace & Co. Its early successes included Sinclair Lewis's *Main Street* and Carl Sandberg's six-volume biography of Abraham Lincoln. Born in upstate New York, Brace graduated from Columbia in 1904 with fellow classmate Alfred

THE WEST 100S   113

Harcourt. They worked together for fifteen years in the publishing house of Henry Holt & Co. before striking out on their own with their eponymous firm. Brace was a supporting and active alumnus of Columbia. He also had two other addresses in the neighborhood: **131 West 103rd Street** (near Amsterdam Avenue) and **504 West 122nd Street** (near Amsterdam Avenue).

200 West 102nd Street (near Amsterdam Avenue)

Abolafia, Louis (1941–1995)
"THE LOVE KING"

Abolafia claimed to have coined the phrase "make love, not war." A fixture in the Lower East Side and Greenwich Village scene, where he organized "love-ins" and "happenings," the press crowned him "the Love King." Allen Ginsberg, Andy Warhol, and Bob Dylan were his friends. Declaring that he had nothing to hide, he ran for president a few times on the tickets of the Nudist Party and the Cosmic Love Party.

248 West 102nd Street (near West End Avenue)

Webb, Roy Denslow (1888–1982) ■
COMPOSER OF FILM MUSIC

In 1925, Webb composed Columbia's fight song, "Roar, Lion, Roar." More famously, he composed or arranged the music for more than two hundred motion pictures, including *Stage Door*; *Bringing Up Baby*; *Abe Lincoln in Illinois*; *Mr. and Mrs. Smith*; *The Magnificent Ambersons*; *Murder, My Sweet*; *Notorious*; *Mighty Joe Young*; *Houdini*; and *Marty*. A New York native, Webb graduated from Columbia in 1910. He also studied painting at the Art Students League for five years. He was nominated for seven Academy Awards. His music can be heard in the newsreel montage in *Citizen Kane*. Film director, screenwriter, and composer Kenneth Seymour Webb is his brother. The brothers also lived at **255 West 108th Street** (near Broadway).

249 West 102nd Street (near Broadway)

Harrigan, Edward "Ned" (1844–1911) ◼
VAUDEVILLE PERFORMER

"H, A, double-R, I, G, A, N spells Harrigan" goes the George M. Cohan song that celebrates half of the popular vaudeville team of Harrigan and Hart. Jimmy Cagney sang and danced to the song in the 1941 motion picture *Yankee Doodle Dandy*. In 1985, the Broadway musical *Harrigan 'n Hart* had a very short run. Born on Manhattan's Lower East Side, Harrigan ran away from home when he was a teenager. By 1867, he was singing and dancing on a stage in San Francisco where he became an audience favorite. After working with earlier partners, he met Tony Hart in Chicago in 1871. With Harrigan writing skits that lampooned Irish, German, African American, and Italian characters, they achieved national success. Their singing, dancing, and comedy worked most markedly in their "Mulligan Guard" routines centered on a neighborhood Irish militia. After the duo split up in 1885, Harrigan continued performing and, in 1890, opened Harrigan's Theater on Herald Square. His son was the physician Anthony Hart Harrigan, and his daughter was the actress Nedda Harrigan Logan.

302 West 102nd Street (near West End Avenue)

Remington, Harold E. (1865–1937) ◼
LAWYER

In 1908, Remington authored the classic nine-volume *Treatise on the Bankruptcy Laws of the United States*. An acknowledged expert on bankruptcy law, his expertise came from being one of the first referees appointed with the Federal Bankruptcy Act of 1898. Many of the amendments made to the Act in 1910 and 1926 were his doing. He chaired the bankruptcy law committee of the Federal Bar Association, was active in similar capacities, and wrote numerous articles. His several texts found their way into law libraries. Born in Illinois, Remington graduated from the University of Michigan with an AB degree in 1888. He attended the Georgetown School of Law and the Columbia School of Law and practiced law in Cleveland until 1910. In New York, his firm of Remington and Twitchell included his daughter's husband, Pierrepont E. Twitchell. In 1918, and with two partners, he founded the Hot Flo Faucet Company that expanded into electric water heaters and related household products.

Townsend, Ralph S. (1854–1921), Architect ■ ▯

(See bio for Townsend at **256 West 100th Street**.)

304 West 102nd Street (near West End Avenue)

Brunette, Harry (1911–1972) ☞
BANK ROBBER AND KIDNAPPER

On December 15, 1936, 25-year-old Harry Brunette exchanged gunfire with the authorities who were trying to capture him. The authorities included twenty-five G-men with submachine guns under the personal command of J. Edgar Hoover and one hundred detectives and policemen who surrounded his ground-floor, rented apartment on West 102nd Street. Brunette surrendered only after his apartment was set on fire by tear-gas bombs and after he ran out of bullets. He was wanted as a suspect in several bank robberies and in the abduction of a New Jersey State Trooper. When arrested, the Wisconsin native implicated himself and his wife, the former Arline LaBeau of 2754 Broadway.

Site between 102nd and 103rd Streets, between Amsterdam and West End Avenues

Willett, Marinus (ca.1740–ca.1830) ★ ▪ ▪
MAYOR AND LANDOWNER

Willett has a loose connection to the Bloomingdale community through a house and barn that he owned on land that would be described today as near 102nd and 103rd Streets between Amsterdam and West End Avenues. In 1786, he advertised the property for sale, and it was purchased by a John Jones. Perhaps Willett stayed in the house when escaping the summer heat at his downtown residence. Perhaps also, he became familiar with the property because of his experience in the nearby Battle of Harlem Heights in 1776. In honor of this Revolutionary War hero, streets in New York City and Albany are named after him, as is the town of Willett, New York. Before the war began, he was a leader of the Sons of Liberty that taunted the British. During the war, he led regiments at the Battle of Quebec, the Battle of Oriskany, the Battle of Monmouth, and the campaign in the Mohawk Valley. He also helped put down Shay's Rebellion, and he served briefly as Mayor of New York City after DeWitt Clinton. A character in Walter Edmond's *Drums along the Mohawk* was based on Willett.

Site near 102nd Street between West End Avenue and Riverside Drive

Le Roy, Herman (1758–1841) ▪
MERCHANT AND LANDOWNER

Le Roy was the first Holland Consul to the United States and head of the commercial firm of Le Roy, Bayard, McKivan & Co. Alexander Hamilton was a lawyer for his firm. Le Roy was a director and president of the Bank of New York. His daughter Caroline Le Roy was the second wife of New Hampshire Senator Daniel Webster. Le Roy came from an old Huguenot family. His fortune was used for land purchases in Bloomingdale in the area between 99th and 107th Streets. Like many others, he invested in land in western New York. The town of Le Roy, New York, is named after him and is known as the birthplace of Jell-O.

313 West 102nd Street (near Riverside Drive)

Roosevelt, Elliott Bulloch (1860–1894) 🖘

BROTHER OF THEODORE ROOSEVELT AND FATHER OF ELEANOR ROOSEVELT

Elliott Roosevelt died in the West 102nd Street brownstone as an alcoholic living with his mistress. The younger brother of future President Theodore Roosevelt, they can be seen together in a Mathew Brady photograph, perched on the ledge of their grandfather Cornelius Roosevelt's mansion on Broadway at 13th Street, watching the Lincoln funeral cortege pass by. Born in New York, Roosevelt didn't finish his education at the prestigious St. Paul's School in New Hampshire because of an illness that might have been related to the onset of alcoholism. His marriage in 1883 produced four children, including Eleanor, and he was the godfather to future President Franklin Delano Roosevelt. As his alcoholism worsened, he was exiled and estranged from his family. In 1891, brother Theodore had him declared insane to put his property into trust for the benefit of his wife and children. Various "cures" in Europe, Illinois, and Virginia, failed. From 1889, he was taking laudanum and morphine, in addition to alcohol, after fracturing his ankle while turning a double somersault during a rehearsal of an amateur circus.

320 West 102nd Street (near Riverside Drive) ★ ▪

Runyon, Damon (1880–1946), Journalist and Short Story Writer

(See bio for Runyon at **251 West 95th Street**.)

West 103rd Street and Columbus Avenue (Mrs. Maguire's Irish Boarding House)

O'Dwyer, Paul (1907–1998), Politician ▪

(See bio for O'Dwyer at **350 Central Park West**.)

12 West 103rd Street (near Manhattan Avenue)

Hall, Edward Hagaman (1858–1936), Historian and Preservationist ▪ ▣

(See bio for Hall at **700 West End Avenue**.)

131 West 103rd Street (near Manhattan Avenue)

Brace, Donald Clifford (1881–1955), Publisher

(See bio for Brace at **74 West 102nd Street**.)

150 West 103rd Street (Manhattan Avenue)

Cadmus, Paul (1904–1999), Super-realist Painter ▪

(See bio for Cadmus at **148 West 95th Street**.)

202 West 103rd Street (Amsterdam Avenue), Hotel Clendening

Chambers, Julius L. (1850–1920), Journalist ☞

(See bio for Chambers at **255 West 97th Street**.)

203 West 103rd Street (near Amsterdam Avenue)

Coltrane, John William "Trane" (1926–1967) ★ ■
JAZZ SAXOPHONIST

Coltrane's 1961 rendition of *My Favorite Things* is one of the high points of recorded jazz. His 1965 album *A Love Supreme* is considered his masterpiece. It was recorded with McCoy Tyner on piano, Jimmy Garrison on bass, and Elvin Jones on drums. Coltrane was born in North Carolina and served in the US Navy in World War II. He played in the growing bebop scene and with such jazz masters as Dizzy Gillespie, Eddie "Clean Head" Vinson, Johnny Hodges, and Earl Bostic. From 1955, he played on and off with Miles Davis in different groups, and in 1957, he was a member of a Thelonious Monk quartet. His 1958 solo album *Blue Train* certified his individuality, and his 1959 *Giant Steps* had musicians and critics noting the incredibly creative chord changes that came to be thought of as distinctive to Coltrane.

206 West 103rd Street (near Amsterdam Avenue)

Rockwell, Norman Percevel (1894–1978) ★ ■
ARTIST AND ILLUSTRATOR

Rockwell illustrated movie posters for *The Magnificent Ambersons*, *The Song of Bernadette*, *The Razor's Edge*, *Cinderfella*, and *Stagecoach*. His most important illustrations might be the 1943 "Four Freedoms" series for the *Saturday Evening Post*. Also well known are the 1943 "Rosie the Riveter," the 1944 "We, Too, Have a Job to Do," the 1951 "Saying Grace," and the 1964 "The Problem We All Live With." Born in the Bloomingdale neighborhood of Manhattan, Rockwell studied at the National Academy of Design and the Art Students League. His earliest illustrations were employed in youth publications such as *Boys' Life* and *St. Nicholas* magazine. At age 19, *Boys' Life* hired him to be their art editor. At age 21, *Saturday Evening Post* magazine chose his submission for their cover. Over the next forty-seven years, he would supply them with 323 cover illustrations. In 1977, President Ford conferred the Presidential Medal of Freedom on him.

234 West 103rd Street (near Broadway)

Bimberg, Bernard K. (ca. 1872–1934) 🖘
BUILDER OF THEATERS

Bimberg built the Belasco Theater in New York, among others. Along with his two brothers, Bernard built the Astor Theater and the Stuyvesant Theater, which was renamed to honor the impresario David Belasco. He also ran a chain of motion picture theaters on upper Broadway including B. K. Bimberg's Broadway Theater at 103rd Street and Broadway (later the Columbia Cinema, now demolished). Born in New York City, Bimberg became a drummer and toured the vaudeville circuit with a group called the Cleveland Minstrels. With the advent of motion pictures, he provided percussive sound effects—hoof beats and the like—from behind the screen. He also put together the Bernard Cycle Band, which was a novelty troupe of one hundred men pedaling musically in parades, notably the parade in 1898 celebrating the city's consolidation. When he died, he was president of the Benkay Amusement Co., the Bim-Green Catering Co., and the Schuyler Amusement Co. His brother was **Meyer R. Bimberg**.

239 West 103rd Street (near Broadway)

Thomas, Harvey Mark (ca. 1871–1957) ▪
PUBLISHER

Harvey Thomas was the founder of the Thomas Publishing Company in 1890. He was president of the company from 1898 to 1956. Their first publication was *Thomas's American Grocery Trades Reference Book*. More popular was their flagship publication: Thomas Register of American Manufacturers, which in its heyday was thirty-four volumes. They were widely known in manufacturing firms as the "big green books." From 1933, Thomas published *Industry Equipment News*, and more publications followed that covered such realms as exports and software. The firm is still family-owned and operated. Thomas was born in Pennsylvania. His wife, Mary Coe Chedsey, graduated from Barnard in 1904. Thomas also lived further up Broadway at **611 West 110th Street** (near Broadway) and **601 West 113th Street** (near Broadway).

245 West 103rd Street (near Broadway)

Bogart, Humphrey DeForest (1899–1957) ★ ▪
ACTOR

Humphrey Bogart was the eldest son of accomplished parents, **Dr. Belmont DeForest Bogart** and **Maud Bogart**. He attended the nearby Trinity School for a while and later became a tournament-level chess player. Although he never actually said "Play it again, Sam" in the film, his performance in *Casablanca* turned him into a cultural icon. However, movies such as *High Sierra*, *The Maltese Falcon*, *The Big Sleep*, *The Treasure of Sierra Madre*, *The African Queen*, and *The Caine Mutiny* confirm that he was one of the great screen actors of all time. Bogart met another Upper West–Sider, Lauren Bacall, on the set of her first film, *To Have or Have Not*, and they married in 1945. Thanks to local cinema champion Gary Dennis and Parks Commissioner Adrian

Humphrey Bogart.

Benepe, West 103rd Street was given the honorific name Humphrey Bogart Place.

Bogart, Maud Humphrey (1868–1940) ▪ ☞
COMMERCIAL ILLUSTRATOR

The urban legend persists that her artistic rendering of her baby son Humphrey was the basis for the Gerber (Foods) Baby. Using her maiden name, Maud Humphrey earned more than her surgeon husband by illustrating children's books, magazine ads, postcards, and greeting cards. Further, she was quite active in the suffrage movement. Born in Rochester, New York, she trained at the Art Students League with James McNeill Whistler. **Dr. Belmont DeForest Bogart** was her husband, and **Humphrey Bogart** was her son.

316 West 103rd Street (near Riverside Drive), Gershwin House

Gershwin, George (1898–1937) ★ ▪
COMPOSER

Rhapsody in Blue not only earned George Gershwin great acclaim, it also garnered about a quarter of a million dollars ($4 million today). Its premiere in 1924 was distinguished in many ways: its commission by the popular bandleader Paul Whiteman, its opening clarinet glissando, the piano part played by the composer himself, the orchestration by Ferde Grofé (who would compose *Grand Canyon Suite* a few years later), and the presence of Sergei Rachmaninoff, John Philip Sousa, Fritz Kreisler, and Leopold Stokowski. Gershwin took an apartment at **501 West 110th Street** to compose *Rhapsody in Blue*, just as he would later take a suite at the Hotel Whitehall at **250 West 100th Street** to finish *An American in Paris*. Born in Brooklyn as Jacob Gershowitz, with a birth certificate indicating "Gershwine," he studied the piano and composition with private instructors. He was so accomplished by the age of 15 that he started earning a living as a "song plugger" on West 28th Street's Tin Pan Alley. At age 20, he and his lyricist, Irving Caesar, had a big hit for Al Jolson, "Swanee." In 1924, George and his lyricist brother, **Ira Gershwin**, collaborated on their first musical, *Lady Be Good*, to be followed by others such as *Funny Face*, *Strike Up the Band*, *Girl Crazy*, and the Pulitzer Prize–winning *Of Thee I Sing*. Gershwin had a decade-long affair with composer Kay Swift, but he never married. His sudden death, at age 38, came just as he was coming into his full creative powers, and way, way too soon.

Gershwin, Ira (1896–1983) ★ ■

LYRICIST

Gershwin's lyrics are so good, several books have been written about them. Consider "You like potato and I like potahto" or "Summertime and the livin' is easy" or "I'm bidin' my time, 'Cause that's the kind of guy I'm." His first collaboration with his brother **George Gershwin** on the 1924 musical *Lady, Be Good* had to be a hit show with songs like "I've Got Rhythm," "They Can't Take That Away From Me," "Someone to Watch Over Me," "The Man I Love," and "Fascinating Rhythm." Ira and George worked on much else together, including the Pulitzer Prize–winning musical *Of Thee I Sing*. After George's untimely death, Ira's lyrical talents graced the music of such masters as Vernon Duke, Burton Lane, Harold Arlen, Kurt Weill, and Jerome Kern. Born Israel Gershowitz in New York City, he graduated from the prestigious Townsend Harris High School and attended City College of New York but dropped out. Fortunately, the Gershwin magic never dropped out; it is part of the great American songbook and a never-ending source of Broadway revivals.

324 West 103rd Street (near Riverside Drive)

Keigwin, Albert Edwin (ca.1868–1951) 🖘
MINISTER

In his day, pastor emeritus Keigwin of the West End Presbyterian Church enjoyed the second-longest pastorate in the history of New York churches. From the inception of radio until 1931, his Sunday services were broadcast. He is thought to have performed the first marriage ceremony broadcast on television. From its start in a tin-roofed chapel on Broadway and 104th Street to welcoming twenty-five hundred worshippers, Keigwin's church may have had the largest Presbyterian congregation in the country. Born in Iowa, Keigwin earned AB and AM degrees from Princeton University and graduated from Union Theological Seminary in 1894. He received a DD degree from Lafayette College in 1906 and an LLD degree in 1928 from Ursinus College, of which he was president from 1907 to 1912. Before beginning his forty-year run at West End Presbyterian Church, he served congregations in Colorado, Iowa, Missouri, and New Jersey. Keigwin also lived at **305 Riverside Drive** (near 103rd Street) and **340 Riverside Drive** (near 106th Street).

Levy, Edward (1878–1947), Medical Doctor and Researcher ▪

(See bio for Levy at **777 West End Avenue**.)

610 West 103rd Street (near Riverside Drive)

Perl, Martin Lewis (1927–2014)
PHYSICIST AND CHEMICAL ENGINEER

Perl credits his parents and his toy erector set for such achievements as discovering the elementary particle known as the tau lepton, for which he was awarded the 1995 Nobel Prize in Physics. He shared the award with Frederick Reines, the co-detector of the neutrino. A native

New Yorker, he graduated in 1948 from Brooklyn Polytechnic Institute with a degree in chemical engineering. He worked with electron vacuum tube technology at General Electric Company in Schenectady and expanded his education into atomic physics at nearby Union College. In 1955, he earned his doctorate in physics at Columbia, where I. I. Rabi was a mentor. That was followed by eight years of expanding research at the University of Michigan. In 1963, he moved on to Stanford University to work with their brand-new nuclear accelerator.

103rd Street and Broadway, a rooming house across from the Hotel Marseilles

Parker, Dorothy (1893–1967) ■

POET, WRITER, AND WIT

Parker left most of her estate to Martin Luther King. She is best known as a member of the legendary Algonquin Round Table and for her wit that was served on a regular basis by Franklin P. Adams in his newspaper column. Consider: "A hangover is the wrath of grapes," or "This is not a novel to be tossed aside lightly. It should be thrown with great force." Born Dorothy Rothschild in New Jersey, she grew up in New York City. (Her uncle Martin Rothschild died in the sinking of the *Titanic*.) At the beginning of her career, she wrote poems for *Vanity Fair* and *Vogue* magazines. After gaining notoriety and connecting to other literary notables at the Round Table, she wrote for the *New Yorker* and, later, *Life*, *McCall's*, and the *New Republic*. Her books of light poetry, starting with *Enough Rope* in 1926, sold very well. She also collaborated on some theater work. In 1929, she won the O. Henry Award for her short story *Big Blonde*, which was much later made into a television movie starring Sally Kellerman. Hollywood provided her with additional work; she co-wrote the movie script for *A Star Is Born* in 1937, among other projects. In time, she achieved legendary status and was often portrayed in movies that convey all that was special about her time. Cole Porter immortalized her nicely by citing her in one of his great songs, "Just One of Those Things."

Smith, James "Thorne" (1892–1934) ◾
WRITER

Before there was the *Topper* television show in the 1950s with Leo G. Carroll, there was the 1937 *Topper* movie with Cary Grant. They were adapted from the novel *Topper* authored by Thorne Smith. Born in Annapolis, Maryland, the son of a Navy commodore, Smith attended Dartmouth College. He served in the US Navy in World War I, struggled for a few years, sometimes working as an advertising agent, and lived on the cheap in Greenwich Village. In 1926, he hit pay dirt with his book *Topper.* In all, he wrote thirteen books, most of them humorous. His last book *The Passionate Witch,* published posthumously, is thought to have inspired the television series *Bewitched.*

1 West 104th Street (near Central Park West)

Friedman, Milton (1912–2006) ★ ◾
ECONOMIST

Friedman described himself as "a libertarian with a small 'l.'<HS>" His 1962 book *Capitalism and Freedom* catapulted him into the world spotlight. The following year, he and Anna J. Schwartz authored *The Monetary History of the United States.* Friedman's economic principles were most notably employed by the Reagan administration and by the Pinochet government in Chile. Born in Brooklyn and raised in New Jersey, Friedman graduated from Rutgers University and went on to earn a master's degree in 1933 at the University of Chicago. At the end of 1933, he studied statistics under a fellowship at Columbia University with some of the best statisticians in the country. In 1946, he earned a PhD at Columbia and then went on to teach at the University of

Chicago for the next three decades. In 1976, he was awarded the Nobel Memorial Prize in Economics. His wife was **Rose Friedman**.

Friedman, Rose Director (1910–2009)

ECONOMIST

President Reagan joked that Rose Friedman was the only person who ever won an argument against her husband, **Milton Friedman**. Years later she indicated that they had their first disagreement ever in 2003, over the invasion of Iraq. She favored invasion; he did not. She advocated for free markets, as did he, and was undoubtedly essential to all his work. She co-authored their 1980 book *Free to Choose: A Personal Statement* and 1984's *The Tyranny of the Status Quo*. Born in the part of Russia that became Ukraine, Friedman came with her family to the United States at age 2. Her higher education began at Reed College and continued at the University of Chicago. There she completed her work for a doctorate, except for a dissertation, and met **Milton Friedman** in 1932. They were married six years later and for sixty-eight years until his death in 2006.

Site of 101 West 104th Street (near Columbus Avenue)

Clendening, John (ca. 1752–1836)

MERCHANT

Clendening lost his shirt when President Andrew Jackson did not renew the charter for the Second Bank of the United States. Clendening, whose staple business was importing linen goods, was a director of the bank, serving under its president, John Jacob Astor. Before the city grid system took over, there was a Clendening Lane. When the Croton water supply system was finished in 1842, it included an aqueduct to carry the water pipe over the Clendening Valley. It was located just west of what would become Columbus Avenue from about 103rd to 99th Streets. For many years, there was a Clendening Hotel on the southwest corner of Amsterdam Avenue and 103rd Street. Clendening lived downtown near Bowling Green. His country residence was in Bloomingdale, near what today would be the corner of West 104th and Columbus Avenue.

126 West 104th Street (near Amsterdam Avenue)

Borglum, Gutzon (1867–1941) ■
SCULPTOR

Best known for creating the sculptures of Mount Rushmore in South Dakota, Borglum also sculpted the angels of the Cathedral of St. John the Divine. He gave the angels female faces, and when the Cathedral clergy objected, he recreated the faces with male features including pronounced Adam's apples. His work in the neighborhood also includes saints and apostles in the Cathedral, cherubs in St. Paul's Chapel on Columbia's campus, and the figure of Colonel Daniel Butterfield in nearby Sakura Park. Borglum was born in what was then Idaho territory and studied very briefly at St. Mary's College in Nebraska. In Los Angeles in 1889, he married one of his art teachers who was nineteen years his senior. For the next decade, they traveled extensively, including Paris where Borglum trained at the Académie Julian and came to know Rodin. By 1901, Borglum was working on the Cathedral. In 1908, he divorced. He was involved with the Armory Show of 1913, and as his talents were in demand. His works can be seen around the country, especially in Washington, D.C., and Newark, New Jersey. Sadly, he was a member of the Ku Klux Klan, and so it is ironic that he was dismissed from the Stone Mountain, Georgia, monumental sculpture paying homage to the Confederacy.

217 West 104th Street (near Broadway)

True, Clarence Fagan (1860–1928) ■ ▣
ARCHITECT

William Van Alen, the designer of the Chrysler Building, trained in
the office of Clarence True. True designed some 270 houses on the
Upper West Side of Manhattan from 1890 to the early 1900s. Many of
them give their blocks a distinctive and elegantly historical look, and
most are in landmarked districts. He specialized in town houses and
row houses, mixing aspects of Romanesque, Renaissance, Tudor, and
similar period styles in their design. From 1894, he built speculatively
to his own designs, taking the risk of lucrative profits or painful
losses. The Roerich Museum resides in one of his buildings. Born in
Massachusetts the son of an Episcopal clergyman, True was raised in
College Point, Queens. Sometime around 1881 he received his training
in the office of architect Richard Upjohn, noted for his Gothic-style
designs, and within a few years he branched out on his own. True also
lived farther uptown at **6 Morningside Avenue** (near 115th Street).

250 West 104th Street (near Broadway)

Leichter, Franz Sigmund (1930–) ■
NEW YORK STATE SENATOR AND ASSEMBLYMAN

The Cook-Leichter Bill was the first in the country to legalize abortion.
Leichter sponsored it with fellow assembly member Constance Cook,
and it impacted the Supreme Court's *Roe v. Wade* decision in 1973.
Born in Austria, Leichter came to the United States escaping from
the Nazi scourge. He graduated from Swarthmore College in 1952 and
left Harvard in 1957 with a doctorate in law. After working in a private
law practice specializing in commercial and foreign interests, he was
elected to the New York State Assembly in 1968 and to the State Senate

in 1974. He retired in 1988 to be succeeded by Eric Schneiderman. He also lived at **600 West 111th Street** (near Broadway).

309 West 104th Street (near West End Avenue)

Levison, Stanley David (1912–1979)
LAWYER AND ACTIVIST

Levison was a close friend and advisor to Dr. Martin Luther King. The FBI had been monitoring Levison since the early 1950s, and President Kennedy warned Dr. King to be wary of Levison because of alleged communist sympathies. Indeed, Levison supported various liberal causes and aided in the defense of the Rosenbergs, who spied for the Soviets. When Levison testified to the Senate Subcommittee on Internal Security in 1962, William Kunstler was his counsel. Born in New York City, Levison attended the University of Michigan, Columbia, and the New School for Social Research. By 1939, he earned two law degrees from St. John's University. He served in the Coast Guard and then achieved wealth through real estate ventures and a Ford dealership in New Jersey. Levison came to know Dr. King in 1956 through Bayard Rustin. He gave King constant, free counsel; raised funds; wrote speeches (including the first draft of his "I Have a Dream" speech); handled publicity; was his literary agent; and even prepared his tax returns. Levison also lived at **225 West 106th Street** (near Broadway).

8 West 105th Street (near Central Park West)

Sullivan, Frank (1892–1976) ▪ ▪
HUMORIST

Sullivan's fictional characters included Martha Hepplethwaite and the "forgotten" Bach who was the tone-deaf member of the famous musical family. His best-known character was the cliché expert, Mr. Arbuthnot, who entertained questions on a wide variety of topical subjects in discombobulated, pretentious blabber. Known as the "Sage of Saratoga," he was born and raised there. After graduating from Cornell University in 1914, he worked for *The Saratogian* newspaper. After his stint in World War I, he moved to New York City and worked as a reporter and feature writer on the *World*, the *Herald*, and the *Evening Sun* newspapers. Ever the wit, and a peripheral member of the Algonquin Round Table, his quotes include "This is either a forgery or a damn clever original!" and "I am in the twilight of a mediocre career." Magazines such as *Harper's*, the *Atlantic Monthly*, the *Saturday Evening Post*, and the *New Yorker* published his humorous pieces as well. He wrote the *New Yorker*'s Christmas greeting poem from 1932 to 1974.

69 West 105th Street (near Columbus Avenue)

Roach, Max (1924–2007), Percussionist ★ ▪

(See bio for Roach at **Park West Village**.)

120 West 105th Street (near Amsterdam Avenue)

Helmreich, William Benno (1945–2020)

PROFESSOR OF SOCIOLOGY, JUDAISM SCHOLAR, AND URBAN WALKING LEGEND

Helmreich is thought to be the first person who walked 6,163 miles of all 121,000 blocks in New York City. Fortunately, he wrote about it and many wonderful encounters with people along the way. His ever-interest in the human spirit is more than evident in the book *The New York Nobody Knows: Walking 6,000 miles in the City* and his companion books on Brooklyn and Manhattan. As a renowned scholar of Judaism in the Graduate Center of the City University of New York, where he chaired the Sociology Department, he wrote *Against All Odds: Holocaust Survivors and the Successful Lives They Made in America*. His first of eighteen books authored in 1973, *The Black Crusaders: A Case Study of a Black Militant Organization* explored the workings of black politics. He was born in Switzerland as his parents fled Nazism, but he arrived in the United States in 1946 and was raised on the Upper West Side. He attended Yeshiva University in Manhattan and did graduate work at Washington University in St. Louis. Like his New York City walk, his classes at City College were legendary. Sadly, he died of COVID-19.

161 West 105th Street (near Amsterdam Avenue)

Jones, Thad (1923–1986)
JAZZ TRUMPETER

There is a street in Copenhagen, Denmark, named after Thad Jones. Jones was born into a musically talented family in Michigan, where he taught himself to play the trumpet. As part of his World War II military service, he played in US Army bands. A continuing association with the US Military School of Music in the Midwest led to his membership in the Count Basie Orchestra. His solo on the Basie rendition of *April in Paris* is particularly notable. He recorded with Thelonious Monk and others before he left Basie in 1963. New York City–based as an arranger and a trumpet player, he teamed up with another giant in jazz to form the Thad Jones/Mel Lewis Orchestra. For twelve years, starting in 1966, they were a feature in one of Greenwich Village's great jazz rooms, the Village Vanguard. They won a Grammy Award in 1978 for a live performance album in Munich, Germany. Jones taught at William Paterson College, where his archives are kept. He lived in Copenhagen from 1979, returning to his home country only to lead the Basie Orchestra after the Count died. His brothers were the jazz drummer Elvin Jones and the pianist **Hank Jones**.

THE WEST 100S 133

172 West 105th Street (near Amsterdam Avenue)

Townsend, Ralph S. (1854–1921), Architect ■ ▮

(See bio for Townsend at **256 West 100th Street**.)

200 West 105th Street (Amsterdam Avenue)

Mumford, Lewis (1895–1990), Urbanist and Intellectual ★ ■
☞

(See bio for Mumford at **59 West 93rd Street**.)

255 West 105th Street (near West End Avenue)

Davies, Marion (1897–1961) ■
ACTRESS, COMEDIENNE, AND PHILANTHROPIST

Marion Davies is probably best known as the mistress of William Randolph Hearst, but she was a first-rate comedienne in her own right. In 1918, Hearst arranged for Marion and her mother and sisters to live in a town house on Riverside Drive. More than just a mistress, she was provided opportunities to further her film career. Although she appeared in some fifty movies, Hearst's controlling attention is thought to have prevented her natural evolution into true stardom. She made a reasonably successful transition from silent pictures to "talkies," despite nervousness associated with a childhood stutter. She was born Marion Cecelia Elizabeth Douras in Brooklyn, where she grew up near Prospect Park. She modeled for illustrators, including Howard Chandler Christy, who executed the murals in Café des Artistes; she worked as a chorus girl and, in 1916, became a Ziegfeld girl on Broadway. After a few film appearances, she was a celebrity with a small fortune. Joseph Kennedy rented her Hollywood mansion during his son's campaign for the presidency. She endowed the Davies

Children's Center at UCLA. Davies also lived at **331 Riverside Drive** (near 105th Street).

15 West 106th Street (near Manhattan Avenue)

Strayhorn, William Thomas "Billy" (1915–1967), Jazz Composer, Arranger, and Pianist ■

(See bio for Strayhorn at **310 Riverside Drive**.)

Gonsalves, Paul (1920–1974)
SAXOPHONIST

Gonsalves is credited with reviving Duke Ellington's career in 1956. At the Newport Jazz festival that year, Gonsalves made the music world take notice when he played a twenty-seven-bar solo in the middle of Ellington's "Diminuendo and Crescendo in Blue." The Duke nicknamed him "the strolling violins" because Gonsalves would walk through audiences while playing his solos. Born in Massachusetts to Portuguese parents, Gonsalves transitioned from guitar to saxophone as a youngster and played in various venues, as well as during his World War II service. His reputation solid, the Count Basie and Dizzy Gillespie bands employed his talents. In 1950, he joined the Duke Ellington Orchestra and stayed there for most of his playing career. Duke Ellington died ten days after Paul Gonsalves.

50 West 106th Street (near Manhattan Avenue)

Cheatham, Adolphus "Doc" (1905–1997)
TRUMPET PLAYER

Cheatham was one of the last trumpet players to play with Louis Armstrong. Born in Nashville, part Choctaw and Cherokee, he started out on drums but shifted to saxophone and cornet. Playing in bands from the 1920s, he backed such greats as Ethel Waters and Bessie Smith. Moving to Chicago, he befriended Louis Armstrong and played with his wife, Lil. He found his way to New York by 1928, and that led to three years of touring in Europe. In 1931, he started an eight-year stint in Cab Calloway's orchestra at the Cotton Club. With big bands fading out over time, his trumpet found its way into Afro-Cuban music. In his seventies, his career was revived, in large part because of his singing ability and delightfully engaging style of talking with his audiences. Like a few greats before him, such as Duke Ellington and Dizzy Gillespie, he was waved into Jazz Heaven from a fitting service at the Cathedral of St. John the Divine.

110 West 106th Street (Columbus Avenue)

Gordon, Taylor Emmanuel (1893–1971)
SINGER AND VAUDEVILLE PERFORMER

Gordon was the singing partner of **J. Rosamond Johnson**, who, with his brother **James Weldon Johnson**, composed "Lift Every Voice and Sing," frequently called the Negro national anthem. Born in Montana, Gordon moved to New York City when he was 17 years old. Gordon and Johnson toured the United States, France, and Europe. They undoubtedly sang selections from the Johnsons' classic *Book of American Negro Spirituals*. In 1927, they gave a concert in Carnegie Hall with the sponsorship of the National Urban League. In 1959, Gordon returned to his hometown, White Sulphur Springs, Montana, to live the rest of his life. Gordon's 1929 autobiography *Born to Be* recounts his life as an African American growing up in a small town and then becoming famous, an important figure in both vaudeville and the Harlem Renaissance.

The Battle of Harlem Heights began here on September 16th, 1776 near the Nicholas Jones house on 106th Street between West End Avenue and Riverside Drive–1890.

203 West 106th Street (near Amsterdam Avenue)

Dresser, Paul (1857–1906) ■
SONGWRITER, SINGER, AND COMEDIC ACTOR

Dresser wrote the official state song of Indiana, "On the Banks of the Wabash, Far Away." Born in Indiana, once destined for the priesthood, he left home at age 16 to join a minstrel act as a piano player. He developed singing and entertaining skills and achieved national recognition. With that, he began writing and publishing songs. Beloved by all, Dresser was characterized by his generosity, his lavish socializing, his large appetites, and his rotund frame. He changed his name from Dreiser to Dresser and was a Tin Pan Alley mainstay. "My Gal Sal" might be his best-known ditty, but occasionally his other chestnuts surface, including "The Letter That Never Came," "The Blue and the Gray," "Just Tell Them You Saw Me," and "The Pardon Came Too Late." Sadly, he died penniless. Dresser was the brother of novelist and journalist **Theodore Dreiser**.

225 West 106th Street (near Broadway)

Levison, Stanley David (1912–1979), Lawyer and Activist

(See bio for Levison at **309 West 104th Street**.)

301 West 106th Street (near West End Avenue)

Bernays, Hella Felicitas (1893–1994) ☞
NIECE OF SIGMUND FREUD

Bernays was the niece of Sigmund Freud. In 1913, she traveled to Europe with her mother Anna Freud Bernays, quite possibly to visit with the great founder of psychoanalysis. A native of New York, Bernays graduated in 1913 from Barnard, where she was president of the Barnard College and Teachers College Social Club, and she began work as a laboratory technician at the Rockefeller Institute for Medical Research. In 1917, she married Maurice "Murray" Cohen, who was attending Columbia's Law School, and who agreed to become Murray C. Bernays so that her family name would be kept alive. They divorced in 1923, and he went on to have the principal responsibility for designing the procedures for the trials at Nuremberg. She was a lifelong friend and sometimes collaborator with **Stella Bloch Hanau**, and she was the sister-in-law of **Doris Fleischman**.

Lauterbach, Edward (1844–1923) ■ ▇

LAWYER

In addition to being one of the great lawyers of his day, Lauterbach was chairman of the board of trustees of the College of the City of New York. Born in New York, Lauterbach graduated from City College in 1864. He learned the practice of law by apprenticing in law firms. He specialized in railroad law and was involved in the creation of the transit system in Brooklyn and New York. His work for J. P. Morgan was extensive, and he was an officer and director of many companies. His philanthropic interests were widespread, including thirty-nine years of service to the Hebrew Orphan Asylum. An active Republican, he is credited with making the gold standard part of the party's platform in the late 1890s, only to be dramatically attacked by William Jennings Bryan in his "cross of gold" speech. Lauterbach also lived at **945 West End Avenue** (near 106th Street) and **2783 Broadway** (near 107th Street).

Untermeyer, Louis (1885–1977) ■

POET AND ANTHOLOGIST

Untermeyer created ninety anthologies of poetry. His *Modern American Poetry* served as the poetry textbook for countless literature classes. Born in New York, he was self-educated and left the family jewelry business to dedicate his life to poetry. In the earliest part of his career, he flirted with Marxism and contributed pieces to the progressive journals the *Liberator* and the *Masses*. In 1916, he founded the *Seven Arts*, a magazine that encouraged emerging writers and introduced his lifelong friend Robert Frost to the public. In the late 1930s he was the poetry editor of the *American Mercury*. He was a prolific writer of poetry all his life, using parody, puns, and wit to rail against the earlier era of Victorian standards and style. More than inspirational when he lectured, he held posts that employed his talents at both Harvard and the Library of Congress. Sadly, he was blacklisted during the McCarthy era for his earlier political sympathies. Fortunately, by then he was already an established part of American literature.

Wilshire, H. Gaylord (1861–1927) ☜

REAL ESTATE DEVELOPER AND SOCIALIST

Wilshire Boulevard in Los Angeles is named after Gaylord Wilshire. He donated the land to the City of Angels in 1895 to create a boulevard, provided they named it after him and banned its use for railroads and trucking. He was born in Ohio and moved to Los Angeles in 1884. His contribution to California is some of its earliest residential development. Around the same time, he became very interested in socialism. After being arrested for speaking in a public park in 1900, he moved to New York where he ran for public office numerous times—including a run for Congress in 1904—but always lost. Emma Goldman worked with him in the Free Speech League. In 1906, he entertained Maxim Gorky when he visited New York. He died destitute, too soon to reap the profits from his "electric belt," marketed as Ionoco, which sold for sixty-five dollars. It was purported to remove toxins from the body but was exposed as quackery.

315 West 106th Street (near Riverside Drive)

Ajello, Gaetan (1883–1983), Architect ■ ▪

(See bio for Ajello at **415 Central Park West**.)

Lamont, Corliss (1902–1995) ★ ■ ☞
CIVIL LIBERTARIAN AND HUMANIST PHILOSOPHER

Author Corliss Lamont Sings for His Family and Friends a Medley of Favorite Hit Songs from American Musicals is the title of a 1977 Folkways record. By no means an accomplished singer, Lamont was a vanguard of secular humanism. A radical at heart with communist sympathies from the 1930s, he matured to become an internationalist. Born in New Jersey when his father was chairman of J. P. Morgan & Co., Lamont was valedictorian at Phillips Exeter Academy and magna cum laude at Harvard. He continued studying at Oxford, where his roommate was the evolutionary biologist Julian Huxley. He subsequently studied at Columbia under John Dewey, and then he taught at Columbia and lectured on philosophy. He also taught at Harvard, Cornell, and the New School for Social Research. His wider activities included running for the Senate in 1952 on the American Labor Party ticket and serving as a director of the American Civil Liberties Union for thirty years. He fought the McCarthy hearings in 1954 but authored *Why I Am Not a Communist*. His brother, Thomas Lamont, Jr., succeeded him as chairman of Morgan. His nephew Ned Lamont ran for the Senate in Connecticut and lost to incumbent Joseph Lieberman, but he was elected to become governor in 2019. Corliss Lamont also lived at **450 Riverside Drive** (near 116th Street) and **454 Riverside Drive** (near 119th Street).

Podhoretz, Norman (1930–), Neoconservative Writer

(See bio for Podhoretz at **924 West End Avenue**.)

318 West 106th Street (near Riverside Drive)

Richter, Gisela Augusta (1882–1972) ■
ARCHEOLOGIST AND ART HISTORIAN

In 1925, Richter was the first woman to hold the title of Curator at
the Metropolitan Museum of Art when she was so appointed. As the
curator of Greek and Roman Art, she was an internationally important
classical art historian. She joined the Met in 1905 and undertook
to catalog their collection of Greek vases. With her expanding
responsibilities, she designed exhibitions and authored some three
dozen related books and museum guides. She also lectured at many
professional and institutional forums, including Oberlin and Bryn
Mawr Colleges, Yale, and Columbia. Born in London, England, she
spent much time in Rome, Italy, with her father, who was a noted
art historian. She graduated from Girton College, University of
Cambridge, and achieved membership in the British School at Athens,
an archeological institute in Athens, Greece. She came to the United
States in 1905 and became a citizen in 1917. In 1952, Oxford University
awarded her an honorary doctor of letters degree.

Townsend, George Alfred (1841–1914) ■
CIVIL WAR CORRESPONDENT

George Townsend is thought to have been one of the youngest
correspondents in the American Civil War. Because of his daily
newspaper coverage, he was widely known, and he came to personally
know every president from Lincoln to Wilson and most of the Civil
War generals from both the North and the South. Born in Philadelphia,

Townsend began his career in journalism at the *Philadelphia Inquirer* in 1859. He moved on to the *New York Herald* in 1861, reporting on the Civil War. In 1865, he became the Washington correspondent for the *New York World* and covered the Lincoln assassination. His account of the subsequent events was published later in 1865 as a best-selling book *The Life, Crime, and Capture of John Wilkes Booth.* He also covered the Austro-Prussian War for the *World.* In the 1870s, he served as a correspondent for the *Chicago Tribune* and the *New York Graphic.* Townsend came to know King Edward VII when he accompanied the Prince of Wales on his tour of the United States, visiting such places as Niagara Falls and Central Park. Townsend's estate in Maryland became Gathland State Park, honoring his pen name "Gath." He also wrote poems, plays, short stories, and novels.

George Alfred Townsend.

14 West 107th Street (near Manhattan Avenue)

Loesser, Frank Henry (1910–1969) ★ ■

SONGWRITER

Anyone who dabbles on the piano undoubtedly plays "Heart and Soul," Frank Loesser's first hit song. He co-wrote it and "Two Sleepy People" with Hoagy Carmichael under contract with Paramount Pictures. Loesser's additional movie hits would include "On a Slow Boat to China"; "Praise the Lord and Pass the Ammunition"; and "Baby, It's Cold Outside." When he returned to New York and Broadway, he gave the world spectacular musicals, including *Guys and Dolls, Most Happy Fella,* and *How to Succeed in Business without Really Trying.* Born on West 107th Street, Loesser was expelled from the prestigious Townsend Harris High School and, later, was expelled from City College. After holding more jobs than one can imagine, he tried songwriting. His first song in 1931, long forgotten, had music by composer **William Schuman**. His half-brother was concert pianist Arthur Loesser.

THE MOST DANGEROUS STREET?

In the Bloomingdale neighborhood, 107th Street between Manhattan and Amsterdam Avenues, might have been the most dangerous street. In an article dated June 19, 1987, the *New York Times* reported that in the early evening of the night before, some two hundred police officers and detectives raided eight apartment houses in the "largest drug sweep conducted in a single city neighborhood." They were aided by search warrants based on previous purchases of drugs in the area, which were videotaped to facilitate arrests. The coordination for the surprise action included a staging area in the Central Park Precinct at 86th Street, rerouting of traffic, police officers on rooftops, mounted police on the streets, and a helicopter. More than fifty people were arrested, and drugs, money, and weapons were seized

Monroe Rosenfeld.

64 West 107th Street (near Columbus Avenue)

Rosenfeld, Monroe H. "Rosey" (ca. 1861–1918) ■ ☞

MUSIC PUBLISHER, SONGWRITER, AND JOURNALIST

Rosenfeld is thought to have coined the phrase "Tin Pan Alley." He was writing a series of articles on popular music for the *New York Herald* newspaper. When fellow songwriter Harry von Tilzer remarked that the tone of Rosey's muffled piano sounded like tin cans, Rosenfeld came up with the name "tin pan alley." Born in Virginia, he came to New York City in the 1880s and became successful as a songwriter. "With All Her Faults I Love Her Still"; "Her Golden Hair Was Hanging Down Her Back"; "Johnny Get Your Gun"; "I'm the Man That Broke the Bank at Monte Carlo"; and "Hush, Little Baby, Don't You Cry" are some of his many songs. In a time of lax copyright laws, Rosenfeld readily employed the names and melodies of others. He also operated his Rosenfeld Musical Bureau, representing songwriters and performers, and he wrote extensively about the emerging music business for newspapers and magazines. In 1917, he was contributing to the ragtime music magazine the *Tuneful Yankee*.

230 West 107th Street (near Broadway), Hamilton Court

Chenoweth, Kristin Dawn (1968–)

SINGER AND ACTRESS

Gorgeous face, petite size, and helium-inflected voice, these only begin to describe the assets of Kristin Chenoweth. Operatically trained, she was only the third musical theater performer to have a solo concert at the Metropolitan Opera House. Despite a lauded Broadway career, she is most likely known for her television roles. An adopted Oklahoman with some Cherokee blood, she attended Oklahoma City University, attaining a bachelor's degree in musical theater and a master's degree in opera performance. A Broadway veteran, she won a Tony Award in 1999

The Lion Brewery spewing smoke behind the erection of the Cathedral of St. John.

THE LION BREWERY

In 1895, the Lion Brewery was the sixth largest in the country. It was a formidable presence, occupying the site where Booker T. Washington School is today. In fact, its full site included most of the block between Columbus and Amsterdam Avenues from 107th to 108th Streets, and the eastern side of Columbus Avenue, where there were picnic grounds for the brewery employees. The brewmaster lived in a house on the north side of 108th Street, where today there is a playground. A map shows two ponds on the site that might have been created to supply ice for the operation, as well as stable buildings for the horses that delivered the barrels of beer.

The Lion Brewery was founded by Emanuel Bernheimer and partner James Speyer in 1857, two years before Central Park was begun. Bavarian Catholics built the brewery and populated the area. Brewery workers also built the Church of the Ascension at 221 West 107th Street, which was completed in 1897. The Lion Brewery survived prohibition in the 1920s but finally closed shop in 1941. The buildings were demolished by 1944.

The Lion Brewery also operated the Lion Music Hall on the southeast corner of Broadway and 110th Street. For years, it was the favorite haunt of Columbia students before the West End Café became

for her role in *You're a Good Man, Charlie Brown*, and originated the role of Glinda in *Wicked*. She had appeared in such popular TV series as *The West Wing*, *Glee*, and *Pushing Daisies*, for which she won a 2009 Emmy Award. Her one-time performances on late-night TV, at sporting events, and especially at the Tony Awards have been more than memorable.

Ebb, Fred (1928–2004) ▪

SONGWRITER

"Start spreading the news . . ." wrote lyricist Fred Ebb, and thus "New York, New York" became one of the five most-sung songs in America. It was introduced by Liza Minnelli in the 1977 movie *New York, New York* and achieved even greater popularity with Frank Sinatra's rendition two years later. A New York native, Ebb graduated from New York University and received a master's in English from Columbia. After some early collaborations, he connected with John Kander in 1962. Their second musical, *Cabaret* premiered in 1966 and earned eight Tony Awards out of eleven nominations, including Best Musical and Best Score. The film adaptation earned eight Academy Awards. He also wrote television specials in the early 1970s for Liza Minnelli and for Frank

their hangout of choice. In 1919, the beer garden site was restructured by the noted theater architect Thomas Lamb. The resulting Nemo Theater, at 2834 Broadway, showed silent films and sat 932 people. It was part of the Fox Theater circuit and lasted until 1963. The theater was then repurposed as a supermarket. Columbia demolished it in 2003 to build an apartment and school building.

There is no connection between the Columbia Lion and the Lion Brewery lion.

Sinatra, coming out of retirement. The Kander-Ebb team wrote other musicals, notably *The Rink*; *Kiss of the Spider Woman*; *Woman of the Year* for Lauren Bacall; *Chicago*, which won both Tony and Academy awards; and *Steel Pier*, which was nominated for eleven Tony Awards.

245 West 107th Street (near Broadway)

Glass, Philip (1937–) ■
COMPOSER

Philip Glass has delved into so many realms of music and art that it should not be surprising that he has collaborated with the likes of Leonard Cohen, Martin Scorsese, Paul Simon, Suzanne Vega, Woody Allen, Richard Serra, Steven Colbert, David Bowie, Linda Ronstadt, Laurie Anderson, and Ravi Shankar. His list of compositions is extensive, including *Einstein on the Beach*, *Piano Etudes*, *Songs from Liquid Days*, *The Low Symphony*, *Koyaanisqatsi*, and *Glassworks*. Glass was born in Baltimore to a family of musicians related to the singer Al Jolson. At age 15, he was admitted to the University of Chicago where he studied mathematics and philosophy. He then went on to Julliard where he concentrated on the keyboard. He extended his development under the instruction of Darius Milhaud at the Aspen Music Festival and received a Fulbright Scholarship that placed him in the midst of a variety of influences in Paris. Glass is a first cousin once removed of Ira Glass the creator of the radio show *This American Life*.

Holbrook, Hal (1925–) ■
ACTOR

Holbrook played the role of "deep throat" in the 1976 movie *All the President's Men*. In 2008, at age 82, he became the oldest person nominated for an Academy Award for his role in *Into the Wild*. Born in Ohio, Holbrook graduated from Denison University where he first performed as Mark Twain. Indeed, most people associate him with his acclaimed Broadway performance in the one-man show *Mark Twain Tonight*. His extensive acting credits also include TV shows such as *The West Wing*, *ER*, *The Sopranos*, *Sons of Anarchy*, *Grey's Anatomy*, *The Sopranos*, and a performance as Abraham Lincoln on the *Ed Sullivan Show*. In Spielberg's 2012 *Lincoln*, Holbrook played the journalist-politician Francis Preston Blair, Sr. Holbrook can also be seen in such movies as *Magnum Force*, *The Great White Hope*, and *Wall Street*.

300 West 107th Street (near West End Avenue)

Neel, Alice (1900–1984) ◼

ARTIST

The 2007 documentary film *Alice Neel* was directed by the artist's grandson Andrew Neel. The film conveys her significance as an artist, which only became widely realized at the end of her life. Best known as a portraitist, her sitters included Joseph Papp, Kate Millet, Frank O'Hara, Faith Ringgold, Bella Abzug, Virgil Thompson, and Ed Koch, among others. She even painted the Greenwich Village character Joe Gould, made famous by Joseph Mitchell in a *New Yorker* piece. Neel was born in Pennsylvania and graduated in 1925 from the Philadelphia School of Design for Women, which is now the Moore College of Art and Design. After a divorce, a nervous breakdown, and a suicide attempt, she established herself in Spanish Harlem. She painted the human form, children, men, and especially women, with shocking introspection.

303 West 107th Street (near West End Avenue)

Fleischman, Doris Elsa (1891–1980) 👉
PIONEER COUNSEL IN PUBLIC RELATIONS AND FEMINIST

Fleischman and her husband advised her uncle Sigmund Freud, as well as such notables as Henry Ford, Thomas Edison, and US presidents from Coolidge to Eisenhower. In her free time, she helped revive the Lucy Stone League and wrote pro-women articles. Born Doris Fleischman in New York, she graduated from Barnard College in 1913 and became a reporter for the *New York Tribune*. In 1922, she married Edward Bernays, keeping her maiden name. In fact, she is thought to be the first married woman to be issued a passport in her maiden name. She was his first hire in his public relations firm and became his lifelong professional partner. Although he became known as "the father of public relations," she cited her own essential role in their success with the 1955 best seller *A Wife Is Many Women*. She was the sister-in-law of **Hella Felicitas Bernays.**

319 West 107th Street (near Riverside Drive)

Bentley, Irene (ca.1870–1940)
STAGE ACTRESS AND SINGER

Miss Irene Bentley.

Evelyn Nesbit, the object of architect Stanford White's affection who got him killed by the jealous Harry K. Thaw, was an actress in the 1902 Broadway musical *The Wild Rose*. Irene Bentley was the star of that show, and her soon-to-be husband, **Harry B. Smith,** co-wrote the show's book and lyrics. Born in Maryland, Bentley first appeared on the Broadway stage in the 1895 production of *Little Christopher*. Within a few years, she was a major stage star in New York and London, headlining such long-forgotten shows as *The Rounders*, *The Casino Girl*, *The Belle of Mayfair*, and others.

Fosdick, Dudley (1902–1957) ▊ 🖎

JAZZ MUSICIAN AND MUSEUM DIRECTOR

Fosdick played the mellophone, a brass instrument not unlike a
flugelhorn, and is considered its first soloist of note. At the time of
his death, Fosdick was the director of the Roerich Academy of Arts.
He donated his house to become the Nicholas Roerich Museum. As
a devoted follower of the artist and mystic **Nicholas Roerich**, Fosdick
employed his musical talents and Roerich's paintings to expound
spiritual development and the value of world peace. Born in Indiana,
Fosdick studied at Northwestern University and graduated from
Columbia University in 1928. He played in an early jazz ensemble, the
Hoosiers, with his brother Gene on saxophone. Thereafter, he played
with bands led by Ted Weems, Don Voorhees, and Roger Wolfe Kahn,
and did some studio session work, notably with Red Nichols and his
Five Pennies. In 1936, he joined the Guy Lombardo Orchestra and was a
valued member for thirteen years.

Roerich, Nicholas (1874–1947) ▮

PAINTER, SCENARIST, AND THEOSOPHIST

An artist and mystic, Roerich mesmerized wealthy Americans who
formed a near-cult. Reportedly, he urged follower Henry Wallace,
Secretary of Agriculture under Franklin Roosevelt, to persuade the
Treasury Department to add the mystic pyramid of the Great Seal
to the dollar bill—a change that was enacted in 1935. Born in Russia,
Roerich attended both St. Petersburg University and the Imperial
Academy of Arts in 1893. In 1897, he received a law degree and began
a long association with the Imperial Society for the Encouragement
of the Arts, where he served as director from 1906 to 1917. In 1913, he
designed the set and costumes for Igor Stravinsky's revolutionary
ballet and music composition *The Rite of Spring*. He came to the United

States in 1920 in reaction to the Russian Revolution. On Riverside Drive at 103rd Street, he built a twenty-four-story, Art Deco building to serve as a combination school, office suite, and museum. Suffering the impact of the Great Depression, his operation was evicted in 1938. Meanwhile, he painted extensively on travels to Tibet and Mongolia, and his 107th Street town house was well-suited to become the Roerich Museum. Roerich also lived at **310 Riverside Drive** (near 103rd Street), the Master Apartments.

Smith, Harry Bache (1860–1936) ★ ● ▮
WRITER, LYRICIST, AND COMPOSER

Smith might have written the words to more songs than anyone ever. He wrote some six thousand lyrics and three hundred librettos, working with such notable Broadway musical composers as Victor Herbert, Reginald De Koven, Sigmund Romberg, Irving Berlin, and Jerome Kern; and with operetta composers Oscar Straus and Franz Lehar; and with bandmaster-composer John Philip Sousa. Born in upstate New York, he wrote his first libretto in 1879. In 1890, he wrote the lyrics to the operetta *Robin Hood*, for which another lyricist wrote the classic wedding song "*Oh Promise Me.*" One of his earliest collaborations with Victor Herbert in 1898, *The Fortune Teller*, produced the operetta standard "Gypsy Love Song." Their 1913 effort *Sweethearts* offered the hit song of the same name and, later, a movie version with Jeanette MacDonald and Nelson Eddy. A charter member of the American Society of Composers, Authors and Publishers, he also wrote the popular song "Sheik of Araby." Smith wrote books on Shakespeare and Charles Dickens, whose works he collected, and he was reputed to have an exceptional wine cellar. His wife was the stage actress **Irene Bentley**.

324 West 107th Street (near Riverside Drive)

Wald, George David (1906–1997)
BIOCHEMIST

Wald was on President Nixon's famous enemies list for his political views. He was most accomplished, however, in his field of biochemistry and was awarded the Nobel Prize in Physiology or Medicine in 1967 for discoveries in the chemistry of vision. A native New Yorker, Wald graduated in 1927 with a BS degree from New York University and, in 1932, with a PhD in zoology from Columbia. His earliest work in Germany and Switzerland began with his discovery of Vitamin A in the retina. His discovery of pigments that were key to light sensitivity explained, amongst other things, color-blindness. After this early research in Europe, he joined the faculty at Harvard in 1934. In his later years, he took active stands against nuclear war and the Vietnam War.

331 West 107th Street (near Riverside Drive)

Miranda, Altinis Schinasi (1907–1999), Sculptor, Filmmaker, and Designer

(See bio for Miranda at **351 Riverside Drive**.)

Schinasi, Moussa or Morris (1855–1928), Cigarette Manufacturer and Philanthropist

(See bio for Schinasi at **351 Riverside Drive**.)

8 West 108th Street (near Central Park West)

Harrison, Robert M. (1904–1978) ● ▮

PUBLISHER OF *CONFIDENTIAL* MAGAZINE

Harrison was a pioneer in exposé journalism, and his magazine is thought to have inspired the title of the James Ellroy novel *L.A. Confidential*. Harrison was born and raised in New York City. He did not graduate from Stuyvesant High School, but he attended night courses at Columbia. After working a beat at the *New York Evening Graphic* newspaper, which also employed Ed Sullivan and Walter Winchell, he worked for a motion picture trade magazine. That experience led to his interest in publishing non-pornographic "cheesecake" magazines. His first magazine in 1941 was *Beauty Parade*, followed by *Eyeful*, followed by the sadomasochistic *Titter*, followed by *Wink*, and then *Whisper*. His masterwork, *Confidential*, launched in 1952, became the fastest-growing magazine of its day when it covered the breakup of Marilyn Monroe and Joe DiMaggio. By 1955, its circulation of five million was greater than that of *Reader's Digest*. During the next few years, Harrison and *Confidential* magazine became mainstays on the front page of national newspapers. The detailed story is too complicated to synopsize, but it is centered on a California court case involving future California governor Pat Brown and lawsuits brought against the magazine totaling more than $40 million, involving Robert Mitchum, Dorothy Dandridge, Errol Flynn, Maureen O'Hara, Mae West, and Liberace. The complications overwhelmed Harrison and his magazine fell into obscurity. Harrison also lived at **15 West 108th Street** (near Manhattan Avenue).

15 West 108th Street (near Manhattan Avenue)

Harrison, Robert M. (1904–1978), Publisher of *Confidential* **Magazine** ◗ ▮

(See bio for Harrison at **8 West 108th Street**.)

61 West 108th Street (near Manhattan Avenue)

Takamine, Jokichi (1854–1922), Chemist ★ ◗ ▮ ☞

(See bio for Takamine at **334 Riverside Drive**.)

200 West 108th Street (near Amsterdam Avenue)

Weaver, Raymond Melbourne (1888–1948) ▮

ENGLISH PROFESSOR

Weaver is credited with reviving interest in the writings of Herman Melville, who had been almost completely forgotten for about fifty years. Today, Melville's *Moby Dick*, Mark Twain's *The Adventures of Huckleberry Finn*, and **F. Scott Fitzgerald**'s *The Great Gatsby* constitute the pantheon of American novels. Born in Baltimore, Weaver graduated from Columbia's Teachers College. After teaching for a few years in Hiroshima, Japan, he taught for a short while at Brooklyn Polytechnic Institute and then joined Columbia's faculty in 1916 to teach English. In 1921, he authored the biography *Herman Melville—Mariner and Mystic*, which started the renewed interest in the author of *Moby Dick*. During his research, he discovered Melville's unfinished manuscript of *Billy Budd*. In 1925, he published *Billy Budd*. His stature grew as a teacher, alongside others like Mark Van Doren and Mortimer J. Adler. He attained tenure in 1937 without ever having completed his doctorate. Possibly because he was an open homosexual, he wasn't made professor until 1946.

255 West 108th Street (near Amsterdam Avenue), the Manchester

Jones, Hank (1918–2010) ■ 🖚
PIANIST

Hank Jones.

When Marilyn Monroe sang Happy Birthday to President Kennedy in 1962 in Madison Square Garden, Hank Jones was playing the piano. Jones was born into a musically talented family in Mississippi but was raised in Michigan where he was playing professionally by age 13. When he came to New York City in 1944, he played with the likes of Andy Kirk, Coleman Hawkins, and Billy Eckstine. From 1948 to 1953, he was Ella Fitzgerald's constant pianist. He was also part of the bebop scene, recording with Charlie Parker and **Max Roach**. He was the "house pianist" for Savoy Records and he was the staff pianist for CBS studios, which included such responsibilities as backing Frank Sinatra on the *Ed Sullivan Show*. In the 1970s, he was the conductor and pianist for the Broadway musical *Ain't Misbehavin'*. The Berklee College of Music awarded him an Honorary Doctorate in Music in 2005. His brothers were the trumpet player **Thad Jones** and the drummer Elvin Jones.

Webb, Roy Denslow (1888–1982), Composer of Film Music ■

(See bio for Roy Webb at **248 West 102nd Street**.)

300 West 108th Street

Brown, Harold (1927–2019)
SECRETARY OF DEFENSE AND NUCLEAR PHYSICIST

Brown graduated summa cum laude with a BS degree from Columbia at age 17, followed by MS and PhD degrees at age 21. Before President Carter appointed him as the first scientist to be Defense Secretary, he was president of the California Institute of Technology for eight years. Before that, he was Secretary of the Air Force under President Johnson with all the complexities of the Vietnam War. His earliest professional endeavors as a nuclear physicist at the University of California, Berkeley, included developing the Polaris missile at its Radiation Laboratory. In 1960, he succeeded his mentor, Edward Teller, as director. Much of his time in government was dedicated to modernizing the military capabilities with better missiles, warheads, and stealth aircraft. He deserves much credit for the success of the Camp David accords that lead to an Israeli-Egyptian peace treaty in 1979, and much sympathy for the tragedy of the failed mission in 1980 to rescue the hostages held by the Iranians.

318 West 108th Street (near Broadway)

O'Gorman, James (1860–1943) ■
SENATOR

A native of New York City, O'Gorman graduated from City College, and then earned a law degree from New York University in 1882. While a student, he favored a single tax on land and other related principles of Henry George. In 1893, he was picked to become a New York District Court justice. In 1900, he was elected to the Supreme Court and, in 1903, was elected head of Tammany. However, Tammany was challenged by upstate Democrats under the leadership of young Franklin Delano Roosevelt. O'Gorman was selected as a compromise candidate for nomination to the US Senate. He became the last senator to be elected by the State Legislature. Thereafter, the Seventeenth Amendment provided for a popular election. After one term in the Senate he resumed practicing law and was president of the New York County Bar Association, president of the Lawyers Club, and trustee of New York University and the College of New Rochelle. Villanova College, Georgetown University, and Fordham University awarded him honorary degrees. His daughter was Alice O'Gorman. His one-time son-in-law was **Dudley Field Malone**.

J. A. O'Gorman.

321 West 108th Street (near Broadway)

Herbert, Victor (1859–1924) ★ ■
COMPOSER

Known for his light operettas, Victor Herbert's compositions also included two grand operas and what was probably the first original symphonic score for a feature film. Born in Ireland but raised in London and Germany where he obtained his musical training, Victor Herbert played in several European orchestras and composed his first pieces of music. In 1886, he came to the United States and achieved recognition rather quickly. He succeeded the bandmaster Patrick Gilmore in one conducting role and became conductor of the Pittsburg Symphony Orchestra. In addition to his efforts on behalf of the Copyright Act of 1909, he was one of the founding members in 1914 of the American Society of Composers, Authors, and Publishers (ASCAP). His string of successful Broadway operettas began in 1903 with *Babes in Toyland*. *Naughty Marietta* and *Sweetheart* are classics that were later reprised on the motion picture screen with Nelson Eddy and Jeanette MacDonald. Senator **James O'Gorman**, who lived at **318 West 108th Street**, across the street from Herbert, was a pallbearer at his funeral. The statue of Victor Herbert in Central Park was commissioned by ASCAP.

142 West 109th Street (near Amsterdam Avenue)

Obama, Barack (1961–) ★ ■
PRESIDENT OF THE UNITED STATES

President Obama spent a night in the alleyway on the west side of the building at 200 West 109th Street. When he arrived in New York to study at Columbia, someone was supposed to leave a key for him to access an apartment. However, because of some mix-up, he didn't get the key and had to sleep alongside the building. Born in Honolulu, Hawaii, he started at Occidental College but graduated from Columbia in 1983. After working as a community organizer in Chicago, he went to Harvard Law School and graduated with the added distinction of being the first black president of the *Harvard Law Review*. He met his wife, Michelle, when working at a Chicago law firm one summer. Next, he taught constitutional law at the University of Chicago Law School. He entered politics with election to a state office, followed by the United States Senate, and the presidency. His history in the Bloomingdale–Morningside Heights neighborhood is yet to be fully documented. Obama also lived at **622 West 114th Street** (near Riverside Drive).

Barack Obama.

174 West 109th Street (near Amsterdam Avenue)

Henderson, Eleanor Curtis (1901–1941), Communist Activist

(See bio for Henderson at **540 West 123rd Street**.)

206 West 109th Street (near Amsterdam Avenue)

Hayden, Richard Miles (ca.1849–ca.1893)
SUPERINTENDENT OF THE LEAKE AND WATTS ORPHAN ASYLUM

Richard Hayden followed **William Henry Guest** as the superintendent of the Leake and Watts Orphan Asylum. As such, he oversaw its movement to Yonkers when the trustees decided to sell the land to the Episcopal Church, which would erect the Cathedral of St. John the Divine on the site. Born in Maryland, Hayden was ordained a minister in 1871 with an AB degree. In 1886, Hayden wrote *An Historical Account of the Founding and Work of the Leake and Watts Orphan House in New York City*. In 1893, he received an MA degree from St. Stephen's College, which would later become Bard College. His widow, Mary A. Maitland, who was the matron at the orphanage, was living on 109th Street when she died in 1925. Hayden also lived somewhere on **110th Street near Amsterdam Avenue**.

214 West 109 Street (near Amsterdam Avenue)

Long, Nick Jr. (1904–1949) 🖛

DANCER

In the 1926 Broadway musical *Oh, Please*, Long jumped headfirst over the backs of ten chorus girls, landing in a net offstage. In the dance segment of the movie "*Broadway Melody of 1936*" entitled "I've Got a Feelin' You're Foolin',"<HS>" Long leapt over six chorus girls and then did eight standing broad jumps in a row over eight dancers. Long and his dance partner, June Knight, grace that movie, which also featured Buddy Ebsen, Eleanor Powell, Jack Benny, and Robert Taylor. Born to vaudevillian parents, Nick Long, Jr., stepped on the stage at age 9 and

Nick Long, Jr., in the "Broadway Melody of 1936" motion picture.

appeared on film at age 11. He attended the Professional Children's School in New York in its earliest years when Joan Blondel, Ruby Keeler, and Milton Berle were also trained there. He lifted weights and trained as a boxer and figure skater. His father wanted him to continue his education at Columbia, but he chose the "school of theater" instead. On Broadway, he shared the stage with the likes of Bob Hope, Clifton Webb, Irene Dunne, Danny Kaye, and Jose Ferrer. However, it was difficult for him to sustain a career in the theater arts or motion picture trade, and he died as a result of an automobile accident on the Henry Hudson Parkway in the Bronx. One of his last appearances was on an early TV show of his friend Ed Sullivan. His father and mother were the vaudevillians Nick Long, Sr., and Idalene Cotton.

237 West 109th Street (near Broadway)

PS 165, a George B. J. Snyder masterpiece–1903.

Duvall, Robert Selden (1931–)
ACTOR

In the 1960s Robert Duvall shared an apartment on 109th Street with **Dustin Hoffman**. Along with Gene Hackman, the trio of aspiring actors made horseplay, pranks, and practical jokes into an art form. Duvall eventually won an Academy Award for Best Actor in his role in the 1984 movie *Tender Mercies*, and he was nominated six other times. Born in California, he was raised in Annapolis, Maryland, because his father was an Admiral in the US Navy. He graduated from Principia College in Illinois with a BA degree in drama. After a brief stint in the army, he studied in New York at the Neighborhood Playhouse School of the Theater alongside students Gene Hackman, James Caan, and **Dustin Hoffman**. After a few years of stock theater, he made his way to off-Broadway, achieving an Obie Award for his role in Arthur Miller's *A View from the Bridge*. The next year, he debuted on Broadway in *Wait Until Dark*. His motion picture career began with a small role in the 1956 film *Somebody Up There Likes Me*, but his first role of consequence was as Boo Radley in *To Kill a Mockingbird*. After other significant roles in *Bullitt*, *True Grit*, and *MASH*, his career took a leap forward with his roles in the two *Godfather* movies.

Hoffman, Dustin Lee (1937–)
ACTOR

In 1970, Hoffman was living in a brownstone on West 11th Street when the building next door blew up and killed three members of the radical group, the Weathermen, who had accidentally detonated a large cache of explosives. Born in Los Angeles, Hoffman attended Santa Monica College but left to join the Pasadena Playhouse. There he met Gene Hackman, and along with **Robert Duvall**, they set out for New York City

A NEW NATIONAL ACADEMY DESIGN?

Some consideration, shortly before World War I, was given to having a National Academy of Design building on Columbia's campus in conjunction with creating a School of Fine Arts with Departments of Painting, Sculpture, and Decorative Arts. Columbia's School of Architecture had conducted a life-drawing course, from 1914 to 1919, at the National Academy of Design school on 109th Street and Amsterdam Avenue. The architects Carrere & Hastings, known for the New York Public Library's Main Branch building, the Frick Museum, and much else, drew plans for an impressive National Academy of Design building on 110th Street at Amsterdam Avenue. Primarily for financial reasons, it was never built.

to pursue their craft. Hoffman took acting classes at the Neighborhood Playhouse and the Actors Studio. His stage work was rather limited, but he debuted on the silver screen in 1967 in *The Tiger Makes Out* with Eli Wallach and Anne Jackson. Next came *The Graduate* and much else followed, including *Midnight Cowboy*, *Lenny*, *All the President's Men*, *Marathon Man*, and *Tootsie*. He was nominated for an Academy Award for Best Actor seven times and won twice for *Kramer vs. Kramer* and *Rain Man*. His return to the Broadway stage was most memorable in the 1984 production of *Death of a Salesman* and in *The Merchant of Venice* in 1989. Hoffman and his friend **Robert Duvall** shared an apartment on West 109th Street in the early 1960s.

300 West 109th Street (near Broadway), the Manhasset Apartments

Kohlberg, Jerome, Jr. (1920–2005), Investor ★ ■ ▪

(See bio for Kohlberg at **924 West End Avenue**.)

McGraw, John Joseph (1873–1934) ★ ■
BASEBALL PLAYER AND MANAGER

McGraw is perhaps best known as the winning manager of the New York Giants from 1902 to 1932, and as a Hall of Famer, inducted in 1937, only its second year. Born in upstate New York, he was only 10 years old when his mother and four of his siblings died of a debilitating fever. Two years later, he ran away from his abusive father. He later became a high school and minor league baseball star and entered the major leagues in Baltimore in 1891. He was a great all-time third baseman, and when he retired in 1907, he had a lifetime batting average of .334, and his on-base percentage of .466 is exceeded only by those of Ted Williams and Babe Ruth. In 1920, he was involved in an altercation that began at the Lambs Club and continued in front of an apartment building on West 109th Street. It sent comedian and actor **John C. Slavin** to St. Luke's Hospital with a fractured skull.

312 West 109th Street (near Riverside Drive)

Georgopulo, Theodore (ca.1883–1935), Cigarette Manufacturer

(See bio for Georgopulo at **865 West End Avenue**.)

415 Central Park West (aka 1 West 101st Street)

Ajello, Gaetan (1883–1983) ◼ ▮

ARCHITECT

Ajello was "found" by *New York Times* architectural writer Christopher Gray. Although Ajello had designed some of the most elegant apartment buildings on Manhattan's Upper West Side, by the 1930s, he seemed to have disappeared off the face of the earth. Gray found him in 1977 living with his sister on the Upper East Side. According to her recollection, Ajello gave another great apartment building architect, Rosario Candella, his first job in New York City. Born in Palermo, Italy, Ajello trained in his home country and came to the United States in 1902. His first significant commissions were for the spectacular cluster of buildings at 25, 29, and 35 Claremont Avenue. He designed nearly forty apartment buildings, with 395 Riverside Drive thought to be his last. His only nonresidential commission was for the landmarked Claremont Theater on Broadway at 135th Street. The entrance can be seen in a 1915 Library of Congress short (see youtube.com). Ajello also lived at **315 West 106th Street** (near Riverside Drive) and **501 West 113th Street** (near Amsterdam Avenue)

Blakey, Art (1919–1990) ■
JAZZ DRUMMER

Blakey played with Dizzy Gillespie, Charlie Parker, and Thelonious Monk, but he is best known for forming and leading the legendary Jazz Messengers. Born in Pittsburgh, he transitioned from piano to drums and found his way to New York City with another Pittsburgh treasure, Mary Lou Williams, as part of the Fletcher Henderson Orchestra. While working with Billy Eckstine's big band, he was introduced to bebop, grooving with Sarah Vaughan and fellow band members Charlie Parker, Thelonious Monk, Dexter Gordon, and Dizzy Gillespie. Art Blakey's Messengers was born in 1947, becoming Jazz Messengers in 1954. Keith Jarrett, Chuck Mangione, Wayne Shorter, and Branford and Wynton Marsalis, among others, earned their stripes in the group. His style of drumming was recognizably unique, and he was one of the first who utilized all four limbs—each arm and each leg playing different rhythms!

Harburg, Edgar Yipsel "Yip" (1896–1981) ★ ■
LYRICIST

Harburg's moniker "Yip" comes from his middle name Yitsel, morphed to Yipsel, meaning squirrel, because he scampered around like one. Born Isadore Hochburg on Manhattan's Lower East Side, he became lifelong friends with Ira Gershwin, with whom he had a common interest in the light verse of W. S. Gilbert. As a young teenager, Harburg wrote parodies for shows at the Henry Street Settlement. He also submitted poems to Franklin P. Adams's newspaper column using the name Yipper. City College graduated him in 1921. His big break came with writing the words to the 1932 song "Brother Can You Spare a Dime." Then came "It's Only a Paper Moon," "April in Paris," and the songs in the 1939 movie *Wizard of Oz*, including the immortal "Somewhere Over the Rainbow." Harburg also wrote for Broadway musicals such as *Bloomer Girl* and *Finian's Rainbow*. And he wrote one of Groucho Marx's favorite songs, "Lydia the Tattooed Lady."

Hart, Lorenz "Larry" Milton (1895–1943) ★ ■
LYRICIST

At only five feet tall, at most, it is no surprise that lyricist Larry Hart was portrayed by the similarly short actor Mickey Rooney in the 1948 movie *Words and Music*. Born in Harlem, Hart came to know and work with both Richard Rogers and **Oscar Hammerstein II** while attending Columbia University for two years. After some work alongside the operetta composer Sigmund Romberg, Rogers and Hart wrote the score for the 1925 Broadway musical *Garrick Gaieties*, which included "Manhattan," their first contribution to the Great American Songbook. Rogers and Hart worked on some twenty-six other musical productions such as *Boys from Syracuse*, *On Your Toes*, *Pal Joey*, and *Babes in Arms*. From those four shows came such classics as "Where or When"; "Isn't It Romantic"; "Bewitched, Bothered, and Bewildered"; "My Funny Valentine"; and "The Lady Is a Tramp."

Lincoln, Abbey (1930–2010), Jazz Singer and Actress ■

(See bio for Lincoln at **Park West Village**.)

Packard, Eleanor Gould (1917–2005), Grammarian ★ ■

(See bio for Packard at **60 West 96th Street**.)

Papp, Joseph (1921–1991) ★ ■
THEATRICAL PRODUCER AND DIRECTOR

Joe Papp gave the world *Hair* and *A Chorus Line*. He is also responsible for Shakespeare in the Park, and for the Public Theater, which introduced such productions as *The Basic Training of Pavlo Hummel*, *That Championship Season*, and *The Mystery of Edward Drood*. He was born Josef Papirofsky in Brooklyn and learned to stage shows while serving in the US Navy during World War II. He joined the Actors' Laboratory

Theater whose students included Lee J. Cobb, Hume Cronyn, Lloyd Bridges, and Marilyn Monroe, and he graduated in 1948 as its managing director. Returning to New York, he worked as a stage manager for CBS television and shortened his name to Papp. In 1954, he began staging free Shakespeare plays in a church in the East Village. With great success, the operation moved to a two thousand-seat amphitheater in a park on the East River, followed by stagings in each of the city's boroughs, and finally, to Central Park by Belvedere Castle. With the help of the courts, Papp won a battle with Robert Moses to keep the Central Park home with a newly built permanent stage. In 1966, the old Astor Library on Lafayette Street became the home of the Public Theater. The success of *Hair* helped it along and paved the way for many up-and-coming playwrights and stars. Papp also lived at **420 Central Park West** (near 102nd Street).

Roach, Max (1924–2007), Percussionist ★ ▪

(See bio for Roach at **Park West Village**.)

Wilson, Teddy (1912–1986) ▪ ▪

JAZZ PIANIST

Wilson played in what many believe to be the most important popular music concert in history. He was part of the Benny Goodman Trio, with Gene Krupa on drums, and a member of Goodman's quartet, with Lionel Hampton on vibraphone, when they played Carnegie Hall in 1938, the first jazz concert ever performed there. Wilson was born in Texas, and after his family moved to Alabama, he learned to play piano, oboe, clarinet, and violin in high school. He studied further at Tuskegee Institute where his father headed the English department and his mother was a librarian. He launched his professional career in Detroit as the pianist for two bands. From there he played with almost every notable jazz musician, and his relaxed and swinging style served numerous singers, including Lena Horne, Billie Holiday, and Ella Fitzgerald. He had his own band for a while, but he wowed the jazz scene with his sextet, playing at the "Café Society" club from 1940 to 1944. He also played with many of the great swing musicians including Coleman, Hawkins, Roy Eldridge, **Buck Clayton**, Ben Webster, and Lester Young. He taught at Julliard for a period of time.

418 Central Park West (near 102nd Street), the Braender

Seidman, Henry L. (1890–1963) ■
ACCOUNTING TEACHER

In 1920 Seidman founded the first school to prepare students to take the examination to become a Certified Public Accountant. For a number of years, he was head of the C.P.A. Examinations Review. Born in Russia, he came to the United States in 1910, graduated from NYU School of Commerce, and earned an LLB degree from the Brooklyn Law School. He began his professional career as a public accountant. Seidman also lived at **890 West End Avenue** (near 104th Street).

420 Central Park West (near 102nd Street)

Papp, Joseph (1921–1991), Theatrical Producer and Director ★ ■

(See bio for Papp at **415 Central Park West**.)

425 Central Park West (near 103rd Street)

Reed, Phil (1949–2008) ■
COUNCILMAN

Reed was the first openly gay, African American New York City Councilman. A native New Yorker, Reed attended Ohio Wesleyan University but did not graduate. He obtained conscientious objector status during the Vietnam War. He participated in the historic Stonewall Riots in Greenwich Village in 1969. After ten years of employment and political activity in San Francisco, he returned to New York and became the project director of an early HIV/AIDS center in East New York, Brooklyn, and Director of Public Affairs for the Hetrick-Martin Institute serving the AIDS community. In 1997, he won election to the City Council representing a constituency that included parts of the Upper West Side, Manhattan Valley, Harlem, and East Harlem. He left office in compliance with term limits. Leukemia and a related complication from pneumonia took his life much too soon.

444 Central Park West (near 104th Street)

Armitage, Norman Cudworth (1907–1972)
CHAMPION FENCER, CHEMICAL ENGINEER, AND PATENT ATTORNEY

In 1928, as a Columbia student, Armitage won the Intercollegiate Fencing Association saber championship. He went on to win the national championship thirteen times, and he competed in six Olympic games: 1928, 1932, 1936, 1948, 1952, and 1956. In 1948, he won his only Olympic medal, a bronze, for his efforts in the team saber event. He was the first person inducted into the National Fencing Association Hall of Fame in 1963. Born Norman Cudworth Cohn in New York, he earned his BA degree at Columbia in 1927; his law degree at New York University in 1937; and his doctor of jurisprudence there in 1939, with a specialty in patent law. He took his mother's maiden name of Armitage, possibly to avoid discrimination for having the Jewish name Cohn. Before and after serving three years in the US Navy during World War II, he worked for Brooklyn Union Gas Company; Colgate-Palmolive; and the textile concern, Milliken & Company.

Brynner, Yul (1920–1985) ■
ACTOR

Brynner performed 4,625 times as the King of Siam in the Rogers and Hammerstein musical *The King and I*. It earned him a Tony Award in 1952 for Best Supporting Actor, an Academy Award for Best Actor in 1956, and a Special Tony Award in 1985. He was born in Eastern Russia of Swiss-German, Russian, and Mongolian heritage. After a childhood that included some time in China, he went to Paris where he found the theater. He arrived in the United States in 1940 and soon appeared on the Broadway stage with a small part in Shakespeare's *Twelfth Night*. He struggled for stage roles but had the good fortune to work with Mary Martin in the 1946 musical *Lute Song*. Finding steady work in early television, he gained exposure, and Martin recommended him for *The King and I*. Although that role, and his shaved head, distinguished him for the rest of his life, he should also be remembered as a distinguished film actor, especially for his roles in such classic movies as *Anastasia*, *The Ten Commandments*, *The Buccaneer*, and *The Magnificent Seven*. He died on October 10, 1985, the same day as Orson Welles, with whom he co-starred in the 1969 movie *The Battle of Neretva*.

Konkle, Oscar E. (ca.1865–1954), Real Estate Operator ☞

(See bio for Konkle at **2720 Broadway**.)

Rosenman, Samuel Irving (1896–1973) ◼

LAWYER, JUDGE, AND POLITICIAN

Rosenman coined the phrase "New Deal" for use by President Franklin Roosevelt. No surprise that Rosenman edited the thirteen volumes of *The Public Papers and Addresses of Franklin D. Roosevelt,* since he wrote most of his speeches. He was also instrumental in assembling Roosevelt's "brain trust" of academic advisors. Born in Texas, Rosenman graduated summa cum laude from Columbia in 1915 with membership in Phi Beta Kappa, went off to serve in World War I, and returned to graduate from Columbia Law School in 1919. As a Democrat, he was elected to the New York State Assembly in 1922 and served through 1926. After a decade of private law practice, he was elected a Justice of the New York Supreme Court in 1936 and served until 1943. In the 1960s, he served as president of the New York City Bar association, director of the New York World's Fair, and director and trustee of the Repertory Theater of Lincoln Center. In his final years, he accepted his last honorary doctorate from his alma mater Columbia, and he played a significant role in blocking Judge Harold Carswell's nomination to the Supreme Court. Rosenman also lived at **610 West 111th Street** (near Riverside Drive).

448 Central Park West (near 105th Street), Larchmont Apartments

Benedict, Ruth Fulton (1887–1948) ★ ◼

PROFESSOR OF ANTHROPOLOGY AND FOLKWAYS

Benedict wrote her anthropology classic *Patterns of Culture* in 1934. The book's foreword was written by her professional colleague, and sometime romantic partner, Margaret Mead. The two were the most important anthropologists of their day. Born in New York City but raised upstate, Benedict graduated from Vassar College in 1909.

After a year in Europe, she moved to California where she developed an interest in Asian cultures. In 1919, she returned to New York to study anthropology at the New School for Social Research. She moved on to Columbia University in 1921 to complete her graduate work under the great Franz Boas. After earning her PhD in 1923, she began teaching at Columbia. Her many field trips to the lands of the Native Americans produced her books *Zuni Mythology* and *Tales of the Cochiti Indians*. Her 1946 work on Japanese culture, which utilized war research, is thought to have influenced the decision to keep Japan's emperor in place. She was president of the American Anthropological Association. Benedict also lived at **616 West 116th Street** (near Claremont Avenue).

Ruth Benedict.

467 Central Park West (near 107th Street)

Ailey, Alvin (1931–1989) ■

DANCER AND CHOREOGRAPHER

Ailey revolutionized dance by infusing African American talent and heritage into modern dance. His Alvin Ailey Dance Theater introduced the audience to new music, innovative staging, and African dance techniques. Born in Rogers, Texas, Ailey was trained as a dancer and mentored by Lester Horton, who founded one of the first racially integrated dance companies in the United States. After Horton's death, Ailey succeeded him as Director of the company. Ailey formed his own dance company in 1958, the Ailey school in 1969, and a repertory company—now Ailey II—in 1974. During the 1950s and '60s, he also performed in four Broadway musicals, including the 1954 Truman Capote/Harold Arlen show *House of Flowers*. Ailey was also a leader in promoting arts education in the schools, especially in underserved

General Memorial Hospital.

areas. Ailey's work and legacy continue through the dance organization he built to include training, choreography, and performance, but his reputation was well established before his tragic death by HIV/AIDS. In 2014, he was posthumously awarded the Presidential Medal of Freedom.

Hasso, Signe (1910–2002)

ACTRESS

Hasso has a star on the Hollywood Walk of Fame. Born in Sweden, Signe Eleonora Cecilia Larsson began acting at age 12 with the Royal Dramatic Theater. She married one of her film directors, Harry Hasso, but divorced in 1941. Coming to the United States in 1940, she was signed to a contract with RKO Studios with promise of becoming "the next Garbo." Her films include *Heaven Can Wait* in 1943; *Johnny Angel* and *The House on 92nd Street*, both in 1945; *A Scandal in Paris* in 1946; and *A Double Life* in 1947. Although her career wound down in the 1950s, she appeared on television in such shows as *Bonanza*, *Starsky and Hutch*, and *Magnum P.I.* She also appeared in a 1978 production of Sondheim's *A Little Night Music* in Stockholm. Her second husband was the actor William Langford.

Warner, Olin Levi (1844–1896) ■ 🖘

SCULPTOR

Warner's residence on Central Park West and 107th Street was the only Venetian-style house in New York City. It also served as the location of his funeral service which was conducted by the Reverend Edward Judson of the Judson Memorial Baptist Church on Washington Square. In attendance were various artists including Edwin Blashfield and Albert Pinkham Ryder, and sculptors including John Quincy Adams

Ward and Augustus St. Gaudens. Warner was born in Connecticut. He was the great-great-grandnephew of Seth Warner, who fought in the Revolutionary War with Ethan Allen and the Green Mountain Boys. He studied sculpture in Paris and, in 1872, set up his own studio in New York. Credit is given to Warner for popularizing the bas-relief, a sculpture form. He designed the souvenir half-dollar for the 1893 Columbian Exposition held in Chicago. His other notable works included the statue of William Lloyd Garrison in Boston; the Skidmore Fountain in Portland, Oregon; the eight portrait busts on the facade of the Brooklyn Historical Society; and the bronze portals for the Library of Congress. He died of an apoplectic fit while riding his bicycle near East 95th Street in Central Park.

60 Manhattan Avenue (near 103rd Street) ▪ ▐

Hall, Edward Hagaman (1858–1936), Historian and Preservationist

(See bio for Hall at **700, 702 West End Avenue**.)

79 Manhattan Avenue (near 104th Street)

Rose, Mary Davies Swartz (1874–1941) ★ ▪ ▐
NUTRITION EDUCATOR

A pioneer in nutritional science, Rose's first book, in 1916, was *Everyday Foods in War Time*. She followed it with *Feeding the Family*, *Foundations of Nutrition*, *Laboratory Handbook for Dietetics*, and *Teaching Nutrition to Boys and Girls*. Born in Ohio, Rose graduated from Denison College with an AB degree in 1901 and from Columbia's Teachers College with a BS degree in 1906. She went on to Yale with a teaching fellowship; met her husband, the future chemist Anton

Richard Rose; and earned her PhD degree there in 1909. Returning to Teachers College, she established a department of nutrition. She was president of the American Institute of Nutrition and, in 1935, was appointed to the League of Nations Health Committee. Her efforts also aided New York City public schools. Mary Rose also lived at **449 West 123rd Street** (near Amsterdam Avenue).

138 Manhattan Avenue (near 106th Street)

Gruppe, Karl Heinrich (1893–1982) ▰ ☞

SCULPTOR

Gruppe was awarded the same "Medal of Special Honor" that the National Sculpture Society gave to Daniel Chester French, Paul Manship, and Malvina Hoffman. Previously, Gruppe had been president of the National Sculpture Society. He was born in Rochester, New York, to a family of artists. He trained at the Royal Academy of Art in Antwerp, Belgium, and at the Art Students League in New York. But his real training came from working with the renowned sculptor Karl Bitter. Bitter did the Carl Schurz Statue on Morningside Drive, the Pulitzer Fountain in front of the Plaza Hotel, and many more works all over the United States. Gruppe was Bitter's right-hand man, who executed much of his work and inherited his materials and papers. When Bitter was assigned full artistic responsibility for the St. Louis World's Fair of 1904, celebrating the centennial of the Louisiana Purchase, Gruppe was indispensable. In that regard, Gruppe designed the bas-reliefs for and finished Bitter's Henry Hudson Monument in the Bronx. Gruppe also sculptured the only statue of Andrew Haswell Green, "the father of Consolidated New York."

164 Manhattan Avenue (near 108th Street)

Auger, George (1881–1922)
CIRCUS GIANT

Auger was thought to be the largest man in the world with a height claim of eight feet, four inches, and a lean weight of 360 pounds. Born in Cardiff, Wales, he was thus called the Cardiff Giant by his employer, the Barnum & Bailey Circus. Intentionally or not, the previous Cardiff Giant was a hoax perpetrated in 1869 in upstate New York wherein a fossilized giant was supposedly found. Auger took his impressive frame to London and became a "Bobby," that is, a policeman. He was often assigned to Queen Victoria's security detail, and she fondly called him "Captain." In 1906, he wrote the play "Jack the Giant Killer," which he performed successfully for ten years. Before he died, the silent film star Harold Lloyd requested his services. He became a US citizen in 1911 and even sold war bonds to support the troops. By all accounts, Auger was very well-liked in the circus community and by the public. After he died, the undertaker, Thomas O'Reilly, who would become a city alderman, had to sue Auger's widow for the cost of building an extra-large coffin.

George Auger.

885 Columbus Avenue (near 104th Street)

McMahon, Bernard "Bennie the Bum" (ca.1893–1934)
GANGSTER

McMahon's specialty was hijacking trucks. In 1933, he hijacked a truck loaded with aspirin. In 1934, he was a part of the largest dollar heist in the country. Author Dan Wakin's book *The Man with the Sawed-off Leg and Other Tales of a New York City Block* recounts McMahon's role in the $427,000 heist and the finding of his body on West 74th Street, with both legs cut off. In gangster land, he acquired the moniker "Bennie the Bum." By some accounts, he was the last member of the Legs Diamond gang.

AMSTERDAM AVENUE
SUBWAY

In 1886, the powers-that-be in
St. Michael's Church ranted
against the proposal to double
the trolley tracks on Amsterdam
Avenue from two to four. Some
thirty-five years later, in 1922, the
Transit Commission gave some
short-lived consideration to
building a subway underneath
Amsterdam Avenue. More
specifically, the Eighth Avenue–
Amsterdam Avenue subway
would have come up Eighth
Avenue to 57th Street, veered
west to 10th Avenue, headed
north as 10th Avenue became
Amsterdam Avenue, then
continued north to 159th Street,
where it would go west to Fort
Washington Avenue, and on up
to 181st Street. About ten years
later, the Independent Subway,
or IND, plowed up Central Park
West.

868 Amsterdam Avenue (near 102nd Street), the Douglass Houses

Carter, Reginald C. "Reggie" (1957–1999)

BASKETBALL PLAYER

Carter's jump shot with five seconds left in the game gave St. John's
University a victory over Duke in the 1979 NCAA tournament.
Unfortunately, St. John's lost their next game by two points and missed
a spot in the "Final Four." From his inner-city youth, Carter became a
high school all-American and a second-round draft pick of the New
York Knicks in the year Magic Johnson was the first draft pick. In the
park on Amsterdam Avenue where he was raised, he likely played with
such basketball greats as Nate "Tiny" Archibald and **Eugene "the Goat"
Manigault**. When he died, way too young, he was an assistant principal
and role model at a Long Island high school. His funeral was hosted at
Riverside Church, where he first played organized ball, and where more
than one thousand friends and colleagues acknowledged his legacy and
reputation as a class act.

2643 Broadway (near 100th Street)

Stedman, Edmund Clarence (1833–1908) ★ ■ ▮

POET, ANTHOLOGIST, AND INVESTOR

Stedman was among the first seven people chosen for membership
in the American Academy of Letters in 1904. Among the others were
William Dean Howells, John La Farge, Augustus St. Gaudens, and
Samuel L. Clemens. Following the death of James Russell Lowell in
1891, Stedman became America's preeminent poet. Born in Connecticut,
Stedman studied at Yale for two years. After a few years of newspaper
experience, he came to New York in 1856. He worked for Horace
Greeley's *New York Tribune*, which included correspondent work in the
early period of the Civil War. He also covered the war for the *New York
World*, but, because of health issues, he found a position in Washington,

D.C., as secretary to Attorney General Edward Bates. Meanwhile, some of his poems began to achieve national attention. After the war, he left journalism for Wall Street, gaining a seat on the New York Stock Exchange. His poetry matured into longer works, and he anthologized Victorian and American poetry. He was an active member of the Century Association and of the Authors and Players Clubs. Yale acknowledged Stedman's literary merits by reinstating him in the class of 1853 and awarding him a master of arts degree.

Broadway and West 101st Street

Peters, Thomas McClure (1821–1893), Episcopal Priest and Rector

(See bio for Thomas Peters at **Broadway and 99th Street**.)

2689–2693 Broadway (near 103rd Street), the Hotel Marseilles

McGuire, James Kennedy (1868–1923) ■ 🖘

MAYOR OF SYRACUSE, NY

Democrat McGuire was elected Mayor of traditionally Republican Syracuse in 1896 at age 28 and served for three terms. The "boy" mayor ran for governor in 1898 and almost derailed Teddy Roosevelt. If McGuire had beaten him, Roosevelt would not have become president when McKinley was assassinated. Born in New York City on the Lower West Side but raised in Syracuse, New York, McGuire was first engaged as a newspaper correspondent, then joined a hardware firm, and was made a partner in a few years. As a teenager, he entered Democratic Party politics and became an exceptional public speaker. In 1892, the party sent him to the Democratic National Convention, and soon he was nominated and elected mayor of Syracuse. In 1902, he retired from politics and, from 1910, made New York City his home. In 1913, he survived an indictment for an illegal campaign contribution, in part by fleeing to Puerto Rico. He spent his remaining years actively supporting the Irish freedom struggle.

Roosevelt, Sara Ann Delano (1854–1941) ■
MOTHER OF PRESIDENT FRANKLIN DELANO ROOSEVELT

The first Delano came to the Pilgrim colony in America in 1621 as Philippe de la Noye. Soon after, he shortened the name to Delano. Family legend has it that he was in love with Priscilla Mullins, who married John Alden. He had known her in Leyden, Holland, where the Pilgrims lived after leaving England. "Why don't you speak for yourself, John?" is Priscilla's famous statement in the Longfellow poem "The Courtship of Miles Standish." Sara Delano was born on the family estate overlooking the Hudson River in upstate New York. She was educated at home and briefly in Paris and at a girl's school in Germany. As a child, she spent three years in Hong Kong consequent to her father's business in trading tea and then-legal opium. She married a widower and businessman twice her age, James Roosevelt, and lived on his estate in Hyde Park. She doted on their only child, Franklin, for the rest of her life and thus made it rather challenging for Franklin's wife, Eleanor.

Thiery, Lewis M. (ca.1871–1934) ☜
REAL ESTATE AGENT AND EQUESTRIAN ENTHUSIAST

Thiery earned the rank of Colonel during his thirty-eight years of service in the National Guard. He commanded the 820 men in the 244th Coast Artillery Regiment based in the armory at 125 West 14th Street. A New York native, he was a real estate agent in the growing Upper West Side area of Manhattan. After working in the real estate business with an established firm, he found a partner and they opened an office at 418 Columbus Avenue, near 80th Street. In addition to general real estate services, they managed estates. Some ten years later, the office was relocated to 2780 Broadway at 107th Street. Thiery served as a Commissioner of Deeds and was active as a member of the Merchants' Association of New York, the New York Society of Military and Naval Officers of the World War, and the Catholic Club. He was also president of the Early Morning Riding Club whose members rode their horses on Central Park's bridle path. Thiery also lived at two other nearby addresses: **925 West End Avenue** (near 106th Street) and at **2752 Broadway** (near 107th Street).

Woolrich, Cornell (1903–1968) ▧

AUTHOR

Woolrich made the generous bequest of $845,000 for writing scholarships to Columbia University in the name of his mother. Born in New York, Woolrich spent much of his early childhood in Latin America with his civil-engineer father. His parents being separated, Woolrich was sent back to New York to finish at Columbia College and live with his rich and controlling mother. But he left Columbia when his first novel *Cover Charge* was published in 1926. The success of a second novel in the same genre of the Jazz Age earned him $10,000 and a job in Hollywood. Although he wrote a few more in the same style, they were not as well-received, so he turned to pulp and detective fiction. Like a machine, he produced books of such good quality that, by some estimations, he was in a class with Raymond Chandler and Dashiell Hammett. Many of his stories were made into movies and television shows. Quite possibly, he sat in his apartment in the Hotel Marseilles, looked out into the courtyard out back, and wrote the thriller *It Had to Be Murder*, which became the Alfred Hitchcock movie *Rear Window*.

Broadway and 103rd to 104th Street

Peters, Thomas McClure (1821–1893), Episcopal Priest and Rector

(See bio for Thomas Peters at **Broadway and 99th Street**.)

2720 Broadway (near 104th Street), the Hotel Regent

Konkle, Oscar E. (ca.1865–1954) ☞
REAL ESTATE OPERATOR

In 1925, Konkle had planned to build the tallest building in the world on the east side of Broadway between 122nd and 123rd Streets. It would have been sixty-five stories and eight hundred feet tall, or eight feet taller than the Woolworth Building. Planned as a not-for-profit housing complex and hotel with forty-five hundred rooms, a hospital on the top floor, swimming pools, and other amenities, the plan was to donate 10 percent of its profits to missionary work. Konkle was motivated by gratitude that his son survived a close call with death. He was also a staff member of the church of the Reverend Billy Sunday. During excavation, a section of rock dislodged and killed five workers, which put an end to the project other than the subsequent litigations. Soon after, the Jewish Theological Seminary was built on the site. Born in Canada, Konkle came to the United States in 1890 and learned the real estate trade. He developed more than a hundred homes in Brooklyn after World War I. In 1923, he moved to Manhattan and built the Regent Hotel at Broadway and 104th Street. He also lived at **444 Central Park West** (near 104th Street).

Wouk, Herman (1915–2019), Author ◼

(See bio for Wouk at **845 West End Avenue**.)

2745 Broadway (near 105th Street)

Straus, Isidor (1845–1912) ★ ◼ ▯
RETAILER AND PHILANTHROPIST

Straus and his wife, Ida, died with the sinking of the *Titanic*. Instead of taking a seat in a lifeboat, she elected to stay with her husband on the sinking ship. That touching end to their loving lives is recounted in the movie and musical of the tragic calamity. Isidor was only one of the three accomplished Straus brothers. His brother Nathan declined to run for mayor even after Tammany Hall selected him with a virtual guarantee to be elected. Instead, Nathan served as Parks Commissioner and Commissioner of Health, where he introduced pasteurized milk for children in the city. Isidor's youngest brother Oscar was the first Jewish Cabinet member, having been selected by President Theodore Roosevelt to be Secretary of Commerce and Labor. Isidor also served two terms in Congress and, in his free time, ran R. H. Macy & Co. department store with brother Nathan.

2783 Broadway (near 107th Street)

Lauterbach, Edward (1844–1923), Lawyer ◼ ▯

(See bio for Lauterbach at **301 West 106th Street**.)

823 West End Avenue (near 100th Street)

Rothschild, Leopold O. (1888–1968) ■ ▇
PRESERVATIONIST AND LAWYER

Rothschild led the effort to block Consolidated Edison's plans to erect a hydroelectric plant on Storm King Mountain. As chairman and founding member of the Scenic Hudson Preservation Conference, he rallied the public against the project. Born in Chicago, Rothschild came to New York in 1901, graduated from Columbia College in 1909, and from Columbia Law School in 1911. From his school days at Columbia, he had hiked all over the New York region and developed an intimate relationship with its scenic areas. In the late 1920s, and in anticipation of the building of the George Washington Bridge, he was instrumental in getting the Rockefeller family to purchase the land that would become Palisades Park and grant it to the Palisades Park Commission. He was not as successful in stopping quarrying on the side of Mount Taurus in what is now Hudson Highlands Park on the East side of the Hudson, opposite Storm King Mountain.

In the 1950s, he advocated against a baseball park in Flushing Meadows and he advocated for the removal of trees suffering from Dutch-elm disease. His extended activities included the New York–New Jersey Trail Conference, the Citizens Union, and the city's Landmark Conservation Commission. Rothschild also lived at three other addresses in the neighborhood: **905 West End Avenue** (near 104th Street), **536 West 111th Street** (near Broadway), and **536 West 113th Street** (near Broadway).

825 West End Avenue (near 100th Street)

Kheel, Theodore (1914–2010) ■
LABOR MEDIATOR

Kheel probably mediated more labor disputes and settled more strikes than anyone. The *New York Times* gave him credit for "deciding more than 30,000 disputes." In 1963, he helped bring an end to New York City's 114-day newspaper strike. In 1966, his skills were employed in ending the city's infamous transit strike that plagued Mayor John Lindsay's first days in office. In 1978, he helped settle the 88-day newspaper strike. Born in Brooklyn, Kheel graduated from Cornell University in 1935 and from its Law School in 1937. Straight out of school, he worked on the legal staff of the National Labor Relations Board and then on the War Labor Board. Mayor William O'Dwyer tapped him for labor relations work in 1946, but after two years his career turned to private practice in the firm of Battle, Fowler, Neaman, Stokes & Kheel. In his spare time, he also served as president of the National Urban League from 1956 to 1960, and as chairman of Republic National Bank. He represented renowned artists like Christo and Robert Rauschenberg and wrote a ten-volume text on labor law.

838 West End Avenue (near 101st Street)

Baum, Lester (1903–1989)
STATE SENATOR AND CITY COUNCILMAN

Lester Baum introduced the legislation to create the New York City Opera. He also proposed the creation of a state arts commission. Like his brother, **Morton Baum**, Lester was born in Manhattan, where his father was a renowned Rabbi. He graduated from New York Law School. For more than thirty years he was a Republican district leader on the West Side. During Mayor La Guardia's administration in 1935, he was elected to the Board of Alderman. In 1938, the aldermen were succeeded by the City Council, and Baum continued in that capacity. He earned election to the State Senate in 1942, and he returned to the City Council in 1965.

Baum, Morton (1905–1968) ◼

FOUNDER AND CHAIRMAN OF NEW YORK CITY CENTER

Baum planned and introduced the New York City sales tax. In that regard, he was consultant to Mayor Lindsay's Commission on City Finances. Years earlier, he provided tax counsel to Mayor La Guardia and most mayors and governors since. Born in Manhattan, where his father was a renowned Rabbi, Baum earned degrees at Columbia College and Harvard Law School. Then he became a city attorney and, like his brother **Lester Baum**, was elected to the City Council. Morton Baum might be best remembered for his instrumental role in making New York City Center (on West 55th Street) a member of the newly formed Lincoln Center. City Center had been created two decades earlier by La Guardia's Parks Commissioner Newbold Morris and Baum. At the time of his death, Baum was Chairman of City Center and an influential board member of Lincoln Center.

Finn, Julius (1871–1931) ★ ◼ ☞

MASTER CHESS PLAYER

In his day, Finn was the second-best blindfolded chess player in North America. One time his skill was demonstrated by playing thirty-one games simultaneously. He was considered the world's leading authority on the chess tactic called "the Rice gambit," named after Isaac Rice, whose mansion on Riverside Drive at 89th Street survives to this day. Finn was born in Poland, came to New York City, and worked as a street peddler on the Lower East Side. After winning some chess tournaments against well-established players, Finn rose to the top of the chess world. He won the New York State Championships in 1901, 1907, and 1908, and he won the prestigious Rice Gambit tournament conducted at the Manhattan Chess Club in 1903. His reputation established, he adjudicated chess for the college league that included Columbia, Yale,

Harvard, and Princeton. He was the referee for the 1921 World Chess Championship. He ran an insurance business, which enabled him to invest in the commercial Bank of the United States. Sadly, that bank started the collapse of banking that brought on the Great Depression. Finn's estate was in the hole for $1,193,489.

Merritt, Mortimer Charles (1840–1931)
ARCHITECT

Before his death at 91, Merritt was the oldest living graduate of the University of the City of New York, known today as New York University. Born in New York, Merritt graduated in 1859 with an MS degree from the University of the City of New York. He began as a solo practitioner of mostly commercial architecture in 1868. In 1887, he designed the Hugh O'Neill department store in the Ladies Mile Historic District. Another of his buildings was the Washington Apartments on Adam Clayton Powell, Jr. Boulevard at 122nd Street. It was designed in 1884 and was home to such notables as Dizzy Gillespie, Erroll Garner, and Billy Eckstine.

Talmey, Dr. Max (1869–1941)
OPHTHALMOLOGIST

Dr. Max Talmey mentored Albert Einstein. When he was attending medical school in Germany, Talmey had a weekly lunch with Einstein's family and gave 10-year-old Albert the science and math books, *Force and Matter* and *Spieker's Geometry*. Einstein maintained a life-long friendship with Dr. Talmey, who recounted the childhood connection in a memoir. He also published a simplified explanation of Einstein's Theory of Relativity. Born in Germany, Talmey left the University of Munich as a faculty member in 1895 to immigrate to New York and practice at Mount Sinai Hospital. He earned acclaim in 1908 for a difficult cataract operation. Other areas of interest for him were infantile paralysis and psychology. He had a strong interest in establishing an international language. He claimed to have been the first to introduce Esperanto into this country, and his 1906 Esperanto textbook was the first. Talmey also lived at **266 West 113th Street** (near Frederick Douglass Boulevard).

839 West End Avenue (near 101st Street)

Cassirer, Ernst (1874–1945) ◾

PHILOSOPHER

Cassirer's *An Essay on Man: An Introduction to a Philosophy of Human Culture* is a highly regarded vindication of human faculties. Cassirer argued that man lives by symbols and that understanding develops his philosophy of culture. Before Nazism ousted him from the University of Hamburg, his credentials included studies leading up to doctorates at the Universities of Berlin, Heidelberg, Hamburg, Munich, and Marburg. After Germany, he taught at Oxford, at Gothenburg in Sweden, and at Yale before arriving at Columbia. Gothenburg and the University of Glasgow gave him honorary degrees. His work with language and the phenomenology of language made him a champion of philosophical idealism. He died while he was Visiting Professor of Philosophy at Columbia.

845 West End Avenue (101st Street)

Grumbacher, Max (ca.1859–1933)

IMPORTER AND MANUFACTURER OF ARTISTS' MATERIALS

Any artist who has painted recognizes the name Grumbacher. Max Grumbacher founded the business in 1905, and today it is part of a larger entity, Chartpak, Inc. Grumbacher was born in Germany and arrived in the United States as a young man. Since artist's materials are extensive, much of the business was importing, warehousing, and supplying. It's fair to state that most of the artists in the country have used Grumbacher products. Sadly, Max Grumbacher's son and heir to the business, Walter Grumbacher, died in 1947 in a six-story plunge from an apartment in San Francisco.

Wouk, Herman (1915–2019) ∎
AUTHOR

The fictional Marjorie Morningstar lived at 740 West End Avenue. She is the main character in Wouk's book of the same name. *The Caine Mutiny,* his other well-known novel, was honored with the Pulitzer Prize. Both books were made into movies.

Wouk was born in the Bronx and went to the prestigious Townsend Harris High School. At age 19, he graduated from Columbia with a BA degree. As editor of his college humor magazine, he was well-positioned to go on to write radio dramas, commercial spots, and gags for comedian Fred Allen. After service in the US Navy in the Pacific theater of World War II, he began writing novels. His first, *Aurora Dawn,* was the Book of the Month Club main selection in 1947. *Youngblood Hawke* was published in 1962, *Winds of War* in 1971, and *War and Remembrance* in 1978. All three were made for the screen, as either a movie or a TV mini-series. There were other novels as well, and numerous honorary degrees. His father was Abraham Isaac Wouk. Herman Wouk also lived at **875 West End Avenue** (near 103rd Street) and **2720 Broadway** (near 104th Street).

850 West End Avenue (near 102nd Street)

Hamlin, Alfred Dwight Foster (1855–1926) ☜

ARCHITECT AND ARCHITECTURAL HISTORIAN

As chairman of the Merchants' Association City Planning Committee, Hamlin predicted that New York City would be forced to build triple-level streets with elevator access in order to handle the vehicular congestion. Sadly, and somewhat ironically, Hamlin was struck and killed by an automobile while he was crossing Riverside Drive at 117th Street. Born in Turkey, the son of the president of Robert College, Hamlin came to the United States in 1871 and graduated from Amherst College with an AB degree in 1875 and an AM degree in 1885. After studying architecture in Boston and Paris, he worked at McKim, Mead & White for a few years and, from 1883, taught architecture in Columbia's School of Engineering. In 1906, he authored *A Textbook of the History of Architecture*, which in its seventh edition is still in print. He also rendered the two-volume *A History of Ornament*. In 1915, he co-authored with New York City's public schools' architect **Charles B. J. Snyder** two volumes entitled *Modern School Houses; Being a Series of Authoritative Articles on Planning, Sanitation, Heating and Ventilation*. He was involved with the construction of the Cathedral of St. John the Divine as chairman of its Arts Committee. His son was the architectural historian Talbot Hamlin. Alfred Hamlin lived at three more addresses in the neighborhood: **1285 Columbus Avenue** (110th Street), **39 Claremont Avenue** (near 119th Street), and **105 Morningside Avenue** (near 123rd Street).

855 West End Avenue (near 102nd Street)

Gussow, Bernard (1881–1957)

ARTIST

Gussow exhibited two works at the Armory Show of 1913. His work was also shown in the 1939–1940 World's Fair in Flushing Meadows. He even contributed to the Federal Art Project in the 1930s by rendering a mural in a Rochester Post Office. Born in Russia, Gussow studied at the Art Students League and the National Academy of Design. Although his earliest works were abstracts, he matured into painting landscapes, human figures, and interiors, and he did portraits and lithographs. Best described as a modern realist, his works are well represented in the Museum of Modern Art, the Whitney Museum of Art, the National Gallery, and the Barnes Foundation collection. In addition to having many private students, he taught at the Newark School of Fine and Industrial Art for forty-five years. That high school shared a building with the Newark Arts School, which means that Gussow would have likely seen students such as Melba Moore, Connie Francis, and Sarah Vaughn.

Landy, Ludwig Lazar (1888–1953) ▪

YIDDISH FILM PRODUCER

Landy co-produced the movie *Green Fields* in 1937. It is thought to possibly be the most commercially successful Yiddish movie. It almost didn't make it when the film laboratory threatened to foreclose because they hadn't been paid. David Dubinsky, as head of the International Garment Workers Union, purchased seventy-five thousand tickets in advance to save the day. Landy was born in Vienna and came to the United States in his youth. By the 1920s, he was active with the International Ladies' Garment Workers' Union (IGWU) and organized efforts to raise funds for striking textile workers in Passaic, New Jersey, and for furriers and cloak makers who were in jail for striking. He also produced the Yiddish movies *The Singing Blacksmith* in 1938 and *Overture to Glory* in 1940. By 1950, he returned to his roots and ran a linen business.

Mitchell, Margaret Julia "Maggie" (1836–1918) ■ ▮
ACTRESS

Born in New York, Mitchell first stepped upon the stage in 1851 on the Bowery. In 1852, she was acclaimed for her performance as the star of *Oliver Twist*. After touring, she returned to the Bowery in 1853 as a member of the James H. Robinson acting company. She performed with the company in a variety of productions, playing in numerous cities. Under new management and in New Orleans, she became famous for her performance in *Fanchon the Cricket*. President Lincoln saw her in this and other plays. Her other successes included *Mignon*, *The Pearl of Savoy*, and *Little Barefoot*. Henry Wadsworth Longfellow praised her in *Jane Eyre* in Boston. Her financial success on the stage enabled her to develop the very apartment building in which she resided. She is the aunt or possibly the mother of Julian P. Mitchell, the stage director of the original 1902 *Wizard of Oz* and Victor Herbert's 1903 *Babes in Toyland*.

865 West End Avenue (near 102nd Street)

Georgopulo, Theodore (ca.1883–1935)
CIGARETTE MANUFACTURER

Georgopulo sold Ramses II Egyptians, the oldest brand of cigarettes in the United States. His family company, opened in 1905, manufactured luxury cigarettes that were sold to private clubs and such wealthy clients as the Astors and Vanderbilts. The cigarette brand names of

years gone by include Andron, Batt Brothers, Brand "X," Campaign
"'88," and Turkish Special. In the cigarette trade, the name of G. A.
Georgopulo & Company continued until 1990 when the company
was acquired and the name changed to G. A. Andron and Company,
reflecting the name of one of its oldest brands. Theodore Georgopulo
committed suicide by jumping off the roof of 865 West End Avenue.
Seven years earlier, his brother George shot and killed himself.
Georgopulo also lived at two other neighborhood addresses: **360
Riverside Drive** (108th Street) and **312 West 109th Street** (near Riverside
Drive).

MacDonald, William J. (ca.1860–1933) ▪ ▪

BUILDER

MacDonald and his contracting firm erected numerous Columbia
buildings including Avery, Livingston, Kent, Furnald, and Brooks
Halls; the Mines and Engineering Building; and the President's
House. They also built hotels; libraries; post offices; dormitories for
New York University; additions to Lenox Hill Hospital, St. Vincent's
Hospital, and the Metropolitan Museum of Art; and numerous private
residences for the likes of Joseph Pulitzer and many others. Born in
Ireland, MacDonald came to the United States at age 13. He learned
the building trades at the night school of the Society of Mechanics and
Tradesmen and by working for his uncle Michael Reid, whose father
built a cathedral in Ireland. It was a "hands-on" business, and in time
MacDonald became the secretary of M. Reid & Co. He worked with and
was praised by Stanford White.

Oliver, Melvin James "Sy" (1910–1988), Trumpeter ▪

(See bio for Oliver at **Park West Village**.)

875 West End Avenue (near 103rd Street)

Motley, Constance Baker (1921–2005) ■ ▣
BOROUGH PRESIDENT AND JUDGE

In 1950, Motley wrote the original complaint in the case of *Brown v. Board of Education*. Working with Thurgood Marshall and as part of the NAACP Legal Defense and Educational Field, she became part of civil rights and legal history. Similarly, in 1962 she became the first African American woman to argue before the Supreme Court to obtain Black student James Meredith's right to attend the University of Mississippi. Born in Connecticut, she began her higher education in Fisk University, Tennessee, but graduated from New York University in 1943 and from Columbia Law School in 1946. In 1964, she was the first African American woman elected to the New York State Senate. She resigned to become the first woman borough president of Manhattan. She left that position when President Lyndon B. Johnson appointed her the first African American woman federal judge. She made history yet again when she ruled in 1978 that a female reporter be allowed into a Major League Baseball locker room.

Wouk, Herman (1915–2019), Author ■

(See bio for Wouk at **845 West End Avenue**.)

878 West End Avenue (103rd Street)

Buchanan, Edgar Simmons (ca. 1872–1932) ☜
PALEOGRAPHER

Buchanan received international attention in 1923 when he discovered a palimpsest (an effaced document) that challenged the King James Bible. He was one of the foremost Latin scholars in the world, and his discovery posited that a Bible script from the first or second century had been erased and rewritten centuries later. The script, known as the Codex Huntington Palimpsestus, was in the collection of the Hispanic Society Library. Buchanan was born in England and lived in New Zealand, the United States, and Australia, where he died. He studied at the Theological College in Salisbury and was ordained in Salisbury Cathedral. After post-graduate work at Oxford, he came to know all of the important existing documents relating to the translation of the Bible from the Vulgate into English by visiting numerous libraries all over the world. He lectured at numerous institutions, including Union and General Theological Seminaries and Columbia University.

Douglas, Jesse (1897–1965)
MATHEMATICIAN

In 1930, Douglas came up with a general solution to the Plateau Problem which had been around since 1760. The problem, sometimes called the soap bubble problem, is in the realm of calculus and geometric measure theory and posited as how to show a minimal surface within a given boundary. In 1936, it earned him one of the first two Fields Medals, which have been described as the mathematician's "Nobel Prize." A native New Yorker, Douglas earned a degree in 1916 from the City College of New York and a PhD in 1920 from Columbia. He taught at Columbia until 1926 when he was awarded a National Research Fellowship. In the 1930s, he had appointments at the Massachusetts Institute of Technology and the Institute for Advanced Study at Princeton. He returned to Columbia in 1942 and taught until 1954. In 1955, he joined the City College faculty as a full professor and taught there until his death. He made other significant contributions to the field of calculus, and the students who took his advanced calculus class were most fortunate.

884 West End Avenue (near 103rd Street)

Klapper, Paul (1885–1952) ■
COLLEGE DEAN AND PRESIDENT

Klapper personally selected the entire faculty and first four hundred students at Queens College when it opened in 1937. Born in Romania, Klapper's family came to the United States in 1892, and at age 14 he enrolled in City College. He earned his BA degree and Phi Beta Kappa membership in 1904, and he earned an MA degree from New York University in 1907. After joining the faculty at City College, he received his PhD at New York University in 1909. By 1917, he was head of the Education Department, and in 1922, he was appointed Dean at City College. When Queens College opened in 1937, he served as its first president. He retired in 1948 after receiving honorary degrees from Queens College, Brooklyn College, Yeshiva University, and Columbia. He was the author of many books on education.

Leonard, Benny (1896–1947), Boxer ★ ■

(See bio for Leonard at 740 West End Avenue.)

885 West End Avenue (near 103rd Street)

Reik, Theodore (1888–1969) ■
PSYCHOANALYST

Reik's doctoral dissertation at the University of Vienna was only the second ever written on psychoanalysis. When he was a student, he met Sigmund Freud, who had just published his book *The Interpretation of Dreams*. For the next few years he was Freud's student, and while explaining and defending him, he made his own mark. His 1925 book, *The Compulsion to Confess*, and his 1932 title, *The Unknown*

Murderer, as well as his 1941 *Masochism in Modern Man*, addressed the unconscious needs surrounding neurotic mannerisms in stuttering, in the guilt of criminals, in religions, and so forth. His 1948 masterwork, *Listening with the Third Ear*, dealt with the mind and process of psychoanalysis. Many will connect Reik with his writings on love and sex. He was born in Vienna, Austria, and studied literature and psychology at the University of Vienna before earning his doctorate there. After coming to the United States in 1938, he established his Theodore Reik Clinic, practicing psychoanalysis and continuing to write.

890 West End Avenue (near 104th Street)

Seidman, Henry L. (1890–1963), Accounting Teacher ∎

(See bio for Seidman at **418 Central Park West**.)

895 West End Avenue (near 104th Street)

Farrell, Frank J. (ca.1866–1926)
OWNER OF THE NEW YORK YANKEES

Farrell owned the New York Yankees for a dozen years before selling the team to Colonel Jacob Ruppert. Farrell had a silent partner in former police superintendent William S. Devery. They built Hilltop Park in upper Manhattan, on the site where Columbia Presbyterian Hospital stands today. There, pitcher Jack Chesbro won forty-one games, and Ty Cobb ran into the stands and beat up a taunting fan that happened to be paraplegic. Farrell was born on the Lower West Side and was educated in the school of hard knocks. His bartending work introduced him to politics; in running a saloon he made the connection to the local police captain at the time, his future partner Devery. Farrell was much involved with real estate, horses, gambling, and politics. He was

NEIGHBORHOOD SING-
ALONG: "WAY OUT WEST ON
WEST END AVENUE"

The 1937 Broadway-smash musical *Babes in Arms* had the wonderful but lesser known tune "Way Out West on West End Avenue." The words were by **Lorenz Hart,** who lived at **415 Central Park West,** and the music was by Richard Rogers. The musical also included such chestnuts as "The Lady Is a Tramp," "My Funny Valentine," and "Where or When." Those familiar with the show will also recognize "I Wish I Were in Love Again" and "Johnny One Note." The original Broadway cast featured Mitzi Green, Ray Heatherton, Alfred Drake, and the tap-dancing Nicholas Brothers, including Bloomingdale resident **Harold Nicholas**. The 1939 film version featured Judy Garland, Mickey Rooney, and Margaret Hamilton, who played the Wicked Witch in "The Wizard of Oz." "Way Out West on West End Avenue" is an awfully catchy tune in the spirit of Cole Porter's "Don't Fence Me In" and Frank Loesser's "Standing on the Corner, Watching All the Girls Go By" and "A Bushel and a Peck."

a longtime friend of the Irish boss, Big Tim Sullivan, and of Thomas F. Foley, a fellow saloonkeeper who became a judge and is memorialized in Foley Square. Farrell was also close to Governor Al Smith, who was mentored by Tom Foley.

Gutkind, Eric (1877–1965), Jewish Philosopher

(See bio for Gutkind at **310 Riverside Drive**.)

900 West End Avenue (near 104th Street)

Rogers, Hugo E. (1899–1974)
MANHATTAN BOROUGH PRESIDENT

Rogers was elected Borough President of Manhattan in 1946 and continued in that capacity until he resigned in 1949. Future mayor Robert F. Wagner, Jr., succeeded him as borough president. Rogers headed up Tammany Hall in 1948 but was replaced by Carmine DeSapio and, the following year, by Mayor O'Dwyer. A New York native, Rogers graduated from NYU School of Engineering in 1922 and the New York Law School in 1925. He served in the infantry in World War I and reenlisted when World War II broke out, rising to the rank of major. In between wars, he gave legal counsel to the Democratic organization in Harlem's Seventeenth Congressional District, and to the office of the New York State Assembly majority leader. His other activities included serving as director of New York University's alumni organization, as trustee of Polyclinic Medical School and Hospital, and as officer of the Hebrew Immigrant Aid Society. He also wrote two books on tax-saving strategies.

905 West End Avenue (near 104th Street)

Rothschild, Leopold O. (1888–1968), Preservationist and Lawyer ▪ ▪

(See bio for Rothschild at **823 West End Avenue**.)

908 West End Avenue (near 105th Street)

Blanck, Max (1867–unknown)
CO-OWNER OF THE TRIANGLE SHIRTWAIST COMPANY

Blanck was co-owner of the Triangle Shirtwaist Company during the horrific fire on March 25, 1911. The fire killed 146 employees, mostly young Italian and Jewish women who died either in the carnage or from escaping the fire by jumping nine stories to their death. Owners Blanck and his partner **Isaac Harris** had the monikers "Shirtwaist Kings" in the 1890s. Despite their responsibility for locked doors that made a stairway exit impossible, they were acquitted of manslaughter charges. They were awarded insurance proceeds that enabled the business to be reestablished in two different locations, but the costs of legal defense ended operations. In 1923 Blanck was convicted of theft and was sentenced to prison.

917 West End Avenue (near 105th Street)

de Teixeira, Eugenio Faria, Marquis de Aguila Branca (1864–1950) ☞▯
ARTIST, WRITER, AND MULTIMILLIONAIRE

In 1896, Brazilian Dom Eugenio Faria Goanzales de Teixeira, Marquis of Aguila Branca, his children, and his mother arrived in New York City. He took up residence in his partially finished mansion on the southeast corner of West End Avenue and 105th Street. He stated that his mansion would become a center of Brazilian art and culture. Being an artist, he painted frescoes inside, built a chapel, and made models of iron dragons to grace the entrance. With his claim of relation to the former Emperor Dom Pedro II, speculation rose that his fortune was between $50 and $100 million. However, within two years his fortune started to dry up when he lost his investment in a large real estate development and was lured into marrying a Barcelona beauty, who disappeared, as did jewels and $70,000. Meanwhile, there was a blackmail attempt on the Marquis, but the perpetrators were caught. In 1899, with new rumors of his wealth reaching $200 million, including gold mines and talk of him building a larger mansion on West End Avenue, and a church in memory of the sailors lost with the sinking of the *Maine*, the Marquis left the house and found his way to lesser splendor in Setauket, Long Island.

Stone, Harlan Fiske (1872–1946), Chief Justice of the Supreme Court ★ ▪ ▯

(See bio for Stone at **435 Riverside Drive**.)

924 West End Avenue (near 105th Street), the Clebourne

Kohlberg, Jerome, Jr. (1920–2005) ★ ▪ ▯
INVESTOR

Kohlberg is the first K in KKR & Co., the preeminent investment firm of Kohlberg, Kravis, and Roberts & Co. They were one of the pioneers in the use of private equity and leveraged buyouts that has become common in the business world. After starting at Bear Stearns in 1955, Kohlberg learned his trade and was party to some of the earliest leveraged buyout transactions in the 1960s. In 1976, he and fellow talents Henry J. Kravis and George Roberts left to form KKR. Born in New York, he graduated from Swarthmore College, served in the US Navy in World War II, and later earned an MBA from Harvard Business School and a bachelor of laws from Columbia Law School. His mother, Edith June Rose, graduated from Barnard in 1924 and was married the same year to Jerome Kohlberg, Sr. They resided at 924 West End Avenue before moving into the Manhasset Apartments. Kohlberg was a cousin of the late congressman James H. Scheuer. He also lived at **300 West 109th Street** (near Broadway), the Manhasset Apartments.

L'Engle (Franklin), Madeleine (1918–2007) ■
CHILDREN'S BOOK AUTHOR

Although she was one of the most successful children's authors, renowned for *A Wrinkle in Time* and much else, L'Engle volunteered as a librarian at St. John the Divine, New York's Episcopal cathedral. A New York native from a prosperous family on the Upper East Side, L'Engle graduated cum laude from Smith College in 1941. She met her husband, Hugh Franklin, when they were performing in a road production of *The Cherry Orchard*. They moved to Goshen, Connecticut, where they raised their family and ran a general store. She had been writing, with some success, for years, but soon after they moved back to city life in the Cleburne, success arrived with *A Wrinkle in Time*. Her writings cover the realms of fiction and fantasy, with a strong underpinning of her religious beliefs. The library at the Cathedral of St. John the Divine is named in her honor.

Podhoretz, Norman (1930–)
NEOCONSERVATIVE WRITER

Podhoretz's 1967 book *Making It* was a bombshell. It tells how he rose from a background of obscurity in the slums into the refined world of the New York intellectuals, such as Lionel and Diana Trilling, Edmund Wilson, Hannah Arendt, Saul Bellow, Norman Mailer, and others. Because the intellectuals didn't appreciate the details he revealed about them, he was shunned. In time he would transition from being a stout liberal to a neoconservative. Born in Brooklyn, Podhoretz attended Columbia University on a Pulitzer scholarship. There he earned a BA degree in English literature, with some mentoring from Lionel Trilling. At the Jewish Theological Seminary, he earned another degree in Hebrew literature. With a Fulbright Scholarship and a Kellit Fellowship from Columbia, he achieved additional BA and MA degrees from the University of Cambridge, England. From 1960 until his retirement in 1995, he was editor-at-large at *Commentary* magazine. He has contributed articles to magazines from *Partisan Review* to the *New Yorker*, and he authored more than twenty books, including *Hannah Arendt on Eichmann: A Study in the Perversity of Brilliance* and *My Negro Problem and Ours*; *Breaking Ranks: A Political Memoir*; and *My Love Affair with America: The Cautionary Tale of a Cheerful Conservative*. His wife is the journalist and author Midge Decter, and his son is John Podhoretz. Norman Podhoretz also lived at **315 West 106th Street** (near Riverside Drive).

Smalls, Charlie (1943–1987)
COMPOSER

Smalls composed the music for the 1975 Broadway musical *The Wiz*, which earned him a Tony Award for best score. The musical was made into the 1978 movie starring Diana Ross and Michael Jackson. The music is extensively used in television and commercial soundtracks. Born in New York, Smalls was a musical prodigy who studied at the Henry Street Settlement and then went on to graduate from Julliard in 1961. For a few years, he was the pianist with the New York Jazz Repertory Company. He also toured with Hugh Masekela and Harry Belafonte, and he recorded with the Harlem Boys Choir and Geoffrey Holder. He died much too young in Belgium from cardiac arrest during emergency surgery for a burst appendix.

925 West End Avenue (near 106th Street)

Shisgal, Murray Joseph (1926–), Playwright and Screenwriter

(See bio for Shisgal at 310 Riverside Drive.)

Thiery, Lewis M. (ca.1871–1934), Real Estate Agent and Equestrian Enthusiast ☞

(See bio for Thiery at 2689–2693 Broadway.)

945 West End Avenue (near 106th Street)

Lauterbach, Edward (1844–1923), Lawyer ◼ ◼

(See bio for Lauterbach at 301 West 106th Street.)

947 West End Avenue (near 106th Street)

Hammerstein, Oscar I (1846–1919) ★ ◼
THEATER IMPRESARIO

Hammerstein owned some eighty patents, most having to do with cigar-making machinery, but he went on to launch a theatrical dynasty. Born in Germany, Hammerstein came to New York City in 1864. He worked in a cigar factory and moonlighted as a theater manager. The cigar business earned him $200,000, which enabled him to start building theaters such as the Harlem Opera House and the Columbus Theater, both on 125th Street. In 1893, he built the Manhattan Opera House on 34th Street, a part of which, known as Hammerstein Ballroom, is still in operation, mostly for rock concerts. Manhattan Opera House was developed to compete with the Metropolitan Opera, which, in 1910, purchased the Hammerstein theater to eliminate the competition. Half a dozen additional theaters in the Times Square area followed, including the massive Olympia Theater. He produced many shows, such as Victor Herbert's *Naughty Marietta*. His grandson was **Oscar Hammerstein II**.

949 West End Avenue (near 107th Street)

Nevins, Bert (1910–1966) ● ▮

ADVERTISING EXECUTIVE AND MRS. AMERICA CONTEST ORIGINATOR

In 1933, Nevins was arrested in the Hotel Knickerbocker for having a turkey strapped to roller skates. He planned to race the turkey in a rink and charge admission. Under the banner of his company, Bert Nevins, Inc., his ability to get publicity was legendary. Nevins was born in New York City. As a student at Columbia Grammar School, he made money by publicizing fellow students. One of them was the tennis ace Frank Shields, whose granddaughter is the model Brooke Shields. As his career got underway, he gained attention for the diaper industry by creating the Diaper Derby race of crawling toddlers. Supposedly, he convinced the etiquette expert Emily Post that dunking donuts was socially proper if the donut was first broken in half. With that groundwork laid, presidential candidate Eisenhower and his wife

HONORARY STREET NAMES— WEST 100S

Humphrey Bogart Place (103rd Street between Broadway and West End Avenue)
Actor **Humphrey Bogart** grew up on the block.
Norman Rockwell Place (at the corner of 103rd Street and Broadway)
Artist and illustrator **Norman Rockwell** was born nearby.
Odessa Steward Street (the corner of Amsterdam Avenue and West 103rd Street)

dunked donuts during the 1952 campaign. In 1938, he created the Mrs. America Pageant for his client, the Palisades Amusement Park.

Thiery, Lewis M. (ca.1871–1934), Real Estate Agent and Equestrian Enthusiast

(See bio for Thiery at **2689–2693 Broadway**.)

Odessa Steward (d. 2010) was a community activist who lived in the nearby Frederick Douglass Houses.

HUDSON RIVE

TWELFTH

NEW YORK CENTRAL AND HUDSON RIVER

RIVERSIDE PA

1897

Nich. De Peyster

RIVERSIDE

Nich. De Peyster

BLOOMINGDALE

Routel

Casper Meier

John Be

G. S. Mumford

1990

CLAREMONT

W.108TH

W.109TH

W.110TH

W.111TH

W.112TH

W.113TH

W.114TH

W.115TH

W.116TH

W.117TH

1989

W.118TH

W.119TH

1893
(1263)

1893
(1266)

1894
(1267)

1894
(1268)

1895
(1299)

1895
(1270)

1896
(1271)

1896
(1272)

(1273)

(1274)

(1275)

(1276)

BOULEVARD

G. S. Mumford

Jas. De Peyler

Nich. De Peyler

New York Hospital
1881

Map 798

Map 110

37

John Jacob Astor

Nich De Peyster

1881
(1150)

1882
(1151)

1883
(1152)

1884
(1153)

1885

1886
(1155)

(1156)

BLOOMINGDALE

INSANE ASYLUM
1974
(1161)

1973

GREEN
HOUSE

AMSTERDAM

(10TH AV.)

CROTON WASTE
WORKS

LEAKE & WATTS

ORPHAN ASYLUM

1865
(1037)

ST.

1865
(1038)

ST.

1865
(1039)

1866
(1040)

ST.

1867
(1041)

1867
(1042)

ST.

1961
(1043)

ST.

1961
(1044)

ST.

1962
(1045)

ST.

1962
(1046)

1863
(1035)

ST.

1864
(1036)

ST.

New York Hospital Farm
L. 61 P. 140 Map 193

Gerard De Peyster

Nich. Kortwright

AV.

MORNINGSIDE

PART OF
WARD 12
NEW YORK CITY

MORNINGSIDE

Scale 150 feet to the inch.

1850

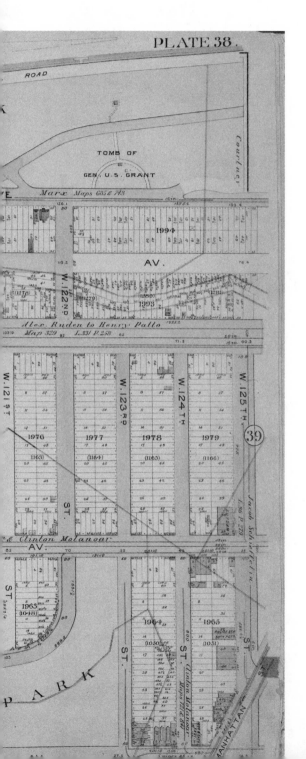

The West 110s

It was in the West 110s that the retreating colonial forces fought the British in the famous Battle of Harlem Heights. In 1821, it was the site of the Bloomingdale Insane Asylum that established the institutional character of the neighborhood, which came to include the Leake and Watts Orphan Asylum, Columbia University, Barnard College, St. Luke's Hospital, and the offices of the Episcopal Diocese of New York on the grounds of the Cathedral of St. John the Divine. These neighborhood institutions contribute to a healthy turnover of population while providing a steadfast stability to the neighborhood. Nestled nicely between Morningside and Riverside Parks, the area inspired some of the most beautiful apartment buildings in the city. This heart of Morningside Heights has no equal in New York or anywhere else in the United States.

204 West 110th Street (near Adam Clayton Powell Jr. Boulevard) ▪

Scheuer, James Haas (1920–2005)

CONGRESSMAN

Liberal congressman James Scheuer contracted polio on his honeymoon in 1948 and walked with a cane for the rest of his life. Born in New York City, he graduated from Swarthmore College in 1942, and he earned an MBA at Harvard in 1943 and a law degree from Columbia's Law School in 1948. He served in the US Army from 1943 to 1945 and then in the Foreign Economic Administration established in the Roosevelt administration. From 1951 he worked in the Office of Price Stabilization and became president of the Renewal and Redevelopment Corporation of New York City, which sponsored housing ventures. After an unsuccessful run for Congress in 1962, he was elected in 1964. He served thirteen terms through much redistricting and was succeeded by Jerrold Nadler in 1993. Scheuer is a cousin of investor **Jerome Kohlberg**. His father was the real estate investor Simon H. Scheuer.

217 West 110th Street (Central Park North, near Adam Clayton Powell, Jr. Boulevard)

Bimberg, Meyer R. (ca.1862–1908) 🖙

THE "BUTTON KING" AND BUILDER OF THEATERS

Meyer Bimberg invented the campaign button. He was a delegate at the 1896 Republican Party convention that nominated McKinley. By having one hundred thousand buttons made with McKinley's picture on them before it was decided that he would be the party's nominee, Bimberg made a fortune and earned his title of "Button King." Two years later he made buttons showing Teddy Roosevelt in a Rough Rider costume with the slogan "Our Choice for Governor," which was reason enough for TR to send flowers to Bimberg's funeral. Meyer Bimberg, along with his two brothers, built the Astor Theater and the Stuyvesant Theater, which was renamed to honor the impresario David Belasco. His brother was **Bernard K. Bimberg**.

307 Cathedral Parkway (110th Street, near Frederick Douglass Boulevard)

Garland, Hamlin (1860–1940) ▪

WRITER

Known in his day as "the dean of American letters," Hamlin Garland won a Pulitzer Prize for Biography in 1922 for the second of his memoirs, *A Daughter of the Middle Border*. In all, he wrote six memoirs. Born in Wisconsin, Garland lived in several different places in the Midwest before arriving in Boston in 1884 to pursue a life of writing. A collection of short stories, *Main-Traveled Roads*, published in 1891, was his first success. The year1893 found him in Chicago where he lectured and wrote essays that championed realistic American literature. To that end, he traveled West, through his home state of Wisconsin, to study Native Americans. These experiences and notes yielded nearly fifty works, which garnered him great acclaim over his lifetime. *The Book of the American Indian* and his two-volume biography of Ulysses S. Grant were indicative of his remarkable skill.

50 Cathedral Parkway, now 350 Cathedral Parkway (110th Street, near Morningside Avenue)

Sinclair, Upton (1878–1968) ★ ▪

AUTHOR AND ACTIVIST

Sinclair is probably best known for his 1906 novel *The Jungle*, built on his seven weeks working undercover in Chicago's meatpacking plants. He sent copies of it to every member of Congress and to President Theodore Roosevelt, who initiated legislation leading to the formation of the Food and Drug Administration. Born in Maryland, Sinclair and his family moved to Queens when he was 10. Five days before he turned 14, he entered City College. He supported himself by writing for pulp magazines and graduated in 1897. Sinclair also attended Columbia for a while, but his appetite for learning and writing were greater than formal schooling. In 1914, Sinclair wrote *The Coal War*, which dealt with the strike against the Rockefeller interests in Colorado. In 1920, he moved his family to the Los Angeles, California, area and ran unsuccessfully on the Socialist ticket for Congress, for the Senate, and for governor. Running a second time for governor in 1934 as a Democrat, he lost with a respectable 44 percent of the vote. In 1943, Sinclair won the Pulitzer Prize for his novel *Dragon's Teeth*. It was one of the eleven novels that he wrote from 1940 to 1953 featuring the protagonist Lanny Budd. His lifetime output would total more than ninety books and thirty plays.

412 West 110th Street (near Columbus Avenue)

Pollak, Walter Heilprin (1887–1940) ● ▪

CIVIL RIGHTS LAWYER

In the 1930s, Pollak appeared before the United States Supreme Court arguing in the famous case defending the Scottsboro Boys. Another of his famous defenses, argued on behalf of the American Civil Liberties Union and before the Supreme Court, was for communist Benjamin Gitlow. He also defended the communist Earl Browder. Born in New Jersey, Pollak attended Columbia but graduated from Harvard with an AB degree in 1907 and a law degree in 1910. In 1914, he married a 1912 Barnard graduate Marion Heilprin. One of the two large law firms that he worked for also employed Benjamin Cardozo, a future US Supreme Court Justice, who became a lifelong friend. For some twenty years, his firm was Engelhard, Pollak, Pitcher, Stern & Clarke. In 1937, he joined the firm that would become Paul, Weiss, Rifkind, Wharton & Garrison. More and more, especially from the 1920s, he argued civil rights cases, often partnering with like-minded "radical" attorneys. He served as counsel to the New York State Park Commission and Robert Moses. In his final year, he was appointed sole trustee for reorganizing the billion-dollar Associated Gas and Electric Company. Pollak also lived at **362 Riverside Drive** (near 109th Street) and at **521 West 112th Street** (near Amsterdam Avenue).

Rademacher, Hans (1892–1969) ■
MATHEMATICIAN AND PROFESSOR OF MATHEMATICS

Rademacher discovered the formula that yields the number of ways that any positive number can be expressed as the sum of whole numbers. In addition to his work with number theory, he delved into quantum theory and the theory of functions, and he developed his theory of Dedekind sums. Born in Germany, Rademacher received his PhD from the University of Gottingen in 1917. He taught at the University of Berlin, the University of Hamburg, and the University of Breslau where he was dismissed for his pacifist views and his hiring of Jewish faculty. From 1934, when he came to the United States, he taught at the University of Pennsylvania. Upon his retirement in 1962, he was awarded an honorary doctor of science. During his retirement years, he was a visiting professor at Rockefeller University and at New York University. Much of his work has been published in two volumes by Massachusetts Institute of Technology.

Women's Hospital, Cathedral Parkway.

501 West 110th Street (near Amsterdam Avenue)

Gershwin, George (1898–1937), Composer ★ ◼

(See bio for Gershwin at 316 West 103rd Street.)

LITTLE CONEY ISLAND

Would you believe there
was an area of ill-repute
called "Little Coney Island"
on West 110th Street? See
Pam Tice's article on the
Bloomingdale Neighborhood
History Group website at
https://bloomingdalehistory.
com/2016/08/27/little-coney-
island-on-west–110th-street/

504 West 110th Street (near Amsterdam Avenue)

Marston, William Moulton (1893–1947), Psychologist and Creator of *Wonder Woman* ★ ◼ ▯

(See bio for Marston at 460 Riverside Drive.)

527 West 110th Street (near Broadway)

Ephron, Henry (1911 –1992) 👉
PLAYWRIGHT, SCREENWRITER, AND PRODUCER

Ephron was the father of Nora, and he became the father-in-law of the
journalist Carl Bernstein. Along with his wife and professional partner,
Phoebe Ephron, Henry wrote classic movie scripts such as *The Desk Set*,
starring Katharine Hepburn and Spencer Tracy, and *Daddy Long Legs*,
featuring Fred Astaire. Born in the Bronx, Ephron attended Cornell
University and started on Broadway as a stage manager on Kaufman and
Hart plays. He also produced some of the movies that he and Phoebe wrote
scripts for, as well as the 1954 movie versions of Irving Berlin's *There's No
Business Like Show Business* and Rogers and Hammerstein's *Carousel*.

Ephron, Phoebe (1914–1971) 👉
PLAYWRIGHT AND SCREENWRITER

Ephron's first success on Broadway was *Three's a Family*, a play based
on her experiences raising her soon-to-be-famous daughter, Nora
Ephron. Opening in 1943, it ran for 497 performances. She wrote a few

more plays, including 1961's *Take Her, She's Mine*, which ran for 404 performances and starred Art Carney and Elizabeth Ashley. Much of her other work, especially in Hollywood, was in collaboration with her husband **Henry Ephron**. Born in the Bronx, she graduated from Hunter College in 1935. She met her husband while they were both working at a summer camp, and they married in 1934. While working as a stage manager and then as secretary to the theatrical producer Gilbert Miller, she began writing plays.

Fiske, Thomas Scott (1865–1944) ▪
MATHEMATICIAN

Fiske was a driving force in establishing the College Entrance Examination Board. As secretary, he championed its acceptance as the standardized testing mechanism for students seeking to gain entrance into colleges or universities. However, Fiske was even more renowned for his work in mathematics. He was a founder and the first long-term secretary of the American Mathematical Society. In addition to numerous articles, he is the author of *The Functions of a Complex Variable*. Born in New York, he earned his doctorate at Columbia in 1888, began teaching there, and was a full professor from 1897 to his retirement in 1935. For a short time, he was acting dean at Barnard. Fiske also lived at **508 West 114th Street** (near Amsterdam Avenue) and **35 Claremont Avenue** (near 119th Street).

601 West 110th Street (near Broadway)

Cobb, Irwin Shrewsbury (1876–1944) ▪ ▪
JOURNALIST AND HUMORIST

Irwin S. Cobb was thought to be the highest-paid newspaper staff reporter in his day. He wrote for Joseph Pulitzer's *New York World* and penned sixty books and three hundred short stories. One of his short stories was adapted into the movie *The Woman Accused,* with Cary Grant. His wit earned him a comparison to Mark Twain and is probably the reason he was selected to host the seventh Academy Awards. Born in Paducah, Kentucky, he honed his journalistic skills at local and regional newspapers before coming to New York City in 1904. He was a serious, in-depth journalist who estimated that he wrote five hundred thousand words in longhand covering the trial of Harry K. Thaw for the murder of architect Stanford White. Cobb was honored by having a bridge, a hotel, and a cigar named after him, and he also received the French Legion of Honor award and two honorary doctorates.

Kunz, George Frederick (1856–1932) ★ ▪ ▯
MINERALOGIST AND GEM EXPERT

Kunz was an expert on gems in the United States, and the mineral "kunzite" was named in his honor. In time, he would receive honorary degrees from Knox College, Illinois; the University of Marburg, Germany; and Columbia University. When he was a teenager, he sold his mineral collection to the University of Minnesota. After he died, his collection of printed materials and precious stones, constituting the Kunz Collection, went to the United States government. He was the honorary curator of the precious stones collection in the American Museum of Natural History. Away from his official responsibilities as an executive of Tiffany & Co., he served as president of the American Scenic and Historic Preservation Society. With that endeavor, he saw to the erection of Anna Vaughn Hyatt Huntington's "Joan of Arc" in Riverside Park. His wife was the charity worker Sophia Handforth Kunz. He also lived at **380 Riverside Drive** (near 111th Street).

Smith, Minnie (ca.1900–?) 👉
REAL ESTATE BROKER

The New York telephone directory of the summer of 1939 listed ten "Minnie Smiths," with nine listed at 601 West 110th Street, and one listed at 501 West 110th Street. Most likely, the 501 West 110th Street listing was an error in the phone book. The number of listings caught the attention of District Attorney Thomas E. Dewey's office as well as that of newspaper columnist Walter Winchell. A *New York Times* reporter visited the building and unraveled the mystery. Mrs. Minnie Smith rented several apartments in the building and sublet them to occupants who requested telephones. Smith installed payphones in each apartment and, without thinking of the consequences, had them listed under her name. She was an otherwise very responsible member of the Morningside Heights neighborhood.

610 Cathedral Parkway (110th Street, near Broadway)

Shattuck, Jane (1865–1948)
BUSINESSWOMAN

Shattuck's brother Frank established the first Schrafft's candy and ice-cream store in New York City in 1898 at 1345 Broadway. Jane Shattuck managed that store with him but then introduced meals in 1909 to the second Schrafft's candy store in New York City at 54 West 23rd Street. She understood that more and more women were entering the workplace, and the genteel atmosphere and pleasant menus catered perfectly to them. By 1927, Schrafft's had grown to twenty-five restaurants in New York City. Shattuck retired in 1933. Shattuck also lived at **21 Claremont Avenue** (near 116th Street).

611 West 110th Street (near Broadway)

Thomas, Harvey Mark (ca.1871–1957), Publisher ▪

(See bio for Thomas at **239 West 103rd Street**.)

West 110th Street near 10th Avenue

Hayden, Richard Miles (ca.1849–ca.1893), Superintendent of the Leake and Watts Orphan Asylum

(See bio for Hayden at **206 West 109th Street**.)

200 West 111th Street (Adam Clayton Powell, Jr. Boulevard)

Loew, Marcus (1870–1927) ★ ▪
MOTION PICTURE INDUSTRY PIONEER

Marcus Loew.

Loew created MGM. In 1920 he acquired the Metro Film Corporation, and in 1924 he acquired the Goldwyn Pictures Corporation and the Louis B. Mayer Company. He didn't live long enough to see his creation become the colossal MGM Studios. Born in Manhattan's East Village, Loew started working when he was 9 years old. Ever the entrepreneur, he failed at a printing venture and in the fur business. After befriending later-to-be-famous actor David Warfield, they tried the penny arcade business. Loew's takeaway idea from that experience was to project motion pictures in vaudeville theaters, first in Cincinnati, then Brooklyn, and then in New York's Lincoln Square and Harlem. His ownership of hundreds of theaters became the chain of Loew's Theaters. Loew also lived at **380 Riverside Drive** (near 111th Street).

Attilio Piccirilli.

320 West 111th Street (near Manhattan Avenue)

Piccirilli, Attilio (1866–1945) ★ ■ ▮
SCULPTOR

Piccirilli created the Maine Monument on Columbus Circle and the Firemen's Memorial on Riverside Drive at 100th Street. He also sculptured figures on the front door of Riverside Church, on the facade of the Brooklyn Museum, on the Custom House, and on the pediment of the Frick Museum. Piccirilli was born in Italy and trained at the Accademia di San Luca of Rome. In 1888, he came to the United States and worked with his father and brothers at their studio in the South Bronx. They worked for such notable architects as McKim, Mead, & White, and Cass Gilbert, and sculptors such as Augustus St. Gaudens, Frederick MacMonnies, and Daniel Chester French. They specialized in taking the sculptors' clay models and plaster castings and carving them into marble, limestone, or granite. As such, they rendered the figure of Lincoln in the Lincoln Memorial in Washington, D.C.; many of the sculptures around the New York Public Library, including the two lions known as Patience and Fortitude; and so much else, from the Washington Square Arch to the Tomb of the Unknown Soldier in Arlington National Cemetery. A first-rate craftsman like his brothers, Attilio Piccirilli was also an artist in his own right.

507 West 111th Street (near Amsterdam Avenue)

Henderson, Eleanor Curtis (1901–1941), Communist Activist

(See bio for Henderson at **540 West 123rd Street**.)

521 West 111th Street (near Amsterdam Avenue)

Johnson, Alvin Saunders (1874–1971), ∎

ECONOMIST AND CO-FOUNDER OF THE NEW SCHOOL

In 1918, Johnson, along with a group of progressive intellectuals including philosopher John Dewey, social economist Thorstein Veblen, historian James Harvey Robinson, economist Wesley Clair Mitchell, and historian Charles A. Beard, founded the New School for Social Research. As the school's director, Johnson created a "university in exile" for scholars, such as the political theorist **Hannah Arendt** and the psychologist Erich Fromm, who had escaped the Nazi wave in Europe. Born in Nebraska and educated at home, he graduated from the University of Nebraska, served in the Spanish-American War, and earned a PhD degree at Columbia University in 1902. After teaching at Bryn Mawr College; Columbia; the Universities of Nebraska, Texas, and Chicago; and Stanford and Cornell Universities; he settled in New York. He edited the *New Republic* in some of its early years, and over his lifetime he wrote about a dozen books, two novels, and over a thousand articles. From 1930, he and Columbia economics professor E. R. A. Seligman edited the fifteen-volume *Encyclopedia of Social Sciences*. Johnson also lived at **395 Riverside Drive** (near 112th Street).

536 West 111th Street (near Broadway)

Rothschild, Leopold O. (1888–1968), Preservationist and Lawyer ∎ ▇

(See bio for Rothschild at **823 West End Avenue**.)

545 West 111th Street (near Broadway)

Chu, Grace Zia (1899–1999), Pioneer Cookbook Author

(See bio for Chu at **370 Riverside Drive**.)

A KISS IN THE DARK

The 1949 comedy flick *A Kiss in the Dark* takes place on 112th Street between Amsterdam Avenue and Broadway. David Niven plays the part of a concert pianist, who, after performing on the road for twenty years, returns to New York City to discover that he owns a building. Hoping for some rest and relaxation, he settles into the building. The fun begins when he meets Jane Wyman, who plays the role of a beautiful model and neighbor, and Broderick Crawford, cast as the building superintendent. It's a mystery why Victor Herbert and Buddy De Sylva are not credited for their 1912 song, "A Kiss in the Dark," as it shares the title, and its melody makes up much of the film's soundtrack.

Kazin, Alfred (1915–1998), Author and Literary Critic ◼

(See bio for Kazin at **46 West 95th Street**.)

600 West 111th Street (near Broadway)

Leichter, Franz Sigmund (1930–), New York State Senator and Assemblyman

(See bio for Leichter at **250 West 104th Street**.)

605 West 111th Street (near Broadway)

Dreiser, Theodore Herman Albert (1871–1945), Novelist and Journalist ◼

(See bio for Dreiser at **6 West 102nd Street**.)

610 West 111th Street (near Broadway)

Rosenman, Samuel Irving (1896–1973), Lawyer, Judge, and Politician ◼

(See bio for Rosenman at **444 Central Park West**.)

507 West 112th Street (near Amsterdam Avenue)

Greene, Belle da Costa (1883–1950), Librarian and Advisor to J. P. Morgan ▮

(See bio for Greene in **The Old Community**.)

Paterno, Joseph (1881–1939) ★ ◼ ▯
APARTMENT BUILDING DEVELOPER

Many apartment buildings in the Bloomingdale–Morningside Heights neighborhood have the signature "J P" inscribed on the buildings' facades, usually in the escutcheon (shield) above the main entrance, but sometimes above windows. Paterno built those buildings and many others, usually employing lesser-known architects like **Gaetan Ajello** and Schwartz & Gross. Born in Italy, he came to the United States as a young boy after an earthquake ruined his father's building business. Young Joseph Paterno finished some of his father's work on 112th Street and then, with his brother Michael, started and finished the ten-story building at 620 West 116th Street. Their brother-in-law, Anthony Campagna, joined the business, and they continued to develop most of the large apartment buildings in the area. They also built and were the primary funders of Columbia's Casa Italiana. The Paterno organization also built some apartment buildings on the East Side and in Riverdale in the Bronx. Paterno also lived at **435 Riverside Drive** (near 116th Street).

521 West 112th Street (near Amsterdam Avenue)

Pollak, Walter Heilprin (1887–1940), Civil Rights Lawyer ◼ ▯

(See bio for Heilprin at **412 West 110th Street**.)

524 West 112th Street (near Broadway)

Capablanca, Jose Raul (1888–1942) ◼ ☞
CHESS CHAMPION

Capablanca was the official world chess champion from 1921 to 1927. His rapid style and endgame skill influenced the future great Bobby

José Raúl Capablanca.

Fischer. Another world champion, Boris Spassky, considered Capablanca the greatest chess player of all time. Born in Havana, Cuba, he came to the United States to attend Columbia. There, he played on the baseball team and led the chess team. He left school to concentrate on chess, returned in 1910 to Columbia's School of Mines, but left again for chess. His first book, published in 1920, was a memoir entitled *My Chess Career*. His book *Chess Fundamentals* is considered one of the best ever.

530 West 112th Street (near Broadway)

Nozick, Robert (1938–2002) ■
PHILOSOPHER

Nozick's first book *Anarchy, State, and Utopia*, published in 1974, was a blockbuster. It argued against the paternalistic welfare state on philosophical grounds. His next book, *Philosophical Explanations*, published in 1981, explored epistemology and individuality. His other four books were *The Examined Life*, *The Nature of Rationality*, *Socratic Puzzles*, and *Invariances: The Structure of the Objective World*. His libertarian leanings were relatively rare in academia at that time. Born in Brooklyn, Nozick graduated summa cum laude from Columbia in 1959 and from Princeton in 1963 with a PhD. He then went on to Oxford as a Fulbright Scholar. He taught at Harvard for most of his career and chaired the philosophy department for a few years. As a teenager, he joined the youth branch of the Norman Thomas Socialist Party, and in college, he was a member of the Student League for Industrial Democracy, which became the Students for a Democratic Society.

542 West 112th Street (near Broadway)

Jaros, Alfred Leopold (1890–1967) ▪

BUILDING ENGINEER AND CONSULTANT

Jaros introduced the idea of radiant heating into the United States in the mid-1920s and created the plans for the first large radiant-cooled office structure, the Alcoa office building in Pittsburgh. A native New Yorker, Jaros graduated from Columbia's School of Engineering in 1911 with a degree in mechanical engineering. He was a founding partner with his Columbia schoolmate Albert Baum in the building engineering firm of Jaros, Baum & Bolles, which is best known for its work on high-rise projects such as the World Trade Center and the Hudson Yards in New York City, and the Sears, now Willis, Tower in Chicago. Baum's long-standing reputation for getting complex mechanical, electrical, and plumbing systems built was based on the firm's involvement with such historic New York structures as the TWA Terminal, the Pan Am Building, the Seagram building, and the Whitney Museum.

545 West 112th Street (near Broadway)

Dewey, John (1859–1952) ★ ▪

PHILOSOPHER, EDUCATIONAL REFORMER, AND PSYCHOLOGIST

Dewey was a champion of the philosophy of pragmatism and progressive reform, especially in education. Arguably, America's most noted philosopher in his day, his progressive beliefs flowed into his extensive political activities. Ever associated with such institutions as the ACLU, the *New Republic*, and those advocating academic freedom, he was a most public intellectual. "Learning by doing" became the core of his progressive education beliefs, and they changed the course of education in the 1930s, not without controversy. His first published work in 1886 was a very early book on psychology. More than thirty books followed, addressing such topics as pedagogy; schools and society; mathematics; China and Japan; German philosophy; empiricism; the process of thinking; and the theory of valuation, ethics, art, and logic. Born in Vermont, Dewey graduated in 1879 from the University of Vermont, where he was elected to Phi Beta Kappa. After attaining a PhD from Johns Hopkins University, he taught at the University of Michigan from 1884 to 1894. For the next ten years, he made the University of Chicago his home. In 1904, he arrived at Columbia University, where he stayed until retirement in 1930. Along with other luminaries such as Thorsten Veblen, and Columbia historians James Harvey Robinson and Charles A. Beard, he founded the New School in 1919. He was awarded some seventeen honorary degrees and made honorary president or chairman of many organizations. At least six schools were named in his honor.

605 West 112th Street (near Broadway)

Schuman, William Howard (1910–1992) ★ ■
COMPOSER AND ARTS EXECUTIVE

Schuman was the founding president of Lincoln Center and the president of the Julliard School of Music. As a composer, he won the Pulitzer Prize for Music in 1943 for his "Secular Cantata No. 2: A Free Song" employing poems by Walt Whitman. In all, he composed ten symphonies, five ballet scores, four string quartets, band pieces, chorus works, concertos for piano and string instruments, and two operas. His Symphony No. 3 and his Symphony for Strings are especially well known. Born in New York, Schuman attended NYU's School of Commerce but dropped out and took up music. He wrote some forty songs with Frank Loesser and studied music privately with the composer Roy Harris. He graduated from Columbia's Teachers College in 1935 with a BS degree and, two years later, with a master's degree.

In 1935, he joined the faculty of Sarah Lawrence College but left in 1945 to become editor-in-chief and director of publications at the music publisher G. Schirmer. Later that year he also became president of the Julliard School of Music, where he stayed until 1962 when he took charge of Lincoln Center.

612 West 112th Street (near Broadway)

Adams, Franklin Pierce (1881–1960) ■

NEWSPAPER COLUMNIST

Adams might have been the most popular American newspaper journalist of his day. He is thought to have been the first bylined columnist who was not a newspaper owner. Adams was a fixture of the legendary Algonquin Round Table and, as editor of the *Evening Mail*, hired two of its other members: Robert Benchley and George S. Kaufman. His poem "Baseball's Sad Lexicon" honored the Chicago Cubs double-play combination we know as "Tinkers to Evers to Chance." Radio aficionados will remember him as one of the witty panelists on the quiz show *Information Please*. Adams also lived at **420 Riverside Drive** (near 114th Street)

266 West 113th Street (near Frederick Douglass Boulevard)

Talmey, Dr. Max (1869–1941), Ophthalmologist ☞

(See bio for Talmey at **838 West End Avenue**.)

278 West 113th Street (near Frederick Douglass Boulevard)

Houdini, Harry (1874–1926) ★ ■
MAGICIAN

Harry Houdini.

Houdini hired the writer H. P. Lovecraft to write a book debunking religious miracles, but Houdini's untimely death ended the effort. Born in Hungary as Ehrich Weiss, Harry Houdini arrived in the United States in 1878 and was raised in Wisconsin. He made his professional debut at the age of 9 as a trapeze artist, calling himself "Ehrich, the Prince of the Air," and later became a champion cross-country runner. His career in magic got off to a slow start, but he worked incredibly hard and had a flair for the extraordinary. His signature tricks and escapes included the Chinese water torture cell, the suspended straitjacket escape, the milk can escape, the buried-alive escapes, the locked-in-the-box-and-tossed-off-the pier escape, and many others.

330 West 113th Street (near Manhattan Avenue)

Runyon, Damon (1880–1946), Journalist and Short Story Writer ★ ■

(See bio for Runyon at 251 West 95th Street.)

511 West 113th Street (near Amsterdam Avenue)

Schwartz, Anna Jacobson (1915–2012) ■ ▋
ECONOMIST

Anna Schwartz co-authored with Milton Friedman the economic classic *A Monetary History of the United States, 1867–1960*. It posits the supply of money, managed mostly by the Federal Reserve Bank, as the primary determinant of the inflation rate and the health of the economy. For this and other works, she might very well be considered the most important woman economist of the twentieth century. A native New Yorker, Schwartz graduated from Barnard College in 1934. She graduated from Columbia with an MA in 1935 and a PhD in 1964, and she was Phi Beta Kappa. She worked briefly for the Department of Agriculture and then for Columbia's Social Science Research Council from 1936 to 1941 before joining the National Bureau of Economic Research in New York. There she met Milton Friedman. In 1953, she collaborated with two other economists to produce a monumental two-volume *Growth and Fluctuations in the British Economy, 1790–1850: A Historical, Statistical, and Theoretical Study of Britain's Economic Development*.

530 West 113th Street (near Amsterdam Avenue)

Swope, Herbert Bayard (1882–1958) ★ ■ ▮

JOURNALIST, EDITOR, AND NEWSPAPER EXECUTIVE

Swope's house in Sands Point, Long Island, was thought to be the basis for Daisy Buchanan's house in F. Scott Fitzgerald's novel *The Great Gatsby*. Swope was the first recipient of the Pulitzer Prize for reporting and is credited with inventing the "op ed" on the page opposite a newspaper's editorial page. The phrase "cold war" is attributed to him. Born in Missouri, he worked as a reporter on the *St. Louis Post-Dispatch*, the *Chicago Tribune*, and the *New York Herald* before making his mark at the *New York World* in 1909. There he covered crime, the Triangle Shirt Waist fire, and World War I, and he was made executive editor in 1920. The talent associated with his newspaper included Franklin P. Adams, Alexander Woollcott, and Heywood Broun. Swope was an intimate of the legendary Algonquin Round Table of intellectuals and wits. In his later years, he served on the State Racing

Commission as a member of the Long Island Park Commission, as a director of the National Conference of Christians and Jews, and as a chairman of the city's Commission on Intergroup Relations. Swope also lived at **411 West 114th Street** (near Amsterdam Avenue).

536 West 113th Street (near Broadway)

Rothschild, Leopold O. (1888–1968), Preservationist and Lawyer ■ ▯

(See bio for Rothschild at **823 West End Avenue**.)

Shotwell, James Thomson (1874–1965) ■ ▯
HISTORIAN

Shotwell was a tireless advocate and toiler for world peace. In 1917 he became an advisor to President Wilson and the director of research at the Carnegie Endowment for International Peace. He was present at the signing of the Treaty of Paris in 1919 and at the inception of many world peace organizations. In 1952, he was a nominee for the Nobel Peace Prize. Born in Canada, Shotwell received a BA degree from the University of Toronto in 1898 and a PhD from Columbia two years later. He joined the Columbia faculty in 1903 and became a full professor in 1908. His long tenure at Columbia was interrupted for only the few years he worked with the Social Science Research Council. In his earliest years at Columbia, he contributed nearly 250 articles to the *Encyclopedia Britannica*. It is estimated that he edited or wrote more than five hundred books—an almost unbelievable achievement! Shotwell also lived at **405 West 117th Street** (near Morningside Drive).

562 West 113th Street (near Broadway), Columbia's McBain Hall

McCain, Meghan (1984–)
TELEVISION PERSONALITY AND AUTHOR

Meghan McCain recounted her road trip across the country with comedian Michael Ian Black in her book *America, You Sexy Bitch: A Love Letter to Freedom.* The daughter of Arizona senator John McCain, she undoubtedly gained special experience working on her father's reelection campaigns. Her other books are *My Dad, John McCain* and *Dirty Sexy Politics.* McCain was born in Arizona and graduated from Columbia University with a bachelor's degree in art history. Her early career experiences included internships at *Newsweek* magazine and *Saturday Night Live* television show. Perhaps best known as a co-host of the popular television show *The View*, McCain was previously a Fox News contributor and co-host of the television talk program *Outnumbered.*

601 West 113th Street (near Broadway)

Thomas, Harvey Mark (ca.1871–1957), Publisher ▪

(See bio for Thomas at **239 West 103rd Street**.)

609 West 113th Street (near Broadway)

Erskine, John (1879–1951) ▪ ▪ ☞
EDUCATOR, AUTHOR, AND MUSICIAN

Erskine was the first president of the Julliard School of Music from 1928 to 1937. However, he is known for many other things. His much-cited 1915 essay, "The Moral Obligation to Be Intelligent," dovetailed with the Great Books movement and Erskine's own creation, the

General Honors Course, at Columbia. His assisting instructors in the early part of this journey were future stars Clifton Fadiman, **Mark Van Doren**, **Rexford Tugwell**, **Raymond Weaver**, and Mortimer Adler. Erskine was born in New York City and earned BA, MA, PhD, and DLitt degrees at Columbia. Later, Erskine would receive a half dozen honorary doctorates. While a student at Columbia in 1900, he showed his piano virtuosity and musical composition skills by producing the 1900 Varsity Show. He was an English Professor at Amherst for seven years before arriving to teach at Columbia. His 1925 novel *The Private Life of Helen of Troy* received acclaim but also controversy for its Freudian bent. It was the first of his novels to be made into a motion picture. In his long, productive life, over one hundred books came from his pen. When he headed up Julliard, he continued to teach at Columbia where he became an institution. Journalist and author Helen Worden was his second wife. Erskine Place in the Bronx is named after him, thanks to the planners of Co-Op City. Erskine also lived at four other addresses nearby: **415 West 115th Street** (near Amsterdam Avenue), **430 West 118th Street** (near Amsterdam Avenue), **39 Claremont Avenue** (near 120th Street), and **130 Claremont Avenue** (122nd Street).

616 West 113th Street (near Riverside Drive)

Clark, John Bates (1847–1938) ■ ▮
ECONOMIST

Before the Nobel Prize for Economic Sciences was awarded in 1968, the most prestigious prize in the field of economics was the John Bates Clark Medal. Clark was the leading classical economist of his day and an original thinker in the evolving science of economics. His notion of marginality developed into a marginal productivity theory used to understand the value of production at different levels and the distribution of wealth. His early socialist leanings transformed into an appreciation for the efficacy of capitalism. Clark was born and raised in Providence, Rhode Island, graduated from Amherst College, and attended the University of Zurich and Heidelberg University. He taught at Smith and Carlton Colleges and lectured at Johns Hopkins, but Columbia was the fortunate recipient of his talents from 1895. He had numerous extracurricular responsibilities, authored many books, and was awarded honorary degrees from Amherst, Princeton, Columbia, and others. His son was the economist **John Maurice Clark**.

Clark, John Maurice (1884–1963) ■
ECONOMIST

In economics, Clark is often credited, probably erroneously, with creating the concept of the multiplier. Although cited most favorably by Keynesian economists including John Kenneth Galbraith, Clark defended capitalism and competition with persistent and rigorous clarity. Sometimes called "an economist's economist," he was the author of a dozen books on the topic. Among them, *Social Control of Business*, published in 1926, was especially influential on economic theory. Born in Massachusetts, John Maurice Clark graduated from Amherst College in 1905 and then achieved his PhD from Columbia in 1910. He taught at Colorado College, at Amherst, and at the University of Chicago before becoming a professor at Columbia in 1923, where he taught until retiring in 1956. He was president of the American Economic Association in 1935. In 1954, Columbia awarded him an honorary degree. He and his father, the economist **John Bates Clark**, worked together on updating his book *The Control of Trusts*.

617 West 113th Street (near Broadway)

Rosoff, Samuel (ca.1882–1951)
SUBWAY CONTRACTOR

"Subway Sam" made his fortune from building subway tunnels. He started as a hustling newsboy living at the Newsboys Home on East 42nd Street. Selling candy on West Shore Railroad, he met former mayor Seth Low's brother, who gave him a job on a lumber road in the Adirondacks. With his savings, he started a salvage operation that raised a sunken steamship from the bottom of the Gulf of St. Lawrence. Anticipating the need for stone for breakwaters on the Cape Cod Canal, Rosoff bought commitments from quarries for their waste stone. Virtually cornering the market, he made his first fortune. He established the Rosoff Sand and Gravel Company, the Manhattan Ash and Garbage Removal Company, and the Rosoff Subway Construction Company. In 1925, he built his first subway under St. Nicholas Avenue from 122nd to 133rd Streets. In addition to becoming the primary contractor of the city's new Independent subway (IND) with some $50 million of contracts, he purchased and refurbished small railroads elsewhere. Born in Russia, Rosoff worked as a cabin boy to come to the United States in 1895. He bragged that he never went to school a day in his life.

625 West 113th Street (near Riverside Drive)

Schickele, Peter (1935–) ★ ■ 🖎
MUSICAL EDUCATOR AND COMPOSER

P. D. Q. Bach was a musical character created by Schickele. P. D. Q's relatively unknown works that Schickele "discovered" in his research include the "Concerto for Horn and Hardart"; "O Little Town of Hackensack"; "Oedipus Tex," featuring the "O.K. Chorale"; and his homage to fellow Julliard classmate, Philip Glass, "Einstein on the Fritz." Born in Iowa, Schickele graduated from Swarthmore College in Pennsylvania in 1957 as its first student awarded a degree in music. He furthered his education graduating from the Julliard School of Music with an MS degree in musical composition. His early interest in the music of Spike Jones led him to perform similar parodies at Town Hall, and that success led to Lincoln Center and other popular venues. His *Schickele Mix*, a program of musical education that ran for a long period on radio, was priceless. In addition to composing more than one hundred works, he produced a few of Joan Baez's albums and contributed to the infamous Broadway show *Oh! Calcutta!*.

351 West 114th Street (near Morningside Avenue)

Van Doren, Carl Clinton (1885–1950) ★ ■
LITERARY EDITOR AND BIOGRAPHER

Van Doren was awarded the Pulitzer Prize in 1939 for his biography of Benjamin Franklin. His 1921 work *The American Novel* helped reestablish Herman Melville in the forefront of American literature. For different periods, he was the literary editor of *The Nation* and *Century* magazines and the *Cambridge History of American Literature*. He championed distinctly American authors such as Edgar Lee Masters, Robert Frost, Eugene O'Neill, **Sinclair Lewis**, and Edna St. Vincent Millay. After achieving his stature as one of the country's most distinguished men of letters, he actively supported world federalism, which flowered into the United Nations. Born in Illinois, he received a BA degree from the University of Illinois at Urbana-Champaign. In 1911 he earned a doctorate from Columbia University and taught there until 1930. His brother was **Mark Van Doren**.

The Site between 113th and 114th Streets, near Morningside Drive

Van De Water (Vandewater), Harmen (1751–1816)
LANDOWNER

Before there was Morningside Heights, there was Harlem Heights, and before that, Vandewater Heights (Vandewater was Anglicized from the Dutch "Van De Water"). The angle on the building at 2869 Broadway between 111th and 112th Street, is an indicator of the country lane that Harmen Vandewater built from his house, where St. Luke's Hospital is today, to the Bloomingdale Road. After the Bloomingdale Insane Asylum came to Morningside Heights, Vandewater's lane was called Asylum Lane. Vandewater purchased his land from Thomas DeKay. Although his father and family had settled in Queens by the early 1700s, Vandewater seems to have been born in Holland. After living in Vandewater Heights and marrying Maria Barnes in 1782, he appears to have migrated to Dutchess County, New York, sometime before 1800.

Site near 114th Street and Morningside Drive

de Peyster, Frederic Augustus, Jr. (1796–1882) ◼ ▮
LAWYER, LANDOWNER, INVESTOR, AND PHILANTHROPIST

On display in the lobby of the New-York Historical Society is sculptor Thomas Crawford's *The Indian: The Dying Chief Contemplating the Progress of Civilization*. The sculpture was donated to the Society by de Peyster, who was a trustee from 1840 and was president from 1870. In 1876, the 100th anniversary of the Battle of Harlem Heights was celebrated at the de Peyster mansion in Morningside Heights. The mansion was near the battle site and ideal for accommodating the five thousand citizens who attended the festivities. Born in downtown Manhattan, de Peyster earned a bachelor of arts and a doctor of laws from Columbia. He practiced law, and from 1820 to 1837 he was Master of Chancery in New York City, a Brigade Major with the state militia, and a colonel on the staff of Governor DeWitt Clinton. In 1824, he began his association with the New-York Historical Society. At the time of his death, he was thought to belong to more organizations than anyone in the city and published a fair number of historical works. He lived at 76 University Place near Washington Square, but he used his uptown house as a country retreat. His only son was **John Watts de Peyster**.

de Peyster, John Watts (1821–1907)
BRIGADIER GENERAL, LANDOWNER, AND PHILANTHROPIST

John Watts de Peyster was actively involved as a volunteer firefighter and with the state's militia. Along with others, he helped shape New York City's police and fire departments. A native New Yorker, John studied law at Columbia but did not graduate because of poor health. In time he would receive an MA degree from Columbia, an LLD from Nebraska College, and a PhD from Franklin & Marshall College. His militia fought in the Mexican War, but when the Civil War broke out, he was more active behind the scenes. In his later years, he focused his philanthropy on Tivoli, New York, the town of his estate, Rose Hill. He wrote extensively about military history and donated his collections to the Smithsonian and to Franklin & Marshall College. He was the only child of **Frederic Augustus de Peyster, Jr.**

411 WEST 114TH STREET (NEAR MORNINGSIDE DRIVE)
Brooks (Pitcher), Harriet (1876–1933) ★ ◼ ▮ ☞
NUCLEAR PHYSICIST

In her day, Brooks was thought to be second only to Marie Curie among women in the field of nuclear physics. Her discovery of the recoil of a radioactive atom led to the discovery of new radioactive elements

Harriet Brooks.

and isotopes. Born in Canada, Brooks graduated from McGill University in 1898 with a BA degree in mathematics and natural philosophy. She continued her studies at McGill under her professor Sir Ernest Rutherford and became the first woman there to attain a master's degree in electromagnetism. Following, she was a fellow at Bryn Mawr College, and a fellow in the Cavendish Laboratory at Cambridge, England. In 1906, she did some work under the direction of Madame Curie at the Sorbonne in Paris. In 1904, she was appointed to Barnard's faculty. Upon announcing her engagement to a Columbia professor, Bergen Davis, Dean Laura Gill demanded she resign. The injustice notwithstanding, and after a fruitless defense by Margaret Maltby, the head of the physics department, Brooks did not marry Davis but did marry a Canadian physicist, Frank Pitcher, and retired to married life in Montreal. Along the way, she befriended the Russian writer Maxim Gorky in New York, and they became part of the small Summer Brook socialist community in the Adirondacks. In 1929, her daughter, Barbara Pitcher, was the subject of an intensive search in Canada and the United States after being reported missing from her studies at McGill. Sadly, she was found drowned in a river near Montreal. Harriet Brooks is a most worthy member of the Canadian Science and Engineering Hall of Fame. Brooks also lived at **44 Morningside Drive** (near 115th Street).

May, Rollo Reece (1909–1994)
PSYCHOLOGIST

Love and Will was one of Rollo May's best sellers in 1969. In the year of Woodstock, it contended that man should affirm his humanity rather than gratify his biological needs. An Ohio native, May graduated from Oberlin in 1930. While teaching at a missionary school in Greece, he was inspired by the Austrian psychologist Alfred Adler to practice psychology in a religious, helping way. The philosopher and theologian Paul Tillich would become a good friend and strong influence on him. May studied at Union Theological Seminary, was briefly a Congregational minister, and then went on to Columbia's Teachers College for his PhD in clinical psychology. His fifteen books constitute a humanistic approach to existential psychology. They touch upon subjects such as the causes of anxiety, positive potential and self-fulfillment, and religion and humanity. May co-founded the Association for Humanistic Psychology. He also lived at **310 Riverside Drive** (near 103rd Street), the Master Apartments, and **601 West 115th Street** (near Broadway).

Rostow, Elspeth Vaughn Davies (1917–2007)
PROFESSOR OF POLITICAL SCIENCE AND PRESIDENTIAL ADVISOR

Elspeth Rostow was known to have composed wickedly funny limericks too racy to be published. She also advised presidents of the United States, as did her renowned husband, Walt W. Rostow, taking heat for their hawkish stands. A native New Yorker, Rostow graduated from Barnard in 1938, and she graduated with master's degrees in history from Radcliffe College in 1939 and from the University of Cambridge, England, in 1949. She started teaching at Barnard in 1939, where she was one of the founders of American Studies as an academic discipline. During World War II, she analyzed dispatches from the French Resistance, working in the Office of Strategic Services. In 1942, she married Walt Rostow. After the war, they lived in Geneva, Switzerland, for three years, and in 1948, she authored the book *European Economic Construction*. During the 1950s, the Rostows taught at the Massachusetts Institute of Technology. In 1961, her husband joined the Kennedy administration, and she taught at Georgetown and American universities in Washington, D.C. From 1969, they were a strong presence at the University of Texas in Austin. Rostow also lived at **39 Claremont Avenue** (near 119th Street).

Swope, Herbert Bayard (1882–1958), Journalist, Editor, and Newspaper Executive ★ ◼ ▮

(See bio for Swope at **530 West 113th Street**.)

Wilson, Edmund Beecher "E B" (1856–1939) ★ ◼ ▮
ZOOLOGIST AND GENETICIST

Wilson is the person who determined that males have XY chromosomes and females have XX. He also discovered the excess or so-called B chromosomes. Wilson is regarded as the first cell biologist in the United States. His 1896 textbook *The Cell*, which ran 1,232 pages, was a classic in its field. It went to three editions and was widely used until sometime after World War II. Born in Illinois, Wilson graduated from Yale in 1878 and earned a PhD degree at Johns Hopkins University in 1881. After lecturing at Williams College and the Massachusetts Institute of Technology, and holding a professorship at Bryn Mawr, he arrived at Columbia University in 1891. He retired with emeritus status after thirty-seven years, having established the department of zoology. Additionally, he was president of the New York Academy of Arts and Sciences, the American Society of Zoologists, the American Society of Naturalists, and the American Association for the Advancement of Science. He was also an honorary fellow at the Royal Society at Edinburgh and the Cambridge Philosophical Society. Many of his summers were spent at the Marine Biological Laboratory in Woods Hole, Massachusetts.

508 West 114th Street (near Amsterdam Avenue), the Arizona

Fiske, Thomas Scott (1865–1944), Mathematician ▮

(See bio for Fiske at **527 West 110th Street**.)

Hayes, Carleton J. H. (1882–1964)
PROFESSOR OF HISTORY AND AMBASSADOR

In 1950, Hayes left his classroom as a teacher at Columbia University exactly fifty years after he began there as a student. He was the Seth Low Professor of History with an aristocratic air that suggested much of his past. Born in upstate New York, Hayes graduated from Columbia in 1904 and earned his PhD there in 1909. From 1907, he taught history at Columbia. He served in World War I with the rank of captain and went back to teaching. He achieved full professorship at Columbia in 1919 and would head up the history department more than once. A converted and devout Roman Catholic, he was always leaning to the right politically and more than partial to nationalism. From 1942 to 1945, he was the Ambassador to Spain and was thought by some to be a little too friendly with Franco. Others thought that he kept Franco from siding with the Axis powers during World War II. He was the first Roman Catholic co-chairman of the National Conference of Christians and Jews, served as head of the New York State Historical Association, and was president of the American Historical Association. The author of thirty books, Hayes was awarded Columbia's Alexander Hamilton medal in 1952 and was presented with nine honorary degrees in his lifetime. He also lived at four other addresses in the neighborhood: **1124 Amsterdam Avenue** (near 115th Street), **427 West 117th Street** (near Morningside Avenue), **430 West 118th Street** (near Amsterdam Avenue), and **88 Morningside Drive** (near 119th Street).

Saltus, Edgar Evertson (1855–1921)
AUTHOR AND PUBLICIST

A fairly well-known and highly acclaimed author in his day, Saltus has been almost completely forgotten. His work was wide-ranging, including his *Historia Amoris: A History of Love, Ancient and Modern*, more than a dozen novels, and books on Honore de Balzac and Oscar Wilde. He also dabbled in poetry. Two of his novels, *The Paliser Case* and

Edgar Saltus.

Daughters of the Rich, were made into silent films in the early 1920s—one produced by **Samuel Goldwyn**. Saltus was part of a bohemian circle in New York that included his half-brother, the minor poet Francis Saltus. In Europe, where he visited several times, he knew the likes of Arthur Conan Doyle and Oscar Wilde, with whom he is sometimes compared. Born in New York City, Saltus studied at the Sorbonne in Paris, at Munich University, at Heidelberg University, and at Yale. In 1880, he graduated from Columbia Law School.

514 West 114th Street (near Amsterdam Avenue)

Buchman, Sidney (1902–1975)
SCREENWRITER

Buchman won the Best Screenplay Oscar for the 1941 film *Here Comes Mr. Jordan.* Three of his other scripts were nominated for Academy Awards: *Mr. Smith Goes to Washington* in 1940, *The Talk of the Town* in 1943, and *Jolson Sings Again* in 1950. After refusing to cooperate with the House Un-American Activities Committee, he was blacklisted until the 1960s. However, he returned to work on the scripts for *Cleopatra* in 1963 and *The Group* in 1966. Born in Minnesota, Buchman attended the University of Minnesota but graduated from Columbia in 1923. From his first screenplay, *Sign of the Cross* for Cecil B. DeMille in 1932, he became one of the most accomplished screenwriters in the country. He also worked on such films as *If I Had a Million* in 1932, *She Married Her Boss* in 1935, and *Lost Horizon* in 1937.

536 West 114th Street (near Broadway)

Ginsberg, Allen (1926–1997) ◼
POET

Beat Generation poet Allen Ginsberg is among the chorus on the John Lennon and Yoko Ono 1969 anti-war hit "Give Peace a Chance." Born in Newark, Ginsberg grew up in Paterson, New Jersey. After a brief period at Montclair State College, he turned to Columbia and earned a BA While at Columbia, he hung out with Jack Kerouac, Lucien Carr, and William Burroughs, who collectively became known as the Beats. Walt Whitman and the literary environment at Columbia were influences, but Ginsberg defied convention and lived a life that seemed to value outrageousness for its own sake. Returning to Paterson after college, he found a mentor in William Carlos Williams. As an early experimenter with LSD and a follower of transcendentalism, he found his way to San Francisco in the mid-1950s where he met his life partner, Peter Orlovsky. It is also where he produced his masterwork "Howl," which gave him national acclaim and notoriety because of the censorship issues arising from its frank descriptions of such matters as homosexuality. He traveled extensively and constantly composed poetry, probably not caring about who might be offended, but undoubtedly aware of the attention he was receiving. Protesting the Vietnam War and supporting other liberal causes just seemed to be a part of who he was. Ginsberg was truly larger than his own life. Ginsberg also lived at **627 West 115th Street** (near Riverside Drive).

611 West 114th Street (near Broadway)

Zukor, Adolph (1873–1976), Motion Picture Pioneer ★ ▪

(See bio for Zukor at **808 West End Avenue**.)

622 West 114th Street (near Riverside Drive), Revere Hall

DeMille, Cecil Blount (1881–1959) ★ ▪
FILM PIONEER

On the same day, DeMille hired William "Hopalong Cassidy" Boyd, **Gloria Swanson**, and Hal Roach. DeMille's film, *The Squaw Man*, completed in 1914, was the first feature film shot in Hollywood and the first to use indoor lighting. It was also the first movie to promote its star Dustin Farnum. DeMille made about sixty silent films including such classics as *The Ten Commandments* and *The King of Kings*. His nearly twenty sound movies included such gems as *Cleopatra,* starring Claudette Colbert; *The Greatest Show on Earth*; and his last film, the 1956 remake of *The Ten Commandments*, starring Charlton Heston. Many will remember that he appeared as himself in Billy Wilder's *Sunset Boulevard*. His numerous awards included Knight of the Legion of Honor from the French. Born in Massachusetts, he first worked as an actor on the Broadway stage. He then directed, produced, and took a troupe out west in 1913 to film the first epic movie, *The Squaw Man*. The film was a big success for his partner, **Jesse Lasky**, whose company would become the foundation for Paramount Pictures. DeMille's older brother was **W. C. DeMille**, and his niece was the dancer and choreographer Agnes DeMille.

Obama, Barack (1961–), President of the United States ★ ■

(See bio for Obama at **142 West 109th Street**.)

205 West 115th Street (near Adam Clayton Powell, Jr. Boulevard)

Schomburg, Arturo Alfonso (1874–1938), Historian, Collector, and Curator ■ ☞

(See bio for Schomburg in **The Old Community**.)

403 West 115th Street (near Morningside Drive).

Greene, Belle da Costa (1883–1950), Librarian and Advisor to J. P. Morgan ▮

(See bio for Greene in **The Old Community**.)

415 West 115th Street (near Amsterdam Avenue)

Erskine, John (1879–1951), Educator, Author, and Musician ● ▪ ☜

(See bio for Erskine at **609 West 113th Street**.)

416 West 115th Street (near Amsterdam Avenue)

Mullins, George W. (1881–1956)
PROFESSOR OF MATHEMATICS

Mullins is responsible for the SAT examination. His work with the College Entrance Examination Board, of which he was executive secretary from 1933 to 1946, advocated for the college and university community to adopt the Scholastic Aptitude Test. Born in Arkansas, Mullins was educated at the University of Arkansas and Columbia, from which he received his PhD in 1917. He came to Barnard in 1913 after teaching at Mount Hope College in Arkansas and Simmons College in Texas. At Barnard, he rose to full professorship and was acting dean from 1929 to 1931. In addition, he was the author of such books as *Answers to Freshman Mathematics* in 1927, and he co-authored *Analytic Geometry* in 1924, *Plane Trigonometry* in 1927, and *College Algebra* in 1930. Mullins also lived at **460 Riverside Drive** (near 119th Street).

419 West 115th Street (near Amsterdam Avenue)

Clapp, Elsie Ripley (1879–1965)
PROGRESSIVE EDUCATION PIONEER

Clapp began her professional career endeavoring to help the children of the workers who were striking against the Paterson silk manufacturers in 1913. She worked alongside John Reed, Carlo Tresca, Elizabeth Gurley Flynn, and Margaret Sanger. The most important influence in her life, however, was the philosopher and educator, John Dewey. She served as his teaching assistant and aide from 1909 to 1913 and from 1925 to 1929. Much influenced by his progressive educational philosophy, she taught in several rural schools through the 1910s and 1920s. In 1934, she was selected to be the director of school and community affairs at the Arthurdale experiment in West Virginia. It was a favorite project of her friend, Eleanor Roosevelt, to house unemployed miners in a self-sufficient community. It was a significant step in the direction of progressive education, but ultimately it was a failure. After leaving Arthurdale in 1936, Clapp edited the journal *Progressive Education* for three years, and she authored two educational books into her retirement. She was born in Brooklyn Heights, and she was educated at Vassar, Barnard, Columbia, and Teachers College. Clapp also lived at **415 West 118th Street** (near Morningside Drive).

Vollmer (Adams, Burroughs), Joan (1923–1951)
BEAT GENERATION FIGURE

Vollmer was accidentally shot in the head and killed by her common-law husband, the writer **William S. Burroughs**. She was central to the Beat Generation history in providing means and rationale for the players to connect. Born in upstate New York, Vollmer attended Barnard. She married a Columbia student who divorced her when he came back from serving in World War II. Meanwhile, she started hanging out with some of the well-known Beat Generation characters such as **Jack Kerouac**, Lucien Carr, **Allen Ginsberg**, and Burroughs, with whom she migrated to Mexico City. Burroughs was arrested for her murder, but he successfully extricated himself, leaving behind mounds of controversy. In the 2000 movie *Beat*, Kiefer Sutherland plays Burroughs, and Courtney Love plays Vollmer. She also lived at **421 West 118th Street** (near Amsterdam Avenue).

600 West 115th Street (near Broadway)

Reichard, Gladys Amanda (1893–1955) ■ ▯

ANTHROPOLOGIST

Reichard studied the Navajo people. In addition to devoting seven years to learning their language, she lived with a Navajo family to better understand their life. She authored more than a dozen books on Navajo language, culture, and customs, which earned her numerous awards from institutions such as the New York Academy of Sciences and the International Folklore Association. Born in Pennsylvania, Reichard graduated from Swarthmore College in 1919 and received her PhD from Columbia University in 1925. The following year, she studied at the University of Hamburg, Germany, on a Guggenheim Fellowship. She joined the Barnard faculty in 1921 and was appointed a full Professor of Anthropology in 1951. Margaret Mead spoke at her memorial service.

601 West 115th Street (near Broadway)

May, Rollo Reece (1909–1994), Psychologist

(See bio for May at 411 West 114th Street.)

627 West 115th Street (near Riverside Drive)

Ginsberg, Allen (1926–1997), Poet ■

(See bio for Ginsberg at 536 West 114th Street.)

633 West 115th Street (near Riverside Drive)

Fox, Dixon Ryan (1887–1945) ▯

EDUCATOR

Before Fox was appointed president of Union College, he was an immensely respected professor of history at Columbia University. He was widely published, his work including the twelve-volume *A History of American Life*, which he co-edited with Arthur Schlesinger. He also edited the *Columbia University Quarterly* and served as president of the New-York Historical Society. Born in upstate New York, Fox graduated from Columbia with a BA degree, an MA degree, and, in 1917, a PhD. He worked as a research assistant at the Carnegie Institute for Historical Research for three years and taught history at Columbia until 1934 when he left to head up Union College in Schenectady, New York. His wife, Barnard graduate Marion Stickley Osgood, was the daughter of Columbia political science professor Herbert Levi Osgood.

404 West 116th Street (near Morningside Drive)

Ginsburg, Ruth Bader (1933–2020) ★ ■
ASSOCIATE JUSTICE OF THE SUPREME COURT

Ginsburg was only the second woman appointed to the United States Supreme Court, the first being Sandra Day O'Connor. As one of the first twenty female law professors in the country, she was more than exceptional. She graduated from high school at age 15, was the highest-ranking female student when she graduated from Cornell, and tied for first in her class when she graduated from Columbia Law School. Her distinguished and continuing tenure on the Supreme Court is worthy of many books yet to be written and has inspired even motion picture representations. Born Joan Ruth Bader in Brooklyn, she graduated in 1954 with a BA degree from Cornell, where she met her husband, Martin Ginsburg. They moved to Oklahoma, where he was stationed in the Reserve Officers' Training Corps, and where she worked for the Social Security Administration. In 1956, she enrolled in Harvard Law School but transferred to Columbia Law School when her husband took employment in New York City. She worked as a research assistant at the Law School until she was appointed a professor at Rutgers

School of Law in 1963. She became general counsel for the ACLU in 1973, where she began arguing before the Supreme Court and earned her reputation as the leading litigator for women's rights. In 1980, President Jimmy Carter appointed Ginsburg to the US Court of Appeals in Washington, D.C. In 1993, President Bill Clinton nominated her for the Supreme Court, and she was confirmed by a Senate vote of 96 to 3.

411 West 116th Street (near Morningside Drive), Wein Hall

Apgar, Virginia (1909–1974) ■ ☞
OBSTETRICAL ANESTHESIOLOGIST

Virginia Apgar.

Dr. Apgar played the violin, often in amateur chamber groups, and made two violins: a viola, and a cello. She was also a golfer, a fly-fisher, a gardener, and a stamp collector. She took flying lessons and stated that she wanted to fly under the George Washington Bridge. By day, she became the first director of Physician and Surgeons' division of anesthesia and its first female full professor. Her clinical and research work at the Sloane Hospital for Women led to the use of the Apgar Score to summarize the health of newborn babies. Born in New Jersey, Apgar graduated from Mount Holyoke College in 1929, from Columbia's College of Physicians and Surgeons in 1933, and she earned a master's degree in public health from Johns Hopkins University in 1959. Ever involved with public health, she was a force in the March of Dimes. In addition to authoring some sixty articles on health topics, in 1973 she and journalist Joan Beck co-authored the popular book *Is My Baby All Right?* In 1994, a stamp was issued in her honor, and the following year she was inducted into the National Women's Hall of Fame in Seneca Falls, New York.

Leo Szilard.

Charles A. Beard.

420 West 116th Street (near Morningside Drive), Royal Crown Hotel

Szilard, Leo (1898–1964) ★ ◾
PHYSICIST

Szilard wrote the letter to President Franklin Roosevelt that was signed by Albert Einstein and gave birth to the Manhattan Project, which developed the atomic bomb. Szilard conceived of the nuclear chain reaction in 1933 and the cyclotron in 1929, and before that, the idea of a nuclear microscope. At the very beginning of nuclear science, he worked with Einstein in Germany and Enrico Fermi at Columbia. Szilard was born in Hungary, studied engineering at the Budapest Institute of Technology, and served in the Austrian Army during World War I. He moved to Berlin and studied theoretical physics to earn a PhD from the University of Berlin. After teaching there for ten years, he migrated away from the growing Nazi threat to London, Oxford, and, in 1938, to New York and Columbia.

430 West 116th Street (near Amsterdam Avenue)

Beard, Charles Austin (1874–1948) ◾
HISTORIAN

Charles Beard was one of the most influential historians of his day. His book *An Economic Interpretation of the Constitution of the United States* posited that the founding fathers were motivated more by a desire to preserve their wealth and less by political principles. Born in Indiana, Beard was educated at Methodist DePauw University, Oxford University, and finally at Columbia University where he received his doctorate and continued to teach. Beard resigned from Columbia, protesting, among other things, its support of involvement in the World War. His wife, **Mary Ritter Beard**, was also a historian and his intellectual partner. The Beards also lived at **400 West 118th Street** (near Morningside Drive).

Beard, Mary Ritter (1876–1958)
HISTORIAN

Mary Ritter Beard.

Mary Beard wrote several books on women's role in history, and collaborated with her husband, **Charles Austin Beard**, on *The Rise of American Civilization*. Born in Indiana, as was her husband, whom she met at DePauw University, she did some graduate work in sociology at Columbia. Her efforts in the suffrage movement were extensive as she organized demonstrations, lectured, edited publications, and testified before Congress. In addition to writing a multivolume work on American history, she also authored works on labor history and women's history. Mary and Charles Beard also lived at **400 West 118th Street** (near Morningside Drive).

Kasner, Edward (1878–1955)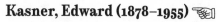
PROFESSOR, MATHEMATICIAN, AND "GOOGLE" ORIGINATOR

It was Edward Kasner's 9-year-old nephew who invented the word "googol" when the professor asked for a suggested word to describe the number one followed by 100 zeros. The Google search engine name is a simplified spelling of "googol." Kasner's forte was making mathematics understandable and interesting. His 1940 bestseller *Mathematics and the Imagination,* co-authored with James R. Newman, inspired countless future mathematicians. A New York native, Kasner graduated from City College with a BA degree and from Columbia with an AM and a PhD. He also studied at the University of Gottingen, Germany. In 1906 he joined Columbia's faculty. Columbia awarded him an Honorary Doctor of Science the year before he died.

Mullan, Helen St. Clair (1877–1936) ■ ▊
LAWYER

Helen Mullan was one of the four Barnard students that founded the international women's fraternity, Alpha Omicron Pi in 1897. In 1899, she married George Vincent Mullin, who was appointed a State Supreme Court Justice in 1916. Previously, Helen and George were lawyers in the firm of Mitchel & Mullan, the first name referring to Mayor **John Purroy Mitchel**. A New York native and daughter of an editor of the *New York Tribune* and the *New York Times*, she graduated from Barnard in 1898 with an AB degree and from New York University in 1901 with an LLB. She was the first chairman of the Barnard Alumnae Council, president of the Associate Alumnae, and, in 1921, became a Barnard trustee. Mullan also lived at **344 West 123rd Street** (near Manhattan Avenue).

439 West 116th Street (near Morningside Drive)

Maltby, Margaret Eliza (1860–1944) ■ ▊
PHYSICIST

Maltby was the first woman to receive a BA degree at the Massachusetts Institute of Technology in 1891. Shortly after, she became the first woman to attain a PhD in Physics at the German University of Gottingen, which had graduated Heinrich Heine, Arthur Schopenhauer, Max Weber, the Brothers Grimm, Carl Friedrich Gauss, John von Neumann, Edward Teller, and J. Robert Oppenheimer. Born in Ohio, Maltby obtained her BA and MA degrees from Oberlin College in her home state. Then she taught physics at Wellesley College, Massachusetts, for four years. She arrived at Barnard in 1900, taught chemistry at first, then physics, and soon chaired the physics department. Her course on the physics of music might have been the first in the country. Maltby also lived at **21 Claremont Avenue** (near 116th Street) and **400 West 118th Street** (near Morningside Drive).

Margaret Eliza Maltby.

600 West 116th Street (near Broadway)

Jackson, Abraham Valentine "A.V." Williams (1862–1937) 📖 ☞
PROFESSOR OF INDO-IRANIAN LANGUAGES

Jackson was one of the world's leading authorities on Indo-Iranian Languages. Columbia gave him his AB AM, LHD (Doctor of Humane Letters), PhD, and LLD. His formal dress, accented with an ascot held in place by a gold stickpin, suggested his uniqueness. Born in New York, Jackson graduated from Columbia in 1883, and for two years was at the University of Halle in Germany. After first teaching English and Literature, Columbia created a professorship of Indo-Iranian languages, which Jackson occupied until his retirement in 1935. He was a member of many organizations and president of some, including the American Philological Society, the American Philosophical Society, the American Institute of Persian Art, the American Oriental Society, the American School for Oriental Research, the Yonkers Board of Education and the Yonkers Public Library. He wrote a nine-volume history of India and edited the thirteen-volume *Columbia University Indo-Iranian Series*. Anyone attempting to read Zoroastrian manuscripts, some of which Jackson received for his work in India, will need to reference his seminal work on the Avestan language.

Rabi, Isador Isaac "I. I." (1898–1988), Physicist ★ ▪

(See bio for Rabi at **450 Riverside Drive**.)

Rudd, Mark (1947–)
STUDENT ACTIVIST

Rudd was elected president of Columbia University's chapter of the Students for a Democratic Society, known as the SDS Castro invited Rudd and other SDS leaders to Cuba. Rudd was both impressed and inspired. Perhaps, this was the impetus that led to the protests on Columbia's campus in 1968. He was arrested along with hundreds of other students and then was expelled from Columbia. He became the leader of an SDS faction, the Revolutionary Youth Movement, which led to the formation of the militant Weathermen. When some of their members accidentally blew up a Greenwich Village Townhouse, Rudd and others went underground. In 1977, he surfaced, moved to New Mexico, taught mathematics at a community college, and on occasion, provides nostalgic insight into all that that happened in the 1960s. Born in New Jersey, Rudd attended Columbia but didn't graduate.

606 West 116th Street (near Broadway)

Norworth, John "Jack" (1879–1959), Vaudeville Performer and Songwriter ▪

(See bio for Norworth at **624 West End Avenue**.)

Reimer, Marie (1875–1962)
ORGANIC CHEMIST AND PROFESSOR

Reimer was the first woman to receive a professional appointment in chemistry from Columbia University, and she established the chemistry department at Barnard College. From 1904, she dedicated more than forty years to teaching at Barnard and retired as emerita professor of chemistry in 1945. She was an honorary member of the American Chemical Society and a fellow of the New York Academy of Sciences. The Marie Reimer Scholarship Fund Prize is awarded each year to an outstanding student majoring in chemistry. Born in Pennsylvania, she received an AB degree from Vassar College in 1897. She studied for two years at the University of Berlin in Germany, but her PhD was earned at Bryn Mawr in 1904.

607 West 116th Street, Brooks Hall on Barnard's Campus and Livingston Hall (116th Street and Broadway) on Columbia's campus

Kemp, William Cullen Bryant (ca. 1850–1929) 🖝
PERENNIAL STUDENT

Kemp earned fourteen degrees from Columbia: MD, AM, AB, LLB, LLM, PhD, CE, EE, MechE, Phar, Chem, and three AB degrees. Born in Wisconsin, he came to New York as a youngster. Enrolled in Columbia in 1872, he initially had an aversion to schoolwork, but a relative's will, which provided him with $2,500 each year that he stayed in school, led him to pursue the academic. When not studying, he played tennis at the Racquet and Tennis Club and traveled extensively.

House on the Grounds of the Bloomingdale Insane Asylum (later the Site of the Columbia University Campus), centered at Broadway and 116th Street

Bloomingdale Asylum, 1881.

Nichols, Charles Henry (1820–1889) ★ ■ ☜
PHYSICIAN AND HOSPITAL ADMINISTRATOR

Nichols was born in Maine, studied medicine at the University of New York (now New York University), and graduated from the medical department of the University of Pennsylvania in 1843. In 1847, he became the associate physician at the New York State Lunatic Asylum in Utica, New York. In 1849, he was appointed the physician and head of the Bloomingdale Insane Asylum, which occupied the land later to become Columbia University's campus. Dorothy Dix came to the Bloomingdale Asylum and gave a report that led to Nichols's dismissal in 1852, but the following year, Dix and Nichols carried on a flirtatious correspondence. With her recommendation, President Millard Fillmore appointed Nichols the first superintendent of the new national mental institution called the Government Hospital, later St. Elizabeth's. In 1877, Nichols returned to the Bloomingdale Insane Asylum as medical superintendent until his death in 1889.

116th Street and Broadway, Columbia University

Cole, Frank Nelson (1861–1926) ☜
PROFESSOR OF MATHEMATICS

Making a presentation in 1903 to the American Mathematical Society, of which he was secretary, Cole showed on a blackboard that 147,573,952,589,676,412,927 was a factor of 193,707,721 <@@ts>× 761,838,257,287. After he completed the calculations, which took an hour, his fellow mathematicians gave him a standing ovation. They knew that the large number was created by raising 2 to the power of 67 and subtracting 1 and might have been a prime number. Cole proved that it wasn't because it could be expressed as the product of two numbers. Born in Massachusetts, he graduated from Harvard in

1881, and continued there to earn his MA and PhD degrees. From 1883 to 1885, he studied in Leipzig, Germany, under the mathematician Felix Klein, of Klein Bottle fame. After receiving tutoring at Harvard, he was tutored at the University of Michigan from 1888 until he was appointed a professor at Columbia in 1895. His few published works on number theory, on group theory, and on the icosahedron affirm his renown. He didn't live at Columbia, but he had all his mail delivered there. Supposedly, he didn't let Columbia know where he lived. At his death, he was living in a small house off the Grand Concourse in the Bronx, under the name of Edward Mitchell, and pretending to be a bookkeeper.

Near Broadway and 116th Street, Superintendent's House on the Grounds of the Bloomingdale Insane Asylum

Earle, Pliny (1809–1892) ■
PHYSICIAN

Dr. Earle was head of the Bloomingdale Insane Asylum, which stood on the site that Columbia University would eventually occupy. Dr. Earle's experience at the asylum would spark his interest in challenging the "curability" rates of mid-nineteenth-century mental hospitals. At the time, mental hospitals were posting cure rates as high as 90 percent. Earle published an important work on the topic, *The Curability of Insanity*, which noted the lack of uniform standards of diagnosis and classification and the negligent manner of counting readmissions. A Massachusetts native, he graduated from the University of Pennsylvania Medical School in 1837, studied in Europe for a year, served on the staff of the Friends Hospital in Philadelphia and in 1844 became Superintendent of the Bloomingdale Insane Asylum, serving until 1849. In 1864, he became Superintendent of the Northampton State

Hospital in Massachusetts. He was president of the Superintendents' Association and a very active member, during its formative years. He also served as president of the American Academy of Medicine and the New York Academy of Medicine.

Near Broadway and 116th Street, Superintendent's House on the Grounds of the Bloomingdale Insane Asylum

MacDonald, James (1803–1849)
PHYSICIAN AT THE BLOOMINGDALE INSANE ASYLUM

Cornelius Vanderbilt sent his wife to the insane asylum in Flushing when MacDonald was in charge. A few years later, Vanderbilt would twice send his son to the Bloomingdale Insane Asylum. Born in White Plains, New York, MacDonald apprenticed to a local physician but also studied under the great Dr. David Hosack, who attended to Alexander Hamilton at his deathbed. MacDonald received his MD degree in 1825 from the College of Physicians and Surgeons, now part of Columbia, and then dedicated his life to the care and treatment of mental illness. From 1825 to 1830 and from 1832 to 1837 he was the physician in charge of the Bloomingdale Insane Asylum. He spent the in-between year of 1831 visiting insane asylums in Europe. Thereafter, he was in private practice and affiliated with New York Hospital. In 1841, he founded an asylum in the Murray Hill neighborhood. He then headed up an asylum in Flushing, Queens, where he died and is buried. His son, James Allen MacDonald, was a financier and an associate of Montana senator William Clark, whose daughter Huguette died in 2012, leaving behind the largest apartment in New York City at 907 Fifth Avenue.

Bloomingdale Insane Asylum, 116th–118th Streets between Broadway and Amsterdam Avenues, the Site That Became Columbia University

Vanderbilt, Cornelius Jeremiah (1830–1882) ☞

SON OF WEALTH

Cornelius Vanderbilt had his son Cornelius Jeremiah Vanderbilt committed to the Bloomingdale Insane Asylum, not once, but twice. The first time was when 18-year-old Cornelius ran off to the California gold strike of 1849 and returned empty-handed, which the senior Cornelius deemed to be evidence that his son was crazy. If not crazy, the youngster was irresponsible. He mooched $50,000 off Horace Greeley to feed his gambling habit, made worse by epileptic seizures. In 1854, his father put him in the Bloomingdale Insane Asylum again. Young Cornelius never measured up to his brother William Henry Vanderbilt, who inherited his father's railroad business and $95 million. Junior inherited only $5 million and wound up committing suicide in 1882.

607 West 116th Street (near Claremont Avenue), Brooks Hall on Barnard campus

Brett, Agnes Baldwin (1876–1955)

NUMISMATIST AND ARCHEOLOGIST

Brett was the first curator of the American Numismatic Society. In 1919, she was only the second recipient of its Huntington Medal. She authored about five catalogs and thirty articles about ancient coins. Her work on Greek and Roman coins and her collection, which included a group of Babylonian Cylinder seals, were especially renowned. She was an honorary curator of Greek Coins for the Boston Museum of Fine

Arts, as well as a Fellow of the Royal Numismatic Society of London and an honorary member of the Belgian and Romanian Numismatic Societies. Brett was born in Newark, New Jersey. She graduated from Barnard in 1897, then earned a master's degree from Columbia three years later and studied further in Paris and Athens. She guest-lectured at Columbia in 1936. Her husband was the philanthropist George Brett and her father-in-law was Professor of Accountancy Philip Brett.

Hutchinson, Emilie Josephine (1877–1938) ▪

ECONOMIST AND HEAD OF BARNARD'S ECONOMICS DEPARTMENT

Hutchinson's books entitled *Women's Wages* and *Women and the PhD*, which was cited in Jill Lepore's book *The Secret History of Wonder Woman*, were at the forefront of the development of women's studies. Born in Canada, Hutchinson graduated from Barnard in 1905, earned AM and PhD degrees from Columbia and attained membership in Phi Beta Kappa. She taught at Mount Holyoke and Wellesley before becoming an associate professor at Barnard. Her additional activities included various roles in occupational and higher academic endeavors. She lived on the Barnard campus in Brooks Hall (3009 Broadway near 119th Street).

Kemp, William Cullen Bryant (ca. 1850–1929), Perennial Student ☜

(See bio for Kemp at **Livingston Hall on 116th Street**.)

616 West 116th Street (near Claremont Avenue)

Benedict, Ruth Fulton (1887–1948), Professor of Anthropology and Folkways ★ ■

(See bio for Benedict at **448 Central Park West**.)

Gold, Grace (ca.1961–1979)

STUDENT

The cross street of 115th Street and Broadway is called Grace Gold Way. Sadly, she was killed when a large piece of terra cotta from a seventh-floor window arrangement at 601 West 115th Street fell and struck her. She was a freshman at Barnard, Class of '82. Columbia owned the building, so a financial settlement, however inadequate to the tragic circumstances, was made with the family. New York City reacted by passing Local Law 10 the following year, and then amended it with Local Law 11 in 1998, both of which required regular, detailed building inspections by licensed architects or engineers. Grace Gold Way came about through the efforts of Grace's older sister Lori, a Barnard graduate, who enlisted the help of Norman Weiss, a professor at Columbia University's Graduate School of Architecture, Planning, and Preservation. In 2013, Lori Gold established the Grace Gold Scholarship Fund in Grace's memory.

Hardwick, Elizabeth Bruce (1916–2007) ■ ▣

WRITER AND LITERARY CRITIC

Hardwick was one of the co-founders of the *New York Review of Books* along with her husband, Robert Lowell; Jason and Barbara Epstein; and Robert B. Silvers. Just three years earlier, in 1959, she wrote an essay in *Harper's* magazine entitled "The Decline of Book Reviewing." Born in Kentucky, Hardwick earned her undergraduate and master's degrees at the University of Kentucky. She dropped out of a doctorate program at Columbia to write short stories and the novel *The Ghostly Lover*. She joined the *Partisan Review* magazine and wrote a wide variety of essays and reviews of fiction, nonfiction, and plays. Her essays were anthologized in four volumes published from 1962 to 1998. She taught writing at Barnard for twenty-five years. In addition to serving on the board of the National Book Critics Circle, she was on many literary award juries, including the Pulitzer Prize, and was a fellow of the American Academy of Arts and Sciences.

Rice, Grantland (1880–1954) ★ ■
SPORTSWRITER

Rice coined the phrase "The Four Horsemen" to describe the backfield of the football team of Notre Dame College. And "not that you won or lost—but how you played the game" came from his poem "Alumnus Football." Born in Tennessee, he received his BA degree from Vanderbilt University where he played football and baseball. He served in World War I as a lieutenant. After starter jobs for newspapers in Atlanta, Cleveland, and Nashville, he became a sportswriter for a few other newspapers before joining the *New York Tribune* in 1914. Acknowledged as the "Dean of American Sports Writers," he was the first sportswriter to become a well-known personality. He advocated for sports figures like Babe Ruth, Knute Rockne, Babe Didrikson Zaharias, and Jack Dempsey to be valued as professionals. Rice shared an apartment on West 116th Street with **Rube Goldberg**. Rice also lived at **450 Riverside Drive** (near 116th Street).

Grantland Rice.

620 West 116th Street (near Riverside Drive)

Hill, Patty Smith (1868–1948) ◼

EDUCATOR AND CO-AUTHOR OF "HAPPY BIRTHDAY"

Patty Hill wrote the words and her sister Mildred wrote the music to a song, "Good Morning to All," that would become popular when the lyrics were changed to "Happy Birthday to You." In 1893, the Hill sisters co-wrote *Song Stories for the Kindergarten*, which included their classic song. The history of the song is a story unto itself, spanning more than a hundred years and famously surrounded by interesting copyright issues. The sisters were born and raised in Kentucky. Mildred died in 1916, but Patty Hill joined the faculty at Teachers College and, in 1924, created the Institute of Child Welfare, which fostered a progressive philosophy in kindergarten teaching. Patty Hill Blocks were large blocks employed in her teaching. Columbia University awarded her an honorary doctorate in 1929. Hill also lived at **21 Claremont Avenue** (near 116th Street).

Trilling, Diana (1905–1996) ◼ ◼

INTELLECTUAL

One of Trilling's five books is *Mrs. Harris: The Death of the Scarsdale Diet Doctor*. Often in the shadow of her husband, **Lionel Trilling**, she wrote books of essays and social criticism. She also co-authored with her husband. For years, she wrote book reviews for the *Nation* magazine, and she allegedly read a book a day for six-and-a-half years. Born Diana Rubin in Westchester County, New York, her family moved into Manhattan. She graduated cum laude from Radcliffe in 1925 majoring in art history. She married **Lionel Trilling** in 1929, and although she belonged to some Communist-front groups in the 1930s, she was critical of the social turbulence in the 1960s. One powerful measure of Diana Trilling's intellect and intellectual stature was her election to the American Academy of Arts and Sciences in 1976. The Trillings also lived at **35 Claremont Avenue** (near 119th Street) and **160 Claremont Avenue** (near La Salle Street).

Trilling, Lionel (1905–1975) ★ ■
INTELLECTUAL

Usually described as a literary critic, teacher, essayist, and writer of short stories, Trilling was more. His essays show how ideas made life exciting. Delving into Matthew Arnold, E. M. Forster, John Keats, Sigmund Freud, and others, Trilling served ideas as stimulants. He was a prolific writer and his book *The Liberal Imagination: Essays on Literature and Society* and *Sincerity and Authenticity* is representative of his modern way of thinking about art, culture, society, and history. Born in Queens, New York, he entered Columbia University at age 16 and graduated in 1925, receiving an MA the following year. He went on to teach at the University of Wisconsin and Hunter College. In 1929 he married a kindred intellectual spirit named Diana Rubin who then became **Diana Trilling**. He returned to Columbia to teach literature and earn a doctorate in 1938. For thirty years he and his colleague Jacques Barzun taught one of the most popular courses on cultural history and criticism, which shaped such students as **Allen Ginsberg**, Cynthia Ozick, and Lucien Carr. When he began writing for the *Parisian Review* in 1937, he became one of the certified New York intellectuals that included the likes of **Hannah Arendt**, **Saul Bellow**, **Alfred Kazin**, **Norman Podhoretz, and Susan Sontag**. It's no small measure of Trilling that numerous books have been written about him. The Trillings also lived at **35 Claremont Avenue** (near 119th Street) and **160 Claremont Avenue** (near La Salle Street).

405 West 117th Street (near Morningside Avenue)

Shotwell, James Thomson (1874–1965), Historian ◼ ▮

(See bio for Shotwell at **536 West 113th Street**.)

409 West 117th Street (near Morningside Avenue)

Morgan, Thomas Hunt (1866–1945) ◼
GENETICIST

Thomas Hunt Morgan.

In the famous fruit fly room at Columbia, Morgan established much of the basis for modern genetics in demonstrating that chromosomes carry genes and their detailed characteristics. That work inspired many others to employ the fruit fly in various experiments, and in 1933, it earned Morgan the Nobel Prize in Physiology or Medicine. His twenty-two books and hundreds of papers cover much of evolution, heredity, and embryology, and evidence his lifelong interest in sex determination. Morgan was born in Kentucky and graduated in 1886 with a BA degree from what would become the University of Kentucky. He earned a master of science degree two years later from the State College of Kentucky. Two years after that, in 1890, and with some field work at the Marine Biological Laboratory in Woods Hole, Massachusetts, he was awarded his PhD at Johns Hopkins University. That same year, he joined the faculty at Bryn Mawr College, while continuing his research and his summer excursions to Woods Hole. In 1904, he was lured to Columbia where he stayed for twenty-five years. In 1927, he accepted an offer to establish the Division of Biology at the California Institute of Technology.

419 West 117th Street (near Morningside Avenue)

Tyson, Levering (1889–1966) ◼
EDUCATOR

In 1924 Tyson made media history by broadcasting the first educational courses over the radio from station WEAF. Born in Pennsylvania, Tyson graduated in 1910 from Gettysburg College in his home state. At Columbia, he earned his master's degree in 1911. In 1931, with the backing of the Carnegie Foundation and John D. Rockefeller, Jr., he developed educational broadcasts under the auspices of the newly organized National Advisory Council on Radio, of which he was the first director. In 1937, he was selected as the fifth president of Muhlenberg College. He left in 1951, and the following year, he was appointed the chancellor of the Free University in Exile in Strasbourg. In 1954, Columbia awarded him an honorary doctorate. He was in good company that year; honorees included Julian Huxley, John von Neumann, Archibald MacLeish, Earl Warren, Konrad Adenauer, David Rockefeller, Dag Hammarskjöld, and the Queen Mother Elizabeth, wife of the Late George VI, and mother of Queen Elizabeth II. Having been a founder of the Columbia University Alumni Federation, in 1956 he was made an assistant on alumni relations to President Grayson Kirk. Tyson also lived at **39 Claremont Avenue** (near 119th Street), **450 Riverside Drive** (near 116th Street), and **520 West 124th Street** (near Morningside Avenue).

423 West 117th Street (near Morningside Avenue)

Williams, Talcott (1849–1928) ◼
JOURNALIST AND EDUCATOR

The Philadelphia artist Thomas Eakins painted portraits of Williams and his wife. Eakins also employed Williams as a model for the reclining nude, amongst six nude men, in his acclaimed 1885 painting "The Swimming Hole." At that time, Williams was an accomplished journalist who would go on to distinguish Columbia's School of Journalism as its director and retired as director emeritus. Williams was born in Turkey, the child of Congregational missionaries. He graduated from Amherst in 1873, was elected to Phi Beta Kappa, and worked for the *New York World*; the *New York Sun*; the *San Francisco Chronicle*; and, in Massachusetts, the *Springfield Republican*. In 1912, after thirty years there, he left the *Philadelphia Press* as editor to become the director of Columbia's new School of Journalism, endowed by Joseph Pulitzer. From 1913, he became the president of the American Conference of Teachers of Journalism. From 1914, he co-edited the twenty-four-volume, second edition of the New International Encyclopedia. He had also been a trustee of Amherst College, the Constantinople Women's College, and the American Bible Society. Amherst College, the University of Pennsylvania, Hobart College, and Western Reserve all conferred honorary degrees upon him.

427 West 117th Street (near Morningside Avenue)

Hayes, Carleton J. H. (1882–1964), Professor of History and Ambassador ☞

(See bio for Hayes at **508 West 114th Street**.)

357 West 118th Street (near Morningside Avenue)

DeMille, William Churchill (1878–1955) ☞

PLAYWRIGHT, MOTION PICTURE DIRECTOR, AND SCREENWRITER

As president of the Academy of Motion Picture Arts and Sciences from 1929 to 1931, W. C. DeMille, along with actor Douglas Fairbanks, hosted the very first Academy Awards in 1929. His 1907 play *The Warrens of*

**ANOTHER CATHEDRAL
TOWER?**

Never mind the two towers
on the west front that
have appeared to be under
construction for some time.
The Central Tower, as originally
proposed, was to have been 455
feet high. That would have made
it the tallest structure in the
Bloomingdale and Morningside
Heights neighborhoods. The
Cathedral's original architects,
Heins & La Farge, went as
deep as 72 feet to support the
heavy load of the freestanding
structure. The later architects,
Cram & Ferguson, were faced
with the incredible challenge
of building the Central Tower,
a challenge they did not meet.
The Central Tower never
materialized.

Virginia had a respectable 308 performances on Broadway. Produced
by David Belasco, it featured two struggling actors: his brother **Cecil
B. DeMille** and **Mary Pickford** in her Broadway debut. In all, he wrote
or co-wrote nine plays, directed more than fifty movies, and wrote
more than thirty movie scripts. Born in North Carolina, he earned a
bachelor's degree from Columbia University and studied further at the
American Academy of Dramatic Arts in New York, as well as at schools
in Germany, and then more at Columbia. His first wife, Anna George,
was the daughter of economist Henry George, who wrote *Progress and
Poverty* and ran for mayor against young Theodore Roosevelt. Dancer
and choreographer Agnes DeMille was his daughter.

364 West 118th Street (near Morningside Avenue)

Stout, Rex Todhunter (1886–1975), Detective Mystery Writer ▪ ▪

(See bio for Stout at **8 Morningside Avenue**.)

400 West 118th Street (near Morningside Drive)

Beard, Charles Austin (1874–1948), Historian ▪

(See bio for Beard at **430 West 116th Street**.)

Beard, Mary Ritter (1876–1958), Historian

(See bio for Beard at **430 West 116th Street**.)

Douglas, William Orville (1898–1980) ★ ▪
ASSOCIATE JUSTICE OF THE SUPREME COURT

Justice Douglas wrote the majority opinion in the landmark case
of *Griswold v. Connecticut* in 1965. The ruling affirmed the basis

for the right to privacy, circling around married couples' access to contraception, with Douglas citing "penumbras" of rights derived from other rights protected in the Bill of Rights of the Constitution. Douglas's record thirty-six years on the Court was characterized by his commitment to civil liberties and environmental rights. Born in Minnesota, Douglas was raised in the state of Washington where he graduated from Whitman College in 1920 with a BA degree and election to Phi Beta Kappa. He came to New York and graduated from Columbia Law School, where he also taught for a short time. Transferring to the Yale Law School, he became the Sterling Professor but left in 1934 to join the Securities and Exchange Commission. In 1939, President Roosevelt nominated Douglas to the Supreme Court to replace the retiring Justice Louis Brandeis. At age 40, Douglas was one of the youngest justices ever appointed.

Maltby, Margaret Eliza (1860–1944), Physicist ● ▤

(See bio for Maltby at 439 West 116th Street.)

401 West 118th Street (near Morningside Drive)

Latham, Minor White (1881–1968) ● ▤
EMERITUS ENGLISH PROFESSOR

Dancer/choreographer Agnes DeMille, actress Jane Wyatt, and actress and Congresswoman Helen Gahagan Douglas were all students of Latham. She founded the theater department at Barnard in 1914 and distinguished it with a novel method of having students performing their plays immediately after they were written. She also taught courses in Elizabethan English and was head of the English department when she retired in 1948. The Minor Latham Playhouse on the Barnard campus was named in her honor in 1954. Born in Mississippi, Latham graduated from the Mississippi College for Women, followed by graduate work at Bryn Mawr College, and a PhD from Columbia in 1914. Latham lived at three other addresses in the neighborhood: **29 Claremont Avenue** (near 119th Street), **509 West 121st Street** (near Amsterdam Avenue) and **140 Claremont Avenue** (near 122nd Street).

405 West 118th Street (near Morningside Drive)

Poffenberger, Albert Theodore (1885–1977) ▪
PSYCHOLOGIST

Poffenberger worked with Columbia Professor **Harry L. Hollingworth** to develop the first psychological tests for the US Army used in World War I. He also designed a psychological test that was required of incoming freshman at Columbia University for many years. In addition to chairing the psychology department at Columbia for a period, he was a president of the American Psychology Association in 1935. Born in Pennsylvania, Albert Poffenberger graduated from Bucknell University with an AB degree in 1909. At Columbia, he earned an AM degree in 1910, and his PhD degree in 1912. He taught there from 1910 until retiring in 1950 as a professor emeritus of psychology. Poffenberger also lived at **29 Claremont Avenue** (near 119th Street).

Yang, Andrew (1975–)
ENTREPRENEUR AND PRESIDENTIAL CANDIDATE

From almost out of nowhere, Yang became a viable presidential candidate with high satisfaction ratings and a range of interesting endorsements from Penn Jillette to Elon Musk. His poll numbers were high enough to earn his presence in the early Democratic Party debates having much coverage on national television. But his poll numbers didn't grow to sustain his campaign, so he chose to drop out and endorse Joe Biden. His professional career began with a very brief stint in a prominent law firm. That was followed with startups in fundraising, part-organizing, and healthcare. Switching to a test preparation company, Manhattan Prep, he became its president and earned a small fortune in its sale to Kaplan, Inc. His next endeavor was Venture for America (VFA), a nonprofit fellowship program that employed top college graduates to seed promising start-up ventures. The idea of a universal basic income, most associated with his presidential crusade arose from his VFA creation. Yang was born in upstate New York. He graduated from Brown University and earned a JD degree from Columbia Law School.

415 West 118th Street (near Morningside Drive)

Clapp, Elsie Ripley (1879–1965), Progressive Education Pioneer

(See bio for Clapp at **419 West 115th Street**.)

417 West 118th Street (near Morningside Drive)

Hollingworth, Harry Levi (1880–1956) ▪
PSYCHOLOGIST

Hollingworth was one of the first to employ psychology in the commercial world. With the understanding that his research and the good name of Columbia University could not be used in advertisements, he did research for the Coca-Cola Company regarding the effect of caffeine in their drink. During World War I, he was the psychologist at the army camp in Plattsburgh, New York, and the Surgeon General had him study soldiers suffering from shell shock. Much of his other research work ushered in the acceptance of industrial and applied psychology. Born in Nebraska, Hollingworth graduated from the University of Nebraska in 1906 with a BA degree in 1906 and election to Phi Beta Kappa. He married Leta Stetter Hollingworth, who would become renowned psychologist in her own right, and they came to New York. He earned his PhD at Columbia in

1909 and taught psychology and logic at Barnard from 1907 until his retirement in 1946 as head of the Department of Psychology, which he had established. He was president of the American Psychological Association for a time. In 1954, the Hollingworth Psychological Laboratories were opened in Millbank Hall at Barnard in his honor. Hollingworth also lived at **90 Morningside Drive** (near 120th Street) and **500 West 124th Street** (near Morningside Avenue).

421 West 118th Street (near Amsterdam Avenue)

Kerouac, Jack (1922–1969) ■
BEAT GENERATION FIGURE AND AUTHOR

As author of the Beat Generation's classic book *On the Road*, Kerouac never had a driver's license, even though he drove long stretches through the deserts on his way back from Mexico with his friend Neal Cassady. A main character in *On the Road* is based on Cassady, whom Kerouac also employed for other characters in other novels. Although *On the Road* was the defining work of the Beat Generation, it wasn't published until 1957. Kerouac wrote much before and after, and he might have even crafted the phrase "beat generation," but he considered himself more of a Catholic with Buddhist leanings, rather than a beatnik. He was born in Lowell, Massachusetts, which honors him with a remarkably interesting memorial. He attended Columbia on a football scholarship, broke a leg playing football in freshman year, and dropped out as a sophomore. He lived with his girlfriend Edie Parker, who would become his first wife in 1944. From life at Columbia, and through Parker, he would meet most of the well-known Beats, notably **Allen Ginsberg** and **William S. Burroughs**, who gave credit to Kerouac for suggesting the title of his book *Naked Lunch*. He died too young, at age 47, from too much drinking. It should not go unnoticed that "Beatles" is an homage to both Kerouac's beat phenomenon and rock and roller Buddy Holly's group, the Crickets. Kerouac also lived at **420 West 119th Street** (near Amsterdam Avenue).

Vollmer (Adams, Burroughs), Joan (1923–1951), Beat Generation Figure

(See bio for Vollmer at **419 West 115th Street**.)

430 West 118th Street (near Amsterdam Avenue)

Erskine, John (1879–1951), Educator, Author, and Musician ■ ■ ☜

(See bio for Erskine at **609 West 113th Street**.)

Hayes, Carleton J. H. (1882–1964), Professor of History and Ambassador ☜

(See bio for Hayes at **508 West 114th Street**.)

400 West 119th Street (near Morningside Drive)

McGregor, James Howard (1872–1954), Anthropologist and Zoologist ■ ■

(See bio for McGregor at **1120 Amsterdam Avenue**.)

420 West 119th Street (near Amsterdam Avenue)

Kerouac, Jack (1922–1969), Beat Generation Figure and Author ■

(See bio for Kerouac at **421 West 118th Street**.)

Morehouse, Ward (1895–1966), Theater Critic ■

(See bio for Morehouse at **Pomander Walk**.)

424 West 119th Street (near Amsterdam Avenue) and

430 West 119th Street (near Amsterdam Avenue)

Coan, Titus Munson (1836–1921) ☞

PHYSICIAN

The Titus M. Coan Prize for Excellence in Research is awarded each year at the graduation ceremonies of Columbia's College of Physicians and Surgeons. Among the dozen books that Coan authored, his memoirs recount his experience in the American Civil War. His correspondence with such notables as Walt Whitman resides in the collections of the New York Historical Society. The son of notable missionary parents in Hawaii, Coan came to the United States in 1856, attended Williams College, and then graduated from Columbia's College of Physicians and Surgeons in 1861. He served in the Civil War as a surgeon, in part with Admiral Farragut's squadron, and thereafter with public charity and correction hospitals on Blackwell's Island, now Roosevelt Island, and at Bellevue Hospital. He even gave his service to the hospital for Civil War veterans, which was established in Central Park in the buildings that were originally the College of Mount St. Vincent.

435 West 119th Street (near Amsterdam Avenue)

Ryan, William Fitts (1922–1972), Congressman ■

(See bio for Ryan at **448 Riverside Drive**.)

280 Manhattan Avenue (near 112th Street)

Wilstach, Frank Jenners (1865–1933) ■
AUTHOR

Wilstach spent twenty-five years compiling a dictionary of fifteen thousand similes from the great works of literature. Similes that compare two different things to make a description more expressive include "about as much privacy as a goldfish" and "as cold as an enthusiastic New England audience." Born in Indiana, Wilstach studied at Purdue University and Seton Hall University. He directed publicity campaigns for such theater notables as the actress **Julia Marlowe** and DeWolf Hopper of "Casey at the Bat" fame. He was also a general press representative for the theater producer and owner Sam H. Harris, and partner to Irving Berlin. After seven years with the Schubert theater organization, he became the assistant to Will H. Hays in the Motion Picture Producers and Distributers of America. His book *A Dictionary of Similes* was published in 1916. He also authored *A Stage Dictionary* in 1923; *Wild Bill Hickok, the Prince of Pistoleers* in 1926; and *The Plainsman, Wild Bill Hickok* in 1937. Wilstach also lived at **320 Manhattan Avenue** (near 114th Street).

Frank Wilstach.

312 Manhattan Avenue (113th Street)

Cantor, Maurice Freeman (1893–1987)
STATE ASSEMBLYMAN AND DEFENSE ATTORNEY FOR MOBSTERS

Cantor was the attorney of Arnold Rothstein when the gangster was dying after being shot in the Park Central Hotel in 1929. In addition to his many organized crime activities, Rothstein is thought to have fixed the 1919 World Series, usually referred to as the "Black Sox" scandal. As Rothstein's attorney who prepared the gangster's will that he signed on his deathbed, Cantor testified that Rothstein did not tell him who shot him. Born in Buffalo, New York, Cantor was engaged in the practice of law since 1916. He was a member of the Monongahela Democratic Club, the Free and Accepted Masons, and the Ancient Arabie Order of the Nobles of the Mystic Shrine (Shriners). He won election to the New York State Assembly in 1927 and introduced legislation to license airplanes and pilots. After he lost his seat in 1930, he moved to Long Beach, Long Island. There he represented such mobsters as Jack Eisenstein, Salvatore Spitale, and Charles "Lucky" Luciano. He resurfaced in 1959 during an investigation of corruption at Roosevelt Raceway.

320 Manhattan Avenue (near 114th Street)

Wilstach, Frank Jenners (1865–1933), Author ◧

(See bio for Wilstach at **280 Manhattan Avenue**.)

6 Morningside Avenue (near 115th Street)

True, Clarence Fagen (1860–1928) ◧ ▉

(See bio for True at **217 West 104th Street**.)

8 Morningside Avenue (near 115th Street)

Stout, Rex Todhunter (1886–1975) ◧ ▉
DETECTIVE MYSTERY WRITER

Stout was active in the early days of the American Civil Liberties Union. He was also a founder of Vanguard Press and he conducted a very public and intensely personal campaign against Hitler's Germany. However, he is best known for his eccentric and corpulent detective Nero Wolfe. From their introduction in 1934, his series of

"MORNINGSIDE" IS NOT IN THE DICTIONARY

"Morningside" is not in the dictionary because it is a proper noun. The word was most likely made up by Frederick Law Olmsted in 1870, when he became involved with the development of what would become Morningside Park. A wonderfully poetic word, "Morningside" refers to how the sun shines on the east side—the morning-side—of the rocky ridge in the park. Olmsted is also thought to have created the word "parkway" to describe a thoroughfare that is lined by green, leafy park lands. He designed the first two parkways, Eastern Parkway and Ocean Parkway, both in Brooklyn. "Parkway" came into general usage and thereby found its way into the dictionary. "Morningside" did not.

Rex Stout.

Nero Wolfe books would sell more than fifty million copies, and it spurred television and movie adaptations. Stout was born in Indiana but raised in Kansas. He attended the University of Kansas but did not graduate and served in the Navy for two years on Theodore Roosevelt's presidential yacht. From 1912, he began writing stories for magazines but turned his attention to convincing banks to start children savings account programs. By 1927, he had retired with $400,000 of savings and devoted himself to writing. Stout was a president of the Mystery Writers of America and received their most prestigious Grand Master Award. His wife was a renowned textile designer, Pola Stout. His sister Ruth Stout was the writer of many gardening books, often promoting her "no work" method.Stout also lived at **364 West 118th Street** (near Morningside Avenue).

44 Morningside Drive (near 115th Street)

Brooks (Pitcher), Harriet (1876–1933), Nuclear Physicist ★ ■ ▉ ☞

(See bio for Brooks at **411 West 114th Street**.)

54 Morningside Drive (near 116th Street)

Gellhorn, Walter Fischel (1906–1995)

LAW PROFESSOR

Gellhorn helped to write the Japanese constitution that was put into place after World War II. He also chaired the mediation panel for New York City's 1980 transit strike. But Gellhorn's renown is more properly based on his long career as a public servant and as a legal scholar. Born in Missouri, Gellhorn graduated in 1927 from Amherst College with a BA degree, and he graduated in 1931 from Columbia Law School with an LLD degree. After serving as a law clerk for Supreme Court

HONORING THE BATTLE OF HARLEM HEIGHTS

On September 16, 1876, the 100th anniversary of the Battle of Harlem Heights was celebrated with a procession of carriages "to the heights of Bloomingdale" where an encampment of tents was arranged on the present site of Columbia's campus. The renowned Seventh Regiment Military Band played as they marched up from 110th Street. Festivities were led by President of the New-York Historical Society **Frederick de Peyster**, whose old family house was nearby. Mayor William H. Wickham was in attendance, and the Honorable John Jay, grandson of his namesake, the first Chief Justice of the Supreme Court, gave the main speech. Attendance was estimated at ten thousand.

Justice Harlan Fiske Stone, he joined Columbia's law school faculty in 1933 and had a sixty-year career there receiving emeritus status on his departure. He is also noted for his sister Martha, a distinguished writer, who was the third wife of Ernest Hemingway.

60 Morningside Drive (near 116th Street), the President's House

Butler, Nicholas Murray (1862–1947) ★ ■
UNIVERSITY PRESIDENT

Butler was the twelfth president of Columbia University, serving for forty-three years from 1902 to 1945. He was a giant in the world of education and a force in diplomatic and political circles. When the 1912 Republican candidate for vice president, James Sherman, died a few days before the presidential election, Butler was designated to receive the electoral votes that Sherman would have received. He co-founded what became Teachers College and helped form the College Entrance Examination Board, which gave us SATs and standardized college entrance examinations. His BA, MA, and PhD were earned at Columbia. Although remembered for imperious ways and some anti-Semitic rants, his significance in the realm of education is undeniable.

Eisenhower, Dwight David (1890–1969) ★ ■
GENERAL, PRESIDENT OF THE UNITED STATES, AND UNIVERSITY PRESIDENT

Eisenhower was the thirty-fourth president of the United States from 1953 to 1961 and the thirteenth president of Columbia University from 1948 to 1953. He offered to resign from Columbia in 1950 when he was appointed Supreme Commander of NATO, but the University trustees refused to accept it. Admittedly, he wasn't a hands-on university president, but he did use his influence in support of closing West 116th

Street between Amsterdam Avenue and Broadway to create the lovely
College Walk on Columbia's campus. Eisenhower was born in Denison,
Texas, the third of seven sons, but he was raised in Kansas, where he
was a high school football star. As a student on West Point's football
team, Eisenhower played against Jim Thorpe. After graduation, he
married Mamie Geneva Doud and was promoted to first lieutenant on
his wedding day. In 1920, early in his military career, he led an army
convoy from Washington, D.C., to San Francisco at the paltry rate of
five miles per hour, which supposedly spurred his presidential efforts
for our national highway system.

Kirk, Grayson Louis (1903–1997)
UNIVERSITY PRESIDENT

Kirk was the fourteenth president of Columbia University from 1953
to 1968. The challenges of 1968, including racial issues, the matter of
a gymnasium to be built in Morningside Park, and student protests
that led to their occupation of university buildings, contaminated
Kirk's place in Columbia's history. After an undergraduate degree at
Miami University in his home state of Ohio, he earned an MA at Clark
University, followed by a PhD at University of Wisconsin–Madison,
where he taught. At Columbia, he doubled the library's holdings, built a
half dozen new buildings, and quadrupled the endowment.

McGill, William James (1922–1997) ● ▪
UNIVERSITY PRESIDENT

McGill was the sixteenth president of Columbia University from 1970
to 1980. After an undergraduate education at Fordham University and
a doctorate from Harvard in experimental psychology, McGill was
recruited to Columbia from the University of California, San Diego.
After a turbulent period on campus in the late '60s and early '70s,

McGill's skills with conflict resolution were much needed. He stabilized Columbia, including its finances, which had taken a hit along with its reputation.

Sovern, Michael Ira (1931–2020)
UNIVERSITY PRESIDENT AND LEGAL SCHOLAR

Sovern was the seventeenth president of Columbia University from 1980 to 1993. He was the Chancellor Kent Professor of Law at Columbia Law School. After graduating from Bronx High School of Science, he began his love affair with Columbia as a student of Columbia College and later Columbia Law School. After a brief stint at the University of Minnesota Law School, he returned to Columbia's Law School as a faculty member and, finally, as president of Columbia. During his tenure, Columbia doubled its unrestricted endowment by selling the land beneath Rockefeller Center. Sovern also lived at **423 West 120th Street** (near Amsterdam Avenue).

Rupp, George Erik (1942–)
UNIVERSITY PRESIDENT

Rupp was the eighteenth president of Columbia University from 1993 to 2002. Previously, he was president of Rice University. He graduated first from Princeton, then Yale Divinity School, and, finally, Harvard with a doctorate in Religion. In fact, he is an ordained Presbyterian minister. After Columbia, he became president of the International Rescue Committee, which was founded in 1933 at the request of Albert Einstein. His tenure at Columbia saw Eric Kandel win the Nobel Prize in Medicine and the loss of forty-one Columbia alumnae in the World Trade Center 9/11 attacks.

88 Morningside Drive (near 119th Street) ☞

Hayes, Carleton J. H. (1882–1964), Professor of History and Ambassador

(See bio for Hayes at **508 West 114th Street**.)

Gutkind, Eric (1877–1965), Jewish Philosopher

(See bio for Gutkind at **310 Riverside Drive**.)

1285 Columbus Avenue (near 110th Street) ☞

Hamlin, Alfred Dwight Foster (1855–1926), Architect and Architectural Historian

(See bio for Hamlin at **850 West End Avenue**.)

1047 Amsterdam Avenue (near 111th Street), the Ogilvie House

Donegan, Horace William Baden (1900–1991)

EPISCOPAL BISHOP

Donegan was the twelfth Episcopal Bishop of New York from 1950 to 1972. He changed the direction of the church from an older, wealthy community to attending to the neighborhood poor. To that end, he diverted resources away from completing the Cathedral to supporting housing in Harlem. He also advanced the prospects of women within the church and ordained the first women as deacons. Born in England, he was made an honorary commander of the Order of the British Empire by Queen Elizabeth II. His family came to the States when he was 10. He studied at St. Stephen's College, known now as Bard, and later at Oxford University. He was ordained a priest in 1928 after

HUNGARIAN RHAPSODY

The Hungarian Pastry Shop (1030 Amsterdam Avenue between Cathedral Parkway and 111th Street) is a neighborhood institution frequented by generations of locals, students, professors, tourists, intellectuals, and writers. The bathroom in the Hungarian has some of the world's most sophisticated, if not always respectable, graffiti. The regulars having their coffee seem oblivious to the framed book covers on the walls. Those books were written in Hungarian, and include such titles as: *The Perfect Storm: A True Story of Men Against the Sea* by Sebastian Junger; *The Death of Satan: How Americans Have Lost the Sense of Evil* by Andrew Delbanco; *The Ministry of Special Cases* by Nathan Englander; and *Between the World and Me* by Ta-Nehisi Coates. The Hungarian has also hosted the filming of several television shows and occasional movies such as Woody Allen's *Husbands and Wives*.

Opened in 1961 by a Mr. and Mrs. Vecony, the Hungarian Pastry Shop was sold to Peter Pangiotis and his two partners in 1976. Peter met his future wife, Wendy, while she was working as a waitress at the shop. When they retired in 2012, their son Philip took over the reins. He knew the business firsthand, and he started working there as a 13-year-old.

Wendy still hosts the most jovial night of the year, the annual Winter Holiday Sing-Along. She distributes words to the standard Christmas,

Hanukkah, and seasonal songs, and the place goes wild. Some 150 or so enthusiastic patrons, accompanied by volunteer musicians, including this author, sing their hearts out, celebrating the joyful season in the spirit of the world-renowned Hungarian Pastry Shop.

receiving his divinity degree at the Episcopal Theological Seminary in Cambridge, Massachusetts. For nearly twenty years in his retirement, his voice for liberal causes continued to be heard.

Manning, William Thomas (1866–1949) ■
EPISCOPAL BISHOP

Manning was the tenth Episcopal Bishop of New York from 1921 to 1946. His demeanor was characterized as "high church," which held to existing formalities and dogmatic theology. He scoffed at attempts to loosen the church's outlook on changing social mores and concentrated on preserving tradition. To that end, he saw to a $10 million campaign to continue building the Cathedral of St. John the Divine. To that same end, he advocated strongly, and successfully, on moral grounds against the appointment of Bertrand Russell to teach math and logic at City College.

Greer, David Hummell (1844–1919)
EPISCOPAL BISHOP

Greer was the eighth Episcopal Bishop of New York from 1908 to 1919. He studied at the divinity school of Kenyon College, receiving a degree there in 1866 and a Doctor of Divinity in 1880. Before becoming Bishop, he was at the renowned St. Bartholomew's Church. At St. Bartholomew's, he managed large personalities and monies on par with significant-sized business enterprises. Greer succeeded Bishop Henry Codman Potter, a tough act to follow. Potter came from a very prominent family, had married Caroline Clark of Singer sewing machine fortune, and arranged for the building of the Cathedral of St. John the Divine. Greer had served as Potter's assistant and was more than up to the challenge. During his lifetime, Greer received numerous honorary degrees, various honors acknowledging his efforts

Rt. Rev. David Hummell Greer.

for international peace, and sat as trustee for select organizations, including Columbia University. He was buried in the crypt of the Cathedral that was not completed in his lifetime.

The Leake and Watts Orphan House, Amsterdam Avenue and W. 112th Street, New York City, undated, ca. 1882-1919.

Guest, William Henry (1808–1876) ☞

SUPERINTENDENT OF AN ORPHANAGE

Guest was the superintendent of the Leake and Watts Orphan Asylum from 1854 to 1876, when it occupied the site that is now 1047 Amsterdam Avenue. The orphanage site was sold in the 1890s to New York's Episcopal Diocese to become the location for the Cathedral of St. John the Divine. Guest was born on the Lower East Side of Manhattan, but his family moved to upstate New York when he was an infant. Around 1825, his family made the seventeen-day journey back to New York City where he was appointed an assistant in the schools at Bellevue Hospital. In 1832, after a cholera outbreak, he was made superintendent

ST. JOHN, ST. LUKE, BARNARD, AND THE OGILVIES

The Ogilvie House in the close of the Cathedral of St. John the Divine is where the bishops of the New York Episcopal Diocese reside. Designed by the noted Gothic architects Cram & Ferguson, it opened in 1914. Helen Slade Ogilvie provided the funding in memory of her husband, Clinton Ogilvie, who died in 1900. They were both landscape painters. When Helen died in 1936, St. Luke's Hospital was the largest institutional beneficiary of her largesse. Clinton's father, William H. Ogilvie, created most of the family fortune by successfully speculating in land as far away as North Carolina and New Hampshire, with proceeds shrewdly invested in the New Jersey Zinc Company.

Helen and Clinton's notable daughter, Ida Helen Ogilvie, graduated from Bryn Mawr in 1896 with a BA degree and from Columbia in 1903 with a PhD. In 1903, she founded the geology department at Barnard and served as chairman of the department until her retirement in 1941. In 1917, she headed up a 150-person Women's Land Army, made up mostly of Barnard students. They worked on a farm in Westchester to produce food for the American war economy. They were called "farmerettes," and they foreshadowed women's future efforts, such as the AWACs, to support the World War II war effort. Ida Helen Ogilvie retired with her partner to the small community of Germantown about one hundred miles up the Hudson.

of the "Farms" in Astoria, the location of the City Nurseries for hundreds of poor children. After those buildings burned, he ventured to Greenpoint, Long Island, and became Justice of the Peace and Tax Collector. In 1854, he was appointed superintendent of the Leake and Watts Orphan Asylum located in the area that would soon become known as Morningside Heights. He died in Wisconsin while visiting his daughter. His remains were brought back to the orphanage and interred in St. Michael's Cemetery in East Elmhurst.

Moore, Paul, Jr. (1919–2003) ★ ■
EPISCOPAL BISHOP

In 1977, Moore was the first Episcopal Bishop to ordain a woman as a priest. He was also responsible for the dramatic changes at the Cathedral of St. John the Divine, including the introduction of concerts, the annual blessing of the animals, artists in residence—including Philipe Petit and Judy Collins—and peacocks. These innovations only begin to suggest his activist liberal influence manifest in civil rights issues, women's rights, and opposition to the Vietnam War. Moore was born in New Jersey into a family of wealth. The Moore side of the family was involved in creating the American Can Company, Bankers Trust, US Steel, Western Union, National Biscuit Company, and a few railroads. Another member of the family is Mark Hanna, who made McKinley president. Paul Moore, Jr., graduated from Yale in 1941 and then served as a captain in the Marine Corps in World War II. He fought at Guadalcanal and earned the Navy Star, the Silver Cross, and the Purple Heart. In 1945, he entered General Theological Seminary and was ordained in 1949. His duties began with a parish in Jersey City, followed by an appointment as Dean of a cathedral in Indianapolis, Indiana, and becoming a bishop in Washington, D.C. In 1972, he was installed as the thirteenth Episcopal Bishop of the New York Diocese and assumed residency at the Cathedral of St. John the Divine, where he served until 1989.

1120 Amsterdam Avenue (near 115th Street), Livingston Dormitory

McGregor, James Howard (1872–1954) ● ▮

ANTHROPOLOGIST AND ZOOLOGIST

At the core of the controversy over the origins of early humans and whether they descended from apes, McGregor argued that there was a connection because, like humans, gorillas could use their thumbs. He was world-famous when, in 1929, he was part of the joint effort by Columbia University and the American Museum of Natural History that brought five gorillas from Africa to the United States. His expertise in this realm culminated in the course that he gave in 1938 entitled "The Evolution of Man." He was affectionately called Columbia's "Mr. Chips" in the latter part of his forty-five years at Columbia. Born in Ohio, McGregor graduated from Ohio State with a BA degree, and from Columbia with AM and PhD degrees. He began teaching zoology at Columbia in 1897. From 1899 to 1906, he was a staff member of the Marine Biological Laboratory at Woods Hole, Massachusetts. By 1916, he was an associate in human anatomy at the American Museum of Natural History. McGregor also lived at **400 West 119th Street** (near Morningside Drive).

1124 Amsterdam Avenue (near 115th Street)

Hayes, Carleton J. H. (1882–1964), Professor of History and Ambassador ☞

(See bio for Hayes at **508 West 114th Street**.)

WHO KNOWS?

Q. Does any part of 1842 Croton Aqueduct still exist?
A. Maybe, but maybe not. Who really knows? It's quite likely that some of the aqueduct remnants are still underground. They would be below Amsterdam Avenue north of 108th Street and between Amsterdam Avenue and Columbus Avenue, south of 108th Street. The aqueduct buildings on Amsterdam Avenue at 113th and 119th Streets were built when the aqueduct was placed underground in the 1870s, '80s, and '90s. The original above-ground aqueduct included the Clendening Viaduct, which ran from around 103rd Street to around 97th Street to cross a valley. Some sources suggest that blocks from the original viaduct were used in building the Church of St. Paul the Apostle on Columbus Avenue at 60th Street. There are large blocks on the west side of Morningside Drive between 111th and 112th Streets behind the Cathedral of St. John the Divine. Might they have come from the 1842 Croton Aqueduct?

2881 Broadway (near 112th Street)

Northrop, John Howard (1891–1987)
BIOCHEMIST

Northrop's father died in a laboratory explosion a few weeks before he was born. The tragic event took place on the Park Avenue side of the School of Mines on Columbia's earlier campus. His father was an instructor of zoology at Columbia, and his mother was a teacher of botany at Hunter College. In 1946, John Howard Northrop and two others were awarded the Nobel Prize in Chemistry for their work with proteins, viruses, and especially enzymes critical to digestion. In 1929, he isolated the gastric enzyme pepsin, and determined that it was a protein. Northrop was born in Yonkers, New York, and educated at Columbia which, in 1915, granted him a PhD in chemistry. His research at the US Chemical Warfare Service during World War I led him toward the study of enzymes. He worked at the Rockefeller Institute for Medical Research from 1916 until he retired in 1961. From 1949, he also had visiting professorial duties at the University of California, Berkeley.

3009 Broadway (near 119th Street)

Gildersleeve, Virginia Crocheron (1877–1965), Educator and Dean ◼

(See bio for Gildersleeve at 404 Riverside Drive.)

Site near Broadway and West 118th Street

Meier, Caspar M. (1774–1839) ★ ◼ ▉
MERCHANT

Born in what is Germany today, Meier came to New York in 1796. In 1798, Meier established the most important German shipping dynasty in

America. In 1852, it would combine with the Oelrichs family interests from Baltimore to become Oelrichs & Co. Meier and Oelrichs had the German Consulate responsibilities. Meier was a board member of the New York Mutual Insurance Co., a vice president of the German Society, and he belonged to the Chamber of Commerce. His son John Diedrich attended Columbia College for two years before joining the family business and died young. Caspar Meier died in his home on the Bloomingdale Road overlooking the Hudson River.

15 Claremont Avenue (near 116th Street)

Bliven, Bruce Ormsby (1889–1977), Editor ▪

(See bio for Bliven at **450 Riverside Drive**.)

Bliven, Bruce, Jr. (1916–2002), Author ▪

(See bio for Bliven at **450 Riverside Drive**.)

Randall, John Herman, Jr. (1899–1980) ● ▪
PROFESSOR OF PHILOSOPHY

In 1933, John Herman Randall, Jr., was one of the thirty-four signers of the first Humanist Manifesto. He also actively challenged and protested the barring of Bertrand Russell from City College in 1940. Randall was born in Michigan but was educated in New York City, graduating from Morris High School in the Bronx. At Columbia University, he earned a BA in 1918, an AM in 1919, and a PhD in 1922. His second book, *The Making of the Modern Mind*, published in 1926 when he was a rather young professor, was a masterwork of philosophical history. Randall's grounding in Western classical values yielded other important works such as his three-volume history of philosophy from the middle ages, *The Career of Philosophy*; his collection of essays, *Nature and Historical Experience*; and his exquisite *Aristotle*. In 1951, Columbia gave him the first Woodbridge Professorship in the history of philosophy. His father was the minister John Herman Randall, Sr.

21 Claremont Avenue (near 116th Street)

Shattuck, Jane (1865–1948), Businesswoman

(See bio for Shattuck at **610 Cathedral Parkway**.)

Hill, Patty Smith (1868–1948), Educator and Co-author of "Happy Birthday" ◼

(See bio for Hill at **620 West 116th Street**.)

Maltby, Margaret Eliza (1860–1944), Physicist ◼ ▪

(See bio for Maltby at **439 West 116th Street**.)

25 Claremont Avenue (near 116th Street)

Hofstadter, Richard (1916–1970) ★
HISTORIAN AND INTELLECTUAL

This DeWitt Clinton Professor of American History at Columbia University won two Pulitzer Prizes, but Richard Hofstadter's authorship of more than two dozen books barely suggests his influence and stature in the understanding of American history. His 1954 book *The Age of Reform* earned him his first Pulitzer, and his 1964 book *Anti-Intellectualism in American Life* brought him his second. Opinionated, ever deducing motives, his writings always seemed to transcend details and render larger themes. His 1948 book *The American Political*

Tradition and the Men Who Made It is one such example of how revisionary his history could be. Born in Buffalo, New York, Hofstadter was educated first at the University of Buffalo, and then at Columbia with an MA degree in 1938 and a PhD in 1942. He taught at Brooklyn College, City College, and the University of Maryland before returning to Columbia in 1946. His earliest works, notably *Social Darwinism in American Thought* and *The American Political Tradition*, brought him much attention.

Kahn, Ely Jacques (1884–1972) ● ▮
ARCHITECT

When Ayn Rand was writing her novel *The Fountainhead*, she researched the architectural profession by working in Kahn's office for six months. Born in New York, Kahn graduated from Columbia University in 1903 and went on to earn a Bachelor of Architecture degree there. He refined his education further by earning a diploma at the École des Beaux-Arts in Paris. With his practice underway, he taught at Cornell and New York University. From 1917 to 1930 he partnered with Albert Buchman and they designed the Art Deco treasures of 2 Park Avenue, the Film Center Building, and the Squibb Building. From 1940, he partnered with Robert Allen Jacobs, with whom he designed the Municipal Asphalt plant, 100 Park Avenue, and the Universal Pictures Building. His hospital work included Montefiore, Hospital for Joint Diseases, and Mount Sinai, in addition to a few of the city's housing projects. He also designed three buildings for the 1939–1940 World's Fair in Flushing Meadows. His son was the *New Yorker* writer **Ely Jacques Kahn, Jr.**

Kahn, Ely Jacques, Jr. (1916–1994)
WRITER FOR THE *NEW YORKER*

When legendary *New Yorker* writer St. Clair McKelway hired him as a Harvard senior, Ely Kahn had the opportunity to get to know A. J. Liebling, Calvin Trillin, and Joseph Mitchell. Born in New York, Kahn graduated from Harvard in 1937. Over five decades, he wrote many pieces at the *New Yorker*, and forty-nine of them were about his experiences in the army during World War II. Several of these stories materialized into his twenty-seven books. His travel writings covered the globe and all forty-eight states that constituted the country at the time. His profiles of noted personalities ranged from **Herbert Bayard Swope** to David Rockefeller to Frank Sinatra. His father was the architect **Ely Jacques Kahn**.

Lee, Tsung-Dao "T. D." (1926–) ◼
PHYSICIST

Lee is the youngest American to have won a Nobel Prize. He shared it in 1957 with C. N. Yang for their work on the violation of the parity law on weak interactions in particle physics. In addition, his work encompassed hydrodynamics, solid state mechanics, astrophysics, and statistical mechanics where the Lee-Yang theorem acknowledges their original modeling in statistical field theory. Born in Shanghai, Lee studied chemical engineering and physics at a few universities in China during the turbulence of World War II. In 1946, his mentor, Professor Wu Ta-You facilitated a fellowship, which took him to the University of Chicago where Enrico Fermi selected him as his PhD student. Lee spent two years at the University of California, Berkeley, as a research assistant and instructor before arriving at Columbia in 1953. He has received numerous prestigious awards and has published a host of technical papers and some eight books.

Moehle, Jean Earl (ca.1889–1964)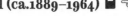
SUFFRAGIST AND PERFORMANCE ARTIST

In James Montgomery Flagg's iconic poster celebrating Wake Up America Day on April 19, 1917, Moehle is dressed up as Paul Revere. On the actual celebration that day, she also dressed up as Paul Revere and rode a horse in the parade. Earlier, in 1914, the Maxwell Motor Company had enlisted suffragists to publicize their new policy of hiring women on equal pay with men. While fellow suffragist Inez Milholland Boissevain spoke publicly, Moehle, dressed in a workman's leather apron and a denim coat, spent an afternoon in the company's showroom on Fifth Avenue, pulling down and reassembling a Maxwell engine. Moehle donated her collection of World War I posters to Columbia's Avery Library in 1919. Born in Newark, New Jersey, Moehle graduated from Barnard in 1915. During World War I, she worked in a YWCA in France. In the early 1920s she was the executive secretary of the American Orchestral Society. Moehle also lived at **39 Claremont Avenue** (near 119th Street) and **490 Riverside Drive** (near 122nd Street).

Jean Earle Mohle.

Shenfield, Lawrence Lewis (1891–1974)
ADVERTISING EXECUTIVE AND PHILATELIST

Shenfield was a world-class stamp collector who specialized in the stamps of the Confederacy. His 1961 book *Confederate States of America, the Special Postal Routes* is the definitive book of its kind. His collection of Confederate stamps was without peer. He wrote numerous articles, lectured extensively, was a member of the Collectors Club, the Philatelic Foundation, and the Royal Philatelic Society of London. Born in Brooklyn, Shenfield graduated from Columbia in 1914 with a degree in architecture. He worked for the firm of Eggers & Higgins, which would be hired by Columbia in the 1960s to design a gymnasium that was never constructed in Morningside Park. In the 1930s, he left architecture for radio advertising and handled shows that featured Orson Welles and Dinah Shore. President of his firm, Doherty, Clifford, Sheers and Shenfield, for years, he retired in 1965, and his firm became part of the Omnicom Group.

27 Claremont Avenue (near 119th Street)

Moore, Douglas Stuart (1893–1969), Composer ■

(See bio for Moore at **464 Riverside Drive**.)

29 Claremont Avenue (near 119th Street)

Dunning, John Ray (1907–1975) ■
PHYSICIST AND ENGINEERING SCHOOL DEAN

Dunning isolated Uranium and was a central figure in the Manhattan Project that led to the development of the atomic bomb. His day job was Dean of the Columbia University School of Engineering. He was born in Nebraska, graduated from Nebraska Wesleyan University, and earned his doctorate at Columbia. He continued at Columbia, teaching and concentrating on the newly discovered neutron particle. After receiving a traveling fellowship, he interacted with the likes of Ernest Rutherford, Niels Bohr, and Werner Heisenberg, and Enrico Fermi. Dunning built the cyclotron that operated in the basement of Pupin Hall. He also directed its 1950 successor at Columbia's location in Irvington-on-the-Hudson: the 385 million electron volt synchro-cyclotron.

Latham, Minor White (1881–1968), Emeritus English Professor ■ ▇

(See bio for Latham at **401 West 118th Street**.)

Poffenberger, Albert Theodore (1885–1977), Psychologist ▇

(See bio for Poffenberger at **405 West 118th Street**.)

Slichter, Walter Irvine (ca.1874–1958), Professor of Electrical Engineering ★ ■ ▇

(See bio for Slichter at **450 Riverside Drive**.)

Urey, Harold C. (1893–1981) ★ ■
PHYSICIST

Urey was awarded the Nobel Prize in Chemistry for his discovery of heavy hydrogen. Born in Indiana, Urey graduated from Montana State University in 1917 with a BA degree. Although he majored in zoology, he began his career in the private sector as a chemical engineer. Pursuing graduate studies at the University of California, Berkeley, in chemistry, with special attention to thermodynamics, he earned a PhD in 1923. For the next couple of years, he worked at the University of

WATER GATE AT 110TH STREET?

In 1609, Hendrick Hudson sailed up the North River, later named in his honor. In 1807, Robert Fulton's steamboat, named the *North River Steamboat of Clermont*, made its way up the North River, to Albany and back. To commemorate these two historical events, the 1909 Hudson-Fulton Celebration was planned. The architect Harold Van Buren Magonigle proposed a water gate complex that would step down from Riverside Drive to the Hudson River at 110th Street. Magonigle had previously designed the Maine Monument at Columbus Circle and the Firemen's Memorial on Riverside Drive at 100th Street. Although the state allocated the land, the subscription funds for the project never materialized, and so the water gate was never built.

TO BUILD OR NOT TO BUILD AT COLUMBIA

Below Uris Hall, which houses Columbia's School of Business, are remnants of University Hall. The architect Charles Follen McKim, of McKim, Mead & White, planned the Hall to be just north of Low Library. It was to be used for large gatherings such as graduations, and it was to seat 2,500 people. A foundation was built, but a shortage of funds frustrated its completion.

In 1969, Columbia hired the architectural firm of Pei Cobb Fried to design a new master plan for the campus. Their proposal called for two 23-story towers for the east and west side of the South Field. After the student protests of 1968, Columbia was in disarray and the plan was never realized.

Copenhagen with Niels Bohr and some of the world's emerging nuclear scientists. After a brief period as a research associate at Johns Hopkins University, he joined the Columbia faculty in 1929. As the world's expert on separating radioactive forms of elements, known as isotopes, Urey was an early and essential player in the Manhattan Project, working on the production of radioactive uranium and the atomic bomb. After World War II, he became a distinguished professor of chemistry at the University of Chicago, and in 1958, he was appointed a professor-at-large at the University of California at La Jolla. His political belief in a world government had him opposing Franco in Spain and denouncing the death sentences of Julius and Ethel Rosenberg.

35 Claremont Avenue (near 119th Street)

Fiske, Thomas Scott (1865–1944), Mathematician ▪

(See bio for Fiske at **527 West 110th Street**.)

Trilling, Diana (1905–1996), Intellectual ▪ ▪

(See bio for Diana Trilling at **620 West 116th Street**.)

Trilling, Lionel (1905–1975), Intellectual ★ ▪

(See bio for Lionel Trilling at **620 West 116th Street**.)

39 Claremont Avenue (near 119th Street)

Chaddock, Robert Emmet (1879–1940) ▪
STATISTICIAN

Dr. Chaddock was part of the effort that created the "census tract" as the primary unit of population measurement in New York. He was one of the nation's most renowned statisticians, having been very influential in the American Statistical Association's efforts in establishing the government's Central Statistical Board for organizing data collection. A native Ohioan, he trained at Wooster College, did graduate work at Columbia, and taught for a while at the Wharton School. At Columbia, he was a professor of statistics and headed up the Sociology Department at one time. He was also a president of the American Statistical Association. Pained by his wife's long-term health problems, he took his own life by a twelve-story plunge from his apartment.

Erskine, John (1879–1951), Educator, Author, and Musician ■ ▮ ☞

(See bio for Erskine at **609 West 113th Street**.)

Hamlin, Alfred Dwight Foster (1855–1926), Architect and Architectural Historian ☞

(See bio for Hamlin at **850 West End Avenue**.)

Jacoby, Harold (1865–1932) ■
ASTRONOMER

Jacoby was known worldwide as an astronomer with a special focus on lunar and solar eclipses. He was the Rutherfurd Professor of Astronomy at Columbia University, and Chairman of the Astronomy Department in his final years. In 1927, during his tenure, Columbia assembled its astronomical equipment on the roof of Pupin Hall and created the Rutherfurd Observatory. A native New Yorker, Jacoby graduated from Columbia with an AB degree in 1885 and a PhD in 1896. After some years of astronomical research, he was made a professor of astronomy at

Columbia in 1894. He authored such books as *Astronomy, A Popular Handbook; Navigation;* and *Practical Talks by an Astronomer*, and he co-authored *The Friendly Stars*. His brother, Oswald Jacoby, was considered one of the greatest bridge players of all time. His great-niece is the author Susan Jacoby.

McBain, Howard Lee (1880–1936), Political Scientist ■ ▪

(See bio for McBain at **448 Riverside Drive**.)

Moehle, Jean Earl (ca.1889–1964), Suffragist and Performance Artist ▪ ☞

(See bio for Moehle at **25 Claremont Avenue**.)

Moley, Raymond C. (1886–1975) ■
POLITICAL SCIENTIST AND HEAD OF F.D.R.'S BRAIN TRUST

Moley is credited with putting the phrase "the forgotten man" into President Franklin Roosevelt's discourse. Quite possibly "New Deal" is his as well. Recruited from Columbia University to advise the president, he, in turn, recruited two other Columbians, **Rexford Tugwell** and Adolph Berle. They constituted the "brain trust" that advised the president in shaping the New Deal policies. Moley advised the president to take the country off the gold standard, to pick Joseph Kennedy as the first Securities and Exchange Commissioner, and to keep J. Edgar Hoover as F.B.I. Director. Moley graduated from Baldwin-Wallace College in his hometown of Berea, Ohio. When he was 21, he was elected Town Clerk of a nearby town, and four years later, mayor. He went on to earn a master's degree at Oberlin College, Ohio, in 1913. After teaching at nearby Western Reserve University, he came to Columbia where he attained his doctorate in 1918. In 1923, he joined the

Barnard faculty to teach government, and in 1928, Columbia made him a Professor of Law. His specialty, the criminal justice system, brought him to the attention of Governor Franklin Roosevelt.

Morgenbesser, Sidney (1921–2004) ■
PHILOSOPHER

In 1968, Professor Morgenbesser was bludgeoned by the police while on a human chain in support of the students who were protesting on Columbia's campus. As the **John Dewey** Professor of Philosophy, he once weighed in on pragmatism: "It's all well in theory but doesn't work in practice." He employed humor to entertain philosophical questions, and his wit was legendary. Like Yogi Berra and **Samuel Goldwyn**, he achieved renown through the quotes and stories attributed to him. A native New Yorker, Morgenbesser was trained at the Jewish Theological Seminary and was ordained a rabbi. He also earned a bachelor's degree from City College and a PhD from the University of Pennsylvania. After teaching at Swarthmore College in Pennsylvania and at the New School for Social Research, he joined the Columbia faculty in 1954. In addition to editing a half dozen anthologies, he edited the *Journal of Philosophy* for many years.

Rostow, Elspeth Vaughan Davies (1917–2007), Professor of Political Science and Presidential Advisor

(See bio for Rostow at **411 West 114th Street**.)

Tyson, Levering (1889–1966), Educator ■

(See bio for Tyson at **419 West 117th Street**.)

Woodbridge, Frederick James Eugene (1867–1940) ■ ▯

DEAN AND PROFESSOR OF PHILOSOPHY

Woodbridge Hall at 431 Riverside Drive is named in honor of the renowned philosopher and Columbia Dean Frederick Woodbridge. Born in Canada, he grew up in Michigan. He graduated from Amherst College in 1889, from Union Theological Seminary in 1892, from Amherst with a master's degree in 1899, and attended the Humboldt University of Berlin to study philosophy. Returning to the United States, he taught at the University of Minnesota, until he joined the Columbia faculty in 1902. In 1904 he co-founded the *Journal of Philosophy*. From 1912 to 1929, he was Dean of the Faculties of Political Science, Philosophy, and Pure Science. Woodbridge, along with John Dewey and George Santayana, introduced philosophical realism to the United States. With a strong underpinning of Aristotle, he founded the philosophical movement of American Naturalism. He authored a number of books on philosophy, and any history of American philosophy should include his contributions. One time he generated some controversy, with much healthy discussion thereafter, when he suggested that most graduate students were merely seeking degrees as proof of their learning, not for passionate scholarship. His son was the architect Frederick James Woodbridge.

130 Claremont Avenue (near 122nd Street)

Erskine, John (1879–1951), Educator, Author, and Musician ■ ▯

(See bio for Erskine at **609 West 113th Street**.)

WHO KNOWS?

Q. Is there a secret tunnel between Columbia and Barnard? A. Who knows? In the book *New York Underground: Anatomy of the City* by Julia Solis, she gives some firsthand detail on the tunnels. However, she does not offer any specific details on tunnels between Columbia and Barnard. Some unauthorized sources on the Internet indicate a connection between the two campuses and offer detailed tunnel maps. But how does a tunnel get under the subway running underneath Broadway?

160 Claremont Avenue (near La Salle Street)

Trilling, Diana (1905–1996), Intellectual ■ ▮

(See bio for Diana Trilling at **620 West 116th Street.**)

Trilling, Lionel (1905–1975), Intellectual ★ ■

(See bio for Lionel Trilling at **620 West 116th Street.**)

175 Claremont Avenue (near La Salle Street)

Rabi, Isador Isaac "I. I." (1898–1988), Physicist ★ ■

(See bio for Rabi at **450 Riverside Drive.**)

HONORARY STREET NAMES— WEST 110S

Barnard Way (the corner of 116th Street and Broadway)
This 2014 designation marks the 125th anniversary of Barnard's founding in 1889.
Grace Gold Way (Broadway between 115th Street and 116th Street)
Grace Gold was the Barnard freshman killed by a falling piece of masonry.

Columbia campus in the Morningside Heights neighborhood ca. 1926.

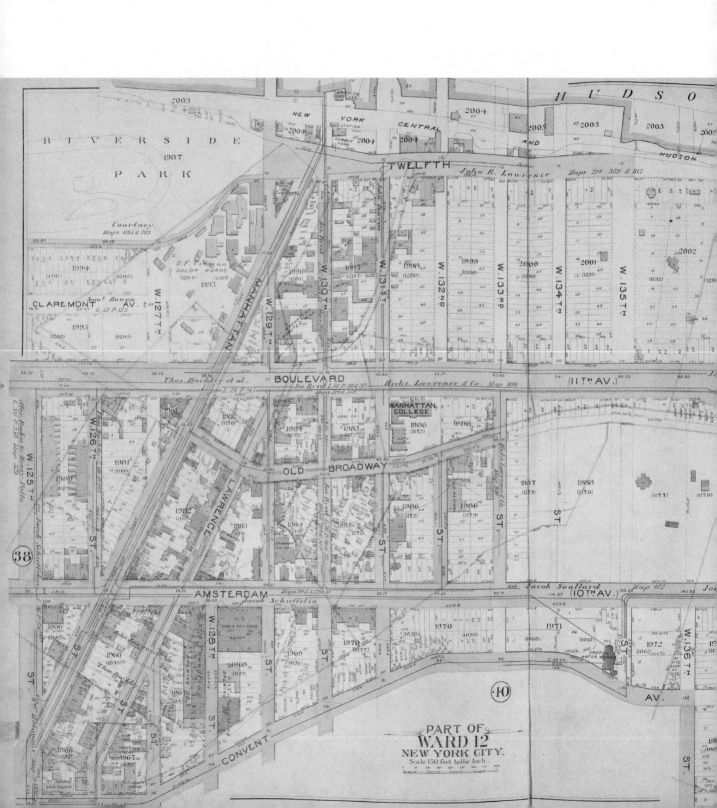

PART OF
WARD 12
NEW YORK CITY.
Scale 150 feet to the Inch.

The West 120s

The West 120s, an area that seems to fight the orderly street-grid, deserves to be better known. It is home to world-class institutions—Teachers College, Union Theological Seminary, Jewish Theological Seminary, the Manhattan School of Music, the Jerome L. Greene Science Center, the Lenfest Center for the Arts, the Forum, and the Columbia Business School. The center of the Columbia campus is clearly shifting north. The West 120s has a fresh vibe with new restaurants and proximity to Harlem's commercial activity. As with any changing neighborhood, the development of new structures that challenge earlier conventions of style and height has not come without conflict.

423 West 120th Street (near Amsterdam Avenue)

Sovern, Michael Ira (1931–2020), University President and Legal Scholar ■

(See bio for Sovern at **60 Morningside Drive**.)

434 West 120th Street (near Amsterdam Avenue)

Britton, Nanna "Nan" Popham (1896–1991)
MISTRESS OF WARREN G. HARDING

DNA testing confirmed Ms. Britton's claim that President Warren G. Harding fathered her daughter, Elizabeth. In 1927, after Harding's death in office, Nan wrote what is thought to be the first kiss-and-tell book, *The President's Daughter*. It received much attention and much skepticism until recently. Britton claimed to have been intimate with Harding for several years in Ohio when he was Governor, as well as during his presidency. She maintained that they were intimate in the White House and that after she moved to New York City, they had dalliances in Central Park and Riverside Park.

Nan Britton.

501 West 120th Street (near Amsterdam Avenue)

Noble, Alfred (1844–1914) ■ ▮
CIVIL ENGINEER

In his day, Noble was the dean of American engineers. He was born in Michigan and graduated from the University of Michigan in 1870 with a degree in civil engineering. He served three years in the Civil War, including at the Battle of Gettysburg. His professional career began with performing harbor surveys on Lakes Michigan and Huron with the US Army Corps of Engineers. Thereafter he built steel truss bridges for railroads. In 1886, he came to New York City to be the resident engineer for the Washington Bridge over the Harlem River. His stature rose as he took charge of the erection of five bridges over the Mississippi, including the one at Memphis, Tennessee. As a member of the Isthmian Canal Commission created by Congress, he is thought to have strongly influenced the use of locks in the design of the Panama Canal. In New York, he consulted on the foundation work for new skyscrapers and was appointed a member of the Board of Engineers of the Pennsylvania Railroad that planned for tunnel access into Manhattan. Furthermore, as chief engineer, he was responsible for the building of the tunnel under the East River to bring the Long Island Railroad into Pennsylvania Station. He was a president of the American Society of Civil Engineers and was awarded honorary doctorates by the University of Wisconsin and his alma mater, the University of Michigan.

Stone, Harlan Fiske (1872–1946), Chief Justice of the Supreme Court ★ ▪ ▮

(See bio for Stone at **435 Riverside Drive**.)

Thorndike, Edward Lee (1874–1949) ★ ▪ ▮
PSYCHOLOGIST AND PROFESSOR OF EDUCATION

Born in Massachusetts, Thorndike graduated from Wesleyan University, Connecticut, with a BA in 1895. He earned an MA at Harvard two years later and studied with an interest in animal learning under the great psychologist and philosopher William James. Thorndike went on to Columbia University, where he completed his PhD with a dissertation on animal psychology and then began teaching at Teachers College. Thorndike was president of the American Association for the Advancement of Science, the American Psychological Society, the Association of Adult Education, and the Psychometric Society. In

1917, he was admitted to the National Academy of Sciences and was elected as a Fellow of the American Statistical Association. He received honorary degrees from seven universities including Columbia and Harvard. Thorndike also lived at **530 West 123rd Street** (near Broadway).

Wood, Thomas Denison (1865–1951) ★ ■ ▉

PHYSICAL EDUCATOR

Wood has been called the Father of Physical Education. From 1891, when he was the first medical director and professor of health and hygiene at the brand-new Stanford University, he began developing some of the earliest education principles of healthful living, including favoring sports and games over the regimen of gymnastics. Born in Illinois, Wood graduated from Oberlin College in 1888, and from Columbia's College of Physicians and Surgeons with a medical degree in 1891. From 1901 to 1927, he was a professor of physical education at Columbia and then a professor of health at Teachers College, where he was awarded emeritus status in 1931. He authored or co-authored numerous books on health and education.

414 West 121st Street (near Amsterdam Avenue)

Wallis, Wilson Allen (1912–1998) ★ ■ ▉ ☜

ECONOMIST, STATISTICIAN, AND EDUCATOR

The Statistical Research Group at Columbia that was put together by Wallis during World War II was the most extraordinary group of statistical talent ever assembled. It operated out of 401 West 118th Street and included Jimmie Savage, the pioneer of decision theory and champion of Bayesian statistics; Frederick Mosteller, who would establish Harvard's statistics department; Norbert Wiener, the noted MIT mathematician and creator of cybernetics; Abraham Wald, who founded the field of statistical sequential analysis; and the future Nobel Prize winner, economist Milton Friedman. Born in Philadelphia, Pennsylvania, Wallis graduated from the University of Minnesota in 1932. He did graduate work there, as well as at the University of Chicago and Columbia University. After working as an economist in the mid-1930s at the National Resources Committee, he was the director of research at the United States Office of Scientific Research and Development through World War II. From 1956 to 1962, Wallis was dean of the University of Chicago Graduate School of Business. He left to become president of the University of Rochester, and in 1970 he was appointed their chancellor. He retired in 1982. Throughout his career, he held various government posts and advised presidents Eisenhower, Nixon, Ford, and Reagan. Wallis also lived at **106 Morningside Drive** (near 121st Street).

501 West 121st Street (near Amsterdam Avenue)

Hanau, Stella Bloch (1890–1972) ▦
PUBLICIST

Stella Hanau managed Paul Robeson's first concert in 1925, and she was a press agent and publicist for such early and experimental theater groups as the Neighborhood Playhouse, the Greenwich Village Theater, Playwrights Theater, and the Provincetown Playhouse. In 1931, she co-authored "The Provincetown: A Story of the Theater." She also worked with Margaret Sanger, editing publications for the American Birth Control League, including *Birth Control Review*, and she served as educational director of the National Committee on Federal Legislation for Birth Control. A New York native, Hanau graduated from Barnard in 1911 with a BA degree. At Barnard, she participated in the College Settlements Association, the Intercollegiate Socialist Society, and Barnard's chapter of the Collegiate Equal Suffrage League of New York.

She was also active with the college's theatrical productions. Hanau was associated, socially and professionally, with fellow Barnard classmates, **Hella Bernays**, Katherine Gay, and **Doris Elsa Fleischman**.

509 West 121st Street (near Amsterdam Avenue)

Latham, Minor White (1881–1968), Emeritus English Professor
■ ▯

(See bio for Latham at **401 West 118th Street**.)

501 West 121st Street (near Amsterdam Avenue)

Yukawa, Hideki (1907–1981)
PHYSICIST

In 1935, Yukawa published his theory that mesons were the carrier particles of nuclear force. In 1947, he predicted the existence of the pi meson, for which he was awarded the Nobel Prize in Physics two years later. In 1949, the pi meson that he predicted was discovered. Yukawa was born in Japan and graduated in 1929 from Kyoto Imperial University. He taught there for four years before becoming an assistant professor at Osaka University in 1933, where he earned his doctorate in 1938. In 1940, he returned to Kyoto as a full professor of theoretical physics and stayed there through the war years. His reputation survived the war, and in 1949, he arrived at Columbia as a professor of physics. In short order, he received honorary memberships in such scientific bulwarks as the Royal Society and an honorary doctorate from the University of Paris. He returned to Kyoto University where he retired as Professor Emeritus in 1970.

WHO KNOWS?

Q. Why was the great lyricist **Oscar Hammerstein II** named Oscar Greeley Clendenning Hammerstein?
A. We can only guess. His mother indicated that he was given Greeley in tribute to the newspaper publisher and presidential candidate, Horace Greeley. The educated guess is that she wanted a distinguished name and heard of Clendening (or Clendenning, as it is also spelled) in the Bloomingdale neighborhood where there was a Clendening Hotel on Amsterdam Avenue and 103rd Street. The hotel and the nearby Clendening Valley took their name from Bloomingdale resident **John Clendening**.

509 West 121st Street (near Amsterdam Avenue)

Hammerstein, Oscar Greeley Clendenning, II (1895–1960) ★ ■

LYRICIST

Hammerstein elevated the American musical by modernizing it with a meaningful story and fully integrated song lyrics. Before him, Broadway musicals were flimsy stories with songs attached, or they were showcases for songs held together by flimsy stories. *Showboat* illustrates this brilliant and revolutionary phenomenon and reminds us that Hammerstein not only collaborated with Rogers but also with Vincent Youmans, Sigmund Romberg, Rudolf Friml, and Jerome Kern. Born and raised in New York City, Hammerstein graduated from Columbia and attended Columbia University Law School for one year. Columbia students produced an annual "Varsity Show" that introduced Hammerstein to **Lorenz Hart** and led to his meeting Richard Rogers. From his partnership with Rogers came *Oklahoma, Carousel, South Pacific, The King and I, The Sound of Music,* and much more. Hammerstein was given the middle name "Greeley" in tribute to the newspaper publisher Horace Greeley. But what about "Clendenning"? (See sidebar, "Who Knows?".) His grandfather was the impresario, **Oscar Hammerstein I**.

Wells, Bettina Borrmann (1874–Unknown)

SUFFRAGIST

In 1908, the New York City Police Commissioner denied a permit to Wells and other suffragists who wanted to march down Broadway. Along with fellow suffragist Maud Malone, she frustrated the police by planning a "silent march" that never really materialized but gained much publicity that led to public discourse and, eventually, full-fledged marches. Having been a member of the British Women's Social and Political Union when she lived in England, she brought the British women's militant approach to the suffragists' cause. Wells was born in Bavaria, Germany, and migrated to England, where she met and married her husband, Herbert James Clement Wells, in 1900. She arrived in the United States a few years later and, in addition to continuing to crusade for suffrage, she studied psychology at Columbia University, graduating with a BS degree in 1915 and an MA in 1916.

519 West 121 Street (near Broadway)

Carlin, George Dennis Patrick (1937–2008) ▇

COMEDIAN

George Carlin.

Carlin will forever be remembered for "The Seven Words You Can Never Say on Television." His early appearances on television revealed a refreshing and witty comic whose commentary made hilarious fun of the simple details of life. With the changing '60s, Carlin pushed the edge and then some, mocking authority, especially in government and religion. He was too risqué for TV or Vegas, but colleges and concerts were ideal for his large followings. His books were more sophisticated than traditional joke books, and they were all best sellers. He was born in New York City, and he honed his irreverent skills as class comedian in the numerous Catholic schools he was kicked out of. Carlin would have had a field day with the controversy that ensued over naming a two-block stretch of West 121St Street "George Carlin Way" in 2014 (see Honorary Street Names).

529 West 121st Street (near Broadway)

Ford, George Barry (1885–1978) ▇

ROMAN CATHOLIC PRIEST

Columbia's Ford Hall recognized his role as its chaplain, and as a champion of civil rights and religious tolerance. With friends such as Eleanor Roosevelt; John D. Rockefeller, Jr.; Robert Moses; and Irving Berlin; Father Ford was beloved, with the exception of many of his fellow Roman Catholic clergy. The archdiocesan authorities reprimanded him for sending flowers to the Riverside Church on its 100th anniversary. Cardinal Spellman officially silenced him for a time, perhaps because he favored the ordination of women as priests, or because he called Senator McCarthy a "demagogue." Born in upstate New York, Ford graduated from Niagara University in 1908. After his training in St. Joseph's Seminary in Yonkers, he was ordained a priest in St. Patrick's Cathedral in 1914. After many years with a Harlem congregation, he was appointed pastor of Corpus Christi Church on West 121st Street. Columbia, Manhattan College, and Seton Hall College awarded him honorary degrees.

630 West 121st Street (near Broadway)

Bates, Blanche (1873–1941)
ACTRESS

Blanche Bates.

In 1905, Bates appeared in a play written and directed by David Belasco, *Girl of the Golden West*, which would be made into an opera by Puccini. Five years previously, she appeared in Belasco's *Madame Butterfly*, which Puccini made into one of his most endearing operas. For some thirty years she was a mainstay of the Broadway stage in leading roles. Her last appearance, in 1933, was with young Katherine Hepburn in *The Lake*. Bates was born in Oregon but was educated in San Francisco where she made her stage debut. She performed in the first West Coast offering of Ibsen's *A Doll House*. She was married to the noted writer and journalist George Creel.

504 West 122nd Street (near Amsterdam Avenue)

Brace, Donald Clifford (1881–1955), Publisher

(See bio for Brace at **74 West 102nd Street**.)

509 West 122nd Street (near Amsterdam Avenue)

Dewey, Thomas E. (1902–1971) ■
LAWYER, DISTRICT ATTORNEY, GOVERNOR, AND PRESIDENTIAL CANDIDATE

Columbia's Law School in the mid-1920s had two accomplished singers:
Paul Robeson and Thomas E. Dewey. Dewey, who sang in his church
choir and college glee club, won the Michigan state singing contest
and finished third in a national singing contest. Though he considered
singing professionally, he opted instead for a career in law. Born in
Michigan, Dewey graduated from the University of Michigan in 1923
and from Columbia Law School in 1925. After some private law practice,
he joined the New York District Attorney's office at age 35 and put away
numerous mobsters, including Charles "Lucky" Luciano. He was elected
governor of New York three times, and he ran for President in 1952,
losing to Harry S. Truman despite the *Chicago Daily Tribune*'s banner
headline: "Dewey Defeats Truman," which proved premature. He was a
third cousin to Admiral George Dewey, and his soprano-singing wife,
born Francis Eileen Hutt, was a grandniece of Jefferson Davis.

514 West 122nd Street (near Amsterdam Avenue)

Lamb, Willis Eugene, Jr. (1913–2008)
PHYSICIST

The Lamb Shift denotes a measurement of differences in energy levels
within the hydrogen atom. It was considered a central theme of physics
and significant in the development of modern quantum electrodynamics.
Accordingly, Lamb was awarded the Nobel Prize in Physics in 1955. Born in
California, Lamb graduated in 1934 with a BS degree in chemistry and in
1938 with his doctorate in physics, both from the University of California,
Berkeley. In 1938, he also joined the faculty of Columbia and worked in its
radiation laboratory, attending to the measurement of the dispersion of
light from the spectrum. From 1951 to 1956, he was a professor of physics

at Stanford University. For the next six years, he was a professor of theoretical physics at the University of Oxford in England, followed by a position as professor of physics at Yale. Lastly, he was appointed professor of physics and optical sciences at the University of Arizona in 1974, from which he retired as professor emeritus in 2002.

Luce, Henry Robinson (1898–1967) ◼

MAGAZINE PUBLISHER

Henry Luce.

Henry Luce and a friend, Briton Hadden, started *Time* magazine in 1922. In 1930, Luce started the business magazine *Fortune*. He acquired *Life* magazine in 1936 and rebuilt it in a weekly, photojournalism format. *Sports Illustrated* didn't launch until 1954, but along the way Luce continued to build his empire with numerous magazines offering a wide variety of content. The man who created the modern magazine was born in China to missionary parents. He graduated from Yale University where he was a member of the secretive Skull and Bones society, and he studied history for a year at Oxford. Clare Boothe Luce, who is thought to have been born somewhere near West 125th Street, became his second wife in 1935. She wrote a hit play, *The Women*, served as an ambassador, and was elected twice to Congress. Henry and Clare were one of the great power couples of their day.

606 West 122nd Street (near Claremont Avenue)

Forbes, Rev James Alexander, Jr. (1935–)

MINISTER

Forbes was the first African American senior minister at Riverside Church, which housed one of the largest and most prominent multicultural congregations in the nation. His stature and accomplishments earned him thirteen honorary doctorates, including ones from Princeton, Dickinson College, Colgate University, Trinity College, and Lehigh University. Born in North Carolina, Forbes earned a BS degree in chemistry from Howard University in 1957, a Master of Divinity degree from Union Theological Seminary in 1962, and a Doctor of Ministry degree from Colgate Rochester Divinity School in 1975. From 1976 to 1989, he taught at Union Theological Seminary. In the 1960s, he held pastorates at three churches in the south and was also campus minister at Virginia Union University. He also lived at **99 Claremont Avenue (near 122nd Street).**

606 West 122nd Street (near Claremont Avenue), Union Theological Seminary residence

Fosdick, Harry Emerson (1878–1969)
PASTOR

Fosdick was the founding pastor of Riverside Church, having arrived after William Jennings Bryan and other fundamentalists pushed him out of First Presbyterian Church on Fifth Avenue at 12th Street. They had problems with Fosdick after he said in his famous sermon, "Shall the Fundamentalists win?" He also said that Darwinism and Christianity were not necessarily in conflict. This constituted the deep split in Protestantism between the Modernists and the Fundamentalists. Fosdick was born in Buffalo and graduated from Colgate University. He also graduated summa cum laude from Union Theological Seminary. Shortly after, he was ordained a Baptist minister. After Fosdick gave his controversial sermon, he underwent a formal church investigation whereby he was defended by future Secretary of State John Foster Dulles. John D. Rockefeller, Jr., seized the opportunity to attract Fosdick to the new Riverside Church that he was building. There his progressive preaching continued, sometimes with controversy, until his retirement in 1946.

344 West 123rd Street (near Manhattan Avenue)

Mullan, Helen St. Clair (1877–1936, Lawyer) ◼ ▮

(See bio for Mullan at **430 West 116th Street**.)

429 West 123rd Street (near Morningside Avenue)

Dreiser, Theodore Herman Albert (1871–1945), Novelist and Journalist ■

(See bio for Dreiser at **6 West 102nd Street**.)

449 West 123rd Street (near Amsterdam Avenue)

Rose, Mary Davies Swartz (1874–1941), Nutrition Educator ★ ■ ▣

(See bio for Rose at **79 Manhattan Avenue**.)

501 West 123rd Street (near Amsterdamn Avenue)

Marshall, Thurgood (1908–1993) ★ ■
SUPREME COURT JUSTICE

Marshall's crowning achievement was successfully arguing the 1954 Supreme Court decision of *Brown v. Board of Education* of Topeka wherein the Supreme Court threw out the "separate but equal" doctrine. In addition to Marshall's stellar legal team, the effort included essential support from historian John Hope Franklin and psychologist Dr. Kenneth Clark. Born in Baltimore, Maryland, Marshall graduated with a BA from Lincoln University, Pennsylvania, where his fellow students were Cab Calloway and Langston Hughes. In 1933, he received his law degree from Howard University School of Law, graduating first in his class. He practiced private law, having a constant and active association with the NAACP. Working under the shadow of the "separate but equal" doctrine of *Plessey v. Ferguson*, he fought against injustice and, at age 32, won a case (*Chambers vs. Florida*) before the Supreme Court. He founded the NAACP Legal Defense and Educational Fund, which advanced more cases that were won in the Supreme Court. President Kennedy appointed him to the US Court of Appeals. President Johnson selected him to be Solicitor General and, two years later, in 1967, appointed him to the highest court in the land. He was the first African American to hold that position, and he served for twenty-four years.

Thurgood Marshall.

528 West 123rd Street (near Amsterdam Avenue)

Sturtevant, Alfred Henry (1891–1970) ◼

PIONEER GENETICIST

In 1913, Sturtevant constructed the first genetic map of a chromosome. In his honor, the distance in an embryo between organs is called a "sturt." Born in Illinois, Sturtevant, as a Columbia student, boarded with his older brother, Edgar Sturtevant, who taught linguistics at Barnard. In 1914, he was awarded a PhD degree at Columbia. Studies he had done as a student determined the frequency of genetic crossing-over rates and sex-linked traits. His work was done in the laboratory of Columbia's future Nobel geneticist Thomas Hunt Morgan. Sturtevant worked at Columbia for the Carnegie Institution of Washington from 1914 until he left for the California Institute of Technology in 1928. In 1967, President Lyndon B. Johnson awarded him the National Medal of Science.

530 West 123rd Street (near Broadway)

Slosson, May Gorslin (1858–1943) ◼ 📖

PIONEER IN EDUCATION AND SUFFRAGIST

In 1880, Slosson became the first woman to obtain a PhD from Cornell, and the first woman in the United States to earn a doctorate in philosophy. Always in the shadows of her renowned husband,

Edward Emery Slosson, and her son, Preston William Slosson, she distinguished herself as a notable and active suffragist. Born in upstate New York but raised in Kansas, she graduated from Hillsdale College with a BS degree in 1878 and an MS degree in 1879, and then she went on to Cornell for her doctorate. After teaching Greek for a few years at Hastings College in Nebraska, she worked as an assistant principal at a high school in Kansas, where she met and married her husband. She became a history professor in Wyoming and developed a program for educating prisoners in the Wyoming State Penitentiary. From 1899 to 1903 she served as the prison's chaplain. In 1903, her family moved to New York, and she threw herself into the women's suffrage movement.

530 West 123rd Street (near Broadway)

Thorndike, Edward Lee (1874–1949), Psychologist and Professor of Education ★ ■ ▣

(See bio for Thorndike at 501 West 120th Street.)

540 West 123rd Street (near Broadway)

Henderson, Donald J. (ca.1902–Unknown)
ECONOMICS PROFESSOR AND COMMUNIST ACTIVIST

Before the student protests at Columbia of 1968, there was the famous protest of 1933 when 1,500 students rallied to demand the reappointment of Professor Henderson, who had been fired for being a communist. The artist Diego Rivera and others spoke to the crowd as fistfights broke out and noses were bloodied. A coffin labeled "Here Lies Academic Freedom" was deposited on the steps in front of Low Library and the Alma Mater sculpture was blindfolded with a piece of black cloth. Henderson's firing caused several protests and split the academic community around the issue of academic freedom. Henderson went on to organize and become president of the United Cannery, Agricultural, Packing, and Allied Workers union, a Congress of Industrial Organizations affiliate. Always an avowed communist, he was an officer in numerous communist front-organizations and thereby received much attention from the House Un-American Activities Committee. He married his wife and fellow communist, **Eleanor Curtis Henderson**, in 1925.

Henderson, Eleanor Curtis (1901–1941)
COMMUNIST ACTIVIST

Henderson ran and lost in New York's Twenty-first Congressional District on the Communist ticket. Born in Manhattan, she was a Columbia graduate student who married the Columbia professor and fellow communist, **Donald Henderson**. Although she weighed less than 85 pounds as an adult, she was constantly agitating for her beliefs and getting arrested. She was arrested for creating a disturbance at a Home Relief Bureau in Harlem. Then she was arrested again for protesting in front of the sentencing magistrate's residence. In Kentucky, she and other students were ejected from the coalfields when they protested the working conditions of the miners and pressed for a congressional inquiry. In New Jersey, she was arrested for a disturbance that came out of a protest against working conditions on farms. Eleanor Henderson also lived at **174 West 109th Street** (near Amsterdam Avenue) and **507 West 111th Street** (near Amsterdam Avenue).

Kusch, Polykarp (1911–1993)
PHYSICIST

Some of Kusch's work was essential in the development of MRI (Magnetic Resonance Imaging) technology. His measurements determined that the magnetic moment of an electron was greater

THE TALLEST BUILDING IN THE WORLD?

In 1925, plans were drawn up for the tallest building in the world, to be built on a site on Broadway and 123rd Street. (See **Oscar E. Konkle**, on page 176, for details.)

than its theoretical value, thus refining thermodynamics and enabling numerous innovations, such as the MRI. His work earned him a Nobel Prize in 1955, which he shared with one-time fellow Columbia physicist **Willis Lamb** for his work on the spectrum of hydrogen. Kusch was born in Germany, but his family brought him to the United States as an infant. In 1931, he graduated with a BS degree from the Case School of Applied Science, now Case Western Reserve, in Cleveland, Ohio. He continued his studies in physics at the University of Illinois, where he earned his PhD degree in 1936. He taught there and at the University of Minnesota for a few years, but as World War II got underway, he joined the effort of the National Defense Research Committee where he concentrated on radar-related technology. From 1944, he worked at the world-famous Bell Telephone Laboratories, until he chose to teach at Columbia in 1946.

549 West 123rd Street (near Broadway)

Dudley, Edward R. (1911–2005)
MANHATTAN BOROUGH PRESIDENT

Dudley was the second Black borough president of Manhattan. Hulan Jack was the first. Dudley was also the first Black ambassador to a foreign country, in his case, Liberia. Born in Virginia, he graduated from Johnson C. Smith College in North Carolina. Soon after he arrived in New York City, he worked on public theater projects, including a stint as stage manager for Orson Welles. Next came his law degree from St. John's University Law School, and that led to politics. **Thurgood Marshall** encouraged him to join the NAACP legal team. During his borough presidency, he ran for state attorney general, but lost to Louis Lefkowitz. His final service was as an administrative judge on the State Supreme Court.

445 West 124th Street (near Morningside Avenue)

Quill, Michael J. (1905–1966) ■
LABOR UNION ORGANIZER AND EXECUTIVE

Older New Yorkers remember Quill as head of the Transport Workers Union and the leader of its strike in the earliest days of Mayor John Lindsay's administration. The city's subways and buses were halted for twelve days, and Lindsay had to swallow some humble pie to end it all. Quill went to jail and died of a heart attack three days after the settlement. Born in Ireland, Quill, as a teenager, served the Irish Republican Army as a dispatch rider. In 1926, he came to the United States and worked for the part of the New York City subway system known as the IRT, the Interborough Rapid Transit Company. Because his work responsibilities had him moving throughout the system, he came to know many transit workers. As the city grew and consolidated its transportation, Quill and others established the Transport Workers Union in 1934. The Union flirted with connections to the Communist Party and national unions, but with powerful leaders like Quill, it was a constant and powerful force.

500 West 124th Street (near Morningside Avenue)

Hollingworth, Harry Levi (1880–1956), Psychologist ■

(See bio for Hollingworth at **417 West 118th Street**.)

503 West 124th Street (near Morningside Avenue)

Van Doren, Mark (1894–1972) ★ ■
POET AND LITERARY SCHOLAR

Jack Kerouac quit Columbia's football team to spend his time studying Shakespeare with Professor Mark Van Doren. Van Doren is generally acknowledged as one of Columbia University's greatest teachers ever, inspiring students such as Kerouac, **Lionel Trilling**, Thomas Merton, Clifton Fadiman, John Berryman, and **Allen Ginsberg**. Van Doren was born in Illinois and was a Phi Beta Kappa student at the University of Illinois at Urbana–Champaign where he received his bachelor's and master's degrees. He earned his doctorate at Columbia, despite serving in World War I during his studies. In 1940, he received the Pulitzer Prize for Poetry. Like Robert Frost, with whom he was often compared, he celebrated America and nature. His brother was the literary editor and biographer **Carl Van Doren**. His son was Charles Van Doren, who was embroiled in a quiz show scandal in the 1950s. His wife was Dorothy Graffe Van Doren.

505 West 124th Street (near Morningside Avenue)

Liebowitz, Benjamin (1890–1977) ■ ☞
ENGINEER AND INVENTOR

Liebowitz invented the semi-stiff collar, thereby eliminating the need to starch a shirt after laundering. His Trubenizing Process Corporation capitalized on the process he invented. A native New Yorker, Liebowitz graduated from Columbia in 1911 with a degree in electrical engineering, and soon thereafter he had his PhD. He worked for Thomas Edison for a time but went on to research in the realms of quantum mechanics and relativity. In 1932, he befriended the physicist **Leo Szilard**, and they worked on getting support for refugees escaping the threat of Nazism in Europe. When Szilard discovered that a uranium-based chain reaction might be possible, Liebowitz loaned him $5,000 to construct an experiment to prove it. Liebowitz focused his efforts on radar development during World War II.

510 West 124th Street (near Morningside Avenue)

Grady, Eleanor Hunsdon (1886–1970) ▪

EDUCATOR

Grady was largely responsible for organizing Hunter College's Bronx campus, now Lehman College, into a four-year co-educational college. Previously, she had been academic dean at Hunter from 1941. Soon after she joined the Hunter faculty in 1915, she served as de facto president while the nominal president was serving in a civilian capacity in Germany after World War I. She taught sociology and economics. A New York native, Grady studied Greek and Latin and graduated from Barnard in 1908. She earned a master's degree in 1911 and a PhD degree in 1930 from Columbia. She taught at Mount Holyoke from 1911 to 1914 before arriving at Hunter.

520 West 124th Street (near Morningside Avenue)

Tyson, Levering (1889–1966), Educator ◼

(See bio for Tyson at **419 West 117th Street**.)

31 Tiemann Place (near Broadway)

Slavin, John C. (ca.1869–1940)

VAUDEVILLE COMEDIAN, ACTOR, AND CHOREOGRAPHER

Slavin played the Wizard in the original production of *The Wizard of Oz* on Broadway in 1902. A native of New York, he began performing as early as 1879 in a singing act called *The Madrigal Boys*. In 1894, he appeared in the play *1492*, a musical extravaganza that ran for four hundred performances. Three years later he was in *The Belle of New York*, and that was followed by many shows. In Florenz Ziegfeld's 1916 production of *The Century Girl*, Slavin played the great Irving Berlin as a character in the show. A few years later, New York Giants baseball team manager **John J. McGraw** got into a drunken rage with Slavin at the Lambs Club.

69 Tiemann Place (near Riverside Drive)

Von Luther, Sidney Albert (1925–1985)

NEW YORK STATE SENATOR

In addition to being known as the "gadfly of the Senate," von Luther was a constant foe of Columbia University, his Democratic primary rival H. Carl McCall, and Borough President Percy Sutton. Born in the Virgin Islands, Von Luther graduated from the University of Maryland and attended the London School of Economics. He worked as a nurse at Grasslands Hospital, worked for the Congress of Racial Equality to register voters, and directed the organizing efforts of Local 1199 of the Drug, Hospital, and Health Care Employees Union. He ran successfully for the State Senate when Basil Paterson gave up his seat to run for lieutenant governor. He lost his seat after two terms, coming in third in the Democratic primary behind H. Carl McCall.

Site of 127th Street, East of Riverside Avenue, Now Tiemann Place, East of Riverside Drive

Tiemann, Daniel Fawcett (1805–1899) ★ ■
MAYOR AND INDUSTRIALIST

Tiemann was the longest-lived ex-mayor of New York City when he died at age 94. He was elected as mayor in 1857 in response to the effects of the Panic of 1857 and as an independent with the support of Tammany Hall. During his mayoralty, the Crystal Palace burned, Central Park was begun, and the Atlantic Cable was laid. He was one of the initial investors in the cable company, and he sent a congratulatory cable message to the mayor of London. He is also credited with placing street names on lampposts. Born in New York, he ran a family paint-works business and married a niece of Peter Cooper. Taking an interest in public affairs, he and Cooper were members of the city's first Board of Education. Later he would be one of the initial trustees of Cooper Union. Tiemann was present for the first arrival of water from the Croton Aqueduct in 1842 and for the building of City Hall, which was completed in 1812. His son was Peter Cooper Tiemann.

92 Morningside Avenue (near 122nd Street)

Rich, Marcus Charles (1881–1941) ■ ▣
STOCKBROKER AND BIRDER

For many years, Charles Rich was the unofficial compiler of birding records in Central Park. In addition to serving as an associate of the American Ornithologists' Union, he was an active member of the Linnaean Society of New York, to which he reported his bird migration data. He was instrumental in having part of Central Park fenced off as a bird sanctuary. Born in New York, he studied chemistry but became a securities broker. He married Eva Jacobs, a 1909 graduate of Barnard who taught music, and volunteered in the women's suffrage movement. Eva introduced him to birding, and the two of them were especially noted for introducing younger people to the New York birding experience.

98 Morningside Avenue (near 122nd Street)

Von Tilzer, Albert (1878–1956) ★ ■
SONGWRITER

Von Tilzer co-wrote with **Jack Norworth** what is thought to be the third most sung song in the English language: "Take Me Out to the Ball Game." It is said that only "Happy Birthday" and "The Star-Spangled Banner" are sung more often. He wrote long-forgotten, popular-in-their-day parlor songs such as "Oh, How She Could Yacki Hacki Wicki Wacki Woo" and "Put on Your Slippers and Fill Up Your Pipe, You're Not Going Bye-Bye Tonight." The Andrews Sisters had success with reviving his "(I'll Be with You) In Apple Blossom Time." Born Albert Gumm or Gummbinsky in Indiana, he worked briefly for his notable songwriting brother Harry von Tilzer's music publishing company. He contributed songs to a couple of dozen Broadway productions and was a charter member of the American Society of Composers, Authors, and Publishers.

105 Morningside Avenue (near 123rd Street)

Hamlin, Alfred Dwight Foster (1855–1926), Architect and Architectural Historian ☞

(See bio for Hamlin at **850 West End Avenue**.)

106 Morningside Avenue (near 123rd Street)

Earhart, Amelia (1897–1937) ★ ■
AVIATRIX

Amelia Earhart.

Earhart lived on the north side of Morningside Park while attending one semester at Columbia in 1920. Later that year, she joined her family in California where she took her first airplane ride, which would change her life. In 1924, she returned to the east coast and attended Columbia for a few months before settling in the Boston area. One year after Lindbergh's flight across the Atlantic, Earhart flew as a passenger, and was the first female to cross the Atlantic with a pilot and a mechanic. Now a celebrity, she was given a ticker tape parade in New York City and a reception with President Coolidge at the White House. In 1932, she became the first woman to make a solo flight across the Atlantic. She set numerous flight records, but tragically in 1937, just before her 40th birthday, she and her navigator, Fred Noonan, disappeared somewhere over the South Pacific Ocean. Born in Kansas, Earhart also lived in Iowa, Minnesota, and Chicago, as her father's job with a railroad moved their family about.

90 Morningside Drive (near 120th Street)

Breslow, Ronald (1931–2017)
ORGANIC CHEMIST

Breslow is the father of biomimetic chemistry, a phrase he coined in the 1950s to describe the use of principles of nature employed in chemistry. His work in this realm yielded, amongst other things, the co-discovery of an inhibitor used in treating certain cancers. The design and synthesis of new molecules occupied his research and produced new avenues in applied organics and pharmacology. His professional awards are too extensive to list but include the National Medal of Science. His professional memberships were many, including Great Britain's Royal Society, the National Academy of Sciences, and the American Chemical Society, of which he was president. Columbia named him its Samuel Latham Mitchell Professor of Chemistry. It also awarded him the Mark Van Doren Medal, the Alexander Hamilton Award, and the Great Teacher Award. Breslow was born in New Jersey, and earned his BAin 1952, MA in 1954, and PhD in 1955, all from Harvard. He arrived at Columbia in 1956, and in time chaired the Department of Chemistry.

Hollingworth, Harry Levi (1880–1956), Psychologist ▣

(See bio for Hollingworth at **417 West 118th Street**.)

Orton, Lawrence M. (1899–1988) ▪ ▣
CITY PLANNER

Orton was an original member of the New York City Planning Commission from its inception in 1938. He was also a general director of the Regional Plan Association from the 1920s, and he was New York City Planning Commissioner in the 1950s. With those responsibilities, he was at the heart of activities creating much of the city's infrastructure, often working directly with the likes of mayors La Guardia and Wagner, governors Lehman and Rockefeller, and "construction czar" Robert Moses. In the Bloomingdale–Morningside Heights area, his support for urban renewal helped enable Park West Village, the Grant Houses, the Douglass Houses, and Morningside Gardens, where he became its executive director. Born in Michigan,

Orton graduated from Cornell University in 1923. He came to New York for work, married, and lived in Queens. In 1960, he became only the third recipient of the Medal of Honor for City Planning, the previous two being George McAneny and Nelson Rockefeller.

106 Morningside Drive (near 121st Street)

Wallis, Wilson Allen (1912–1998), Economist, Statistician, and Educator ★ ■ ▮ ☞

(See bio for Wallis at 414 West 121st Street.)

114 Morningside Drive (near 122nd Street)

Dingwall, Andrew (1892–1980) ☞
CHEMIST

On June 30, 1931, Professor Andrew Dingwall blew up a chemistry laboratory on the third floor of Havemeyer Hall on Columbia University's campus. He was conducting an experiment when a tube of acid exploded, smashing the windows facing Broadway and causing a ruckus heard several blocks away. Dingwall was taken to nearby St. Luke's Hospital for treatment of burns and lacerations. Born in Scotland, he arrived in the United States in 1921. His wife was the speech and dramatics professor Ariel Dingwall, his son was the inventor **Andrew G. F. Dingwall**, and his grandson is the biochemist and molecular biologist Andrew K. Dingwall.

Dingwall, Andrew Gordon Francis (1928–2003) ■
INVENTOR

Andrew G. F. Dingwall is in the New Jersey Inventor's Hall of Fame along with Nikola Tesla, Thomas Edison, and Albert Einstein. The fact that he held more than one hundred patents doesn't begin to convey his problem-solving skills and his strong competitive spirit. He received his undergraduate degree at Princeton University, earned numerous master's degrees, was a Fulbright scholar, and obtained his doctorate from the University of Sheffield in England. He was the son of the speech and dramatics professor Ariel Dingwall and the chemist **Andrew Dingwall**, and he was the father of the biochemist and molecular biologist Andrew Dingwall.

130 Morningside Drive (near Amsterdam Avenue)

Arendt, Hannah (1906–1975), Political Theorist ★ ■

(See bio for Arendt at **370 Riverside Drive**.)

Runyon, Marie M. (1915 –2018)

STATE ASSEMBLYWOMAN

Marie Runyon's 100th birthday party was held in her apartment and attended by former Governor David Paterson, Manhattan Borough President Gale Brewer, New York State Senator Bill Perkins, New York State Assemblyman Daniel O'Donnell, and lawyer-activist Lynne Stewart. Starting in 1961, Columbia waged a long battle to evict her from her apartment. In 2002, Columbia settled with her; she stayed put and the building was renamed Marie Runyon Court. Born in North Carolina, Runyon came to New York in 1947 and soon became involved in the rent strike movement in Harlem. On a record of fighting for tenants' rights, she was elected to the New York State Assembly in 1975 for one term. She was executive director of the Harlem Restoration Project, Inc. Not surprising for a woman with so much energy, Runyon made cameo appearances in the 2004 movie remake of *The Manchurian Candidate* and in the 2008 movie *Rachel Getting Married*.

80 Claremont Avenue (near 120th Street)

Brown, Francis (1849–1916)

THEOLOGIAN

Brown was one of the country's most renowned theologians and Semitic scholars. President of the faculty of Union Theological Seminary from 1908 until his death, he was awarded honorary doctorates by Harvard, Yale, Hamilton College, Williams College, the University of Glasgow, and Oxford University. In 1911, he found his way onto the front pages of the country's newspapers after being accused, tried, and exonerated of heresy by his Presbyterian Church. Brown was born in New Hampshire, graduated from Dartmouth with an AB degree in 1870, and an AM degree in 1873. He then attended Union Theological Seminary and studied in Berlin for two years. In 1879, he began his career at Union as an instructor.

McGiffert, Arthur Cushman (1861–1933) ■

THEOLOGIAN

Union Theological Seminary's McGiffert Hall at 99 Claremont Avenue is named after him. With part of the $4 million he raised for the seminary, he built a place to house furloughed missionaries. In 1917, he became the eighth president of Union. He was noted for his knowledge of the history of church dogma, and two of his works especially attest to his stature: *History of Christianity in the Apostolic Age* authored in 1897, and his two-volume *History of Christian Thought* completed in 1933. The son of a minister, McGiffert was born in upstate New York. He graduated from Western Reserve College in Ohio in 1882 and from Union Theological Seminary in 1885. Three years later, he earned a doctor of philosophy degree at Marburg University in Germany. After teaching at Lane Theological Seminary in Ohio for a few years, he became the Washburn professor of church history at Union Theological

Seminary in 1893. His wife was the poet Gertrude Huntington Boyce McGiffert.

99 Claremont Avenue (near 122nd Street)

Forbes, Rev. James Alexander, Jr. (1935–), Minister

(See bio for Forbes at **606 West 122nd Street**.)

Tillich, Paul Johannes (1886–1965) ★ ■
PHILOSOPHER AND THEOLOGIAN

Tillich is one of the most important Protestant theologians of the twentieth century. As an existential philosopher, he wrote of an ontological understanding of God that contrasted with the earlier view espoused by Thomas Aquinas. His realms of theology and philosophy manifested in his dozen or so nuanced writings such as *The Courage to Be* in 1952 and *The Dynamics of Faith* in 1957. His three-volume masterwork is *Systematic Theology*, published in 1963. Born in Prussia, Tillich studied theology in the Universities of Berlin, Tubingen, and Halle, and he received a doctorate in philosophy degree at the University of Breslau. In 1912, he was ordained a minister in the Evangelical Lutheran Church. During World War I, he served as a chaplain in the German military, and through the 1920s he taught at the University of Berlin. In 1933, he came to Union Theological Seminary at the request of **Reinhold Niebuhr**. He taught there until 1955 and was also a special instructor at Harvard's Divinity School. From 1962 he taught at the University of Chicago Divinity School.

130 Claremont Avenue (near 122nd Street)

Freas, Thomas Bruce (1868–1928) ◧
PROFESSOR OF CHEMISTRY

Freas's portrait, painted by Michael De Santis, is in the National Portrait Gallery in Washington, D.C. A photograph of him is also in the collection of the Smithsonian. He was considered an authority on thermodynamics and an expert on chemical laboratory design, being an inventor and manufacturer of precision equipment for chemical and industrial research. Born in Ohio, he graduated from Leland Stanford University in California. After serving as a high school principal for two years, he joined Western Electric Company as a chemist in 1898. That same year, he began teaching at the University of Chicago where he would become a full professor and, in 1911, earn a PhD. Subsequently, he came to Columbia and became the president of Thermo-Electric Instrument Company in Newark. Freas designed the chemistry laboratory in Columbia's Chandler Building.

140 Claremont Avenue (near 122nd Street)

Latham, Minor White (1881–1968), Emeritus English Professor ● ◧

(See bio for Latham at 401 West 118th Street.)

195 Claremont Avenue (near Tiemann Place)

Broun, Heywood Campbell (1888–1939) ●
JOURNALIST

Broun was an original member of the Algonquin Round Table of literary notables and wits. Ever the champion of the underdog, his column "It Seems to Me" was one of the most widely read of its day. In his final days, he received a "get-well" telegram from President Roosevelt. Bishop Fulton Sheen presided at his funeral in St. Patrick's Cathedral with three thousand mourners in attendance. Earlier in the year, Sheen had baptized Broun into the Roman Catholic faith. Born in Brooklyn, Broun attended Harvard but did not graduate. His career in journalism began with covering sports for the *New York Morning Telegraph*. At the *New York Tribune* from 1912 to 1921, he rose to drama critic and then moved on to the *New York World-Telegram* for eight years. He ran for Congress in 1930 as a socialist and lost. In 1933, he founded the American Newspaper Guild.

200 Claremont Avenue (near Tiemann Place)

Fitzgerald, F. Scott (1896–1940) ★ ■
WRITER

Fitzgerald's *The Great Gatsby* was made into a movie in 1926, 1949, 1974, 2000, and 2013. He coined the term "The Jazz Age" to describe the 1920s, and he wrote some first-rate literature that reflects the era, as exemplified by his own life. Motion picture portrayals of Fitzgerald were a virtual industry. He is portrayed by Jeremy Irons in *Last Call* (2002), by Gregory Peck in *Beloved Infidel* (1959), by Timothy Hutton in *Zelda* (1993), and by Richard Chamberlain in *The Last of the Belles* (1974), among others. Born in St. Paul, Minnesota, Fitzgerald attended Princeton University, but he quit to enlist in the US Army during World War I. He was never deployed, and after being discharged, he worked for an advertising firm and lived in Morningside Heights. In 1920, his first novel, *This Side of Paradise*, based on his years at Princeton, was successful and he married socialite Zelda Sayre. Although he wrote short stories for magazines like *Saturday Evening Post*, *Esquire*, and *Collier's Weekly*, the couple's extravagant lifestyle, which included traveling to Italy and France, left them constantly in debt. *The Great*

Gatsby was published in 1925 but was not a financial success. In 1926, he migrated to Hollywood, where Zelda's mental breakdown and his own alcoholism followed. After Fitzgerald's death, his friend Edmund Wilson edited the unfinished novel *The Last Tycoon*.

Morningside Heights

DeKay or DeKey, Jacob (ca.1659–1708)
LANDOWNER

In 1701, Jacob DeKay purchased virtually all of the land in present-day Morningside Heights from the City of New York. In 1735, the DeKay family sold the western section to Adrian Hoaglandt and the eastern section to Harmon Vandewater. The DeKays were party to land deals up and down the Hudson River Valley, including the land near Chatham Square on which Sheareth Israel established the first Jewish Cemetery in the colonies. Jacob Dekay increased his wealth by marrying into the Van Brugh family of prosperous merchants. A notable DeKay descendent was the zoologist James Ellsworth DeKay (1792–1851), who was a good friend of the literati, including Joseph Rodman Drake, Fitz-Greene Halleck, and William Cullen Bryant. He is the namesake of DeKay's snake, which is native to the New York area.

HONORARY STREET NAMES— THE 120S

George Carlin Way (on West 121st Street between Amsterdam Avenue and Morningside Drive)
Comedian **George Carlin** lived one block away on West 121st Street between Amsterdam Avenue and Broadway. Carlin was raised as a Roman Catholic, and the Catholic Church was often the object of his humor. Apparently, the location of George Carlin Way was moved one block east so as not offend the community of Corpus Christi Church, which Carlin attended in his youth.
Teachers College Way (West 120th Street between Amsterdam Avenue and Broadway)
Honors the oldest and largest graduate school of education in the country.

Proposed World's Fair of 1883, from 110th to 125th Streets
between Morningside Park and the Hudson River.

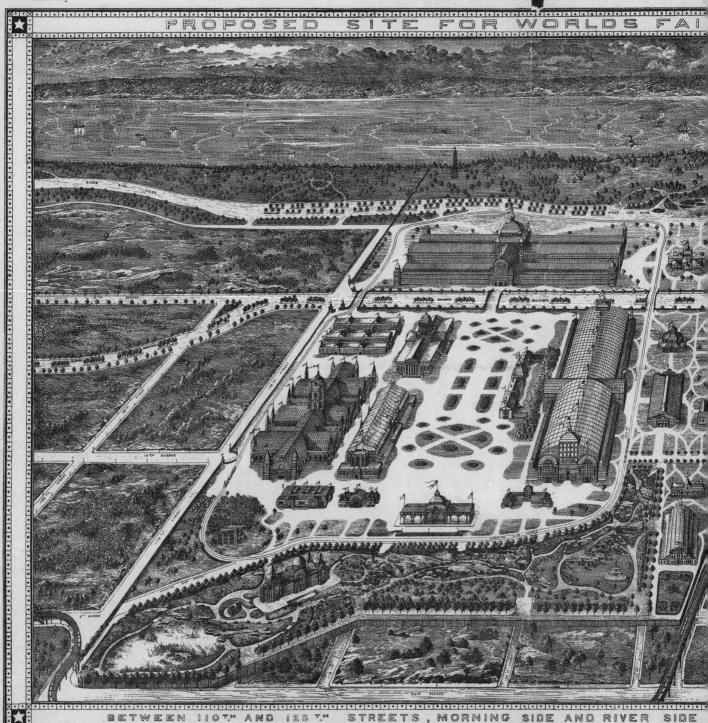

PROPOSED SITE FOR WORLDS FAIR

BETWEEN 110TH AND 125TH STREETS, MORNING SIDE AND RIVER SIDE

[1879.

1883.

BROADWAY

10TH AVENUE

N.Y. AREA 300 ACRES.

Riverside Drive

Riverside Drive from the West 90s to the West 120s at the Riverside Viaduct is one of the world's great thoroughfares. In addition to housing so many notables, it is a virtual museum of architecture with majestic apartment buildings, Riverside Church, and Grant's Tomb. There are not many other places where buildings curve to the streets. Riverside Drive not only curves, it undulates over a series of small hills. The M5 bus trip on Riverside Drive is always a surprise, and it has a hundred-year history. Riverside Drive also showcases one of the largest and oldest collections of surviving American Elm trees.

155 Riverside Drive (near 88th Street)

Oppenheimer, Julius Robert (1904–1967), Theoretical Physicist ★ ▪

(See bio for Oppenheimer at **250 West 94th Street**.)

194 Riverside Drive (near 91st Street)

Sheffer, Isaiah (1935–2012) ▪

ACTOR, PLAYWRIGHT, THEATER DIRECTOR, AND CULTURAL ENTREPRENEUR

Sheffer created the Upper West Side neighborhood treasure, Symphony Space, at Broadway and 95th Street. That site started as the Astor Market in the early twentieth century and later became an ice-skating rink and finally a movie theatre and a temporary boxing venue. Sheffer and his orchestral director friend Allan Miller found the old abandoned Symphony Theatre in need of a nurturing owner, and they launched its reopening in 1978 with "Wall-to-Wall Bach," a twelve-hour music marathon. In the next thirty-two years, Sheffer, as artistic director, created a modern cultural complex for music, literature, theatre, and community, and it is widely recognized as a major arts venue on the West Side and in New York. It is nationally known for its radio broadcast "Selected Shorts: A Celebration of the Short Story" and for Bloomsday (the annual celebration of James Joyce's Ulysses). It is also known for its numerous music marathons, ranging from classical to jazz to musical theatre. Born in the Bronx, Sheffer began his career in the theater as a young actor and later became a producer, playwright, theater director, and a teacher of theater studies for hundreds of students, while he served as the creative force behind Symphony Space. He has been called one of New York's Renaissance men who left an indelible mark on New York's cultural and artistic life.

202 Riverside Drive (near 93rd Street)

Allison Skipworth

Skipworth, Alison (1863–1952) ◼

ACTRESS

As Margaret Dumont was to Groucho Marx, Alison Skipworth was to W. C. Fields. She usually played the grand dame as a foil to Fields, as in *If I Had a Million*, *Tillie and Gus*, *Six of a Kind*, or *Alice in Wonderland*, in which she played the Duchess. Some of her other fifty film appearances include *The Girl from Tenth Avenue*, featuring Bette Davis, and *Shanghai*, with Loretta Young. Born in London, England, Skipworth didn't make her first stage appearance until 1894 in London. The following year she debuted on the Broadway stage and became a regular fixture in more than forty dramas, comedies, musicals, and operettas. She made her first silent film in 1912.

214 Riverside Drive (near 94th Street)

Cady, Josiah Cleaveland (1837–1919) ◼

ARCHITECT

J. Cleaveland Cady, as he was known, designed the large impressive south side of the American Museum of Natural History and the original Metropolitan Opera House, which was razed after the new theater opened in Lincoln Center. He was a partner in the firms of Cady, Berg & See, and Cady & Gregory, which designed numerous churches, hospitals, and campus buildings. One of his gems, the Church of the Good Shepard, is tucked in the Lincoln Center complex on West 66th Street. Born in Providence, Rhode Island, he graduated

from Trinity College. He was a trustee of Berea College, a governor of
the Presbyterian Hospital, a vice president of the New York Mission
Society, president of the National Federation of Churches, and
president of the Skin and Cancer Hospital. He died in his Riverside
Drive apartment.

Dos Passos, John (1896–1970) ■
NOVELIST AND ACTIVIST

In 1932, John Dos Passos wrote an article in *The New Republic* arguing
that Franklin D. Roosevelt was not liberal enough to be president.
In 1964, Dos Passos supported Barry Goldwater for president. The
transition from left to right is especially dramatic given his earlier
activism in the Spanish Civil War, as a member of the Dewey
Commission defending Leon Trotsky, and as a one-time backer of
communist candidate William Z. Foster. Dos Passos was born in
Chicago, graduated from Harvard in 1916, and served in the Army
Medical Corps in World War I. His first novel *One Man's Initiation:
1917,* published in 1920, was followed by *Three Soldiers*, which received
attention for its anti-war sensibility. In 1925, he wrote his best seller,
Manhattan Transfer, while living on Riverside Drive. The year 1930
marked the start of his *U.S.A.* trilogy.

John dos Passos.

Gilman, Charlotte Perkins (1860–1935) ▋
POET, WRITER, AND FEMINIST

Gilman was cited as one of the twelve greatest American women
by Morningside Heights suffragist Carrie Chapman Catt. Catt also
defended Gilman's suicide as justified to avoid a painful death from
breast cancer. Gilman's revolutionary book, *Women and Economics*,
published in 1898, advocated for the economic independence of women.
Some of her other nonfiction books were *The Man-Made World, The*

Charlotte Perkins Gilman.

Home, Its Work and Influence, *His Religion and Hers*, and *Our Brains and What Ails Them*. She also wrote nine novels, much poetry, nearly fifty short stories, and she lectured extensively. Born in Harford, Connecticut, Gilman's father's aunts were the author Harriet Beecher Stowe, suffragist Isabella Beecher Hooker, and the educationalist Catherine Beecher. She grew up mostly in Providence, Rhode Island, where she attended the Rhode Island School of Design for a short period. After a brief marriage to the artist Charles Walter Stetson, she found her way to California and feminist organizations such as the Woman's Alliance and the Pacific Coast Women's Press Association. Eight years later, in 1893, she returned to the east coast, found true love with a first cousin and married him, and then occupied herself with writing and feminist organizations, political activities, and lectures. Gilman also lived at **223 Riverside Drive** (near 95th Street).

Hillquit, Morris (1869–1933)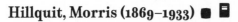

SOCIALIST, LABOR LAWYER, AND MAYORAL CANDIDATE

Hillquit received 22 percent of the vote for mayor in 1917, running as an anti-war Socialist candidate. He ran again and lost in 1932, just before his death from tuberculosis. Born Moishe Hillkowitz in Latvia, Hillquit came to the Lower East Side of Manhattan in 1886. At age 18 he joined the Socialist Labor Party of America and began his lifelong commitment to his political beliefs. In 1893, he graduated from the New York University Law School. He became as prominent as Eugene V. Debs, in large part by being at the center of the socialist movement. He was an able figure for the cause who spoke and wrote well. His *History of Socialism in the United States* is a classic.

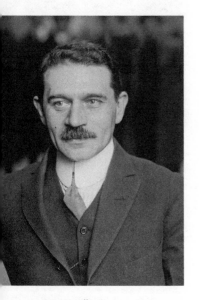

Morris Hillquit.

223 Riverside Drive (near 95th Street)

Gilman, Charlotte Perkins (1860–1935), Poet, Writer, and Feminist ▪

(See bio for Gilman at **214 Riverside Drive**.)

230 Riverside Drive (near 95th Street)

Perelman, Simeon Joseph "S. J." (1904–1979)
HUMORIST

Supposedly, Perelman popularized the phrase "crazy like a fox" with the title of a book he wrote in 1944. He is also credited with popularizing Joseph Heller's novel *Catch-22* with a singularly favorable review. Perelman might be best known for his screenwriting contributions to the Marx Brothers' movies *Monkey Business* and *Horse Feathers*. He wrote the screenplay for many other films such as *Sweethearts*, *Around the World in 80 Days*, and *One Touch of Venus*, which won him an Academy Award. But a full appreciation of his oeuvre is best achieved by reading his *New Yorker* magazine pieces that reveal his extraordinary ability to explode a common idea or hackneyed phrase into riotous humor. The creator of such playful characters as Sir Hamish Sphincter said, "I don't know much about medicine, but I know what I like." Born in Brooklyn, Perelman grew up in Rhode Island. He attended Brown University but dropped out to begin a career in New York City. A school friend from Brown introduced him to his younger sister Linda West, nee Loraine Weinstein, who became Perelman's wife. The cartoonist Al Hirschfeld was an early collaborator and lifelong friend. By the early 1930s, he had engaged with many notable writers, most of whom were honored members of the Algonquin Round Table.

234 Riverside Drive (near 97th Street)

Macfadden, Bernarr (1868–1955) ■ 👉
PHYSICAL FITNESS GURU

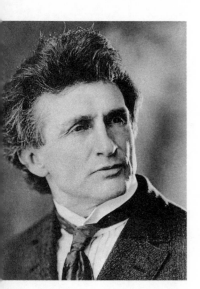

Bernarr MacFadden.

À la President George H. W. Bush, Macfadden made a parachute jump into the Hudson River on his 83rd birthday. Decades before Charles Atlas and Jack LaLanne, there was Bernarr Macfadden. He raised physical fitness to a lifestyle and even, unsuccessfully, to a religion that he called "cosmotarianism." Fasting, exercise, and vegetarianism were his core beliefs. In fact, he was very physically fit, and his physique was extensively photographed, sometimes featuring his cord-and-pulley Macfadden Exerciser. His vegetarian restaurant, Physical Culture, was one of the first in the country when it opened in 1902. "Physical Culture" was also the name of the magazine that he founded in 1902, the start of his empire that included such other publications as *True Detective*, *Ghost Stories*, *Photoplay*, *True Romances*, and *Sport*, which presaged *Sports Illustrated*. His empire grew to include the daily newspaper the *New York Evening Graphic*, a few hotels, and numerous commercial properties. The five-volume *Macfadden's Encyclopedia of Physical Culture* was but one of the more than on hundred books that he authored. He was born Bernard Adolphus McFadden (note the abbreviated prefix "Mc" and the uppercase "F") in Missouri and overcame being orphaned as an 11-year-old in part by adopting the lion-sounding name of "Bernarr" and the more masculine last name with "Mac" and a small "f."

244 Riverside Drive (near 97th Street)

Rowan, Joseph Charles (1870–1930)
CONGRESSMAN

Rowan was a one-term congressman from 1919 to 1921. He supported the National Women's Party in seeking women's right to vote. As president of the Manhattan Club, he was ever present at Tammany functions and constantly employed as a toastmaster for other Democrat dignitaries. A New York native, Rowan graduated from Columbia Law School in 1891. He practiced business law and one of his clients was the West Side Savings Bank of which he was an officer and trustee. In 1905, he married Cora Cook, the daughter of the chief surgeon of the New York City Police Department.

258 Riverside Drive (near 98th Street)

Mitchel, John Purroy (1879–1918) ★ ■ ▯ ☞
MAYOR

Mitchel Field on Long Island was named in honor of Mayor Mitchel, whose bust adorns the entrance to Central Park at Fifth Avenue and 90th Street. In 1913, at age 34, he was elected Mayor of New York City by the largest plurality up to that time. In 1917, he lost by even more and only had ten thousand votes more than Socialist candidate **Morris Hillquit**. By all accounts, he was a good mayor, but a poor politician. He died tragically by falling out of an airplane during a US Army Air Corps training flight in Louisiana. His uncle, Henry Purroy, was Fire Commissioner, and his name is on many firehouses, such as one from 1889 located at 502 West 113th Street. His aunt was Salome Purroy, namesake and principal of PS 53 on East 79 Street. His wife, Olive, is thought to be one of the first persons ever photographed in color in 1916. As a widow in 1924, her hair was accidentally set on fire (and extinguished) at a charity ball.

John Purroy Mitchel.

Scribner, Charles E. (1858–1926) ★ ■ ▯
ELECTRICAL ENGINEER AND INVENTOR

Scribner had more patents than anyone else in the electrical industry, including Thomas Edison. His multiple switchboards, which enabled a single operator to connect calls, was adopted throughout the world. Underpinning his switchboard was his 1878 invention of the "jackknife switch." The research and development department that he established at Western Electric was the forerunner of Bell Labs. He initiated the acquisition of the **De Forest** Audion and then oversaw its refinement into the first modern vacuum tube, which enabled telephone communication to other continents. He was born in Ohio and began working for Western Electric Manufacturing Company in 1877. Charles E. Scribner was a distant relative of the Charles Scribner of book publishing fame.

269 Riverside Drive (near 99th Street)

Ponselle, Rosa (1897–1981) ★ ■
SOPRANO

Although she had hardly any formal training, Ponselle's first performance on an opera stage was in Verdi's *La Forza del Destino*, opposite Enrico Caruso. She was considered to have one of the most beautiful voices of the century. Born Rosa Ponzillo in Connecticut, Ponselle started in vaudeville with her older sister. As the Ponzillo Sisters, they became a headlining act that sang the range from popular music to opera. After an introduction to Enrico Caruso, Rosa was contracted to sing with the Metropolitan Opera in the 1918–1919 season. She sang in four productions that first season, including her debut with Caruso, and continued performing through the 1930s. Her title role in Bellini's *Norma* in 1927 was perhaps her crowning achievement. In her long and accomplished career, she also won praise in some of the great opera houses in Europe. In her later years, she guided the Baltimore Civic Opera, which provided opportunities in the early careers of Beverly Sills, Placido Domingo, and Sherrill Milnes.

270 Riverside Drive (near 99th Street)

Barrie, Elaine (1915–2003)
ACTRESS

Barrie became the fourth and final wife of the great Shakespearean actor, John Barrymore, after writing a letter to him while he was hospitalized. They were married a year later in 1936 and divorced in 1940. When he died in 1942, she was the only ex-wife who went to the funeral. Born Elaine Jacobs in New York City, she attended Hunter College where she wrote and directed plays. Her infatuation with Barrymore began as a teenager when she saw him on the screen in *Svengali*. Shortly after, and with obvious significance, she changed her name to Barrie. Her film career was limited to one movie in 1939, *Midnight*, and two 1937 film shorts, *How to Take a Bath* and *How to Undress in Front of Your Husband*.

Madonna (1958–) ★
ROCK AND ROLL SINGER, PERFORMER, AND ACTRESS

In 2008, Madonna was inducted into the Rock and Roll Hall of Fame by Justin Timberlake. In 1996, she and David Byrne inducted David Bowie. Born Madonna Louise Ciccone in Michigan, she dropped out of the University of Michigan School of Music, Theater & Dance to start her career in New York City. She did some modern dancing, having taken dance classes at **Alvin Ailey** and **Pearl Lang**, and formed a rock band, the Breakfast Club, in which she played drums and guitar and sang. Going solo with a remarkably fresh sound and look that was perfect for the emerging music video phenomena, she became an overnight success story. Her 1984 hit "Like a Virgin" was a milestone in Rock's chronology. Many hits followed, such as "Crazy for You," "Vogue," "Take a Bow," "Like a Prayer," "Papa Don't Preach," "Material Girl," and "Who's That Girl." With all her talents and use of advancing stage technology, she raised the bar for the rock concert experience. Her television and film appearances have been wide-ranging and include *Desperately Seeking Susan*, *A League of Their Own*, and *Evita*. She also appeared on Broadway in David Mamet's *Speed the Plow*.

Malone, Dudley Field (1882–1950)
LAWYER AND ACTIVIST

Malone resembled Winston Churchill, whom he portrayed in the 1943 movie *Mission to Moscow*. His political career began with an appointment by President Wilson in 1913, but he resigned in protest when Wilson didn't support the Woman Suffrage Amendment to the Constitution. As an internationally renowned lawyer who handled famous divorce cases, his own divorce in 1921was front-page news. In 1925, he joined Clarence Darrow in the famous Scopes trial, rendering the best speech in the trial defending academic freedom. He fought Tammany Hall yet defended his friend Mayor Jimmy Walker against removal from office. Son of a Tammany Hall Democratic official, Malone was born on the West Side of Manhattan. He graduated from St. Francis Xavier College in 1903 with a BA degree and from Fordham Law School in 1905. In 1908, he married the first of three wives, May Patricia O'Gorman, the daughter of Senator **James A. O'Gorman**. His second wife was the suffragist Doris Stevens.

Dudley Field Malone.

Pickford, Mary (1892–1979) ★ ▪

ACTRESS

In 1919, Mary Pickford, along with her soon-to-be-husband, Douglas Fairbanks, **D. W. Griffith**, and Charlie Chaplin, founded the United Artists motion picture company. She is thought to be the first subject of a cinematic close-up and the first actress to receive a percentage of a film's earnings. She is one of the thirty-six founders of the American Academy of Motion Picture Arts and Sciences. Born Gladys Louise Smith in Canada, Pickford began acting at age 7. She toured extensively in theater with her family and arrived on the Broadway stage in 1907. The stage producer David Belasco gave her the stage name Mary Pickford. In 1909, she was noticed by D. W. Griffith and signed to Biograph Studios, appearing in fifty-one films that year. In 1912, she helped start the film careers of **Dorothy** and **Lillian Gish** by introducing them to D. W. Griffith. By 1916, she was earning $10,000 a week, and only Charlie Chaplin was thought to be more popular with film audiences. Among her 250-plus film credits are classics such as *The Poor Little Rich Girl* in 1917, *Rebecca of Sunnybrook Farm* in 1917, *Daddy-Long-Legs* in 1919, and *Coquette* in 1929, for which she won an Academy Award for Best Actress.

Mary Pickford.

Riverside Drive at 100th Street, Site of the Furniss Mansion

Stein, Gertrude (1874–1946) ★ ∎

AUTHOR AND ART COLLECTOR

Stein's *Autobiography of Alice B. Toklas* is considered by many to be one of the greatest books of the twentieth century. The tongue-in-cheek title conceals the wonderful memoirs of Stein herself but includes her loving relationship with her partner Alice; it is a delightful entrance into their engaging world. In 1903 Gertrude Stein was a resident in the Furniss Mansion along with other residents, such as theater manager Paul Wilstach and the writer brothers Vaughn and Paul Kester. The mansion operated as sort of an artists' colony. One of the Furniss sisters, Sophia, rented the mansion to Alma Walker, and she rented the

Gertrude Stein.

rooms and served meals to Stein and the others. Born to a wealthy family in Pennsylvania, Stein was raised in Oakland, California, where her father became director of San Francisco's streetcar lines. Her parents died while she was a teenager, so she moved to Baltimore, Maryland, to live with relatives. She was educated at Radcliffe College and, with encouragement from psychologist William James, went on to Johns Hopkins School of Medicine in 1897. Just short of graduating, she took up residence in Paris where she and her brother Leo Stein collected the art of Cézanne, Matisse and Picasso, among others. Gertrude Stein met her partner Alice B. Toklas in Paris in 1907, on Toklas's first day there. For nearly four decades, they lived together and were the center of a remarkable circle of artists, writers, and intellectuals. Among Stein's numerous novels, portraits, poetry, and plays are *Tender Buttons*, *The Making of Americans*, *Four Saints in Three Acts*, and *Paris*.

Furniss Mansion near Riverside Drive at 100th Street ca. 1903

Zimmerman, Margaret Elizabeth Furniss (1829–1918)
PHILANTHROPIST

Zimmerman left half of her $2 million estate to St. Michael's Church to buy five Tiffany windows and build St. Jude's Chapel on West 99th Street. The windows still grace St. Michael's on Amsterdam Avenue at 99th Street, but St. Jude's Chapel is gone. It was built for the African Americans in St. Michael's congregation and destroyed by urban renewal the building of Park West Village. Margaret Zimmerman lived in the Furniss mansion with her elderly sisters, Sophia and Clementina. After being in possession for sixty-six years, the sisters decided to sell the mansion and the property. In the early 1900s, it was used as an artists' colony where **Gertrude Stein** was a resident. After the mansion came down in 1910, the apartment building at 276 Riverside Drive was built.

On the Site of 280 Riverside Drive (near 100th Street)

Doelger, Peter (1832–1912) 🖛
BREWER

In 1903, someone left a pipe bomb on the front steps of Peter Doelger's mansion. It might have been a practical joke. Doelger built one of the largest breweries in New York on East 55th Street, opened several saloons, and bought the Grimm building on the corner of 100th Street and Broadway to operate as a restaurant. (Today, it is the Metro Diner.) Doelger was born in Bavaria, Germany. He came to New York in 1850 and learned the brewery business from his father. With his brother, they started a brewery in what is today the East Village. It was successful enough to justify building one of the largest breweries in the city on East 55th Street. Doelger died leaving an estate of more than $7 million, including his mansion on Riverside Drive at 100th Street. In 1925, it was sold for $900,000 and razed to make way for the apartment building at 280 Riverside Drive. The brewery in New York ran until

FIREMEN'S MEMORIAL

On September 5, 1913, some 7,000 firefighters, including 1,500 from New York City, and some from as far away as Oregon, marched to the dedication of the Firemen's Memorial on Riverside Drive at 100th Street. Jesse Isidor Straus spoke for his father, Isidor Straus, who, while serving as chairman of the Firemen's Memorial Committee, died on the *Titanic* the previous year. Former President Taft spoke for President Wilson. The estimated attendance at the dedication ceremony was 10,000.

NEIGHBORHOOD HEADS
OF STATE

Nicholas D. Avxentieff (ca. 1879–1943) was president of the Russian Republic for a few months in 1917. He lived at 294 Riverside Drive (near 102nd Street).

Joseph Bonaparte (1768–1844) was King Giuseppe I of Naples and Sicily from 1806 to 1808, and King Jose I of Spain from 1808 to 1813. He was supposedly offered the position of Emperor of Mexico in 1820 by revolutionaries there, but he declined. He lived near the site at **Riverside Drive near Tiemann Place**.

Dwight David Eisenhower (1890–1969) was the thirty-fourth president of the United States from 1953 to 1961. As president of Columbia University, he lived at **60 Morningside Drive, the President's House** (near 116th Street).

Barack Obama (1961–) was the forty-fourth president of the United States from 2009 to 2017. As a Columbia student, he lived at **622 West 114th Street**, at **Revere Hall** (near Riverside Drive), and at **142 West 109th Street** (near Amsterdam Avenue).

1937, operated in New Jersey for a bit, and ceased operations in 1947. Doelger's daughter Matilda married a boxer named John Patrick West, and one of their daughters was the notorious Mary Jane "Mae" West.

280 Riverside Drive (near 100th Street)

Bergman, Bernard (1911–1984)
RABBI AND NURSING HOME MAGNATE

In 1976, Bergman was convicted on Medicare and tax fraud charges resulting from a New York State Senate investigation of his Towers Nursing Home. It operated in what was formerly the New York Cancer Hospital on Central Park West and 106th Street. The details of patient abuse and neglect in Bergman's nursing home operation occupied the news for weeks. He was sent to prison and forced to make punitive reimbursements. Born in Hungary to a family with a long lineage of Hasidic rabbis, Bergman came with his family to Brooklyn in the 1920s. In the 1930s he traveled to Palestine for studies that led to his ordination as an Orthodox Rabbi. He got his start as a rabbi at a nursing home on the Lower East Side and also published the Yiddish-language newspaper, the *Jewish Morning Journal*. Using a small family inheritance, he acquired nursing homes, which he built into an empire large enough to warrant the 1955 purchase of the property at Central Park West and 106th Street. The building later received landmark status and became a luxury apartment building.

285 Riverside Drive (near 101st Street)

Fokker, Anton Herman Gerard "Anthony" (1890–1939) ★ ■ 🖘
INVENTOR

Fokker invented the synchronized device that allows aircraft to fire bullets through a rotating propeller. He taught himself to fly on an airplane that he built for himself. He was born of Dutch heritage in what is now Indonesia and grew up in the Netherlands. At age 20 he went to Germany to attend a school that trained auto mechanics, but he discovered the thrill of aviation. In 1911, he became a celebrity by flying in his hometown of Haarlem during a celebration of Queen Wilhelmina's birthday. The following year he started his airplane company near Berlin and designed some forty airplanes that were used by the German government in World War 1. After the war, he started up a new aircraft company in the Netherlands. Since he was selling aircraft to the United States military, he established the Fokker Aircraft Corporation of America in 1922, which was eventually acquired by General Motors. One of Fokker's many innovations was a three-engine aircraft, one of which carried Commander Richard Byrd and Floyd Bennett to the North Pole. In 1929, his second wife fell fifteen stories out of their Riverside Drive apartment, an apparent suicide. She was only 29 years old and when he died ten years later, he was only 49.

Anthony Fokker.

290 Riverside Drive (near 101st Street)

Farrar, Geraldine (1882–1967) ★ ■

SOPRANO OPERA SINGER AND ACTRESS

Farrar often performed with Enrico Caruso. She appeared in the American debut of Puccini's *Madame Butterfly* at the Metropolitan Opera. She sang 29 roles in 672 performances at the Met from 1906 to 1922. She also appeared in a dozen films, including **Cecil B. DeMille**'s 1915 adaptation of Bizet's *Carmen*. In 1907, she sang in an experimental radio broadcast years before commercial radio arrived in the 1920s. Her voice was extensively recorded on cylinders and discs made by the Victor Talking Machine Company. Born in Massachusetts, the daughter

Geraldine Farrar.

of a professional baseball player, Farrar began singing at age 5 and
was giving recitals by the time she was 14. She studied voice in Paris
and Berlin, and then earned her stripes with three years at the Monte
Carlo Opera Company before returning to New York and joining the
Metropolitan Opera. In the early part of her career, she was thought to
have had a relationship with Crown Prince Wilhelm of Germany. Later,
she was known to have had a seven-year affair with Arturo Toscanini.

294 Riverside Drive (near 102nd Street)

Avxentieff, Nicholas D. (ca.1879–1943)
PRESIDENT OF THE RUSSIAN REPUBLIC

Avxentieff was president of the Russian Republic, which lasted less
than eight months—from the abdication of the Emperor Nicholas II
in March of 1917 to the Russian Revolution in October of the same
year. He was also Interior Minister under Alexander Kerensky in the
same period. After being hounded and arrested by the Communists, he
escaped to Paris and attempted to establish a Russian Democracy. In
1921, he came to New York and continued his political activities.

Mansion on Riverside Drive at 102nd Street

Foster, William F. (1841–1895)
INVENTOR AND GLOVE MANUFACTURER

The Foster Mausoleum in Woodlawn Cemetery in the Bronx is 38 feet
in diameter, 50 feet high and is constructed from 1,100 tons of granite,
including some of the largest single stones quarried in the United
States. He commissioned it as he was dying from cancer in his mansion
on Riverside Drive. In 1922, his mansion would be razed to build 300
Riverside Drive. Foster had planned to move into the larger Dudley
Field estate in Hastings-on-Hudson, which he had purchased, but it

was not meant to be. Born in England, Foster came to the United States in 1856, started a business in Chicago, and was ruined by the fire there in 1871. In 1876, he invented a way for a glove to be laced at the wrist instead of buttoned. With that, he built his fortune by importing gloves from Grenoble, France, and affixing his device on them in his New York City factory. Foster, Paul & Company, at Broadway and Grand Street occupied a five-story building, employed five hundred workers, and sold to all the major department stores in the country.

305 Riverside Drive (103rd Street)

Keigwin, Albert Edwin (ca.1868–1951), Minister 👆

(See bio for Keigwin at 324 West 103rd Street.)

Levy, Edward (1878–1947), Medical Doctor and Researcher ▪

(See bio for Levy at 777 West End Avenue.)

310 Riverside Drive (near 103rd Street), Masters Apartments

Bloom, Sol (1870–1949) ▪ 👆
CONGRESSMAN

Bloom is thought to have introduced belly dancing to the United States. At age 23, he was hired to run the mile-long Midway amusement venue at the 1893 World's Columbian Exposition. One of the attractions that he offered was "Little Egypt" and the "hoochie coochie" dance. Earlier, he was a theatrical stage manager who also staged boxing matches, including one with world champion "Gentleman Jim" Corbett. After the fair, he was Chicago branch manager for M. Witmark & Sons, the largest publisher of sheet music in the country. In 1903, he came to

McGavin, Ossie Davis, Lee Grant, and Harvey Korman.

Founded by actor Sam Jaffe in 1943 as an outgrowth of the Actors' Equity Association to showcase actors, ELT performed in neighborhood library spaces until it acquired a permanent home on the East Side in 1949. It arrived at the Master Apartment building (310 Riverside Drive, near 103rd Street) in 1961. The Master had a theater space that seated about two hundred people. Its long-term director, George Wojtasik, produced an incredible 196 shows for the company and was awarded a special Tony in 1977. Tony Randall was chairman of the Board of ELT for a number of years and was in a 1948 production with Charlton Heston. Anne Jackson and Eli Wallach met in a 1946 ELT production. When ELT closed during its 1989–1990 season, it was one of the longest continuously operating theater groups in the country.

Sol Bloom.

New York and was successful in theater and real estate. Leaving his
Chicago Republican Party roots behind, he joined the Democratic Party
of Tammany Hall and was elected to Congress in 1923. In addition to
chairing the House Committee on Foreign Affairs from 1939, he oversaw
the George Washington Bicentennial in 1932 and the US Constitution
Sesquicentennial Exposition in 1937. His activities with foreign affairs
had him a strong Zionist and much involved with the creation of the
United Nations. His own *Autobiography of Sol Bloom* recounts a most
amazing life.

Gutkind, Eric (1877–1965)
JEWISH PHILOSOPHER

Albert Einstein's letter to Gutkind has received much attention,
especially since it sold at action for more than a million dollars. In
1952, Gutkind authored a book, *Choose Life: The Biblical Call to Revolt*.
Einstein got around to reading it in 1954 and wrote to Gutkind that
he didn't have much appreciation for God or the Bible. Gutkind's
earlier works appealed to students of Judaism who were searching for
something between orthodoxy and liberal leanings. His wide range of
interests, including general philosophy, mathematics, art history, and
anthropology, placed him among such modern intellectuals as Martin
Buber, Walter Benjamin, Henry Miller, and Upton Sinclair. Born in
Germany, Gutkind studied at the University of Berlin. He came to the
United States in 1933 and taught at the City College of New York, the
New School for Social Research, and Yeshiva University. Gutkind also
lived at **895 West End Avenue** (near 104th Street) and **88 Morningside
Drive** (near 119th Street).

May, Rollo Reece (1909–1994), Psychologist

(See bio for May at **411 West 114th Street**.)

Roerich, Nicholas (1874–1947), Painter, Scenarist, and Theosophist ■

(See bio for Roerich at **319 West 107th Street.**)

Shindle, Katherine Renee "Kate" (1977–)

ACTRESS, AUTHOR, AND PRESIDENT OF ACTORS' EQUITY ASSOCIATION

Shindle was Miss America 1998. Previously, she was Miss Illinois 1997. Her book, *Being Miss America: Behind the Rhinestone Curtain,* is a delightful memoir, history of the pageant, and essay on life values. Acting ever since, she has taken on major roles on Broadway in *Legally Blonde, Wonderland of Oz, Dracula: The Musical*, and a revival of *Cabaret*. Her regional theater work has been extensive, and her television work includes *Gossip Girl, White Collar*, and *Law & Order: Special Victims Unit*. Born in Ohio, Shindle was raised in New Jersey, graduated from Northwestern University after studying sociology and theater, and has done graduate work at NYU and UCLA.

Shisgal, Murray Joseph (1926–)

PLAYWRIGHT AND SCREENWRITER

Murray Shisgal and Larry Gelbart co-wrote the screenplay for the 1982 motion picture *Tootsie*. In 1965, Shisgal's first Broadway play, *Luv,* garnered two Tony Award nominations—for Best Play and for Best Author (Dramatic). He ventured off Broadway with a double bill of *The Typists* and *The Tiger*, which earned a Drama Desk Award. These plays also featured the actors Anne Jackson and Eli Wallach, who would reprise their roles in the 1967 movie *The Tiger Makes Out* and the 1971 movie version of *The Typist*. Jackson and Wallach also played in Shisgal's *Twice Around the Park* in 1982. A native New Yorker, Shisgal was raised in Brooklyn. His 2011 play *74 Georgia Avenue* honors his old neighborhood. Shisgal also lived at **925 West End Avenue** (near 106th Street).

Strayhorn, William Thomas "Billy" (1915–1967) ■
JAZZ COMPOSER, ARRANGER, AND PIANIST

Strayhorn composed **Duke Ellington's** theme song "Take the A Train." Often called Ellington's alter ego, he worked with him from 1938 to 1966, and together they composed numerous songs. Strayhorn's arrangements distinguish many of Ellington classics, such as "Satin Doll," and he also arranged jazz interpretations of classical pieces, such as Tchaikovsky's "The Nutcracker," for Ellington's orchestra. Strayhorn also arranged for Lena Horne, who affectionately called him "sweet pea." Born in Ohio, he was raised in North Carolina and Pittsburgh, and trained at the Pittsburgh Music Institute. He composed the exquisite composition "Lush Life" when he was only 16 years old. Strayhorn also lived at **15 West 106th Street** (near Manhattan Avenue).

Tune, Tommy (1939–) ■
DANCER, CHOREOGRAPHER, ACTOR, SINGER, DIRECTOR, AND PRODUCER

In his youth, Tune worked closely with Mary Highsmith, mother of the novelist Patricia Highsmith, at the Point Summer Theater in Texas. Known for his work on Broadway, Tune has earned ten Tony Awards. In fact, he is the only person to win in two categories, two years in a row, and he is the first to win in four categories. His Tonys began with *Seesaw*, and they continued coming with *The Best Little Whorehouse in Texas*, *A Day in Hollywood/A Night in the Ukraine*, *Nine*, *My One and Only*, *Grand Hotel*, *The Will Rogers Follies*, and included the Lifetime Achievement Award. He has respectable television and movie credits as well, with his 1971 film performance in *The Boy Friend* with the famous actor and model Twiggy. Born in Texas, he attended Lon Morris College, but went on to receive a

BFA degree in Drama from the University of Texas at Austin. Coming to New York, he made his debut in the 1965 musical *Baker Street*.

Wiesel, Elie (1928–2016) ■
HOLOCAUST SURVIVOR AND WRITER

Among his various teaching experiences, Wiesel was the Ingeborg Rennert Visiting Professor of Judaic Studies at Barnard. Wiesel came to personify the uncommon experience of surviving the Holocaust. He was born in a vibrant Jewish community in Romania. During World War II, his family was sent to the Auschwitz concentration camp where his mother and one of his three sisters were killed. Wiesel and his father were relocated to the Buchenwald concentration camp and there his father was killed. Wiesel was saved in 1945 when Buchenwald was liberated by US forces. He found his way to France where he met literary and intellectual luminaries, and began writing. His nine hundred–page memoir *And the World Remained Silent* was written in Yiddish, but it was shortened in the French translation; then it was published in English in 1960 as *Night*. In 1955, he moved to the United States and continued writing, totaling more than forty books. With world attention on the Eichmann trials, Wiesel came into prominence as a Holocaust survivor, and he continued to place the Holocaust in the forefront of modern history. In 1986, he was awarded the Nobel Peace Prize for speaking out against violence, repression, and racism.

314 Riverside Drive (near 104th Street)

Meyers, Augustus (1841–1919) ☞
SOLDIER, ARCHITECT, AND DEVELOPER

Meyers joined the United States Army as a 14-year-old for a five-year turn—although, in fact, he was only 12 years and 9 months old and 4

Augustus Meyers.

feet 10 inches in height. Born in Switzerland, his amazing experiences included beating a desertion rap and having nearly five years of contact with the Native American Sioux, from whom he learned their language. He returned to New York in 1860 and reenlisted. During the Civil War, he served at the battles of Manassas, Antietam, Chancellorsville, Fredericksburg, and Gettysburg. Later he wrote *Ten Years in the Ranks, U.S. Army*, a classic memoir of his military training experiences on Governors Island. After the war, he enrolled in night school at Cooper Union and earned a degree in architecture. He made a fortune in the building trades, and some of the warehouses that he designed still exist and are part of the Chelsea historic district.

315 Riverside Drive (near 104th Street)

Coco, James (1930–1987)
ACTOR

Coco may best be remembered for his Tony-nominated lead in *Last of the Red Hot Lovers*. A superb character actor, he might also be recalled for his movie roles in *Only When I Laugh* or *Murder by Death*, and for TV characters in *The Love Boat* and *Who's the Boss?* Born in New York City, he received intensive acting training from Uta Hagen. In addition, the playwright Terence McNally was a friend and provided opportunities for roles in some of his early plays. Neil Simon wrote *Last of the Red Hot Lovers* for him, and Coco also lent his talents to other Neil Simon plays and films. Despite his lifelong struggle with obesity, he wrote some very popular cookbooks.

Harris, Cyril Manton (1917–2011)
PROFESSOR OF ARCHITECTURE, PROFESSOR OF ELECTRICAL ENGINEERING, AND ACOUSTICS SPECIALIST

In 1976, Harris earned his reputation as a wizard of acoustics with the reopening of Avery Fisher Hall at Lincoln Center after a desperately needed renovation. It was challenged with poor acoustics from the day it opened in 1962. Fisher also put his talents to use, and to great acclaim, at the Metropolitan Opera, the three theaters at the Kennedy Performing Arts Center in Washington, D.C., and more than one hundred other concert halls throughout the country. He had taught in Columbia's engineering school, but from 1974 to 1984, at the top of his field, he served as chairman of the division of architectural technology in the graduate school of architecture and planning. Born in Michigan, Harris was raised in Los Angeles, where he came to know Warner Brothers studios. In 1938, he graduated from UCLA with a bachelor's degree in mathematics, followed two years later with a master's degree in physics. In 1945, he earned his doctorate in physics from MIT. His career began at the world-famous Bell Telephone Laboratories, where he co-authored *Acoustical Design in Architecture*. His loss to Bell Labs was Columbia's gain in 1952. He also lived at **425 Riverside Drive** (near 114th Street).

316 Riverside Drive (104th Street)

Brady, Alice (1892–1939)
ACTRESS

In 1937 Alice Brady won an Oscar for Best Supporting Actress for her performance in *In Old Chicago*. She began acting on the Broadway stage in 1911, appearing with such luminaries as John Barrymore and appearing in the premiere of Eugene O'Neill's *Mourning Becomes Electra*. Her transition into silent films was likely inevitable, given her stage credentials and her father's connections. From 1923 to 1933 she withdrew from films to concentrate on the stage. But before her early death from cancer, she appeared in twenty-five films, including such classics as *The Gay Divorcee*, *Gold Diggers of 1935*, *My Man Godfrey*, and *Young Mr. Lincoln*. Her father was the theatrical producer **William A. Brady**, and her stepmother was the actress Grace George.

Alice Brady.

Brady, William Aloysius (1863–1950) 👈

THEATRICAL PRODUCER AND SPORTS PROMOTER

Brady is thought to be the only person to manage two heavyweight boxing champions: James J. Jeffries and James J. Corbett. Born in San Francisco, California, Brady started out as an actor. Soon he turned to producing shows, and after casting boxer Jeffries in a play, he discovered sports promotion. In 1897, he produced a boxing match between James J. Corbett and Bob Fitzsimmons in Carson City, Nevada. That fight resulted in what was then the world's longest feature film, running about one hundred minutes. He estimated that he produced over 260 plays. One of them was Elmer Rice's *Street Scene*, which ran for 600 performances on Broadway and won the Pulitzer Prize in 1930. Brady also gave **Humphrey Bogart** his first job in the theater. Brady was married to the Broadway actress Grace George, and his daughter from a previous marriage was the Oscar-winning actress **Alice Brady**.

Mansfield, Richard (1857–1907) ★ ● ▮

ACTOR AND PRODUCER

Richard Mansfield.

Richard Mansfield was the renowned actor of his age. He was born in Berlin but was raised in England where he studied painting. He later switched to acting and light opera, joining the D'Oyly Carte Opera Company where he appeared as Sir Joseph Porter in *H.M.S. Pinafore* on tour. He also created the role of Major-General Stanley ("I am the very model of a modern Major-General") in *The Pirates of Penzance*. In 1886, he started producing plays in New York and introduced audiences to the plays of George Bernard Shaw and Ibsen, acting in the lead role in *Peer Gynt*. Audiences flocked to see him in Shakespeare's plays, but he is most remembered for his dual role on the London stage of *Dr. Jekyll and Mr. Hyde*. In 1898, he purchased his town house at 316 Riverside Drive for $80,000.

317 Riverside Drive (104th Street)

Tierney, Myles (1841–1921) ★ ■
CONTRACTOR AND BANKER

Tierney built the Washington Bridge, which spans the Harlem River at 181st Street and was opened in 1888. He also built several buildings on Fordham's Rose Hill campus in the Bronx, as well as Harlem Hospital, Gouverneur Hospital, and numerous public buildings in New Jersey. He also built the waterworks in Boston, Massachusetts; in Norfolk, Virginia; and in Kingston, Long Island City, and New Rochelle, New York. His contracting work for railroads led to his presidency of the North Hudson Railway Company, and his various projects led to his directorships on numerous banks. He was president of Hudson Trust Company in Hoboken and an executive vice president of the Immigrant Savings Bank in New York City. He was a member of the 1901 Tenement House Commission, as well as a trustee of Bellevue Hospital and of St. Patrick's Cathedral. Tierney was born in Pennsylvania and joined an uncle's contracting firm in Jersey City. From digging cellars and grading streets, he learned how to build larger structures.

320 Riverside Drive (104th Street)

McMillin, Emerson (1844–1922)
FINANCIER AND ART COLLECTOR

McMillin's art collection included paintings by Corot, Daubigny, Millet, Rousseau, and Inness. Born in Ohio, he fought on the side of the North in the Civil War and was wounded five times in thirty-eight battles. His first work experience was at an iron furnace, but he shifted to the gas business where he became manager and later president of several companies. After gaining experience as president of the Columbus Street Railway Company in Ohio and establishing the banking house of Emerson McMillin & Co. on Wall Street, he founded American Light and Traction Company, which controlled forty gas and streetcar entities. Entering the New York City market, McMillin made gas in Queens to be sold in Manhattan. He served as president of the Arbitration Society of America and helped fund the establishment of the Columbia School of Business in 1916.

Mills, Hayley Catherine Rose Vivien (1946–)
ACTRESS

Mills was the last recipient of the Academy Juvenile Award for her performance in the 1960 Disney film *Pollyanna*. Previous winners of the Juvenile Oscar included Shirley Temple, Mickey Rooney, and Judy Garland. Since Mills could not be present to accept the award, former Mouseketeer, Annette Funicello, accepted it on her behalf. Disney next cast Mills in *The Parent Trap*, in which she played twins and sang the 1961 chart hit "Let's Get Together," harmonizing with herself. She was born into a family of prominent actors. Hayley's older sister is actress Juliet Mills. Her mother, Mary Hayley Bell, Lady Mills, was an actress who wrote the novel *Whistle Down the Wind*, which was adapted into a 1961 movie starring her daughter Hayley. Her father was actor Sir John Mills, who appeared in more than 120 films and won the 1970 Academy Award for Best Supporting Actor in *Ryan's Daughter*. Hayley Mills made nearly 30 movies; 2 from 1964 stand out: *The Chalk Garden* and *The Moon-Spinners*. She could also be seen on television and stage from time to time.

330 Riverside Drive (105th Street)

Davis, Robert Benson (1843–1920) 🖘
BAKING POWDER MANUFACTURER

Davis Baking Powder can be found today in most grocery stores. Robert Benson Davis founded his company in 1881. The manufacturing plant was in Hoboken, New Jersey. Davis was born in Pompey, New York, and he fought in the Civil War. In 1881 he married Jennie Weed, who was twenty years younger. By 1908, after many of her relatives had moved into their mansion on Riverside Drive and a few doctors had questioned his mental faculties, she made him a virtual prisoner in his own house. She pressed him to adjust his will in her favor. He would not, and two years later he dropped a letter out of the bedroom window addressed to a friend. Some solid citizen found it, delivered it, and with the help of his accomplice friend, Davis escaped disguised as a physician with two women in nurse's outfits. He made it to California and sued for divorce. She remarried but died before him in 1915.

331 Riverside Drive (near 105th Street)

Ahnelt, William Paul "W.P." (1864–1949)
PUBLISHER

Ahnelt's *Pictorial Review* magazine was read by over three million people, mostly women. It featured illustrators, such as Howard Chandler Christy, and serialized novels by Mary Roberts Rinehart and by Edith Wharton. His business occupied a twelve-story building on West 39th Street that took up half the block. Ahnelt was born in Berlin and came to New York in 1890. He developed a new type of fashion magazine that illustrated garments on complete figures. From this, he published several journals that also provided patterns of the garments displayed. He is also thought to be the first person to bring Paris fashion models to New York. Ahnelt also lived at **431 Riverside Drive** (near 115th Street).

Davies, Marion (1897–1961), Actress, Comedienne, and Philanthropist ●

(See bio for Davies at **255 West 105th Street**.)

333 Riverside Drive (near 105th Street)

Bellow, Saul (1915–2005) ●
WRITER

Saul Bellow is the only writer to win the National Book Award for Fiction three times. He also won the Pulitzer Prize and the Nobel Prize for Literature and is widely known for such best sellers as *Herzog* and *Humboldt's Gift*. Quebec-born Bellow wrote several novels, novellas, short stories, and a play. His Chicago experiences are well represented, yet as a self-professed historian of society, his years in New York City served him well. He wrote his fourth novel, *Seize the Day*, published in 1956, while living on Riverside Drive.

Canavan, David Patrick (ca.1867–1914) 🖎
EXCAVATOR

Canavan's specialty was excavating rock. He excavated from 16th to 30th Streets for the IRT's #1 Line, part of the New York City subway system that runs along Seventh Avenue and Broadway, and for the construction of many prominent buildings in the city. These included the Candler building for Coca-Cola on West 42nd Street, the Astor Hotel, the Apthorp and Belnord apartments on Broadway, the University Club and the St. Regis Hotel on Fifth Avenue, the Society for Ethical Culture and the Century Theater on Central Park West, and the Schwab mansion that was on Riverside Drive. He also excavated for the largest office building in the world in 1915, the Equitable Life Building on Lower Broadway. Born in Hell's Kitchen, Canavan was educated in a public school and entered into his father's excavation business, located in the West 50s, which was reestablished under his leadership as Canavan Brothers. From an early age, he became involved in politics, and was an active member of such organizations as the Society of St. Tammany, the National Democratic Club, the Catholic Club of New York, the Friends of Ireland, the Knights of Columbus, the New York Athletic Club, and the Nameoki Club at 233 West 100th Street (near Broadway), where he sometimes lived.

334 Riverside Drive (near 106th Street)

Forhan, Richard J. (1866–1965)
DENTIST AND TOOTHPASTE MANUFACTURER

Dr. Forhan was a dentist who made a fortune from making toothpaste. The Forhan formula, which contained an astringent, ran ads citing gum disease with the slogan "Four out of five get it." Forhan established his company in New York in 1913 and sold it in 1929 for $5 million plus stock just before the market crashed. His fortune was expanded to include extensive real estate holdings. He was born in Ireland and raised in Colorado. He graduated from the University of Denver School of Dentistry and had a dental practice in Denver for eighteen years. His five-story town house on Riverside Drive was known to have an exquisite Japanese interior, thanks to its previous owner, **Dr. Jokichi Takamine**. Regrettably, the interior suffered extensively from a fire in 1928.

Takamine, Jokichi (1854–1922) ★ ◼ ▮ ☞
CHEMIST

Takamine is sometimes called the father of American biotechnology and the Japanese Pasteur. In addition to his professional accomplishments, his efforts and donations gave us the blossoming

Jokichi Takamine.

cherry trees in Riverside Park, Sakura Park, and on the Mall in Washington, D.C. To Americans, he was not only the best-known Japanese person of his day, but he was known for fostering friendly relations between Japan and the United States. Takamine was a wonder in his field of chemistry. In 1894, he discovered the starch-digestion remedy Takadiastase. In 1900 he discovered adrenaline, which enabled bloodless surgery in minor operations. Born in Japan, Takamine was one of the first graduates of the Imperial University of Japan at Tokyo where he received a degree in engineering and chemistry. He also did post-graduate studies at the University of Glasgow and Anderson College in Scotland. In 1906, the University of Japan would honor his accomplishments by making him a Doctor of Chemical Engineering and a Doctor of Pharmacology. Takamine also lived at **61 West 108th Street** (near Manhattan Avenue).

335 Riverside Drive (near 106th Street)

Faber, John Eberhard, Jr. (1859–1946) ◼

PENCIL MANUFACTURER

At the age of 20, Faber began running his family's pencil business, which had been founded in Germany in 1761. When John Eberhard Faber, Sr., died in 1879, Junior took over the company and made it international, employing over one thousand workers. With his brother **Lothar Washington Faber**, he expanded their Greenpoint, Brooklyn, operation into Newark, New Jersey, to capitalize on their innovation of attaching rubber erasers to the pencils. John Jr. was born in New York City, entered Columbia University School of Mines at age 15, and finished his education in Europe. As a lifetime athlete, he was a senior member of the New York Athletic Club, a founder and honorary member of the Richmond County Country Club, and president of the Staten Island Boat Club. Knowing a thing or two about the importance of a valued product name, he was honorary chairman of the United States Trademark Association.

Marlowe, Julia (1865–1950) ★ ■ ▮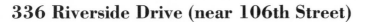
ACTRESS

Marlowe was the most successful actress of her day, appearing in more than seventy productions on Broadway starting in 1895. Her philanthropic activities were extensive and acknowledged by George Washington University with an honorary doctorate in law degree in 1921. Born Sarah Frances Frost in England, Marlowe came to the United States in 1870. By 1879, she was playing the part of Sir Joseph Porter in a children's opera touring group production of Gilbert and Sullivan's *H.M.S. Pinafore*. After garnering some experience with Shakespeare's plays, she came to New York for voice training and took the name of Fanny Marlowe. In 1891, she survived a bout of typhoid fever. She was married twice to actors, but did her best-appreciated work, mostly Shakespeare, with her second husband, E. H. Sothern. After he died in the Plaza Hotel in 1933, she became a recluse until 1944 when she donated seventeen trunks of their costumes to the Museum of the City of New York. She also died in the Plaza Hotel.

Julia Marlowe.

336 Riverside Drive (near 106th Street)

Simone, Nina (1933–2003) ★ ■
SINGER, SONGWRITER, AND PIANIST

Known as the High Priestess of Soul, Simone is not easy to classify. There is soul and there is jazz, and there is always a classical foundation, emphasized in her own piano accompaniment. But her music is unique and widely influential. Born Eunice Kathleen Waymon in North Carolina, Simone won a scholarship to study piano at the Julliard School of Music. She left school due to a lack of funds and began singing, first in Atlantic City, New Jersey, where her Billie Holiday–influenced style was rather special. In 1958, she recorded the first of forty some-odd albums, which received growing acclaim. From 1964 her music became fused with her fervor for civil rights. She was given three honorary degrees and a special Grammy Award. She has a long list of acting credits, but the recent documentary, *Nina Simone*, may be the start of renewed interest in her particular talent.

337 Riverside Drive (near 106th Street), the River Mansion

Faber, Lothar Washington (1861–1943) ■

PENCIL MANUFACTURER

Lothar Faber invented the clamp tip type of pencil that had a removable and adjustable eraser. Lothar ran the manufacturing part of the family pencil business. Faber pencils were the first to have erasers, and Lothar expanded their products to include fountain pens, mechanical pencils, and refills. Lothar Faber was born in New York City and graduated from the Columbia University School of Mines. He was always next in line after his older brother, **John Eberhard, Jr.**, to run the company. Along the way, Lothar also ran Eberhard Faber Rubber Company in Newark. His son, Eberhard Lothar Faber had the misfortune to be thrown from his horse in Central Park. Worse, in 1945, he died while saving his 8-year-old son from drowning in the New Jersey surf.

340 Riverside Drive (near 106th Street)

Feather, Leonard Geoffrey (1914–1994) ■ ▉
COMPOSER AND JAZZ CRITIC

Any owner of jazz albums from the 1950s would be familiar with
Leonard Feather's liner notes. An early advocate of bebop, he was
the most significant jazz critic of his day and wrote the liner notes
for numerous albums. He organized the first Carnegie Hall jazz
performances and the only two jazz concerts in the old Metropolitan
Opera House. His monumental work *The Encyclopedia of Jazz*,
published in 1955, was followed by a dozen other important books on
the subject. Born in London, Feather studied piano and clarinet and
taught himself arranging. He settled into New York City in 1939 and
developed into a record producer and jazz talent scout, composing and
producing for the likes of Dinah Washington and Louis Jordon. He even
penned a tune in 1952, "Get Rich Quick," for future rock and roll legend
Little Richard. The Berklee College of Music awarded him an honorary
doctorate in music. He was married to vocalist and jazz writer Jane
Feather.

Johns, Jasper (1930–) ■
ARTIST

Johns's 1958 painting *Flag* is thought to have sold privately for $110
million in 2010. His 1958 *Three Flags* painting had fetched the highest
price for a work by a living American artist when the Whitney Museum
of Art purchased it in 1980 for $1 million. His first American flag
painting from 1954 is in the Metropolitan Museum of Art. Born in
Georgia, he studied briefly at the University of South Carolina, and
after arriving in New York in the late 1940s, he studied at the Parsons
School of Design. Part of a vibrantly creative community, including
his long-term lover Robert Rauschenberg, along with composer John

Cage and choreographer Merce Cunningham, who were a couple, Johns employed popular images in abstractly playful ways. The legendary gallery owner, Leo Castelli, found and championed Johns's work, and Alfred Barr, who was one of the founders of the Museum of Modern Art, sanctioned Johns's significance with a number of purchases.

Keigwin, Albert Edwin (ca.1868–1951), Minister 🖎

(See bio for Keigwin at **324 West 103rd Street**.)

Marvin, Henry "Harry" Norton (1862–1940) ■ ▯
INVENTOR AND FILM PIONEER

In 1895, Marvin, along with Herman Casler and W. K. L. Dickson, formed the American Mutoscope Company, which successfully competed with Thomas Edison's Kinetoscope for individual "peep shows." "Mutoscope" became "Biograph," and as its vice president, Marvin hired the pioneer film director **D. W. Griffith**. The company launched the film careers of John Barrymore, **Lillian Gish**, **Mary Pickford**, and others. He was later the president of the Motion Picture Patents Company, which combined the resources of Edison and Biograph. Born in upstate New York, Marvin graduated from the University of Syracuse, where he later became a trustee. He worked with Edison in 1888, installing New York City's electric generating system, and he was present with him when the city's lights were first turned on. At General Electric Company in Schenectady, he invented the Marvin Electric Rock Drill. He officially retired a wealthy man in 1912 but continued to invent an automatic radio-tuning device and an automatic palm-reading device that was very popular in penny arcades.

Sontag, Susan (1933–2004) ▣
WRITER, TEACHER, AND INTELLECTUAL

Susan Sontag.

Sontag is buried in Montparnasse Cemetery in Paris. So are Jean-Paul Sartre, Simone de Beauvoir, Camille Saint-Saens, Guy de Maupassant, Frederick Bartholdi, Cesar Franck, and Eugene Ionesco. Born in New York City as Susan Rosenblatt, she took her mother's remarried name of Sontag. She was raised on Long Island and in California. Her education began at the University of California, Berkeley, but she graduated Phi Beta Kappa at age 18 from the University of Chicago with a BA degree. Married at age 17, she taught English at the University of Connecticut for two years, and then earned MA degrees in English and in philosophy at Harvard. The philosopher Herbert Marcuse lived with Sontag and became her husband in 1955 while working on a book. In 1959, Sontag came to New York and was an editor at the journal *Commentary* while teaching at Sarah Lawrence College, City College, and Columbia. Her reputation soared with almost everything that she wrote, but she was often in controversial territory. Her fiction included her 1990 play *The Way We Live Now* about the AIDS epidemic and her 1992 novel *The Volcano Lover*. Her other writings included numerous essays in the *New Yorker* and other magazines, six anthologies of her essays, the 1977 treatise *On Photography*, and the 1978 *Illness as Metaphor*. Photographer Annie Liebovitz was Sontag's companion for many years.

343 Riverside Drive (near 106th Street)

Roosevelt, James R. "Tadd" (1879–1958)
BOY MILLIONAIRE

He was a grandson of William Astor and cousin to President Theodore Roosevelt. His father was Franklin Delano Roosevelt's half-brother and a noted philanthropist. His parents disapproved of his marriage in 1900 to a Hungarian-born prostitute, Sadie Messinger, known as "Dutch Sadie." He was receiving a family income of $15,000 a year as a Harvard senior when he married. A year later he received $500,000 in real estate from his father's estate, and then $750,000 from his mother when he turned 30. In 1917, he was arrested in Florida, living under an assumed name while undergoing divorce proceedings. At that time, he was reportedly paying the highest income taxes in the state. He and Sadie separated, but never divorced. Sadie died in 1940. When Tadd died in 1958, his fortune went to the Salvation Army.

351 Riverside Drive (near 107th Street), the Schinasi Mansion

Schinasi, Moussa or Morris (1855–1928) ■ 🖎
CIGARETTE MANUFACTURER AND PHILANTHROPIST

The Schinasi Brothers produced 250 million cigarettes a year. Established in 1893, they were one of the first three US manufacturers of Turkish cigarettes. Their factory building at 309–311 West 120th Street is still standing as of 2020. Born in Turkey, Schinasi went to Alexandria, Egypt, at age 15, where he learned the tobacco trade. At age 30, he came to the United States and exhibited cigarettes made by his patented cigarette-rolling machine at the 1893 Chicago World's Fair. Their success was based on selling ready-made cigarettes that had Turkish tobacco. He and his brother Abraham sold their business for $3.5 million in 1916. Morris bequeathed $1 million to build a hospital in his hometown in Turkey and the rest of his $5 million fortune to health care institutions including Beth Israel Hospital and the nearby Sydenham Hospital at 124th Street and Manhattan Avenue. His daughter was **Altina Schinasi Miranda**. Schinasi also lived at **331 West 107th Street** (near Riverside Drive).

Miranda, Altina Schinasi (1907–1999)

SCULPTOR, FILMMAKER, AND DESIGNER

Schinasi designed the 1930s sensational Harlequin eyeglass frame. One of the first pairs was sold to Clare Boothe Luce. Schinasi was born in the Schinasi mansion on Riverside Drive. After her mother took her to Paris where she took art lessons, she eschewed college for art instruction, including lessons at the Roerich Museum given by the American painter Samuel Halpert. In the 1940s, she moved to the Los Angeles area and made a short film about another of her art teachers entitled "George Grosz' Interregnum." With narration by Lotte Lenya, it was nominated for an Academy Award. After some involvement with the civil rights movement in the 1960s, she married her fourth husband, painter Celestino Miranda, in 1981, and they spent their final days in Santa Fe, New Mexico. In 2014, her grandson Peter Sanders produced a documentary about her and some of her sculptures that are pieces of furniture with heads and torsos called "chairacters." Her father was **Morris Schinasi**. Miranda also lived at **331 West 107th Street** (near Riverside Drive).

355 Riverside Drive (near 108th Street)

Bayne, Samuel Gamble (1844–1924)

OIL PIONEER AND BANKER

Bayne lived in one of the few mansions on Riverside Avenue (renamed Riverside Drive in 1909). Born in Ireland, he was schooled in Belfast before entering the linen business. He came to America in the 1860s and purchased the second oldest oil well in the country in Titusville, Pennsylvania. In 1883, he established the Seaboard National Bank to handle the burgeoning oil business. After he died, Seaboard would merge with the Bank of the Manhattan Company, which is now part of JP Morgan Chase & Co. In addition to banking, Bayne traveled the world, wrote extensively, and patronized the arts. His impressive Romanesque Revival mansion at 355 Riverside Avenue, designed by noted architect Frank Freeman, was larger than his first one at 360 Riverside Avenue. Bayne's mansion was sold in 1921. His son-in-law, architect Alfred C. Bossom, designed the fourteen-story apartment building that now occupies the site. Socialite Emily Bayne was his daughter.

Feldman, Hyman Isaac (1896–1981) ■ ▮
ARCHITECT

Feldman designed functional and economical apartment buildings that disappoint critics looking for artistic style. His building at 1025 Fifth Avenue, across from the Metropolitan Museum of Art, seems to get the most negative attention, as do his other buildings from the 1950s and 1960s, including the Schwab House on Riverside Drive from 73rd to 74th Streets. But Feldman's earlier buildings in neighborhoods from Inwood in upper Manhattan to Brooklyn, and especially on the Grand Concourse in the Bronx, constitute an Art Deco extravaganza that is yet to be fully appreciated. Feldman was born in what is now Poland. He first attended Cornell to study landscape architecture and completed his education at Yale. By providing scholarship funding and donating rare books, he was an early supporter of the Yale School of Architecture when it was established in the 1950s. Columbia and City College awarded him honorary degrees.

Fellheimer, Alfred T. (1875–1959) ■ ▮
ARCHITECT

Fellheimer headed up the design team of architects from Warren & Wetmore, and Reed & Stem that produced Grand Central Terminal. As part of Stem & Fellheimer, he designed the magnificent Union Station in Utica, New York. As part of Fellheimer & Wagner, he designed the Union Station in Erie, Pennsylvania, the towering Buffalo Central Terminal, and the Art Deco masterpiece Cincinnati Union Terminal. They designed some seven other train terminals, the Farragut and Albany Houses in Brooklyn, Elmhurst General Hospital and Thomas Edison Vocational High School in Queens, the Beekman Theater on the Upper East Side, The Hoffmann-LaRoche Pharmaceutical Plant and the Becton, Dickinson & Co. facility in New Jersey, and much else. Born in Chicago, Fellheimer graduated from the University of Illinois School of Architecture in 1895. After working in Chicago, he based his evolving career in New York.

Uris, Harris H. (ca. 1867–1945) ■
IRON WORKS MAGNATE AND COMMERCIAL DEVELOPER

Uris owned one of the few mansions on Riverside Drive, having purchased it from **Samuel G. Bayne** in 1921. Although he might not have lived there, he is included here because of his ownership and because the neighborhood would be proud to claim him. Soon after acquiring the Bayne mansion he built a fourteen-story apartment building on the site using Bayne's son-in-law architect Alfred C. Bossom. Uris's wealth came from owning and operating the Harris H. Uris Iron Works, which supplied structural and ornamental ironworks for numerous buildings, public schools, and the city's subways. The business grew into commercial development that included such well-known structures as the Washington Hilton, the New York Hilton, the JC Penney Building, 55 Water Street, and 1633 Broadway (a.k.a. the Uris Building), which includes the Uris Theater.

360 Riverside Drive (near 108th Street), the Rutherfurd

Burroughs, William S. (1914–1997) ■
BEAT WRITER

Burroughs is included among the influencers pictured on the album cover of the Beatles' *Sargent Pepper's Lonely Hearts Club Band*. He was one of the great writers of the twentieth century. Most well-known for *Naked Lunch*, his nonlinear 1959 novel that defined hip, his writings were extensive and challenging, to say the least.

Georgopulo, Theodore (ca.1883–1935), Cigarette Manufacturer

(See bio for Georgopulo at **865 West End Avenue**.)

Riverside Drive and 108th Street

Townsend, Ralph S. (1854–1921), Architect ■ ▊

(See bio for Townsend at **172 West 105th Street**.)

362 Riverside Drive (near 109th Street)

Lybrand, William M. (1867–1960) ★ ■ ▊
ACCOUNTING PIONEER

In 1898, Lybrand and others formed the accounting firm of Lybrand, Ross Brothers and Montgomery, which over time would become Coopers & Lybrand and, since 1998, PricewaterhouseCoopers LLP, one of the "big four" auditing firms. Its papers from 1891 to 2000 are archived at Columbia University. Lybrand was a giant in the accounting world for half a century. Born in Philadelphia, he began his business career with a tool and die company where he assisted a seasoned accountant in installing a cost accounting system. His experience spurred him on to promoting the development of integrated cost systems so that businesses would know whether or not products were profitable. In 1919, he was an organizer and early president of the National Association of Cost Accountants, and he held Certified Public Accounting certificates in ten states. He wrote extensively on accounting matters and co-authored the 1922 business book classic, *Accounting for Modern Corporations*.

Pollak, Walter Heilprin (1887–1940), Civil Rights Lawyer ■ ▤

(See bio for Pollak at **412 West 110th Street**.)

Robson (Belmont), Eleanor (1879–1979) ☞
ACTRESS AND ARTS PATRON

Eleanor Robson was born in England but moved to the United States as a young girl and became an actress of note. She acted in at least fifteen shows on the Broadway stage from 1900 to her retirement in 1910, when she married August Belmont, Jr. He built Belmont Park racetrack and the first subway in New York City, the IRT line that includes the #1 train, which runs through the Bloomingdale and Morningside Heights neighborhoods. In 1912, with Anne Tracy Morgan, Eleanor founded the Society for the Prevention of Useless Giving. In 1924, she wrote *In the Next Room*, a play that was produced on Broadway and ran for 159 performances. That same year, Mr. Belmont died, and Eleanor engaged with the Metropolitan Opera, joining its Board of Directors and starting the Metropolitan Opera Guild. She lived to be 100 years old.

Eleanor Robson.

Walker, William Baker (1867–1922) ● 🖝

INDUSTRIALIST

Walker was the founder of the thermos bottle industry in the United
States. As President of the American Thermos Bottle Company, he
began operations in Brooklyn in 1907. In 1912, he moved the company
and it became the largest employer in Norwich, Connecticut. In 1910,
while living in the Bona Vista Apartments at 362 Riverside Drive,
he survived a crowd in Harlem threatening to lynch him after his
car accidentally struck and killed a child in a baby carriage. A few
years later, in 1914, his wife committed suicide by shooting herself in
their Bona Vista apartment. In 1915, his skull was fractured when an
automobile in which he was riding near Providence, Rhode Island,
turned over on him. He died in 1922 in New London, Connecticut, near
his company.

370 Riverside Drive (near 109th Street)

Arendt, Hannah (1906–1975) ★ ●

POLITICAL THEORIST

Arendt is mostly known for her classic study, *The Origins of
Totalitarianism*. Many will also cite her phrase "banality of evil," used
in her reportage of the Eichmann trial for the *New Yorker* magazine.
The 2012 movie *Hannah Arendt* centers on the controversy associated
with the phrase. Born Johanna Cohn Arendt in Germany, she studied
there at the University of Marburg where she had a romantic
relationship with her philosophy professor Martin Heidegger. This
brought her controversy because of his support for the Nazi party.
She wrote her dissertation under the philosopher Karl Jaspers in
Heidelberg. In France for a few years, she met and married Heinrich
Blucher, and they immigrated to the United States in 1941. She was
connected to several universities, including the University of Chicago

and Princeton, where she was the first female lecturer. Her last teaching post was at the New School for Social Research. Her husband taught at Bard College. They are both buried on the Bard Campus. She also lived at **130 Morningside Drive** (near Amsterdam Avenue) and **317 West 95th Street** (near Riverside Drive).

Chu, Grace Zia (1899–1999)
PIONEER COOKBOOK AUTHOR

Mrs. Chu introduced Chinese cooking to America, pure and simple. Her classes in Chinese cooking and her landmark book *The Pleasures of Chinese Cooking*, published in 1962, corrected the all-too-typical misunderstanding of Chinese food as chop suey. As the first American instructor of Chinese cuisine, Mrs. Chu had the daunting task of making unfamiliar foods into easy-to-make, tasty meals. She did that and more, as evidenced by her popularity. She gave her cooking instructions at the China Institute, at the Mandarin Institute, and in her apartment. Born in Shanghai, Chu attended Wellesley College in Massachusetts on a scholarship, earned a degree in physical education, and returned to China where she became an executive in the Young Women's Christian Association. She married an army officer who was assigned to the Chinese Embassy in Washington, D.C. There she began her mission to demonstrate the artistry of Chinese cooking. Meals in America would never be the same. Chu also lived at **545 West 111th Street** (near Broadway).

Gutzwiller, Martin C. (1925–2014) ■ ▪
PHYSICIST

The Gutzwiller approximation, the Gutzwiller wave function, the Gutzwiller projection, and the Gutzwiller trace formula, all suggest Martin C. Gutzwiller's significance in the realm of modern physics.

More specifically, he focused on field theory, quantum chaos, and complex systems. With chaotic systems, he was the first to study the relationship between classical and quantum mechanics. His work in field theory, celestial mechanics, wave propagation, and the physics of crystals, all with extra-complex mathematics, produced novel solutions. The Max Planck Institute for the Physics of Complex Systems awards the Gutzwiller Fellowship to acknowledge and promote exceptional research in this field. Gutzwiller was awarded the prestigious Max Planck Medal in 2003, following in the footsteps of Max Planck, Albert Einstein, Werner Heisenberg, Enrico Fermi, and Wolfgang Pauli. Born in Switzerland, he studied under Wolfgang Pauli at the Swiss Federal Institute of Technology. He earned his PhD at the University of Kansas under Max Dresden. He taught in Stockholm, Zurich, Paris, and at Columbia and Yale universities. His interest in the history of science fueled his collection of rare books on astronomy and mechanics.

Pfeiffer, Henry (1857–1939) ▪
PHARMACEUTICAL EXECUTIVE

Pfeiffer was president of one of the largest pharmaceutical companies in the world, William R. Warner & Co. That firm grew into Warner-Lambert, which was acquired by Pfizer in 2000. The Smithsonian Institution heralds Warner's invention of the tablet-coating process that encases harsh-tasting medicines in sugar shells. Pfeiffer founded the Pfeiffer Chemical Company in 1901 in St. Louis. He purchased the Warner Company in Philadelphia and built it into one of the leading manufacturers of drugs. His retirement was marked by philanthropy to numerous organizations, most connected to the Methodist Episcopal Church, including Brooklyn's Methodist Hospital.

Thompson, Robert G. (1915–1965) 👉
COMMUNIST LEADER

Thompson was an important American communist whose life could make for a compelling movie. Born in Oregon, he joined the Communist Party as a teenager in Oakland, California. After working two years, he traveled to Moscow to participate in the Young Communist International Congress. Then he went on to Spain where he joined the International Brigade and commanded a battalion. Back in the United States by 1938, he became secretary of the Young Communist League in Ohio and was eventually selected to the party's National Board. After Germany attacked the Soviet Union in 1941, Thompson joined the United States Army. His actions in the South West Pacific earned him the Distinguished Service Cross. But in 1948, a Federal grand jury indicted him as chairman of the New York State Communist Party, along with ten other members of the National Board. The charge was violation of the Smith Act, which prohibited teaching or advocating overthrow of the government by force or violence. The conviction of all defendants came after nine months of testimony. Thompson received the lightest sentence of three years in prison because of his war record. Rather than showing up to begin his sentence, he obtained false identification papers, grew a mustache, dyed his hair strawberry blonde, and holed up in a secluded cabin 8,000 feet up in the Sierra Mountains near Sonora, California. The FBI captured him and a comrade without a shot and sent them off to Alcatraz. While in the Federal House of Detention in New York City awaiting trial for a related charge, a fellow inmate attacked him with a lead pipe for no apparent reason and cracked his skull. After his release from prison in 1960, he lived quietly until his death at age 50 from a heart attack.

Isamu Noguchi, with a model for
contoured playground planned for
Riverside Park.

375 Riverside Drive (near 110th Street)

Morris, Bernadine (1925–2018) ▤
FASHION JOURNALIST AND CRITIC

When she retired in 1995, Bernadine Morris was the chief fashion
writer of the *New York Times*. During her thirty-plus years there,
she often worked with the likes of famed *Times* photographer Bill
Cunningham and illustrator Antonio Lopez, among others. Many
designers, such as Donna Karan, Ralph Lauren, Calvin Klein, Claire
McCardell, Geoffrey Beene, and Halston, owed some of their success to
her approval. She authored such books as *The Fashion Makers*, *Scaasi:
A Cut Above* and *Universe of Fashion: Valentino*, as well as over four
thousand articles for the *Times*. She is credited with elevating fashion
journalism and was honored with the Medal of the City of Paris is 1985
and a Council of Fashion Designers of America (CFDA) award in 1987.
She was born Bernadine Traub in Harlem, and she graduated from
Hunter College in the Bronx before it became Lehman College. She also
earned a master's degree in English from New York University. Before
arriving at the *New York Times* in 1963, she worked at *Fashion Trades*
magazine, the *New York Journal-American* newspaper, and *Women's
Wear Daily*.

380 Riverside Drive (near 111th Street), the Hendrick Hudson

Gilbreth, Frank Bunker, Sr. (1868–1924), Industrial Engineer ▬

(See bio for Frank Gilbreth at **310 West 94th Street**.)

Gilbreth, Lillian Moller (1878–1972), Psychologist and Industrial Engineer ■

(See bio for Lillian Gilbreth at **310 West 94th Street**.)

Jerome, William Travers (1859–1934) ■
LAWYER AND POLITICIAN

Jerome prosecuted Harry Kendall Thaw for the murder of architect Stanford White. Born in upstate New York, Jerome attended but did not graduate from Amherst College in Massachusetts. He studied law at Columbia, was admitted to the bar in 1884, and began his practice. Avowedly anti-Tammany, he worked for the Lexow Committee that probed police corruption. He was elected New York County District Attorney in 1901. As the prosecutor of Harry Thaw in two trials, he was on the front pages of the newspapers constantly and came to have one of the earliest interests in criminal psychiatry. Winston Churchill was Jerome's first cousin once removed through Churchill's mother, Jennie Jerome, who became Lady Randolph Churchill when she married Winston's father. Jennie's father and William's uncle was the financier Leonard Jerome. His son, William Travers Jerome, Jr., also lived next door.

William Travers Jerome.

Kunz, George Frederick (1856–1932), Mineralogist and Gem Expert ★ ■ ▉

(See bio for Kunz at **601 West 110th Street**.)

Lefcourt, Abraham E. (1876–1932) ■ ▉
COMMERCIAL DEVELOPER

Lefcourt is thought to have built more New York skyscrapers than anyone else. He is also most responsible for the development of the

Garment District in Manhattan's West 30s and 40s. Lefcourt was born in England but grew up on the Lower East Side, where he sold newspapers and polished shoes. After success in the garment industry, he shifted his energies to real estate. Numerous buildings followed in the Garment District, many with his name attached. It is thought that he might have destroyed more structures destined for landmark status than any other developer. For example, his buildings replaced the earlier Temple Emanuel, the Spanish Flats apartments on Central Park South, and the Consolidated Stock Exchange building. He also built the Brill Building, which is famous for housing many rock and roll songwriters, and the Newark Building, which still defines the Newark skyline.

Loew, Marcus (1870–1927), Motion Picture Industry Pioneer ★ ■

(See bio for Loew at **200 West 111th Street**.)

Weber, Joseph Morris (1867–1942) ★ ■
VAUDEVILLE PERFORMER

Neil Simon's play *The Sunshine Boys* may be based on the popular vaudeville team of Weber and Fields. Weber was born and raised on the Lower East Side in New York. His partnership with Lew Fields, which lasted decades, began in their childhood. They teamed up in part to earn money to see the dime shows on the Bowery. Weber and Fields performed a so-called Dutch act, which lampooned German immigrants initially but evolved to include dialects of any group worthy of their humor. They were the perennial stars of vaudeville shows all over the country and expanded their success to three road companies. In 1894, they debuted on Broadway as it came into the Times Square area. In 1895, they operated their own theater, the Weber and Fields Broadway Music Hall, and featured stars such as DeWolf Hopper of "Casey at Bat" fame, and Lillian Russell. Their partnership broke up in 1904, with Weber continuing to run the theater, for a time with Florenz Ziegfeld. Reunions in 1912 and 1932 in Radio City Music Hall were warmly received, but times had changed.

390 Riverside Drive (near 111th Street)

King, Carole (1942–) ■
PERFORMING ARTIST AND POPULAR SONG COMPOSER

Most rock and roll aficionados know that the artist who sang "You're So Vain" in 1971 was the same person who wrote "Will You Still Love Me Tomorrow" for the Shirelles in 1960. Her "Tapestry" album, recorded in 1971, introduced "I Feel the Earth Move," "You've Got a Friend," and "It's Too Late (Baby)." With her one-time husband, Gerry Goffin, she composed such rock and roll classics as "Take Good Care of My Baby"; "The Locomotion"; "Up on the Roof"; "Go Away, Little Girl"; "Crying in the Rain"; "(You Make Me Feel Like) A Natural Woman"; and "One Fine Day." Born Carol Joan Klein, she attended Queens College. She had perfect pitch at age 4, played the piano, dated Neal Sedaka in her teenage years, and recorded with Paul Simon while beginning to compose her string of well-known rock and roll hits. It is no surprise that such an amazing talent is a Rock and Roll Hall of Fame inductee and the subject of the successful Broadway show "Beautiful: The Carole King Musical."

Newman, Hugo (1867–1951) ■
EDUCATOR

PS 180 at 370 West 120th Street in Harlem is named Hugo Newman Prep in his honor. Newman was an assistant superintendent of schools and the last principal of the former New York Training School for Teachers. A native New Yorker, Newman graduated from City College with a BS degree in 1885, and soon after from New York University with a master of pedagogy degree. He taught at various public schools in the Bronx and Manhattan and served as principal of Morris Evening High School. He developed many pedagogical devices including some for teaching numbers and converting tables for laboratory purposes. As principal of New York Teachers Training School, he helped design its building on West 135th Street near the City College Campus. The training school ended in 1933 because there was a surplus of teachers, and the building became the High School of Music and Art. Newman also composed piano music, was an organist at numerous churches, and was a director of choruses.

Pannell, Anne Thomas Gary (1910–1984) ■ ▪
EDUCATOR

Born in North Carolina, Pannell graduated from Barnard in 1931, where she was editor of the school newspaper *Motorboard* and was elected to Phi Beta Kappa. She taught history at the Barnard Summer School for Women Workers, and went off to Oxford, England, to earn a PhD degree in 1936. She taught at the Alabama College for Women and, was a professor of history at the University of Alabama. In the late 1940s, Pannell was dean of Goucher College in Baltimore. In 1950, she was appointed president of Sweet Briar College in Virginia, a position she served in until her retirement in 1971. In the 1960s she was president of the American Association of University Women. From 1969 to 1972, she was also a Barnard trustee.

395 Riverside Drive (near 112th Street)

Johnson, Alvin Saunders (1874–1971), Economist and Co-founder of The New School ▣

(See bio for Johnson at 521 West 111th Street.)

Smith, Elinor Regina (1911–2010) ★ ▣ ☞

AVIATION PIONEER

Smith is thought to be the only person to have flown an airplane under all four East River bridges. That was in 1928, and it took the intercession of Mayor Jimmy Walker to prevent the suspension of her flying license. In 1927, when she was only 16 years old, Orville Wright helped her get an international flying license. Later that year, she became the youngest licensed pilot in the United States. In 1929, she set the women's flying endurance record, thirteen-and-a-half hours. She bested it the next year with twenty-six-and-a-half hours. She set the women's altitude record in 1930, flying to 27,419 feet. Within a year, she bested that by flying as high as 32,576 feet. In 1934, she became the first woman on a Wheaties cereal box. Born Elinor Regina Patricia Ward in New York City, she changed her last name after her actor father changed his name to Tom Smith. He traveled the vaudeville circuit and used airplanes any chance he could. When she was just 6 years old, her father strapped her into an airplane that took off from a potato patch on Long Island. In 1933, she married New York State assemblyman Patrick H. Sullivan, ceased flying, and raised a family.

Elinor Regina Smith.

404 Riverside Drive (113th Street), the Strathmore

Beeson, Jack (1921–2010)
CLASSICAL MUSIC COMPOSER

Beeson is best known for his operas, especially *Lizzie Borden*. An Indiana native, he was trained in piano and music theory at the University of Toronto and took private lessons from Bela Bartok in New York. Columbia University enabled his first opera productions that led to his teaching there. After composing orchestral and other pieces, he created and recorded *Lizzie Borden*. It was televised by NET and later revived by New York City Opera. At about the same time, Columbia made him the MacDowell Professor of Music. He continued composing and inspiring the next generation of composers even after he retired from Columbia.

Catt, Carrie Chapman (1859–1947) ★ ■ ▣
SUFFRAGIST

Catt co-founded the League of Women Voters. Eleanor Roosevelt dedicated one of her books, *This Troubled World*, to Catt. She was a giant in the suffragist movement alongside Elizabeth Cady Stanton and Susan B. Anthony. Catt was born Carrie Clinton Lane in Ripon, Wisconsin, the birthplace of the Republican Party in 1854. She earned a BS degree from Iowa State Agricultural College, now Iowa State University, was valedictorian of her class and the only female. Starting as a teacher, she rose to become school superintendent in Mason City, Iowa, the model for River City in the Broadway musical *The Music Man*. She married San Francisco newspaper editor Leo Chapman, but he died in 1886. She worked as the first female reporter in the city and married an Iowa State University alumnus, George Catt, whose wealth came from running the American Dredging Company. She succeeded Susan B. Anthony as president of the National Woman Suffrage

Association. Her friend, Mrs. Frank Leslie, whose husband was a noted magazine publisher, left Catt $900,000 to use for the suffragist cause. Such efforts led to the passage of the Nineteenth Amendment in 1920, giving women the right to vote. Her companion was fellow suffragist **Mary Garrett Hay**.

Delacorte, George Thomas, Jr. (1894–1991) ★ ◼ ▣
BOOK PUBLISHER AND PHILANTHROPIST

Shakespeare in the Park is performed in the Delacorte Amphitheater in Central Park. The 400-foot geyser in the East River south of Roosevelt Island is the Delacorte Fountain. The Delacorte Clock adorns the entrance to the Central Park Zoo. The Alice-in-Wonderland sculpture in Central Park, and the fountains at Columbus Circle, Bowling Green, and City Hall are all Delacorte bequests. Some $3 million that he gave to Columbia established the George T. Delacorte Center for Magazine Journalism, two endowed professorships, the 116th Street gates, and the fountain near Hamilton Hall. Born in Brooklyn, Delacorte went to Harvard, but transferred to Columbia where he graduated in 1913. After a brief stint at a publishing company, he struck out on his own and established Dell Publishing in 1921. It published pulp magazines and three hundred million comics a year that featured the likes of Mickey Mouse, Woody Woodpecker, and Bugs Bunny. After World War II, Dell became a major publisher of paperbacks with a cadre of authors that included Danielle Steel, Kurt Vonnegut, Elmore Leonard, and many, many others.

Gildersleeve, Henry Alger (1840–1923) ☞📖
JUDGE

Judge Gildersleeve authored a book entitled *Rifles and Marksmanship* and was so accomplished a marksman that he was sent to Ireland in

1874 to participate in an international competition. As a lieutenant colonel after the Civil War, he was in command of the State Arsenal in New York City. Born in upstate New York, Gildersleeve raised a regiment to fight in the Civil War. He saw action at Gettysburg, in the Maryland and Virginia campaigns, and with General Sherman and the march through Georgia to the sea. He was educated at College Hill near Poughkeepsie and at Columbia Law School. He practiced law on and off when he was not elected or appointed to a judgeship. In 1891, he filled a vacancy in New York State's Supreme Court. He was considered a mayoral possibility from time to time. When Colonel John Jacob Astor did not survive the sinking of the *Titanic* in 1912, Gildersleeve was made special guardian of Astor's widow. There is a street in the Bronx named after him. He was the father of Dean **Virginia Crocheron Gildersleeve** and a distant relative of **William P. S. Earle**.

Gildersleeve, Virginia Crocheron (1877–1965) ◼

EDUCATOR AND DEAN

Gildersleeve was the only woman in the United States delegation to work on writing the charter for the United Nations. During World War I, she was instrumental in creating the Women's Land Army of "farmerettes," which enabled women to support the war effort by farming. With the founding of the WAVES (Women Accepted for Volunteer Emergency Service) during World War II, she helped start a similar effort. A native New Yorker, Gildersleeve earned her undergraduate degree in 1899 at Barnard before it arrived at Morningside Heights. Her master's in medieval history and her doctorate in comparative literature were earned at Columbia. She taught at both Barnard and Columbia. In 1911, she was made Barnard's dean and served for thirty-six years—longer than anyone else in that capacity. She hired the revolutionary economist Charles Beard and anthropologist Franz Boas when his objection to World War I

Virginia C. Gildersleeve.

jeopardized his position at Columbia. Her dedication to Barnard notwithstanding, her purview was larger and included politics and the education of women. She was a driving force behind creating an international organization that raised the stature of women's education. Gildersleeve was the daughter of Judge **Henry Alger Gildersleeve** and the distant relative of **William P. S. Earle**. Gildersleeve also lived at **3009 Broadway** (near 119th Street).

Hay, Mary Garrett (1857–1928) ▪
SUFFRAGIST

After the Nineteenth Amendment was adopted in 1920, Hay became one of the first women in the country to join a political party and was appointed chairman of the Republican Women's National Executive Committee. Born in Indiana, Hay studied for two years to become a pharmacist at Western College for Women in Ohio. Following her father's political activities, she became an active worker for the Woman's Christian Temperance Union. That led to her interest in the suffrage movement, where she met her eventual companion, Carrie Chapman Catt. Her exceptional organizing ability made her a significant force in the movement leading to the presidency of the New York City Woman's Suffrage Party in 1909, which eventually became the League of Women Voters. She also served as president of the New York Federation of Women's Clubs and president of the New York Women's City Club.

Mary Garet Hay.

Hogan, Frank Smithwick (1902–1974) 👈
DISTRICT ATTORNEY FOR NEW YORK COUNTY

In 1971, on Riverside Drive near 106th Street, two police officers assigned to guard Frank Hogan were critically injured by gunfire when they chased a suspicious car connected to the Black Panthers.

Born in Connecticut, Hogan studied journalism at Columbia, went on to graduate from Columbia's Law School, and served on its board of trustees. He changed his career path several times from professional baseball player to journalist to lawyer. At age 33, he joined the staff of Thomas E. Dewey, who was appointed special prosecutor to investigate mob-related rackets. Dewey was elected district attorney, but when he left to become governor, Hogan, then aged 39, was elected his successor. He served in that capacity for thirty-two years, due in part to an unsuccessful bid to get elected to the US Senate. Hogan prosecuted numerous notable cases during his tenure, including mobsters, college basketball game-fixing, television game show-rigging, the Lenny Bruce obscenity case, and the students involved in the Columbia riots of 1968.

Hotelling, Addison "Harold" (1895–1973)
STATISTICIAN AND ECONOMIST

Hotelling's Law explains why producers make their products as similar as possible. Hotelling's rent is the maximum rent that can be efficiently exploited from a nonrenewable resource. Hotelling's dilemma shows the relationship of the supply of a good to the profit of the good's producer. These only suggest how Hotelling advanced the use of statistics to measure economic phenomena in a wide range of realms from public policy and administration to applied sciences and economics. At Columbia University, when Hotelling was co-head of Columbia's Division of War Research, he was a significant influence on Milton Friedman. Born in Minnesota, Hotelling graduated from the University of Washington with bachelor's and master's degrees, and from Princeton in 1924 with his PhD. He joined the Columbia faculty in 1927 and left there in 1946 as a professor of economics to finish his career at the University of North Carolina.

Morris, Augustus Newbold (1902–1966) ◼ ▮

POLITICIAN AND LAWYER

In 1960, Morris was named New York City's Parks Commissioner, succeeding Robert Moses. He was also the first president of the City Council, a position established in 1938. He ran for mayor in 1945 and lost. He was a descendant of Lewis Morris, signer of the Declaration of Independence and half-brother to Gouverneur Morris. He was related to Edith Wharton, to *the* Mrs. Astor of "the 400" notoriety, to Mayor Ambrose Kingsland (elected in 1851), and to Frederick J. De Peyster, whose family owned much of Morningside Heights at one time. Born Augustus Newbold Morris in New York, he never used his first name. A Yale graduate, he helped to establish the New York City Opera and to make City Center their home theater. He later served as chairman of the board of Lincoln Center.

Niebuhr, Reinhold (1892–1971) ★ ◼

THEOLOGIAN

Niebuhr claimed that he wrote the serenity prayer used frequently by alcoholics seeking recovery. Its familiar words are "God grant me the serenity to accept the things I cannot change, the courage to change the things I can, and the wisdom to know the difference." Niebuhr was born the son of a Lutheran minister in Missouri. After attending Elmhurst College in Illinois and Eden Seminary in Missouri, he went to Yale Divinity School to earn Bachelor of Divinity and Master of Arts degrees. For the next thirteen years in Detroit, Michigan, he attended to his only congregation. After preaching against the industrialist Henry Ford, he became a prominent leader in a militant faction of the Socialist Party of America. Eventually he recanted on socialism, but not on the "social gospel." In 1928 he became a professor of practical philosophy at Union Theological Seminary, where he remained until his retirement in 1960. He weighed in on many political and social issues, often clashing with Columbia Professor John Dewey. He authored numerous books, and much recognition is given to his contribution to the "just war theory." His wife was the religious studies professor Ursula Keppel-Compton Niebuhr.

Rossellini, Isabella Fiorella Elettra Giovanna (1952–) ◼
ACTRESS, MODEL, AND ANIMAL BEHAVIORIST

In 1992, Rossellini was featured in rock star **Madonna's** book *Sex* and in her music video *Erotica*. She has been captured on film by many famous photographers, including Annie Liebovitz, Bruce Weber, Richard Avedon, and Robert Mapplethorpe. Born in Italy, the daughter of Swedish actress Ingrid Bergman and Italian film director Roberto Rossellini, she attended Finch College on East 78th Street. She has a fraternal twin sister who has been a professor of literature at Harvard, Princeton, New York University, and Columbia. The television journalist Pia Lindstrom is her stepsister. In her late twenties, her modeling career began and resulted in many magazine covers and a twenty-year connection with the Lancôme cosmetics brand. Meanwhile she was married to Martin Scorsese for three years and appeared in numerous movies and on television. Her appearance in David Lynch's 1987 *Blue Velvet* was memorable, as was her role as Alec Baldwin's first wife in the television series *30 Rock*. Her love of animals has led her to pursue a master's in conservation and animal behavior from Hunter College.

Simon, Robert Edward, Sr. (1877–1935) ◼ ▮
REAL ESTATE ENTREPRENEUR

PS 165 on 109th Street, was JHS 165 in 1935 when it was named the Robert E. Simon School in recognition of the founder and president of the United Parents Association. A New York native, Simon was related to both Ambassador Henry Morganthau, Sr., and Secretary of the Treasury Robert Morganthau, Sr., through his mother Pauline Morganthau Simon. After attending City College of New York, he began his long career in real estate. He brokered the move of the *New York Times* from downtown to Longacre Square, thereafter designated Times Square. In 1905, he joined his uncle's real estate firm, but went into business for himself in 1919. In 1925, Simon purchased Carnegie Hall from Andrew Carnegie's widow. His son, **Robert E. Simon, Jr.**, sold it to the City of New York in 1960.

Simon, Robert Edward, Jr. (1914–2015) ★ ■ ▇

REAL ESTATE ENTREPRENEUR AND PHILANTHROPIST

Robert Edward Simon, Jr., developed Reston, Virginia, which is an acronym of his name—that is, "R E S ton." He also developed Columbia, Maryland. Both are fully modern communities planned for tens of thousands of residents, with schools, religious institutions, and shopping facilities. Born in New York City, Simon graduated from Harvard in 1935. Later that year his father **Robert Edward Simon, Sr.,** died, and so he took over the reins of the family's real estate business, which included ownership of Carnegie Hall. When World War II came along, he joined the United States Army and served a few years in Europe, rising to the rank of captain. In the 1950s, he developed properties all over the United States. For twenty-five years, he kept the financially struggling Carnegie Hall afloat, but in 1960, he arranged for its sale and transfer to New York City.

410 Riverside Drive (near 113rd Street)
Said, Edward Wadie (1935–2003)

PROFESSOR OF LITERATURE AND INTELLECTUAL

Edward Said wrote four books about music, one co-authored with the renowned conductor Daniel Barenboim. He was also the music critic for the *Nation* magazine and a consummate pianist. His book on Joseph Conrad illustrates the underpinning of culture and imperialism in his literary work and political stance—he is mostly known for his support of the Palestinian cause. Ever present in media discussions of the Israeli-Palestinian conflict, Said's views are perhaps best elaborated in his 1978 book *Orientalism*, which argues that the Arab-Islamic world is mistakenly understood because of Western-created prejudices and stereotypes. Said was born in Jerusalem during the British Mandate in Palestine. He came to the United States as a teenager, was expelled from Victoria College in Egypt, but went on to obtain a BA degree from Princeton, and MA and PhD degrees in English Literature from Harvard. His distinguished career brought him numerous awards and twenty honorary degrees. Said also lived at **435 and 448 Riverside Drive** (near 116th Street).

Schell, Jonathan Edward (1943–2014)

AUTHOR

Schell is best known for the 1982 blockbuster book *The Fate of the Earth*, which drew attention to the nuclear arms race and its implications. More specifically, it posed the argument for nuclear disarmament as a choice between the continuation of sovereign nation states and survival of the earth. Born in Manhattan, Schell graduated from Harvard with a bachelor's degree in Far Eastern history. He also studied Japanese for a year at the International Christian University in Tokyo.

Joining the *New Yorker* magazine in 1967, he was a protégé and favorite of its editor Wallace Shawn and was employed to write much of its editorial content. Schell's first two books espoused an anti–Vietnam War view and were followed by another ten or so books.

413 Riverside Drive (near 113rd Street)

Noakes, George (ca. 1865–1941) 🖘
RESTAURATEUR AND REAL ESTATE INVESTOR

Noakes was born in New York City, attended City College, and ran the Noakes Hotel and Restaurant at 219 Greenwich Street, which was founded by his father, also named George Noakes. In 1883, his father purchased the home of former mayor Philip Hone at 233 Broadway. Our George Noakes must have realized a substantial windfall when the property was sold in 1910 to enable the construction of the Woolworth building. By 1900, he was living on Riverside Drive, in a house known by the name of its 1884 original owner, the Stephen F. Sherman house. Noakes invested in real estate and in apartment building development on the Upper West Side. When his house was demolished in 1906, he moved his family into the Ansonia Hotel for a while, and later into a town house on West 71st Street. In 1926, he became a salesman for a coal and oil company. Perhaps his fortunes were turning for the worse with the onset of the Great Depression, because by 1930 and until he died, he was living with some family members on a modest street in Bayside, Queens.

Gottheil, Richard James Horatio (1862–1936) 📕 🖘
ORIENTALIST SCHOLAR AND ZIONIST

As president of the American Federation of Zionists from 1898 to 1904, Gottheil worked with Theodor Herzl and Rabbi Stephen Wise in activities that would flower decades later into the State of Israel. He taught Hebrew, Arabic, Syriac, and Abyssinian languages as well as Near Eastern history and archeology at Columbia and earned an international reputation. He headed the Oriental Department of the New York Public Library, was an editor of the twelve-volume *Jewish Encyclopedia*, and a vice president of the American Jewish Historical Society. His father, Gustav Gottheil, was the rabbi of Temple Emanu-El for many years. Born in England, Gottheil came to the United States as a 10-year-old and graduated from Columbia in 1881 at the age of 19. In 1929, he would earn a Litt.D. at Columbia. He joined Columbia's faculty in 1886 to teach the Syriac and Semitic languages. Meanwhile, he continued his studies at the Universities of Berlin, Tuebingen, and Leipzig, where he received his PhD degree in 1904. At the time of his death, he was reported to be the oldest member of Columbia's faculty. He was also the founder of the first Jewish fraternity in the United States, Zeta Beta Tau.

417 Riverside Drive (near 114rd Street)

Laemmle, Carl (1867–1939) ★ ■
MOTION PICTURE PIONEER

Laemmle founded the iconic motion picture company, Universal Studios. Born in Germany, he came first to Chicago, buying nickelodeons and starting one of the first movie theaters there. But when he moved to New York, he began producing movies and, with other partners and investors, created Universal in 1912. The studios were in Fort Lee, New Jersey, but Universal established a presence in California as early as 1915. Although *Jaws* and *Jurassic Park* are the two of the movies most associated with Universal today, in Laemmle's day there were silent classics such as *The Phantom of the Opera* and *The Hunchback of Notre Dame*.

Carl Laemmle.

Stephanopoulos, George (1961–)
POLITICAL COMMENTATOR

An image of Stephanopoulos can be found on a postage stamp issued by Greece in 2016. He entered the national spotlight in 1993 as the White House Director of Communications under President Bill Clinton. His earlier experiences with politics included working on the 1988 presidential campaign of Democrat Party candidate Michael Dukakis and as floor manager for Congressman and Democrat Party House Majority Leader Dick Gephardt. After Clinton was elected for a second term, Stephanopoulos decided to teach at Columbia and became a political analyst for ABC News. With increased visibility at ABC, he co-moderated the final 2008 Democrat Party debate between Barack Obama and Hillary Clinton. Born in Massachusetts, Stephanopoulos was the salutatorian of his class at Columbia and Phi Beta Kappa. He earned a master's degree in theology at Oxford University, England, on a Rhodes scholarship.

420 Riverside Drive (near 114th Street), the Hamilton

Adams, Franklin Pierce (1881–1960), Newspaper Columnist ▪

(See bio for Adams at **612 West 112th Street**.)

Bourdain, Anthony (1956–2018) ▪
CHEF AND FOOD AND TRAVEL AUTHOR

Bourdain ate an entire cobra, took LSD and used heroin, and advised against ordering fish in a restaurant on Mondays. The range of his experience and all-too-honest insights, especially about other chefs, made him a most entertaining new breed of celebrity. A New York native, Bourdain attended Vassar College for two years, but graduated from the Culinary Institute of America in 1978. He ran the kitchens at such noted restaurants as One Fifth Avenue, Sullivan's, Supper Club, and Brasserie Les Halles. As the restaurant industry grew and became more sophisticated, he gained much attention for his unconventional and refreshing ways and opinions. His article in the *New Yorker* in 1999 entitled "Don't Eat Before Reading This," and his first best-seller book in 2000, *Kitchen Confidential: Adventures in the Culinary Underbelly*, sealed his stature at the top of the food-writing chain. Many books, articles, and radio and television appearances followed, including his acclaimed shows on the Food and Travel channels, and his CNN show *Anthony Bourdain: Parts Unknown*.

Carter, Elliott (1908–2012) ■
COMPOSER

Carter was a Pulitzer Prize winner in 1960 for his String Quartet No. 2 and in 1973 for his String Quartet No. 3. His range of composing was extraordinary and included orchestral pieces; concertos for varied instruments; and piano, chamber, and voice compositions. In the last ten years of his remarkable life of 103 years, he composed dozens of works. Although influenced by all the great "moderns" such as Igor Stravinsky and Aaron Copland, and the American "ultra-moderns" such as Edgard Varese and Henry Cowell, Carter's music was uniquely characterized by layers of intricate rhythms and modulating metrics. As testimony to his stature, his works are extensively performed and recorded. Born in Manhattan but raised in Europe, Carter attended Harvard and attained a master's degree in music. Living in Paris, he earned a doctorate in music from the École Normale de Musique de Paris. Back in the States in the late 1930s, he composed ballet music for Lincoln Kirstein. Throughout the 1940s, he taught at St. John's College and the Peabody Conservatory in Maryland. He then taught at Columbia and Queens College throughout 1950s. From 1960, he made

Yale and Cornell his workplace, followed by Julliard from 1972. He was an esteemed member of the American Academy of Arts and Letters from 1967.

Clark, John Bates (1847–1938), Economist ■ ▪

(See bio for Clark at **616 West 113th Street**.)

Danto, Arthur C. (1924–2013) ▪

ART CRITIC AND PHILOSOPHER

Danto told the world that Andy Warhol's "Brillo Box" was art. He figured out that art is what we say it is, especially if shown in an art gallery. No joke here—Danto spoke to the very question of what makes something art, and Hegel, Schopenhauer, and Nietzsche helped him find his answer. *Beyond the Brillo Box* and his other thirty or so books elaborate his thinking. He was the art critic for *The Nation* and would typically be supportive, understanding, and philosophical about any challenging art, including the work of such artists as Yoko Ono and Damien Hirst. He was born and raised in Michigan, studied art and history at Wayne State University, and topped it off with a doctorate in philosophy at Columbia. There he taught for years until his retirement in 1992, after which he was labeled emeritus.

Goldberg, Reuben "Rube" Garrett Lucius (1883–1970) ■

CARTOONIST

By 1915, Goldberg was earning $50,000 a year as the most popular cartoonist in the country. Today we are still amused by his ridiculously complicated thingamajigs that made mockeries of simplicity. These are now generally and respectfully known as Rube Goldberg contraptions. In his cartoon world, they were the creations of Professor Lucifer

Rube Goldberg.

Gorgonzola Butts. Goldberg did other memorable cartoons including "Lala Palooza," "Ike and Mike—They Look Alike," and "Boob McNutt." Another standout was "The Foolish Question" employing absurdities to create playfully hilarious destinations. Goldberg was born in San Francisco where his father was a banker, a real estate developer, and a police and fire commissioner. Goldberg earned an engineering degree from the University of California, Berkeley. However, he became interested in creating cartoons and came to New York in 1907 to realize his dreams. Goldberg also lived at **309 West 99th Street** (near West End Avenue).

Liebowitz, Benjamin (1890–1977), Engineer and Inventor

(See bio for Liebowitz at **505 West 124th Street**.)

Moskowitz, Eva (1964 –)
EDUCATOR AND CITY COUNCILMEMBER

Moskowitz is the founder and CEO of Success Academy Charter Schools, serving New York City. There are almost fifty schools and 15,000 "scholars" selected by lottery from more than 100,000 applicants. Moskowitz was born in Manhattan, and raised in Morningside Heights with her father, Martin Moskowitz, teaching mathematics at Columbia. She earned a BA degree at the University of Pennsylvania, and an MA degree and PhD in American history at Johns Hopkins University. After teaching history at the University of Virginia, Vanderbilt University, and the College of Staten Island, she entered politics in the mid-1990s volunteering to help Gifford Miller get elected to the City Council. In 1999, she was elected to the City Council. She focused on education, but with opposition from the United Federation of Teachers, she lost in a bid to be the Democratic nominee for borough president in 2005. Undaunted, she committed herself to improving public education and founded Success Academy in 2006. She has authored three books: *In Therapy We Trust: America's Obsession with Self-Fulfillment*; *Mission Impossible: How the Secrets of Success Academies Can Work in Any School* with co-author Arin Lavinia; and *The Education of Eva Moskowitz: A Memoir*.

Rothafel, Samuel Lionel "Roxy" (1882–1936)
IMPRESARIO AND THEATER ENTREPRENEUR

Rothafel's own theater, the Roxy, was the grandest in New York until Radio City Music Hall came along. He was hired to get Radio City going, so he brought over his precision dance troupe the Roxyettes, which became known as the Rockettes. His reputation for making spectacular theater experiences was based on some of the innovations attributed to him, such as employing multiple projectors to make seamless reel changes, replacing incidental piano music with an orchestra, and using pipe organs. Born in Germany, he came first to Minnesota before arriving in New York City. While a teenager, he enlisted in the United States Marine Corps and spent time in Santo Domingo and China during the Boxer Rebellion. Back in New York, he did house-to-house peddling and drifted to Pennsylvania where he met his wife and began his theatrical career. In time, he returned to New York and in 1913 gained the responsibility of managing the Regent Theater. He brightened it by dispensing of the dropping stage curtain, employing innovative lighting, and introducing live entertainment in between the showings of silent movies. In a similar fashion, he managed such notable theaters as the Rivoli, the Rialto, the Capitol, and the Strand.

S. L. Rothapfel.

425 Riverside Drive (near 115th Street)

Harris, Cyril Manton (1917–2011), Professor of Architecture, Professor of Electrical Engineering, and Acoustics Specialist

(See bio for Harris at **315 Riverside Drive**.)

431 Riverside Drive (near 115th Street), the Columbia Court Apartments

Ahnelt, William Paul (1864–1949), Publisher

(See bio for Ahnelt at **331 Riverside Drive**.)

Earle, William "P.S." (1882–1972)
SILENT FILM DIRECTOR

William P. S. Earle directed nearly fifty silent films from 1915 to 1926. Born in New York, his father was a military officer and a proprietor of numerous prominent hotels. At one time, his father owned Jumel Mansion in Washington Heights. Young William attended Columbia University, but became interested in the early movie business. The Vitagraph Company of America gave him his first chance at directing *For Honor of the Crew*, a short flick about a Columbia crew race. Some of his later work was with **David O. Selznick** (of *Gone with the Wind* fame) who, though twenty years younger, grew up nearby at 449 Riverside Drive. Earle lost all his money in the 1929 stock market crash and had to resort to selling vacuum cleaners door-to-door. His brother Ferdinand P. Earle was also a film director and is credited with discovering and first publishing the work of Edna St. Vincent Millay. William's daughter Valerie De Blois Earle married the business and economics journalist Henry Hazlitt. Earle was a distant relative of **Virginia Crocheron Gildersleeve**.

Riverside Drive near 115th Street (no street address in 1894)

Smith, Edmund Munroe (1854–1926) ■ ▤
LEGAL HISTORIAN

Meg Whitman, who headed Hewlett Packard and eBay, and ran for governor of California, is a great-granddaughter of Edmund Smith. Columbia's president, **Nicholas Murray Butler**, along with Columbia board members George A. Plimpton, and other notables such as Supreme Court Justice **Harlan Fiske Stone**, were honorary pallbearers at his funeral. As a renowned historical scholar, he authored *The Law of Nationality*, *Bismarck and German Unity*, *American Diplomacy in the European War*, and *Militarism and Statecraft*. Born in Brooklyn, he graduated from Amherst with an AB degree in 1874, and from Columbia's Law School with an LL.B. in 1877. Returning to Amherst, he graduated with an AM degree, and then he went off to Germany to earn a JUD degree from the University of Gottingen in 1880. He lectured on Roman law, history, and comparative jurisprudence at Columbia, was appointed a full professor in 1891, and didn't retire until 1924. In addition to being one of the founders of the *Political Science Quarterly*, he was its managing editor for nearly twenty years. Louvain University in Belgium, along with Columbia and Amherst, awarded him honorary degrees. His brother Henry Maynard Smith was dean of Columbia's School of Mines from 1891 to 1915.

435 Riverside Drive (116th Street), the Colosseum

Bushman, Francis Xavier (1883–1966) ■
ACTOR

Bushman was advertised as "the handsomest man in the world." He was a giant film star in the 1910s and early 1920s. From his weightlifting

Francis X. Bushman

regimen, he developed a physique that enabled him to model for the statues of Lord Baltimore in Baltimore, his hometown, and Nathan Hale at Harvard. His first public performance was as an altar boy for Cardinal Gibbons. After moving to New York, he worked as a model and entered the emerging film business. He appeared in nearly two hundred films, the 1925 version of *Ben Hur* being especially memorable. Bushman could also be seen quite frequently on television in the 1950s and 1960s.

Paterno, Joseph (1881–1939), Apartment Building Developer ★ ▪ ▤

(See bio for Paterno at **507 West 112th Street**.)

Said, Edward Wadie (1935–2003), Professor of Literature and Intellectual

(See bio for Said at **410 Riverside Drive**.)

Stone, Harlan Fiske (1872–1946) ★ ▪ ▤
CHIEF JUSTICE OF THE SUPREME COURT

Stone was known as one of the "great dissenters" and for being outspoken on the liberal side of the bench. He was a Columbia Law School alumnus selected in 1941 by President Franklin D. Roosevelt to replace another Columbia Law School alumnus, Charles Evans Hughes, as Chief Justice of the Supreme Court. Born on a farm in New Hampshire, Stone graduated from Amherst College in 1894 and the Columbia University School of Law in 1898. He rose to partnership in

Harlan Fiske Stone.

the Wall Street law firm of Satterlee, Canfield & Stone, lectured on law at Columbia, was named the prestigious Kent Professor of Law, and then became dean of the Law School. In 1924, he resigned to become a partner in Sullivan & Cromwell for one year. He was first selected by President Calvin Coolidge in 1925 to be an Associate Justice of the Supreme Court. At the time, William Howard Taft was Chief Justice and Oliver Wendell Holmes, Jr., and Louis Brandeis were Associate Justices. In time, he would serve with Associate Justices Benjamin Cardozo, Hugo Black, Felix Frankfurter, and William O. Douglas. Stone received honorary degrees from Amherst, Yale, Columbia, Williams College, Syracuse University, and Harvard. Stone lived at two other addresses in the area: **917 West End Avenue** (near 105th Street) and **501 West 120th Street** (near Amsterdam Avenue).

440 Riverside Drive (near 116th Street), the Paterno

Holloway, Ralph Leslie, Jr. (1935–) ◼
PROFESSOR OF ANTHROPOLOGY

Holloway had some seventy-five human skulls in his laboratory. In his forty-plus years at Columbia, he argued that humanoid brains expanded millions of years ago, and yet factors other than size are necessary to explain human thinking. His research on cranial matters and evolution of the brain is considered second to none. His counsel is sought every time a new human fossil skull is discovered. The BBC has employed his talents, as has the American Museum of Natural History. Raised in Philadelphia, he developed his interest in anthropology at the University of New Mexico and obtained his PhD in 1964 at the University of California, Berkeley. His daughter is Marguerite Holloway, the author of *The Measure of Manhattan*, about the surveyor John Randel, Jr., who gave Manhattan its street grid.

Kirchwey, Freda (1893–1976) ◼

ACTIVIST PUBLISHER

Kirchwey is mostly responsible for the banishment of sororities at Barnard. In addition, her classmates rated her "best looking, the one who has done the most for Barnard, most popular, most militant and the one most likely to be famous in the future." After starting as a cub reporter for the liberal weekly journal *The Nation*, she became its editor and, in 1937, its owner. She published the country's oldest liberal journal to much acclaim and controversy, especially with allegations of communist sympathies that led to its ban in public schools for two years. By 1955 she moved on and became active with the National Association for the Advancement of Colored People, the Women's International League for Peace and Freedom, and the League of Women Voters. Born in upstate New York, Kirchwey graduated from Barnard in 1915, and she married Princeton University professor Evans Clark. She was lured to *The Nation* by the magazine's owner and editor Oswald Garrison Villard.

Lazarsfeld, Paul Felix (1901–1976) ★ ◼

SOCIOLOGIST

Paul Lazarsfeld made the use of mass media research into a science. He implemented some of the first studies of radio-listening, television-watching, and voting habits. His attention to the processes of research, including focus-group interviewing, employment of data into scatter plotting and contingency analyses, and statistical survey analysis, earned him the title "founder of modern empirical sociology." Born in Vienna, Lazarsfeld was educated at the University of Vienna where he earned his Ph.D. in 1925. He founded a research institute for applied psychology in Vienna but came to the United State in 1933 where he directed a Rockefeller endeavor, the Office of Radio Research. It was transferred from Princeton to Columbia in 1940 and became the Bureau of Applied Social Research. Collaborating with Hadley Cantril and Frank Stanton, he authored the 1940 book, *Radio and the Printed Page: An Introduction to the Study of Radio and Its Role in the Communication of Ideas.* Columbia awarded him a distinguished professor title and created a social science chair in his honor. He was awarded numerous honorary degrees including the first conferred by the Sorbonne on an American sociologist.

Runyon, Damon (1880–1946), Journalist and Short Story Writer ★ ■

(See bio for Runyon **at 251 West 95th Street**.)

445 Riverside Drive (near 116th Street)

Moffatt, James (1870–1944) ▪

THEOLOGIAN

The "Moffatt Bible" refers to his translation of the New Testament in 1913 and of the Old Testament in 1924. If there is any confusion, one can read his other twenty books or delve into his seventeen-volume work, *Moffatt New Testament Commentary*, published from 1928 to 1949. Moffatt was born in Scotland and educated at the University of Glasgow. Pursuing a religious life, he trained at the Free Church College in Glasgow and received a Doctor of Divinity degree from the University of St. Andrews in 1902. He was a professor of Greek for a few years at Oxford in England, and a professor of church history at Union Free College in Glasgow from 1915. In 1927, he joined the faculty at Union Theological Seminary in New York as the Washburn Professor of Church History.

448 Riverside Drive (near 116th Street)

Collins, George R. (1917–1993) ▪
ARCHITECTURAL HISTORIAN

Collins was the leading champion of the Barcelonan architect Antonio Gaudi. His book on Gaudi in 1960 was the first in the United States. He wrote twenty-six books and articles about Gaudi and his "modernism" style while teaching at Columbia for forty years. Born in Massachusetts, Collins graduated from Princeton in 1939 with a BA degree, and in 1942 with an MFA degree. He served in World War II before joining Columbia's faculty in 1946. After the death of his first wife in 1948, he married Christiane Crasemann Collins. Together they supported the integrity of Morningside Park against Columbia's attempted intrusion with a gymnasium.

McBain, Howard Lee (1880–1936) ● ▪
POLITICAL SCIENTIST

McBain originated the phrase "living constitution." It was the title of his 1927 book, published the year Columbia granted him an honorary doctor of laws degree. He was one of the country's leading constitutional scholars. His talents were employed by New York City, by its Charter Commission, the Board of Education, and even the government of Cuba. McBain was born in Toronto, Canada, but he grew up in Virginia, where he graduated Phi Beta Kappa from Richmond College with a BA in 1900 and an MA in 1901. He studied briefly at the University of Chicago but came to New York and was an honorary fellow at Columbia where he received an MA in 1905 and a PhD in 1907. Then he taught at George Washington University and became dean of the College of Political Sciences. After a few years at the University of Wisconsin, he came to Columbia in 1913. He taught municipal science and administration, but especially constitutional law. McBain also lived at **456 Riverside Drive** (near 116th Street) and **39 Claremont Avenue** (near 119th Street).

Ryan, William Fitts (1922–1972) ■
CONGRESSMAN

Ryan was the first Reform Democratic congressman from New York City and the first member of Congress to vote against funds for the Vietnam War. He established the Gateway National Urban Recreational Area that included the waterfront from Jamaica Bay to Sandy Hook, New Jersey. Born in upstate New York, the son of a judge and the grandson of Alabama's attorney general, Ryan served as an artillery lieutenant in World War II, graduated from Princeton in 1947, and from Columbia Law School in 1949. From 1950 to 1961 he was an assistant district attorney in New York County. In 1961, he was elected as a Democrat to Congress, succeeding Ludwig Teller. In 1965, he failed to win his party's nomination for Mayor. In 1972, he won his party's primary for Congress, but died two months later before the general election. His wife, **Priscilla Ryan**, attempted to retain the seat.

Ryan, Priscilla (1929--2017)
POLITICIAN

Priscilla Ryan ran for Congress after the death of her husband, **William Fitts Ryan**. She was on the Liberal Party line but lost to her opponent Bella Abzug in the general election. Priscilla Ryan was a relative of William Marbury, who was known for the historic 1801 Supreme Court case of *Marbury vs. Madison*. Born in Maryland, the daughter of a judge, Priscilla Ryan attended Bryn Mawr College for three years but graduated from Barnard in 1950. Along with her husband, **William Fitts Ryan**, whom she married in 1949, she was a founder of the Riverside Democratic Club. Ryan also lived at **435 West 119th Street** (near Amsterdam Avenue).

Said, Edward Wadie (1935–2003), Professor of Literature and Intellectual

(See bio for Said at **410 Riverside Drive**.)

449 Riverside Drive (near 116th Street)

Selznick, David O. (1902–1965) ★ ■
MOTION PICTURE PRODUCER

David Selznick

Selznick is most known for producing the motion picture *Gone with the Wind*. He is also responsible for *King Kong*, *The Third Man*, *A Star is Born*, *A Farewell to Arms*, *The Prisoner of Zenda*, *Dinner at Eight*, *A Tale of Two Cities*, *David Copperfield*, and more. He supposedly said that he wouldn't hire anyone who could take dictation at less than two hundred words per minute because it would interrupt his train of thought. He was born in Pittsburgh but grew up on Riverside Drive. He studied at Columbia, but after his father went bankrupt, he moved to Hollywood. At age 29, after working at Metro-Goldwyn-Mayer and Paramount Pictures, he became head of production at RKO. In 1935, he became an independent producer. The 1939 Academy Awards were kind to *Gone with the Wind*. It received eight Oscars, two special awards, and for Selznick, the Irving G. Thalberg Memorial Award.

450 Riverside Drive (near 116th Street)

Barr, William (1950–)
ATTORNEY GENERAL OF THE UNITED STATES

Barr plays the bagpipes well enough to have competed in Scotland as a member of an American pipe band. He is much better known as an attorney general under two noncontinuous presidents, George H. Bush and Donald Trump. He began his long career in government in 1973 with the Central Intelligence Agency, after which he clerked for a federal judge for two years. The 1980s had him in private law practice, but with a short stint on the domestic policy staff of President Reagan. President George H. W. Bush appointed him an assistant attorney general in 1989 and elevated him to attorney general in 1991. After leaving the Department of Justice when President Clinton assumed office, Barr served as general counsel to the telecommunications giant GTE Corporation for fourteen years until he was tapped by President Trump to be attorney general again. A native New Yorker, Barr grew up in Morningside Heights and, in 1971, graduated from Columbia with a BA degree, majoring in government. In 1973 he earned an MS in government and Chinese studies from Columbia, and a Juris Doctor degree in 1977 from George Washington University Law School.

Bliven, Bruce Ormsby (1889–1977) ▪

EDITOR

Bliven was managing editor of the *New Republic* in its early days. On the pages of that magazine and on the lecture circuit, he actively advanced liberal ideas. Born in Iowa, he was educated at Stanford University and at the University of Southern California, where he stayed for two years to run its department of journalism. He joined the *New Republic*, where one of his articles led to exposing the Teapot Dome scandal during the Harding administration. He continued to write and lecture through the Depression, and until he retired to Stanford for health reasons. His son was author **Bruce Bliven, Jr.** Bruce Ormsby Bliven also lived at **15 Claremont Avenue** (near 116th Street).

Bliven, Bruce, Jr. (1916–2002) ▪

AUTHOR

Bliven's book *Battle for Manhattan* offers a detailed account of the Battle of Harlem Heights. He was the author of other books on New York City history, on the Revolutionary War, and on World War II. Most curious and delightful is *The Wonderful Writing Machine*, a history of the typewriter. Many other subjects that received his attention can be found in the *New Republic* and various other publications, including the *New Yorker* for which he wrote regularly. The son of **Bruce Ormsby Bliven**, Bruce Bliven, Jr., was born in Los Angeles, raised in New York City, and educated at Harvard. Bruce Bliven, Jr., also lived at **15 Claremont Avenue** (near 116th Street).

Lamont, Corliss (1902–1995), Civil Libertarian and Humanist Philosopher ★ ■ ☞

(See bio for Lamont at **315 West 106th Street**.)

Merton, Robert King (1910–2003) ★ ■
SOCIOLOGIST

Merton gave us the "focus group," the idea of "unintended consequences," and the "reference group," as well as the terms "self-fulfilling prophecy" and "role model." It is no surprise that he is considered the father of modern sociology. He was born Meyer Robert Schkolnick in Philadelphia. An interest in magic resulted in his name change. He modified "Merlin" into Merton, like Houdini, who honored his hero Jean-Eugène Robert-Houdin by adapting his name. Merton received a BA degree from Temple University and an MA and a PhD from Harvard University. His teaching career began at Harvard, and then he moved to Tulane University in New Orleans for a few years where he chaired the Sociology department. He arrived at Columbia University in 1941 and so much followed. His numerous books, articles, and awards only begin to suggest the range and depth of his influence. In 1957, he was elected president of the American Sociological Association. In 1976, with colleague **Paul F. Lazarsfeld**, he created the Bureau of Applied Research, which gave birth to focus groups. He was awarded nearly thirty honorary degrees. His son, Robert C. Merton, was awarded the Nobel Prize in economics in 1997.

Rabi, Isador Isaac "I. I." (1898–1988) ★ ■

PHYSICIST

Rabi received the Nobel Prize in Physics in 1944. But his under-appreciated achievement was his role in developing a physics department at Columbia that has received four Nobel Prizes. Born in what is now Poland, Rabi came to the United States with his family as a toddler and was raised on the Lower East Side of Manhattan and in Brownsville, Brooklyn. He graduated from Cornell University, majoring in chemistry. After doing graduate work there, he transferred to Columbia University and concentrated on physics, earning a doctorate in 1927. That same year, he was appointed a Barnard Fellow and went to Europe to study the newest realms of physics and to meet the likes of Wolfgang Pauli, John von Neumann, **Leo Szilard**, Nils Bohr, and Werner Heisenberg. He returned to Columbia in 1929 as a full-time faculty member and began his profoundly important work with nuclear physics and chemistry. His work with nuclear magnetic resonance was especially useful for the development of scanning techniques in medicine. His work in measuring the magnetic properties in atoms enabled the atomic clock. The creation of Brookhaven Laboratories on Long Island and the way that physics is taught bear his imprint, as did the Manhattan Project and the Atomic Energy Commission, which he headed in the 1950s. Rabi also lived at **600 West 116th Street** (near Broadway) and **175 Claremont Avenue** (near La Salle Street).

Rice, Grantland (1880–1954), Sportswriter ★ ■

(See bio for Rice **at 616 West 116th Street**.)

Slichter, Walter Irvine (ca.1874–1958) ★ ■ ▪

PROFESSOR OF ELECTRICAL ENGINEERING

In 1926, Slichter authored *Principles Underlining the Design of Electrical Machinery*. An authority on alternating current, especially in the design of electrical machinery, he oversaw the installation of electrical turbines in battleships for the United States Navy. He also served as associate editor of handbooks on electrical engineering and mining engineering. Born in Minnesota, Slichter received his degree in science from Columbia University in 1896. After graduation, he joined General Electric Company and worked under the legendary Charles Steinmetz until 1905, when he began working as an engineer in the company's railway and traction department. He joined the faculty of Columbia, was appointed Professor of Electrical Engineering, headed up the department, and retired with emeritus status. He was a fellow of the Society of Mechanical Engineers as well as the Institute of Electrical Engineers where he also served as a vice president and treasurer. Slichter also lived at **29 Claremont Avenue** (near 119th Street).

Tyson, Levering (1889–1966), Educator ■

(See bio for Tyson **at 419 West 117th Street**.)

454 Riverside Drive (near 119th Street)

Lamont, Corliss (1902–1995), Civil Libertarian and Humanist Philosopher ★ ■ ☞

(See bio for Lamont at **315 West 106th Street**.)

456 Riverside Drive (near 119th Street)

McBain, Howard Lee (1880–1936), Political Scientist ■ ▮

(See bio for McBain at **448 Riverside Drive**.)

460 Riverside Drive (near 119th Street)

Marston, William Moulton (1893–1947) ★ ■ ▮
PSYCHOLOGIST AND CREATOR OF "WONDER WOMAN"

William Moulton Marston.

In 1915, Marston invented the lie detector. His device measured systolic blood pressure and was improved by John Augustus Larson to become the modern polygraph machine. Marston might be better known for creating the comic strip character "Wonder Woman." His psychological beliefs centered on the essence of females versus males. He seemed to hold that women were stronger than men, yet submission and eroticism were central to his "live, love, and laugh" doctrine. Marston, his wife, and his mistress lived in a ménage à trois. Both had children by him, whom they cared for jointly. Born in Massachusetts, Marston graduated Phi Beta Kappa from Harvard with a BA in 1915, an LLB in 1918, and a PhD in 1921. He taught at American University in Washington, D.C., and Tufts University in Massachusetts. He also taught psychology at Columbia and New York University. Marston also lived at **504 West 110th Street** (near Amsterdam Avenue).

Mullins, George W. (1881–1956), Professor of Mathematics ★

(See bio for Mullins at **416 West 115th Street**.)

Tugwell, Rexford Guy (1891–1979) ■
ECONOMIST, PRESIDENTIAL ADVISOR, AND HISTORIAN

In 1938, Tugwell was the first head of the New York City Planning Commission. He is more likely known, along with fellow Columbia professors **Raymond Moley** and Adolph A. Berle, Jr., as part of President Franklin Roosevelt's "brains trust." Tugwell's influence on national policy was profound and included suburban planning, paying farmers not to produce; creating the Soil Conservation Service; and formulating the Federal Food, Drug, and Cosmetic Act. Born in upstate New York, he received his bachelor's, master's, and doctorate degrees from the University of Pennsylvania and its Wharton School of Finance and Commerce. After teaching in Pennsylvania, at the University of Washington, and in Paris, he became a professor of economics at Columbia University. He would go on to teach at the University of Chicago and the University of California at Santa Barbara, but only after being tapped in 1934 to be Assistant Secretary of Agriculture. Tugwell was integral to shaping the New Deal, and Roosevelt later appointed him governor of Puerto Rico. He authored more than twenty books; *The Brains Trust* won the Bancroft Prize in 1967.

Moore, Douglas Stuart (1893–1969) ■
COMPOSER

Moore won the 1951 Pulitzer Prize for Music for his opera *Giants in the Earth*. He is better known for his 1938 opera *The Devil and Daniel Webster*, written with fellow Yale alumnus Stephen Vincent Benét. And he is best known for his 1956 opera *The Ballad of Baby Doe*, a collaboration with one-time Columbia student John La Touche, and now a staple of the American opera repertoire. Born on Long Island, Moore received a BA degree in 1915 and a BMus degree in 1917, both from Yale. He served in World War I as a lieutenant in the Navy and then studied music in Paris. After some work with the Cleveland Art Museum and the Cleveland Orchestra, he arrived at Columbia in 1926. He was awarded a Guggenheim Fellowship and guest-conducted a few orchestras, all the while composing chamber and orchestral music, incidental and ballet music, and an operetta, *The Headless Horseman*, based on Washington Irving's *The Legend of Sleepy Hollow*. Moore served as a president of the National Institute of Arts and Sciences; president of the American Academy of Arts and Letters; and director of the American Society of Composers, Authors, and Publishers. Moore also lived at **27 Claremont Avenue** (near 119th Street).

490 Riverside Drive (near 122nd Street)

Moehle, Jean Earl (ca.1889–1964), Suffragist and Performance Artist ▪ ☞

(See bio for Moehle at **25 Claremont Avenue**.)

528 Riverside Drive (near Tiemann Place)

Leigh, Robert Devore (1891–1961) ▪
BARNARD PROFESSOR AND PRESIDENT OF BENNINGTON COLLEGE

Leigh was the first president of Bennington College in Vermont, appointed in 1928 and serving until 1941. Born in Nebraska, Leigh graduated summa cum laude from Bowdoin College, Maine, in 1914. Before earning a PhD at Columbia in 1927, he lectured on government there and at Williams College, Massachusetts. Columbia made him acting dean at Bard College to study its educational program. After taking on various responsibilities for the United States, the United Nations, and other entities, he became a professor and acting dean at Columbia's library school.

ARE OTHER PRESIDENTS ENTOMBED IN NYC?

James Monroe was. After he died in 1831, his coffin was placed in the Gouverneur Vault in Marble Cemetery in the East Village area. In 1858, his coffin was exhumed and his remains were entombed in Hollywood Cemetery in Richmond Virginia. Nearby is the grave of President John Tyler, who was married in New York City.

THE US CAPITOL?

The rise above the Hudson River, where Grant's (Grants') Tomb is now located, was known as Claremont. See the notable **Michael Hogan** for some background details. Legend has it that George Washington thought this might have been a possible location for the Capitol of the United States.

STANDING ROOM ONLY!

Grant's funeral ceremony at Claremont on August 8, 1885—President U. S. Grant's funeral cortege of 60,000 people marched seven miles from City Hall to the site of a temporary tomb at Claremont, near present day Riverside Drive and 123rd Street. The newspapers reported that one million people turned out to watch the cortege, which is remarkable since New York City's population, before the inclusion of Brooklyn and other parts in the consolidation of 1898, was about 1.3 million people. The ceremonies at the tomb were attended by then President Grover Cleveland, the two living ex-presidents, Chester A. Arthur and Rutherford B. Hayes, Grant's entire cabinet, all the Supreme Court Justices, almost all of Congress, and almost every person who had a prominent role in the Civil War. The attendance at the ceremony was likely **100,000**.

Dedication of Grant's Tomb on April 27, 1897—Selected as the day that Grant would have been 75 years of age, then President William McKinley led the dedication. Some 60,000 public officials, military, and others assembled at Madison Square and marched to then Riverside Avenue at 72nd Street and north to the completed Grant's Tomb. The newspapers reported the presence of one million onlookers. The attendance at the ceremony was likely about **100,000**.

549 Riverside Drive (near Tiemann Place)

Papanastassiou, John M. (ca.1948–)

RARE BOOK THIEF

In 1981 Papanastassiou was a Columbia University student studying for an advanced economics degree when he was arrested by US Customs officials on a charge of stealing rare books worth over two million dollars. Customs officials employed a rare bookseller wearing a bulletproof vest to transact with Papanastassiou in a "sting" operation at the Princeton Club on West 43rd Street. The books were pilfered from various institutions, with 267 reported missing from the library of the University College in London. They included rare items by Giordano Bruno and Galileo. A search of Papanastassiou's apartment on Riverside Drive turned up more of the stolen goods. Brought to trial in New York, he received a three-year sentence with a fine and would then face extradition to Great Britain for further criminal proceedings.

Weil, Simone (1909–1943)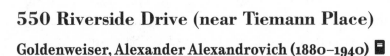
PHILOSPHER AND POLITICAL ACTIVIST

Weil was born in Paris where her intellect developed at a very early age. It was said that she read Ancient Greek at age 12, and Sanskrit soon after. Her extensive education at some of the best schools in Paris widened her interests from philosophy into world religions. Her political and social sympathies were with workers, and as an activist with the workers' movement, she participated in strikes against Franco in the Spanish Civil War. Undoubtedly a pacifist and a Marxist, she called herself an anarchist. By the time she came to the United States in 1942, she had experienced a religious "ecstasy" and had embraced mysticism as a value system. Her empathy for those suffering in France during the war, compelled her to take an active part of the French Resistance, but tuberculosis overtook her, and perhaps her ascetic ways contributed to her early death.

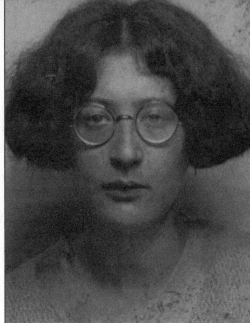

Simone Weil

550 Riverside Drive (near Tiemann Place)

Goldenweiser, Alexander Alexandrovich (1880–1940)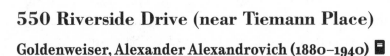
ANTHROPOLOGIST AND SOCIOLOGIST

Goldenweiser's 1922 book, *Early Civilization*, renamed *Anthropology* in 1937, was one of the first such textbooks in the United States. His work on totemism made him famous. He promoted the notion that all cultures are closed systems, all fundamentally the same, and that their mystical relationships and their manifestation in totemic practices constitute their unique identity. Born in the part of Russia that became Ukraine, Goldenweiser came to the United States in 1900, studied under Franz Boas at Columbia University, and graduated with an AB degree in 1902, an AM degree in 1904, and a PhD in 1910. He then taught anthropology at Columbia until he went to the New School for Social

Josef Bonaparte.

Research in 1919. His other teaching experiences included the Rand School of Social Science, Oregon State, the University of Wisconsin at Madison, the University of Washington, and Reed College in Oregon.

Somewhere on Riverside Drive Near Riverside Church (490 Riverside Drive at 120th Street)

Adler, Pearl "Polly" (1900–1962), Madam

(See bio for Adler at 303 West 92nd Street.)

Site Just North of Grant's Tomb (122nd Street) on Riverside Drive

Hogan, Michael (1766–1833)
SEAMAN AND CONSUL FOR UNITED STATES

Hogan was born in Ireland but gained employment in the British Royal Navy shortly after the American War of Independence ended. He engaged in the maritime trade that took him to India and China, but by 1802 had settled in New York. Hogan served as US Consul at Cork, Ireland, from 1815 to 1817; as US Consul in Havana, Cuba, from 1819 to 1820; and from 1823 until his death he was the US Consul and Navy Agent at Valparaíso, Mexico. Hogan's estate was on the hill just north of Grant's Tomb. He named it Claremont and built a home that would be later occupied by such notables as **Aaron Burr's daughter Theodosia, Napoleon's older brother Joseph**, and the Claremont Inn from 1872 where Admiral Dewey and President McKinley were entertained. Alas, it burned down in 1951.

Site at Riverside Drive near Tiemann Place

Alston, Joseph (1779–1816)
GOVERNOR OF SOUTH CAROLINA

In 1801, Joseph Alston married Aaron Burr's daughter, **Theodosia**, and they were the first recorded married couple to honeymoon at Niagara Falls. He purchased the Claremont estate from George Pollock, whose son was the "Amiable Child" **St. Claire Pollock** (of the Riverside Park memorial). Alston was born in South Carolina, and studied at the College of New Jersey, which was later renamed Princeton. He apprenticed with Edward Rutledge, was admitted to the bar, and turned his attention elsewhere to become one of the most prosperous planters in South Carolina. Then he was elected to Congress, served multiple terms, was elected Speaker of the House, and left to become governor of his state. In 1812 their only son, 10-year-old Aaron Burr Alston died. The following year, **Theodosia Burr Alston** was lost at sea.

Alston, Theodosia Burr (1783–1813)
DAUGHTER OF AARON BURR

Theodosia Burr was born to Aaron Burr and his first wife, Theodosia Bartow Burr. More than a thousand letters between Aaron and his daughter evidence their special relationship. In 1801 Theodosia married **Joseph Alston**, who would become Speaker of the House of Representatives and governor of South Carolina. They were the first recorded married couple to honeymoon at Niagara Falls. For a while they lived at the Claremont estate, which was purchased from George Pollock, whose son was the "Amiable Child" **St. Claire Pollock** (of the Riverside Park Memorial). Theodosia's only son, 10-year-old Aaron Burr Alston, died in 1812. The following year, Theodosia was lost at sea.

Theodosia Burr Alston

Bonaparte, Joseph (1768–1844)
KING OF NAPLES AND SICILY AND KING OF SPAIN

Bonaparte's tenure as a monarch was brief (1806–1807). After his younger brother, Napoleon, lost the Battle of Waterloo, things went downhill for Joseph. Soon he lost high kingship of Spain, but not without taking a few jewels and hightailing it to New York. He moved into the house called Claremont in 1815. There is speculation that he entertained Talleyrand, Louis Phillipe, and Lafayette there. Although he was supposedly offered the position of Emperor of Mexico, he eventually made Bordentown, New Jersey, his home in the United States. At the end of his life he returned to Europe.

Post, George Browne (1837–1913) ★ ■
ARCHITECT

Post designed the Pulitzer Building on Park Row, which was the tallest building in the world when it was finished in 1890. Post also designed the New York Stock Exchange, the Brooklyn Historical Society, the old Bronx Borough Hall, the *New York Times* building on Park Row (now a part of Pace University), the north campus of the City College of New York, two buildings in the 1893 Chicago Exposition, and the Wisconsin State Capitol. A New York City native, Post was raised on his family's estate, which was near where Grant's Tomb is today. He received a degree in civil engineering when he graduated from New York University in 1858. For the next few years, he apprenticed to the renowned architect Richard Morris Hunt. He also partnered for a while with Charles D. Gambrill, whom he met in Hunt's office. Post served in the Civil War with the rank of captain, progressing to colonel, in battle and on the staff of General Burnside. Numerous awards were bestowed upon him, including an LLD from Columbia University in 1908, and he served as the sixth president of the American Institute of Architects.

His grandfather was Joel Post. His great uncle was the renowned physician and surgeon Wright Post, who was an associate of such other notables as **Valentine Mott** and David Hosack, who, amongst many other things in his remarkable life, attended to Alexander Hamilton after being shot by Aaron Burr.

George Browne Post.

Riverside Drive at 124th Street

Pollock, St. Claire (1792–1797) ☞

"AN AMIABLE CHILD"

The monument to 5-year-old Pollock is thought to be the only single-person, private grave on any New York City property. The monument is in the form of memorial urn on Riverside Drive West, just north of Grant's Tomb. In its day, the area was called Strawberry Hill. On July 15, 1797, Pollock fell off a cliff. His body was found the following day washed up on the rocks at the edge of the water. Since there are no records of his mother, Catherine Yates Pollock, after 1792, she might have died in childbirth. She and other Yates family members were the subjects of portraits by Gilbert Stuart. There is also some question whether George Pollock, or his brother James Pollock, was the father of St. Claire.

Bloemendael

Bedlow, Isaac (1598–1672)

LANDOWNER

Bedlow might be the earliest individual landowner in the Bloomingdale area when it was known by its original Dutch name of Bloemendael. In 1667, after the British takeover of New Amsterdam and their acknowledgement of Dutch land interests, Governor Richard Nicholls granted a patent to Isaac Bedlow that extended from roughly West 89th Street to West 107th Street and from the Hudson River to the

A BOLD MOVE FOR RIVERSIDE PARK?

It looked like something out of *Star Wars*. The 1960 design product of sculptor-designer **Isamu Noguchi** and architect Louis Kahn could not have been bolder, especially in Riverside Park. It originated with the Bloomingdale Neighborhood Conservation Project and had the support of Mayor Wagner. It would have honored Adele Rosenwald Levy, a philanthropist who had recently died and was a founder of the Citizen's Committee for Children of New York. After six years of failure to win approvals from the city, the ambitious proposal was withdrawn.

middle of the island. In that same year of 1667, Nichols also awarded to Isaac Bedlow an island that would reflect a slightly different spelling. It would later become the site of the Statue of Liberty and be renamed Liberty Island.

Unknown Location in Bloomingdale

Kortright, Lawrence (1728–1794) 🖎
MERCHANT AND LANDOWNER

Kortright's daughter, Elizabeth Kortright Monroe, was First Lady to the fifth president of the United States. Kortright's associate merchant, Isaac Sears, was central to the Sons of Liberty activity in New York during the Revolutionary War. Kortright's son, Captain John Kortright, was engaged in the Revolutionary War, and after he died, his widow married Supreme Court Justice **Henry Brockholst Livingston**, whose estate, Oak Villa, was at the foot of West 91st Street. Kortright was born in New York and made his fortune in privateering in the French and Indian War. After injuries in the Revolutionary War, he concentrated on managing his land interests, which were extensive in the Bloomingdale area. The town of Kortright in upstate New York is named in his honor.

Unknown Location Near the Bloomingdale Road

Peale, Charles Willson (1741–1827)
PORTRAITIST

The Peale Museum in Baltimore, Maryland, still functioning, is one of the oldest in the country. In 1801, Peale organized the first scientific expedition in the country. He is most well known for his portraits of a number of the "founding fathers," including George Washington, Benjamin Franklin, Alexander Hamilton, and Thomas Jefferson. Born in Maryland, Peale studied for a short time under John Singleton

Copley, and he studied for three years in England under Benjamin West. He was personally engaged in the American Revolution by raising troops and serving as a captain of a militia. His second wife was Elizabeth de Peyster (1765 to 1804), and her brother was Nicholas de Peyster, who died in the Bloomingdale area. For a period, Peale had a studio in a former schoolhouse in Bloomingdale, where he gave instruction called "Art's Delight."

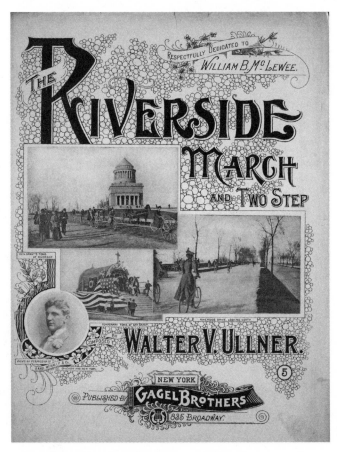

The Riverside March and Two Step.

Acknowledgments

This book began when Andy Russakoff, a friend and professor, told me I *could* write a book. Then my friend Joanna Clapps Herman told me in no uncertain terms, "You've got to write a book!" Joanna gave massive encouragement and endless guidance and invaluable advice. I am so thankful to her and her partner of inspiration, Bill Herman.

Books rule a good part of my life. Peter Salwen's book *Upper West Side History* prompted my interest in local history. He has my gratitude for what is still the most comprehensive history of Manhattan's Upper West Side. Other New York City history stalwarts—Francis Morrone, Justin Ferate, and the "Daytonian" Tom Miller—inspired this budding historian.

Many friends and family members have over the years listened to me talk about history. My memory is good, a parlor trick of facts and trivia that I use in social situations, sometimes perhaps too much. I thank all those who listened with interest and those who out of politeness pretended to. Your kind words encouraged me to write this book.

At the New-York Historical Society, I have expanded my historical horizon by volunteering for more than a dozen years and favoring the marvelous evening programs that feature renowned historians. The credit goes to Dale Gregory, the Vice President and Director of Evening Programs, and her team of Alex Kassl, Heather Whittaker, and Cat Schwartz. I also salute my fellow volunteers at the Society who donate their service to a most special place.

The New York Society Library has me as a proud member and constant user. The professional staff; the head librarian, Carolyn Waters; and the very high caliber of its collection explain its special reputation. Wandering the library's stacks is one of life's great pleasures. For a New York City buff, The New York Society Library has it all.

My fellow members of the Bloomingdale Neighborhood History Group and all my fellow members there have my warmest appreciation. Mary Lee Baranger introduced me to the group some dozen years ago, and I was warmly welcomed by Win Armstrong, Hedda Fields, and Barbara Earnest. I am thankful to these hardworking group members—Win Armstrong, Dan Armstrong, Peter Arndtsen, Marjorie Cohen, Michael Gonzalez, John Gorham, Lisa Krisman, Nancy Macagno, Batya Miller, Gil Tauber, Pam Tice, and Vita Wallace. We work diligently to offer numerous presentations, neighborhood tours, and archivings of local history. Pleasant surprises await visitors to our website, bloomingdalehistory.com. Member Pam Tice outdoes herself with researching and writing most of our history blog, upperwestsidehistory.org.

My historical outlook has been widened by many of those who made presentations at the Bloomingdale Neighborhood History Group. Most appreciated are the presentations made by Joan Adler, Jean Arrington, Cynthia Brenwall, Cynthia Copeland, Gary Dennis, Bert Hansen, William Helmreich, Marguerite Holloway, Sidney Horenstein, Celedonia "Cal" Jones, Fran Leadon, Judith Martin, Charles McKinney, Thomas Mellins, Sara Cedar Miller, Robin Nagle, Margaret Oppenheimer, Robert Pigott, Andrea Renner, Jan Rubin, Barnet Schecter, Kara Murphy Schlichting, Kurt Schlichting, William Seraile, Matthew Spady, John Touranac, Michael Susi, and Dan Wakin, Stephen Wolf, and Kate Wood.

In preparing this book I received invaluable input and critique from Michael Miscione, the former Manhattan Borough Historian. Much appreciation to Michael for opening my eyes to deeper city history. Likewise, my good friend, fellow Bloomingdale Neighbor History Group member, and occasional singing partner, Gil Tauber, rendered most valuable editorial details to this book. In my opinion, Gil is the most knowledgeable person when it comes to Bloomingdale history.

Lisa Krisman gave me wise counsel, great friendship, and heartfelt support. Sylvia Helm is a lifelong friend and counselor who gave direction in the world of book publishing. Others who contributed in various ways to enable this work include Mel Bauer, Gary Cohen, George Calderaro, Deb Cohen and Edgar Masters, Angela and Bruce Darling, Bernard A. Drew, Lesley Doyel and Nick Fritsch, Melanie Edwards, Lynne Elizabeth, Jim Epstein, Joshua Freeman, Laura Friedman, Steve Friedman., Laurence Frommer, Donna Gill, Jane Olian, James Goldberg, Caitlin Hawke, Bob Krisman, Robert and Lisa Leicht, Dan McSweeney, Fred Myers, Peggy Raferty and Tim O'Connor, Louis Phillips, Frank Roosevelt, Valerie Thaler and Bob Petrie, Ethel Sheffer, and Jim Wunsch.

Special thanks go to my longtime WeekdayWalkers: Alan, Bruce, Carol, Ed, Gladys, Holly, Jane, Jim, Jodi, Joel, Judy, Marie-Caroline and Martin, Mark, Mary, Michael and Carol, Morrie, Nancy, Peter, Rikki, Scott, Teri, Victoria, and Walter.

Robert A. McCaughey, professor of history and the Janet H. Robb Chair in the Social Sciences at Barnard, allowed me to attend three of his courses. Everyone should be so fortunate to experience such first-class instruction by the author of Columbia University's standard histories *Stand Columbia, A Lever Long Enough: A History of Columbia's School of Engineering and Applied Science since 1864* and *A College of Her Own: The History of Barnard*.

Much of my writing was done at the world-famous Hungarian Pastry Shop in my neighborhood. The owner, Philip, and the charming waitresses Betty, Crenora, Ida, Losa, Noemi, and Sophia, made my work there so warm and friendly. The Hungarian provided me with not only "office space" but also a number of good friends. Two of my long-term coffee regulars gave much more than good company: Jon Horvitz, professor of neuroscience at CUNY and master of comic observation, and Cal Lobel, a master of more things than I can remember and a true friend. I love them for brightening my days and bantering to no particular end.

Thanks to Fred Nachbaur, the Director of Fordham University Press, who took a chance on me, an unpublished author. I am a Fordham graduate, and it is a great honor to have my alma mater for a publisher. To Fred and his board, and his entire team, especially Mark Lerner and Eric

Newman, as well as copyeditor Mildred Sanchez, I gratefully appreciate the opportunity to have my book in the prestigious Empire State Editions imprint.

My biggest thanks go to Katharine Bernard. She was a "Christmas present" given to me by my wife, Janet, who knew I needed help with the book. Not everyone gets a copyeditor for Christmas, but I did, and it was the best gift I ever got. I thank Kathy for her smile and knack for making editing a no-pain, encouraging process. She turned a bulky mass of pages into a streamlined book.

My son Ethan and his wife, Aviva, have given me what history can't—the future. Seeing the world through their eyes offers confidence that the world will be a better place. They also feed me well with good food and rich conversation. I love them both dearly.

Janet Mackin and I have known each other since 1954 and our approaching fifty-year marriage grows stronger and blossoms constantly into endeavors such as this book. *Notable New Yorkers of Manhattan's Upper West Side*, as all that I do, is inspired by Janet and flavored by her enthusiasm, creativity, judgment, and an endless supply of goodness. This book is dedicated with so much love to Janet.

Image Credits

121 Humphrey Bogart. (Published by The Minneapolis Tribune-photo from Warner Bros. Public Domain, https://commons.wikimedia.org/w/index.php?curid=37858916.)

136 The Battle of Harlem Heights began here on September 16th, 1776 near the Nicholas Jones house on 106th Street between West End Avenue and Riverside Drive–1890. (By Keystone View Co. [picture credit]—National Police Gazette [Jan. 28, 1922] on the Internet Archive, Public Domain.)

141 George Alfred Townsend. (By unknown—George Alfred Townsend. *Poems of Men and Events.* New York, E. F. Bonaventure, https://archive.org/details/poemsofmeneventsootownrich. Public Domain, https://commons.wikimedia.org/w/index.php?curid=4142805.)

142 Monroe Rosenfeld. (Source [WP:NFCC#4]. Fair use, https://en.wikipedia.org/w/index.php?curid=53758851.)

143 The Lion Brewery spewing smoke behind the erection of the Cathedral of St. John. (Broken negative, Photo, George P. Hall & Son photograph collection, ca. 1876-1914, New-York Historical Society. Geo. P. Hall & Son, photographer.)

146 Miss Irene Bentley. (By Macfadden, Bernarr Aldolphus, 1858––, https://www.flickr.com/photos/internetarchivebookimages/14782393212/. Source book page: https://archive.org/stream/physicalculture201908macf/physicalculture201908macf#page/n311/mode/1up. No restrictions, https://commons.wikimedia.org/w/index.php?curid=42700403.)

152 Hank Jones. (Photograph by Brian Mcmillen—Own work, CC BY-SA 4.0, https://commons.wikimedia.org/w/index.php?curid=52043476.)

153 J. A. O'Gorman. (By Harris & Ewing, photographer—Library of Congress Catalog: https://lccn.loc.gov/2016857994. Image download: https://cdn.loc.gov/master/pnp/hec/16900/16930a.tif. Original url, https://www.loc.gov/pictures/item/2016857994/. Public Domain, https://commons.wikimedia.org/w/index.php?curid=66836879.)

155 Barack Obama. (By SEIU Walk a Day in My Shoes 2008, edit by Matthias.kötter—Sen. Barack Obama smiles, CC BY 2.0, https://commons.wikimedia.org/w/index.php?curid=1980017. Licensed under the Creative Commons Attribution 2.0 Generic license.)

156 Nick Long, Jr., in the "Broadway Melody of 1936" motion picture. (By unknown.)

157 PS 165, a George B. J. Snyder masterpiece–1903. (By Jacob A. Riis. Licensed from the Museum of the City of NY.)

167 Ruth Benedict. (By World Telegram staff photographer—Library of Congress. New York World-Telegram & Sun Collection, http://hdl.loc.gov/loc.pnp/cph.3c14649. Public Domain, https://commons.wikimedia.org/w/index.php?curid=1276865.)

168 General Memorial Hospital. (Wurts Bros. [New York, NY]. Licensed from the Museum City of New York.)

171 George Auger. (By Apeda [Photography Studio]—J. Willis Sayre Collection of Theatrical Photographs. Public Domain, https://commons.wikimedia.org/w/index.php?curid=80649095.)

200 Map bounded by Hudson River, W. 125th St., 9th Ave., W.1 08th St. (George Washington Bromley, Cartographer.)

206 Women's Hospital, Cathedral Parkway. (Photograph by Irving Underhill. Licensed from the Museum City of New York.)

211 Marcus Loew. (By Broadway Pub. Co.—Robert Grau. The business man in the amusement world: a volume of progress in the field of the theatre. NY: Broadway Pub. Co., 1910. Public Domain, https://commons.wikimedia.org/w/index.php?curid=18640661.)

212 Attilio Piccirilli. (By unidentified photographer—Catalogue of an Exhibition of Contemporary American Sculpture, Held under the Auspices of the National Sculpture Society; June 17–October 2, 1916. [The Buffalo Fine Arts Academy, 1916], page 16.[1]. Public Domain, https://commons.wikimedia.org/w/index.php?curid=50987338.)

216 José Raúl Capablanca. (By unknown, http://www.gettyimages.co.uk/detail/news-photo/cuban-chess-champion-jose-raul-capablanca-news-photo/3378095. Public Domain, https://commons.wikimedia.org/w/index.php?curid=43321121.)

220 Harry Houdini. (By the National Portrait Gallery/Smithsonian Institution http://collections.si.edu/search/results.jsp?q=record_ID:npg_NPG.2000.15. Public Domain, https://commons.wikimedia.org/w/index.php?curid=11922039.)

230 Harriet Brooks. (The original uploader was QueenAdelaide at English Wikipedia. Transferred from en.wikipedia to Commons by Armando-Martin using CommonsHelper. Public Domain, https://commons.wikimedia.org/w/index.php?curid=15692007.)

234 Edgar Saltus. (By unknown—Famous American Men and Women: A Complete Portrait Gallery of Celebrated People: https://archive.org/stream/bub_gb_4-E-AAAAYAAJ#page/n399/mode/2up. Public Domain, https://commons.wikimedia.org/w/index.php?curid=58265891.)

241 Virginia Apgar. (By March of Dimes—Library of Congress. Public Domain, https://commons.wikimedia.org/w/index.php?curid=43770603.)

242 Leo Szilard. (By unknown photographer Furfur—Leo_Szilard.jpg. Public Domain, https://commons.wikimedia.org/w/index.php?curid=25055865.)

242 Charles A. Beard. (By George Grantham Bain Collection—Library of Congress. Original url, https://www.loc.gov/pictures/item/2005690097/. Public Domain, https://commons.wikimedia.org/w/index.php?curid=66695961.)

243 Mary Ritter Beard. (By unknown. Public Domain, https://commons.wikimedia.org/w/index.php?curid=45785725.)

244 Margaret Eliza Maltby. (By JaneRayGill75—Own work, CC BY-SA 4.0, https://commons.wikimedia.org/w/index.php?curid=48929399.)

247 Bloomingdale Asylum, 1881. (By unknown.)
254 Grantland Rice. (By Paul Thompson—Library of Congress. Original url, https://www.loc.gov/pictures/item/2013646402/. Public Domain, https://commons.wikimedia.org/w/index.php?curid=67977733.)
257 Thomas Hunt Morgan. (By unknown—http://wwwihm.nlm.nih.gov/. Public Domain, https://commons.wikimedia.org/w/index.php?curid=549067.)
267 Frank Wilstach. (By no later than 1917—The Bookman: https://babel.hathitrust.org/cgi/pt?id=uc1.$b623131;view=1up;seq-364. Public Domain, https://commons.wikimedia.org/w/index.php?curid=63000811.)
269 Rex Stout. (By CBS Radio and photographer uncredited—Self scan of original promotional glossy photograph date-stamped December 2, 1942. Public Domain, https://commons.wikimedia.org/w/index.php?curid=32960030.)
274 Rt. Rev. David Hummell Greer. (By Churchman Company—The Churchman Company. House of Bishops; the latest portraits of the living Bishops of the Protestant Episcopal Church in the United States, also the Archbishop of Canterbury and the Bishops of Ripon and Hereford. New York, Churchman Company, 1904. Original in Princeton University Library. Courtesy HaithiTrust. Public Domain, https://commons.wikimedia.org/w/index.php?curid=52888787.)
275 The Leake and Watts Orphan House, Amsterdam Avenue and W. 112th Street, New York City, undated, ca. 1882-1919. (Robert L. Bracklow Photograph Collection. Licensed by the New-York Historical Society.)
283 Jean Earle Mohle. (By Bain News Service, publisher—Library of Congress. Original url, https://www.loc.gov/pictures/item/2014704432/. Public Domain, https://commons.wikimedia.org/w/index.php?curid=67444892.)
291 Columbia campus in the Morningside Heights neighborhood ca. 1926. (Fairchild Aerial Surveys, Inc.)
292 Map bounded by Hudson River, West 124th Street, Convent Avenue, West 125th Street (Bromley, George Washington Cartographer)
295 Nan Britton. (Source [WP:NFCC#4], Fair use, https://en.wikipedia.org/w/index.php?curid=54450863.)
301 George Carlin. (By ABC Television. Public Domain, https://commons.wikimedia.org/w/index.php?curid=18155121.)
302 Blanche Bates. (By Bain Collection. Public Domain, https://commons.wikimedia.org/w/index.php?curid=28430226.)
304 Henry Luce. (By New York World-Telegram and the Sun staff photographer: Phil Stanziola, photographer—Library of Congress Prints and Photographs Division. New York World-Telegram and the Sun Newspaper Photograph Collection. http://hdl.loc.gov/loc.pnp/cph.3c24600. Public Domain, https://commons.wikimedia.org/w/index.php?curid=74446928.)
307 Thurgood Marshall. (By unknown; photograph distributed by the NAACP—the *Detroit Tribune*, November 23, 1946. On file at the Library of Congress. Public Domain, https://commons.wikimedia.org/w/index.php?curid=72631160.)

317 Amelia Earhart. (By Underwood & Underwood [active 1880–c. 1950]. Public Domain, https://commons.wikimedia.org/w/index.php?curid=57938262.)
326 Outline and Index map of New York City, Manhattan Island ca. 1891. Cropped for RSD only. (George Washington Bromley, Cartographer.)
330 Allison Skipworth. (By my own screen capture—*Satan Met a Lady* DVD, 1936 public domain trailer. Public Domain, https://commons.wikimedia.org/w/index.php?curid=16969550.)
331 John dos Passos. (Creative Commons Attribution-Share Alike 3.0 Unported license.)
332 Charlotte Perkins Gilman. (By C. F. Lummis [Original copyright holder, presumably photographer]. Restoration by Adam Cuerden. Public Domain, https://commons.wikimedia.org/w/index.php?curid=2638416.)
332 Morris Hillquit. (Public Domain, https://commons.wikimedia.org/w/index.php?curid=46837474.)
334 Bernarr MacFadden. (By unknown author. Public Domain.)
335 John Purroy Mitchel. (By unknown author. Public Domain, https://commons.wikimedia.org/w/index.php?curid=3871036.)
338 Dudley Field Malone. (Public Domain, https://commons.wikimedia.org/w/index.php?curid=1798486.)
339 Mary Pickford. (By Rufus Porter Moody. Public Domain, https://commons.wikimedia.org/w/index.php?curid=5048087.)
340 Gertrude Stein. (By George Eastman House, https://www.flickr.com/photos/george_eastman_house/3334091978/. No restrictions, https://commons.wikimedia.org/w/index.php?curid=53595951.)
340 Furniss Mansion near Riverside Drive at 100th Street ca. 1903. (By unknown. Licensed from the Museum City of New York.)
343 Anthony Fokker. (By Fritz Heuschkel. Public Domain, https://commons.wikimedia.org/w/index.php?curid=53464.)
344 Geraldine Farrar. (By Addie K. Robinson [Addie Kilburn], 1860–1935. Public Domain, https://commons.wikimedia.org/w/index.php?curid=9049391.)
345 Sol Bloom. (By National Photo Company Collection [Library of Congress]. Public Domain, https://commons.wikimedia.org/w/index.php?curid=6264224.)
350 Augustus Meyers. (By unknown, family photo. Public Domain, https://commons.wikimedia.org/w/index.php?curid=6979777.)
351 Alice Brady. (By Photoplay magazine, http://silentladies.com/BBrady.html. Public Domain, https://commons.wikimedia.org/w/index.php?curid=7845909.)
352 Richard Mansfield. (By Internet Archive Book Images, https://www.flickr.com/photos/internetarchivebookimages/14597966357/. Source book page: https://archive.org/stream/lifeartofrichard01wint/lifeartofrichard01wint#page/n308/mode/1up. No

Index

Jim Mackin is a New York City historian and founder of WeekdayWalks, which provides tours of New York neighborhoods. Jim is co-leader of the Bloomingdale Neighborhood History Group, and he is the recipient of the Mayor's Award for Volunteer Service and the Morningside Heights Historic District Committee Award for Contributions.

EMPIRE STATE EDITIONS

Revolution: Stretch Johnson, Harlem Communist at the Cotton Club.
Foreword by Mark D. Naison

Joseph B. Raskin, *The Routes Not Taken: A Trip Through New York City's Unbuilt Subway System*

Phillip Deery, *Red Apple: Communism and McCarthyism in Cold War New York*

North Brother Island: The Last Unknown Place in New York City.
Photographs by Christopher Payne, A History by Randall Mason, Essay by Robert Sullivan

Richard Kostelanetz, *Artists' SoHo: 49 Episodes of Intimate History*

Stephen Miller, *Walking New York: Reflections of American Writers from Walt Whitman to Teju Cole*

Tom Glynn, *Reading Publics: New York City's Public Libraries, 1754–1911*

Craig Saper, *The Amazing Adventures of Bob Brown: A Real-Life Zelig Who Wrote His Way Through the 20th Century*

R. Scott Hanson, *City of Gods: Religious Freedom, Immigration, and Pluralism in Flushing, Queens.* Foreword by Martin E. Marty

Dorothy Day and the Catholic Worker: The Miracle of Our Continuance.
Edited, with an Introduction and Additional Text by Kate Hennessy, Photographs by Vivian Cherry, Text by Dorothy Day

Pamela Lewis, *Teaching While Black: A New Voice on Race and Education in New York City*

Mark Naison and Bob Gumbs, *Before the Fires: An Oral History of African American Life in the Bronx from the 1930s to the 1960s*

Robert Weldon Whalen, *Murder, Inc., and the Moral Life: Gangsters and Gangbusters in La Guardia's New York*

Joanne Witty and Henrik Krogius, *Brooklyn Bridge Park: A Dying Waterfront Transformed*

Sharon Egretta Sutton, *When Ivory Towers Were Black: A Story about Race in America's Cities and Universities*

Pamela Hanlon, *A Wordly Affair: New York, the United Nations, and the Story Behind Their Unlikely Bond*

Britt Haas, *Fighting Authoritarianism: American Youth Activism in the 1930s*

David J. Goodwin, *Left Bank of the Hudson: Jersey City and the Artists of 111 1st Street*. Foreword by DW Gibson

Nandini Bagchee, *Counter Institution: Activist Estates of the Lower East Side*

Carol Lamberg, *Neighborhood Success Stories: Creating and Sustaining Affordable Housing in New York*

Susan Celia Greenfield (ed.), *Sacred Shelter: Thirteen Journeys of Homelessness and Healing*

Elizabeth Macaulay Lewis and Matthew M. McGowan (eds.), *Classical New York: Discovering Greece and Rome in Gotham*

Susan Opotow and Zachary Baron Shemtob (eds.), *New York after 9/11*

Andrew Feffer, *Bad Faith: Teachers, Liberalism, and the Origins of McCarthyism*

Colin Davey with Thomas A. Lesser, *The American Museum of Natural History and How It Got That Way*. Foreword by Kermit Roosevelt III

Wendy Jean Katz, *Humbug! The Politics of Art Criticism in New York City's Penny Press*

Lolita Buckner Inniss, *The Princeton Fugitive Slave: The Trials of James Collins Johnson*

Mike Jaccarino, *America's Last Great Newspaper War: The Death of Print in a Two-Tabloid Town*

Angel Garcia, *The Kingdom Began in Puerto Rico: Neil Connolly's Priesthood in the South Bronx*

Matthew Spady, *The Neighborhood Manhattan Forgot: Audubon Park and the Families Who Shaped It*

For a complete list, visit www.fordhampress.com/empire-state-editions.

R I V E R S I D E

RIVERSIDE

Nich. De Peyster

G. S. Mumford

BLOOMINGDALE

W. 109TH
W. 110TH
W. 111TH
W. 112TH
W. 113TH
W. 114TH
W. 115TH
W. 116TH

1893
(1265)

1893
(1266)

1894
(1267)

1894
(1268)

1895
(1269)

1895
(1270)

1896
(1271)

1896
(1272)

(1273)

ST. CHRISTOPHER'S HOME

G. S. Mumford
Jas. De Peyter
Nich. De Peyter

Map 7.98
Map 110

Nich. De Peyster
Map 110

1882
(151)

1883
(1152)

1884
(1153)

1885
(1154)

1886
(1155)

(1156)

ENG. RO.
CROTON WATER WORKS

AMSTERDAM

LEAKE & WATTS

ORPHAN ASYLUM

1865
(1037)

1865
(1038)

1865
(1039)

1864
(1036)

1866
(1040)

1867
(1041)

1867
(1042)

ST.
ST.
ST.
ST.
ST.

Gerard De Peyster